UNITED NATIONS CONFERENCE ON TRADE AND DEVELOPMENT

THE LEAST DEVELOPED COUNTRIES REPORT 2013

Growth with employment for inclusive and sustainable development

UNITED NATIONS
New York and Geneva, 2013

Note

Symbols of United Nations documents are composed of capital letters with figures. Mention of such a symbol indicates a reference to a United Nations document.

Material in this publication may be freely quoted or reprinted, but full acknowledgement is requested. A copy of the publication containing the quotation or reprint should be sent to the UNCTAD secretariat at: Palais des Nations, CH-1211 Geneva 10, Switzerland.

The designations employed and the presentation of the material in this publication do not imply the expression of any opinion whatsoever on the part of the Secretariat of the United Nations concerning the legal status of any country, territory, city or area, or of its authorities, or concerning the delimitation of its frontiers or boundaries.

The overview of this report can also be found on the Internet, in all six official languages of the United Nations, at www.unctad.org/ldcr

UNCTAD/LDC/2013

UNITED NATIONS PUBLICATION

Sales No. E.13.II.D.1

ISBN 978-92-1-112864-2
eISBN 978-92-1-054116-9
ISSN 0257-7550

> "Don't let your past dictate your future"
>
> *Proverb from Sierra Leone*

What are the least developed countries?

Forty-nine countries are currently designated by the United Nations as "least developed countries" (LDCs). These are: Afghanistan, Angola, Bangladesh, Benin, Bhutan, Burkina Faso, Burundi, Cambodia, Central African Republic, Chad, Comoros, Democratic Republic of the Congo, Djibouti, Equatorial Guinea, Eritrea, Ethiopia, the Gambia, Guinea, Guinea-Bissau, Haiti, Kiribati, Lao People's Democratic Republic, Lesotho, Liberia, Madagascar, Malawi, Mali, Mauritania, Mozambique, Myanmar, Nepal, Niger, Rwanda, Samoa, Sao Tome and Principe, Senegal, Sierra Leone, Solomon Islands, Somalia, South Sudan, Sudan, Timor-Leste, Togo, Tuvalu, Uganda, United Republic of Tanzania, Vanuatu, Yemen and Zambia.

The list of LDCs is reviewed every three years by the United Nations Economic and Social Council in the light of recommendations by the Committee for Development Policy (CDP). The following three criteria were used by CDP in the latest review of the list, in March 2012:

(a) a per capita income criterion, based on a three-year average estimate of the gross national income (GNI) per capita, with a threshold of $992 for possible cases of addition to the list, and a threshold of $1,190 for graduation from LDC status;

(b) a human assets criterion, involving a composite index (the Human Assets Index) based on indicators of: (i) nutrition (percentage of the population that is undernourished); (ii) health (child mortality rate); (iii) school enrolment (gross secondary school enrolment ratio); and (iv) literacy (adult literacy rate); and

(c) an economic vulnerability criterion, involving a composite index (the Economic Vulnerability Index) based on indicators of: (i) natural shocks (index of instability of agricultural production; share of the population that has been a victim of natural disasters); (ii) trade-related shocks (index of instability of exports of goods and services); (iii) physical exposure to shocks (share of the population living in low-lying areas); (iv) economic exposure to shocks (share of agriculture, forestry and fisheries in gross domestic product (GDP)); index of merchandise export concentration); (v) smallness (population in logarithm); and (vi) remoteness (index of remoteness).

For all three criteria, different thresholds are used for identifying cases of addition to, and graduation from, the list of LDCs. A country will qualify to be added to the list if it meets the addition thresholds on all three criteria and does not have a population greater than 75 million. Qualification for addition to the list will effectively lead to LDC status only if the Government of the relevant country accepts this status. A country will normally qualify for graduation from LDC status if it has met graduation thresholds under at least two of the three criteria in at least two consecutive triennial reviews of the list. However, if the per capita GNI of an LDC has risen to a level at least double the graduation threshold, the country will be deemed eligible for graduation regardless of its performance under the other two criteria.

The General Assembly, through a resolution adopted on 18 December 2012, endorsed (with immediate effect) CDP's March 2012 recommendation to add South Sudan to the list of LDCs. South Sudan became an independent State on 9 July 2011 and a Member State of the United Nations five days later.

Only three countries have so far graduated from LDC status: Botswana in December 1994, Cape Verde in December 2007 and Maldives in January 2011. In March 2009, CDP recommended the graduation of Equatorial Guinea. This recommendation was accepted by the Council in July 2009, but as of September 2013, the Assembly had not confirmed the decision. In September 2010, the Assembly, giving due consideration to the unprecedented losses Samoa suffered as a result of the Pacific Ocean tsunami of 29 September 2009, decided to defer to 1 January 2014 the graduation of that country. The Council in July 2012 endorsed CDP's recommendation to graduate Vanuatu from LDC status, a decision the Assembly had not yet confirmed as of September 2013.

After a recommendation to graduate a country has been endorsed by the Economic and Social Council and confirmed by the General Assembly, the graduating country is granted a three-year grace period before graduation effectively takes place. This grace period, during which the country remains an LDC, is designed to enable the graduating State and its development and trading partners to agree on a "smooth transition" strategy, so that the loss of LDC status at the time of graduation does not disrupt the country's socio-economic progress. A "smooth transition" measure generally implies extending for a number of years after graduation, for the benefit of the graduated country, a concession from which the country used to benefit by virtue of its LDC status.

Acknowledgements

The Least Developed Countries Report 2013 was prepared by a team consisting of Agnès Collardeau-Angleys, Junior Davis, Pierre Encontre, Igor Paunovic, Madasamyraja Rajalingam, Rolf Traeger and Heather Wicks (the LDC Report team). The work was carried out under the guidance and supervision of Taffere Tesfachew, Director, Division for Africa, Least Developed Countries and Special Programmes, who also made significant inputs to the structure and content of the Report.

An ad hoc expert group meeting on "Growth with employment for inclusive and sustainable development" was held in Geneva on 3 and 4 July 2013 to peer-review the Report and its specific inputs. It brought together specialists in the fields of labour economics, development policies, public works, industrial policy and financing for development. The participants in the meeting were: Ludovico Alcorta (United Nations Industrial Development Organization), Christoph Ernst (International Labour Office), Charles Gore (University of Glasgow), Massimiliano La Marca (International Labour Office), Woori Lee (International Labour Office), Moazam Mahmood (International Labour Office), Pedro Martins (Overseas Development Institute), Irmgard Nübler (International Labour Office) and Aurelio Parisotto (International Labour Office), as well as the members of the LDC Report team and the following UNCTAD colleagues: Chantal Dupasquier, Mahmoud Elkhafif, Samuel Gayi, Ricardo Gottschalk, Kalman Kalotay, Jörg Mayer, Patrick Osakwe and Astrit Sulstarova. The papers reviewed at the meeting had been prepared by Junior Davis, Igor Paunovic and Rolf Traeger.

The Report draws on background papers prepared by Chalapurath Chandrasekhar, Jayati Ghosh and Anna McCord. Jayati Ghosh provided the substantive editing and contributed to the overall Report. Evangelia Bourmpoula, Marie-Claire Sodergren and Christina Wieser (International Labour Office) made available the ILO Laborsta and Employment Trends (EMP/TRENDS) econometric model databases.

Erica Meltzer edited the text. Sophie Combette designed the cover. Heather Wicks and Maria Bovey provided secretarial support.

Madasamyraja Rajalingam did the overall layout, graphics and desktop publishing.

Contents

What are the least developed countries? v

Explanatory notes xi

Abbreviations xii

Classifications used in this Report xiv

Overview .... I-XIII

CHAPTER 1: Recent Trends and Outlook for the LDCs 1

A. Introduction 2

B. Recent trends in the global economy and implications for the LDCs 3

    1. Global growth and international trade 3

    2. Recent trends in financial flows 4

    3. Recent trends in commodity prices 5

    4. Recent developments in special and differential treatment of the LDCs 6

C. Recent economic performance of the LDCs 7

    1. Trends in the real economy 7

    2. Trends in current account and international trade 10

    3. Trends in external finance 15

D. Outlook for the LDCs 18

Notes 22

References 22

CHAPTER 2: Exploring Demographic Dynamics in the LDCs 23

A. Rationale for addressing growth with employment for inclusive and sustainable development
    in the LDCs 24

B. Exploring demographic dynamics in the LDCs 28

    1. Key demographic trends in the LDCs 28

    2. Urbanization and rural–urban labour migration 36

    3. Conclusions 39

Appendix 1 41

Notes 42

References 43

CHAPTER 3: Employment Trends in LDCs 45

A. The quantity of employment in the LDCs 46

    1. Introduction 46

    2. The LDC employment challenge 46

    3. Gross employment trends in the LDCs 47

    4. Sectoral distribution of employment by status 49

    5. LDC labour productivity 55

6. Labour force participation rates 59

7. LDC employment-to-population ratios 61

8. Rural non-farm employment: panacea, or Pandora's box? 63

9. Unemployment and inactivity 67

B. The quality of employment in the LDCs 70

1. The LDC working poor 70

2. Employment status and vulnerable work in the LDCs 71

3. Informal sector employment 75

C. Employment growth and estimated net job creation 76

D. Conclusions 85

Notes 88

References 89

CHAPTER 4: A Framework for Linking Employment Creation and Development of Productive Capacities in the LDCs 93

A. Introduction 94

B. Investing to develop productive capacities: capital accumulation 97

1. Capital accumulation and the role of the investment-growth-employment nexus 97

2. The nexus in the short term: the primary role of the public sector 102

3. The nexus in the long term: the primary role of the private sector 105

4. Formation of human capital 106

C. Enterprise development and technological change 108

1. Enterprise development and the employment challenge: Firm size matters 109

2. Technological change and the employment challenge: the choice of technology matters 110

D. Structural change 113

1. Structural change and employment challenge: the three-pronged approach ... 113

2. Agriculture and the employment challenge: modernizing subsistence activities in rural areas ... 117

3. Tradable activities: the employment challenge in an open economy 121

4. Non-tradable activities: the employment challenge in low-productivity activities 122

E. How to adjust the framework to conditions in different LDCs 123

1. Fuel and mineral producers and exporters 124

2. Producers and exporters of agricultural products 124

3. Producers and exporters of manufactured goods 125

4. Small island developing States 126

F. Conclusions 126

Notes 128

References 129

CHAPTER 5: Policies for Employment-Intensive Growth in the LDCs 131

A. Introduction 132

B. Macroeconomic strategies 134

C. Managing the external sector 139

D. State-led employment creation.. 141

E. Enterprise development 146

   1. Industrial policies.. 146

   2. Policies to foster entrepreneurship.. 153

F. Summary and conclusions.. 160

G. International support measure: Bolstering youth employment in LDCs through private sector development 162

Notes.. 164

References 164

Statistical Tables on the Least Developed Countries **169**

Boxes

1. Graduation of Samoa from LDC status.. 11

2. Changing growth model in China and possible consequences for the LDCs 20

3. Observations on rural non-farm employment in Bangladesh 52

4. Focusing on smaller-scale projects to foster job creation: the case of Mozambique............. 155

Charts

1. Terms of trade indices of LDCs, regional groups of LDCs and ODCs, 2000–2012 12

2. Food, meat and cereal price indices, January 2005-June 2013... 14

3. Concentration indices of exports of country groups, selected years 15

4. Private financial flows to the LDCs, 2000–2012... 16

5. Official capital flows to LDCs, 2000–2011 17

6. LDC population, 1970–2050 29

7. Average annual population growth rate in the LDCs, 1970–2012....................................... 30

8. Average annual increase in the LDC working-age population 2010-2050............................ 31

9. LDC population by age groups, 1990–2050 33

10. LDC dependency ratios, 2010 and 2050 34

11. Youth population, (10–24 years), 1950–2050 35

12. Age distribution of LDC and ODC populations, 2015 and 2050 36

13. LDC rural-urban population trends and forecasts, 1970–2050.. 37

14. LDC GDP, employment and population growth trends, 2000–2018 47

15. Labour force dynamics in the LDCs, 1990–2020.. 48

16. Growth of agricultural and non-agricultural labour force in LDCs, 1990–2020................... 51

17. Employment in major economic sectors, 2000–2018.. 53

18. LDC labour productivity, by country groups and by export specialization, 2000–2012 56

19. LDC output per worker as a share of more developed economies, 1990–2012 57

20. Agricultural labour productivity trends in LDCs, developed and other developing countries, 1985–2011.. 58

21. LDC labour force participation rates by gender and region, 2012...................................... 60

22. LDC Labour force participation rates, by region and age, 1980–2009 61

23. Labour force participation rates for women in LDCs, 1990–2012 62

24. Employment-to-population ratios, LDC regional averages by gender, 2012 63

25. Youth and adult employment-to-population ratios in selected LDCs, 2000 to 2012 64

26. Household participation and shares in rural non-farm income-generating activities in four selected LDCs 66

27. LDC total unemployment rate by region, gender and youth, 1991–2012 68

28. LDC inactivity rates for youths and working-age population, 2009 69

29. Share of the working poor in LDCs living on less than $1.25 per day in total employment, 2000–2017 ..71

30. Share of vulnerable employment in LDCs and ODCs, 2000–2018 72

31. Distribution of employment by status in selected LDCs, 2012 73

32. Employment by economic class in the LDCs and ODCs (various years).......................75

33. Growth elasticity of employment in LDCs, 2004–2008 78

34. Elasticity of total employment to total GDP in the LDCs, 2000–2008 80

35. Policy framework for linking development of productive capacities with employment creation in LDCs...96

36. Investment ratios in LDCs and ODCs, 1985–2011 98

37. The investment-growth-employment nexus in a closed economy 99

38. Primary sector as a share of GDP, 2009–2011..116

39. Rural population as a share of total population, 2010–2012 119

40. Cereal yield in LDCs and ODCs, 1990–2011 120

Tables

1. Real GDP and real GDP per capita growth rates for LDCs, advanced economies, emerging and developing economies and world, selected years.................................3

2. Price indices for selected primary commodities of importance to LDCs, 2008–2013.................6

3. Real GDP and real GDP per capita growth rates for LDCs, by groups, selected years 7

4. Exports and imports of merchandise and services in LDCs.....................................12

5. Composition of merchandise exports and imports in LDCs, average 2010–2012 13

6. Real GDP growth rates for LDCs, developing and advanced economies, selected years and forecasts. 18

7. Broad demographic trends in the LDCs, 1980–2011...32

8. LDC distribution of population and labour, 2000–2020 37

9. Urbanization and pressure on land in the LDCs, 1980–2011.....................................38

10. Changing locus of the labour force in LDCs 1990–2020 50

11. Sectoral share of total employment for selected LDCs, various years 54

12. Labour force participation rates, 1980–2009 59

13. LDC Inactivity rates, 1980–2009 69

14. Employment and poverty dynamics in the LDCs, 2000–2018....................................70

15. Distribution of employment by status, 2012 73

16. Contribution of informal sector to total non-agricultural employment in selected LDCs.................77

17. Decomposition of GDP per capita in selected LDCs, 2000–2010 81

18. Growth decomposition, percentage contribution to total growth in GDP.......................83

19. Indicators of human capital formation in LDCs and ODCs, 1995 and 2011 107

Annex Tables

1. Indicators on LDCs development, 2012..170

2. Real GDP growth rates for individual LDCs, selected years..171

3. Real GDP per capita growth rates for individual LDCs, selected years............................172

4. Gross capital formation, gross domestic savings and resource gap in LDCs, by country, and by LDC groups, selected years...173

5. Share of value added in main economic sectors in LDCs, by country and country groups, 1999–2001 and 2009–2011...174

6. Foreign direct investment inflows to LDCs, selected years...175

7. Total workers remittances to LDCs, by country and groups..176

8. Selected indicators on debt burden in LDCs..177

9. Indicators on area and population, 2011 178

10. Selected indicators on education and labour, 2011...179

11. Selected indicators on demography in LDCs 180

12. LDC selected population indicators, 2012..181

13. New entrants to the labour market in LDCs 182

14. Total employment trends in LDCs..183

15. Countries and data sources for LDC sub-sample RNF income analysis........................184

EXPLANATORY NOTES

The term "dollars" ($) refers to United States dollars unless otherwise stated. The term "billion" signifies 1,000 million.

Annual rates of growth and changes refer to compound rates. Exports are valued f.o.b. (free on board) and imports c.i.f. (cost, insurance, freight) unless otherwise specified.

Use of a dash (–) between dates representing years, e.g. 1981–1990, signifies the full period involved, including the initial and final years. An oblique stroke (/) between two years, e.g. 1991/92, signifies a fiscal or crop year.

The term "least developed country" (LDC) refers, throughout this report, to a country included in the United Nations list of least developed countries.

In the tables:

Two dots (..) indicate that the data are not available, or are not separately reported.

One dot (.) indicates that the data are not applicable.

A hyphen (-) indicates that the amount is nil or negligible.

Details and percentages do not necessarily add up to totals, because of rounding.

Abbreviations

AfDB	African Development Bank
AFRICATIP	Association Africaine des Agences d'Exécution des Travaux d'Intérêt Public
AGETIP	Agence d'Exécution des Travaux d'Intérêt Public contre le Sous-emploi
CDP	Committee for Development Policy
DAC	Development Assistance Committee
EAP	economically active population
ECOWAS	Economic Community of West African States
EIF	Enhanced Integrated Framework
EIIPs	Employment-Intensive Investment Programmes
EMP/TRENDS	Employment Trends
EPZ	export processing zone
ERRA	Ethiopian Rural Roads Authority
EU	European Union
EVI	Economic Vulnerability Index
FAO	Food and Agriculture Organization of the United Nations
FDI	foreign direct investment
GDP	gross domestic product
GNI	gross national income
GVC	global value chain
HIPC	Heavily Indebted Poor Countries Initiative
HYV	high-yielding variety
ICT	information and communication technology
ILO	International Labour Organization
IMF	International Monetary Fund
IPoA	Istanbul Programme of Action (IPoA) for the Least Developed Countries for the Decade 2011–2020
IPR	Investment Policy Review
IPRs	intellectual property rights
ISIC	International Standard Industrial Classification
ISM	international support measure
JoGGs	Job Generation and Growth Decomposition Tool
KEP	Karnali Employment Programme
KILM	Key Indicators of the Labour Market
LDC	least developed country
LDC-IV	Fourth United Nations Conference on the Least Developed Countries
LDCR	Least Developed Countries Report
LFPR	labour force participation rate
LIC	low income country
LSMS	Living Standards Measurement Study
MDG	Millennium Development Goal

MDRI	Multilateral Debt Relief Initiative
MSE	micro and small enterprise
MSME	micro, small and medium-sized enterprise
NEETs	Not in education, employment or training
NEPAD	New Partnership for Africa's Development
NGO	non-governmental organization
NICs	newly industrialized countries
ODA	official development assistance
ODCs	other developing countries
OECD	Organisation for Economic Co-operation and Development
ppm	parts per million
PPP	purchasing power parity
PSNP	Productive Safety Nets Programme
PWPs	public works programmes
R&D	research and development
RIGA	Rural Income Generating Activities
RNF	rural non-farm
RNFE	rural non-farm economy
SADC	Southern Africa Development Community
SDRs	special drawing rights
SIDS	small island developing States
SMEs	small and medium-sized enterprises
SSA	Sub-Saharan Africa
TNC	transnational corporation
TRIPS	Trade-related Aspects of Intellectual Property Rights
UNCTAD	United Nations Conference on Trade and Development
UN/DESA	United Nations Department of Economic and Social Affairs
UNECA	United Nations Economic Commission for Africa
UNEP	United Nations Environment Programme
UNFPA	United Nations Population Fund
UNICEF	The United Nations Children's Fund
UNIDO	United Nations Industrial Development Organization
VAT	Value Added Tax
VUP	Vision 2020 Umurenge Programme
WDI	World Development Indicators
WEO	World Economic Outlook
WESP	World Economic and Social Prospects
WFP	World Food Programme
WIR	World Investment Report
WTO	World Trade Organization

Classifications used in this Report

Least developed countries

Geographical/structural classification

Unless otherwise specified, in this Report the least developed countries (LDCs) are classified according to a combination of geographical and structural criteria. Therefore, the small island LDCs which geographically are in Africa or Asia are grouped together with the Pacific islands, due to their structural similarities. Haiti and Madagascar, which are regarded as large island States, are grouped together with the African LDCs. South Sudan declared its independence on 9 July 2011, and became both an independent state and a Member of the United Nations on 14 July 2011. Therefore, from 2011, data for South Sudan and Sudan (officially the Republic of the Sudan), where available, are shown under the appropriate country name. For periods prior to the independence of South Sudan in 2011, data for Sudan (former) include those for South Sudan unless otherwise indicated. The resulting groups are as follows:

African LDCs and Haiti: Angola, Benin, Burkina Faso, Burundi, Central African Republic, Chad, Democratic Republic of the Congo, Djibouti, Equatorial Guinea, Eritrea, Ethiopia, Gambia, Guinea, Guinea-Bissau, Haiti, Lesotho, Liberia, Madagascar, Malawi, Mali, Mauritania, Mozambique, Niger, Rwanda, Senegal, Sierra Leone, Somalia, Sudan (former) or South Sudan and Sudan, Togo, Uganda, United Republic of Tanzania, Zambia.

Asian LDCs: Afghanistan, Bangladesh, Bhutan, Cambodia, Lao People's Democratic Republic, Myanmar, Nepal, Yemen.

Island LDCs: Comoros, Kiribati, Samoa, Sao Tome and Principe, Solomon Islands, Timor-Leste, Tuvalu, Vanuatu.

Export specialization

For the purpose of analysing current trends in chapter 1, UNCTAD has classified the LDCs into six export specialization categories, according to which type of exports accounted for at least 45 per cent of total exports of goods and services in 2010–2012. The group composition is as follows:

Agricultural and Food exporters: Guinea-Bissau, Malawi, Solomon Islands, Somalia.

Fuel exporters: Angola, Chad, Equatorial Guinea, Sudan, Yemen.

Manufactures exporters: Bangladesh, Bhutan, Cambodia, Haiti, Lesotho.

Mineral exporters: Democratic Republic of the Congo, Eritrea, Guinea, Mali, Mauritania, Mozambique, Zambia.

Mixed exporters: Benin, Burkina Faso, Central African Republic, Kiribati, Lao People's Democratic Republic, Myanmar, Niger, Senegal, Sierra Leone, Togo, United Republic of Tanzania.

Services exporters: Afghanistan, Burundi, Comoros, Djibouti, Ethiopia, Gambia, Liberia, Madagascar, Nepal, Rwanda, Samoa, Sao Tome and Principe, Timor-Leste, Tuvalu, Vanuatu, Uganda.

Other groups of countries and territories

Developed economies: Andorra, Austria, Australia, Belgium, Bulgaria, Bermuda, Canada, Cyprus, Czech Republic, Denmark, Estonia, Faeroe Islands, Finland, France, Germany, Gibraltar, Greece, Greenland, Holy See, Hungary, Iceland, Ireland, Italy, Israel, Japan, Latvia, Lithuania, Luxembourg, Malta, Netherlands, New Zealand, Norway, Poland, Portugal, Romania, Saint Pierre and Miquelon, San Marino, Slovakia, Slovenia, Spain, Sweden, Switzerland, United Kingdom, United States.

Other developing countries (ODCs): All developing countries (as classified by the United Nations) which are not LDCs.

Transition economies: Albania, Armenia, Azerbaijan, Belarus, Bosnia and Herzegovina, Croatia, Georgia, Kazakhstan, Kyrgyzstan, Moldova, Montenegro, Russian Federation, Serbia, Tajikistan, The former Yugoslav Republic of Macedonia, Turkmenistan, Ukraine, Uzbekistan.

Product classification

Goods: The figures provided below are the codes of the Standard International Trade Classification (SITC), revision 3.

Agriculture and Food: section 0, 1, 2 and 4 excluding divisions 27 and 28.

Minerals: section 27, 28 and 68 and groups 667 and 971.

Fuels: section 3.

Manufactures: section 5 to 8 excluding group 667.

Section 9 (Commodities and transactions not classified elsewhere in the SITC) has been included only in the total export of goods and services, but not in the goods classification above, except for group 971 (Gold, non-monetary (excluding gold ores and concentrates)), which has been included in Minerals.

Services: Total services cover the following main categories: transport, travel, communications, construction, insurance, financial services, computer and information services, royalties and license fees, other business services, personal, cultural, recreational and government services.

Taxonomy of LDCs according to their employment challenges

The UNCTAD secretariat has classified LDCs according to their employment challenges on the basis of three criteria: 1. geographical location of the population (which provides a proxy of the type of economic activity available to the labour force); 2. structure of output; and 3. structure of exports.

Rural economies: Countries whose rural population is higher than 60 per cent and/or whose primary sector contributes more than 50 per cent of gross value added (GVA) and which do not fall under one of the categories below: Afghanistan, Burkina Faso, Burundi, Central African Republic, Ethiopia, Guinea-Bissau, Lao People's Democratic Republic, Liberia, Madagascar, Malawi, Nepal, Niger, Rwanda, Sierra Leone, Somalia, United Republic of Tanzania, Uganda.

Small island developing States: LDCs recognized as members of the SIDS category by the United Nations: Comoros, Kiribati, Samoa, Sao Tome and Principe, Solomon Islands, Tuvalu, Vanuatu.

Fuels producers and exporters: Countries whose mining, utilities and construction sector accounts for more than 25 per cent of GVA and/or whose fuel exports account for more than 45 per cent of total exports of goods and services: Angola, Bhutan, Chad, Equatorial Guinea, Sudan, Timor-Leste, Yemen.

Minerals producers and exporters: Countries whose mining, utilities and construction sector accounts for more than 25 per cent of GVA and/or whose mineral exports account for more than 45 per cent of total exports of goods and services: Democratic Republic of the Congo, Eritrea, Guinea, Mali, Mauritania, Mozambique, Zambia.

Major manufactures producers and exporters: Countries whose manufacturing sector accounts for more than 15 per cent of GVA and/or whose manufactures exports account for more than 45 per cent of total exports of goods and services: Bangladesh, Cambodia, Haiti, Lesotho, Myanmar.

Five LDCs for which data were available have not been classified because they do not fall into any of the above categories. According to their export specialization, they are mixed exporters (Benin, Senegal and Togo) or service exporters (Djibouti and Gambia). Data for South Sudan are not yet available, but it can be surmised that it would have been classified as fuels producer and exporter.

Data were drawn from UNCTAD's UNCTADStat and FAO's FAOSTAT databases and the time coverage for data was 2009–2012.

OVERVIEW

Introduction

Despite the sluggish global economic performance of recent years, the least developed countries (LDCs) in general have enjoyed moderate economic growth. Per capita income for the group as a whole has been expanding steadily, raising hopes that some of them may even be able to graduate from the category within the decade. However, there are worrying signs that this growth trend has not been inclusive and that its contribution to poverty reduction has been limited. The main explanation for the lack of inclusiveness is that growth in LDCs has not generated enough "quality" jobs — that is, jobs offering higher wages and better working conditions — especially for the young. Creating employment opportunities is critical because of the fundamental role that work plays in economic development and in people's lives. Not only does it influence income, aggregate demand and investment decisions, it is also the best and most dignified pathway out of poverty.

Since the onset of the global financial and economic crisis in 2008, employment generation — and especially the phenomenon of jobless growth — has increasingly been recognized as a major policy concern worldwide. This is particularly true of the LDCs, where the challenges posed by demographic patterns, persistent poverty, accelerated urbanization and rising inequalities make the absence of remunerative employment a source of significant social and political tension. Not all LDCs are rich in mineral resources or other natural endowments. For most of these countries, their most valuable asset is their people, in particular the young. It is only by engaging their people in productive employment that LDCs can achieve lasting and constructive growth.

This *Report* examines the link between investment, growth and employment. More specifically, it considers how LDCs can promote growth that generates an adequate number of quality jobs and that enables them to reach what UNCTAD believes are their most urgent and pivotal goals, both now and in the post-2015 development agenda: poverty reduction, inclusive growth and sustainable development.

Recent economic trends and outlook for the LDCs

With the global economy still struggling to return to a strong and sustained growth path, the external environment faced by the LDCs has been less propitious in the past five years than previously. The recent slowdown of world trade, which is now at a near-standstill, has weakened the demand for LDC imports, most notably in the case of developed countries but also in emerging economies. In addition to weaker demand for their exports, the LDCs have been confronted with a heightened volatility of commodity prices and capital flows.

As a result, economic growth in the LDCs has been weaker by a full two percentage points in the past five years (2009–2013) than during the previous boom period (2002–2008). It has also been below the target rate of 7-per-cent annual growth established in the Istanbul Programme of Action (IPoA) for the Least Developed Countries for the Decade 2011–2020.

Despite the slow global recovery, however, real gross domestic product (GDP) growth in the LDCs has picked up somewhat, from 4.5 per cent in 2011 to 5.3 per cent in 2012. International Monetary Fund (IMF) forecasts point to a similar growth rate in 2013, in the 5-to-6 per cent range. The real GDP growth rates for different groups of LDCs continued recent trends in 2012, with African LDCs lagging behind their Asian and island counterparts. The growth rates of African LDCs' real GDP per capita have also lagged, a result of their higher population growth rate.

The heterogeneous performance of LDC groups has been reflected not only in real GDP growth rates, but also in the growth rates of individual countries. There were 15 countries with growth rates exceeding 6 per cent, but also 10 countries with growth rates below 3 per cent. Given the high population growth rate, the latter countries had stagnant or negative growth in per capita terms. This has severe consequences for their poverty reduction, for their achievement of the Millennium Development Goals (MDGs) and more broadly for their human development. Three LDCs experienced a recession in 2012, since they had negative growth rates of real GDP.

The heterogeneity in real GDP growth rates among the LDCs is a consequence of wide disparities in other macroeconomic indicators. Most notably, and most importantly for economic growth, the rates of gross capital formation differ widely across individual LDCs. The IPoA identified a gross capital formation rate of 25 per cent of GDP as a prerequisite for attaining real GDP growth rates of 7 per cent. Seventeen LDCs managed to reach, or even exceed, that benchmark in 2011. However, 31 others had an investment rate below the 25-per cent benchmark, and the rate in still other LDCs was even below the 10-per cent mark. Given the close relationship between investment and economic growth, these countries' growth prospects are not very bright.

Analysing developments over the course of a decade allows us to explore the extent and direction of the process of structural change in the LDCs. For these countries as a group, the average share of agriculture in GDP declined from 31.4 per cent in 1999–2001 to 25.6 per cent in 2009–2011. The share of manufacturing stayed the same, at around 10 per cent of GDP, while the average share of services declined somewhat. More generally, the trends suggest that for the LDCs as a group, over the period between 1999–2001 and 2009–2011 — which was characterized by the most rapid economic growth in decades — there was little structural change of the type that results in strong increases in productivity, incomes, technological intensity and high value added.

The current account deficit for the LDCs as a group also widened substantially, from $10.5 billion in 2011 to $28.8 billion in 2012. The deterioration of their current account was due mainly to a significant worsening of the merchandise trade balance, which expanded from a $3.7-billion deficit in 2011 to a much larger one of $18.5 billion in 2012. Their terms of trade continued to improve in the three years since the sharp deterioration of 2009. In 2011 and 2012 they reached a higher level than during the previous peak of 2008, just before the adverse impact of the crisis was first felt.

With respect to exports, the strong growth of about 25 per cent in both 2010 and 2011 stalled to a mere 0.6 per cent in 2012 for the LDCs as a group. This is in line with the worldwide deceleration of trade in goods mentioned earlier. While imports expanded by 21.9 per cent in 2011, one year later their growth had slowed to 7.8 per cent. Nonetheless, that was enough to widen the LDCs' merchandise trade deficit substantially.

External finance is of particular importance to the LDCs, given their low level of domestic savings relative to investment. Inflows of foreign direct investment (FDI) to LDCs hit a record high of almost $26 billion in 2012, about 20 per cent more than in 2011. Inflows to African LDCs and Haiti rose from $16.9 billion to $19.8 billion over the same period. Asian LDCs also saw an increase, from $4.2 billion to $5.6 billion, while island LDCs suffered a reversal, from $320 million to $235 million.

The flow of workers' remittances to LDCs continued to expand in 2012, reaching a new record of $30.5 billion. Remittances to these countries are much more stable than FDI inflows, and have risen even during the worst stage of the crisis. With respect to regional distribution, remittances are mostly a feature of Asian LDCs, where they increased from $16.3 billion in 2010 to $17.8 billion a year later.

After playing an important countercyclical role during the financial crisis, official development assistance (ODA) to the LDCs began to decline in 2011. According to data from the Development Assistance Committee (DAC) of the Organisation for Economic Co-operation and Development (OECD), net ODA disbursements from all donors to LDCs, excluding debt relief, fell slightly, from $41.7 billion in 2010 to $41.6 billion in 2011. According to preliminary data for 2012, bilateral net ODA to the LDCs shrunk by 12.8 per cent in real terms. If these estimates are confirmed, they will mark the largest decline in ODA to LDCs since 1997.

The total external debt of the LDCs expanded in 2012 to an estimated $183 billion, up 6.7 per cent in nominal terms from 2011. The debt-to-GDP ratio grew slightly as well, from 26.3 per cent in 2011 to 26.7 per cent in 2012, while the ratio of total debt to exports rose from 78.7 to 82.5 per cent; both ratios were higher than those in other developing countries. The stock of short-term debt was up by $2.5 billion in 2012, a 14-per-cent increase.

According to IMF forecasts, real GDP worldwide will expand by 3.3 per cent in 2013, a slight improvement over the 3.2 per cent of 2012. For the LDCs as a group, IMF forecasts a 5.7-per-cent growth rate for 2013, compared to 5.3 per cent for emerging and developing economies. The growth of the world economy should increase to 4.0 per cent in 2014 and to around 4.5 per cent in the subsequent four years. LDC growth should be around 6 per cent in the medium term.

For the LDCs, international trade has been the single most important channel of transmission of the recessionary impulses from the developed countries since the start of the crisis. The recent slowdown of world trade will thus have further negative impacts on the LDCs' prospects. While the demand for imported goods in developed countries has been weak at best, the LDCs have avoided a sharp deceleration of growth by relying more on their domestic demand and on South-South trade. Both will continue to be necessary in the future, but the recent deceleration of economic growth in the large emerging economies will seriously limit further possibilities for such reorientation.

The availability of external financing is another precondition for strong growth of real GDP in the LDCs. As the analysis in chapter 1 of this Report suggests, external financing has undergone considerable fluctuations since the beginning of the crisis. Moreover, the prospect of a tighter monetary policy in developed countries over the course of 2014 and 2015 will change the relative profitability of investments between developed and developing countries' assets. Reduction in the interest rate differential between the two country groupings will also make it more difficult to finance the current account deficits. LDCs with large such deficits should start now to prepare for these future developments.

The third major factor affecting the external conditions for the LDCs is movements in international commodity prices. IMF projections suggest continued declines for prices of both oil and non-fuel primary commodities over the long term. But the short-term outlook for commodity prices is highly uncertain, not only because of possible supply-side disruptions (such as energy and food), but also because of demand uncertainties.

Against this background, the outlook for the LDCs in the short to medium term is not very good. Even if none of the downside risks materialize and the IMF growth rate forecasts prove accurate, the growth of the LDCs as a group will be below the 7-per-cent IPoA target. In that scenario, responding effectively to the employment challenge, whose future magnitude is analysed in this Report, will be even more difficult for the LDCs.

Demographic dynamics in the LDCs

Demographic change affects the environmental and socio-economic development of all countries, but especially the most vulnerable of the LDCs. Although the proportion of people in these countries who live on less than US$ 1.25 per day (i.e., in extreme poverty) has declined, the number has continued to rise due to high population growth.

The LDCs face a stark demographic challenge as their population, about 60 per cent of which is currently under 25 years of age, is projected to double to 1.7 billion by 2050. The LDC youth population (aged 15 to 24 years) is expected to soar from 168 million in 2010 to 300 million by 2050, an increase of 131.7 million. By 2050, one in four youths (aged 15–24 years) worldwide will live in an LDC.

As to the LDC working-age population, it will increase on average by 15.7 million people per year between 2010 and 2050, and in 11 LDCs, by at least 0.5 million a year. The projected increases are highest in African LDCs — Democratic Republic of the Congo, Ethiopia, Uganda and United Republic of Tanzania — where that population will expand by more than 1 million people a year. If, as expected, an additional 630 million people (equivalent to 37 per cent of the LDC population in 2050) enter the labour market by 2050, this will pose a major employment and development challenge for the LDCs.

LDC population growth rates also greatly surpass those of other country groupings: At 2.2 per cent per annum in 2011, they were roughly double those of other developing countries (ODCs) (1.2 per cent), and five times those of developed countries (0.4 per cent). Furthermore, LDCs have the highest fertility rates in the world, averaging 4.4 children per woman during the period 2005–2010, as compared to 2.4 in ODCs and 1.7 in developed countries.

For most LDCs, the realization of a potential demographic dividend (where the dependency ratio is at its lowest) will require increased investment in the training, education and employment of youths. Although LDC primary and secondary education enrolment and youth literacy rates have improved since 1990, they are still below the equivalent levels in ODCs and developed countries. In the medium term, LDC demographic growth dynamics, together with the expanding youth bulge, will mean declining dependency ratios but a growing labour supply.

Urbanization trends are another key factor in LDC demographics. The level of urbanization in LDCs in 2010 was 28 per cent, or about 20 percentage points below the world average (50.5 per cent). LDC urbanization should reach 39 per cent by 2020, largely as a result of rising rural–urban migration, high fertility rates and population growth.

Many LDCs are now at a critical stage of development where population growth is high and the nature of the employment challenge, especially in rural areas, is changing. In the past, most new labour markets entrants were typically absorbed in low-productivity agriculture. However, as population densities rise, farm sizes decline, and farmers increasingly shift towards the cultivation of more ecologically fragile land, both on-farm incomes and agricultural productivity are likely to remain perilously low. Because of these factors, the LDCs' urbanization and emigration rates are expected to remain high.

Given the clear demographic challenges highlighted in this Report, then, the LDCs will need to make significant efforts to generate a sufficient quantity of jobs and offer decent employment opportunities to their young population in the medium term. The potential benefits arising from the demographic dividend are not automatic. Successful exploitation of the potential will depend on the ability of the LDC economies to absorb and productively employ both new labour market entrants and those who are presently unemployed or underemployed.

Employment challenges in the LDCs: Creating quality employment in sufficient quantities

The central employment challenge in the LDCs is to create productive jobs and livelihoods for the millions of people who enter the labour force each year. Given the above-mentioned demographic trends, the scale of this challenge will be even greater in the coming years. To illustrate the magnitude of the problem, it is worth considering the estimated number of new labour market entrants in selected countries. In Ethiopia, for example, there were an estimated 1.4 million new entrants to the labour force in 2005, and their number will increase to 3.2 million by 2050. Similarly, in Haiti, new entrants in 2005 numbered about 204,000 — a figure that will reach 229,000 by 2035. In Bangladesh, there were 2.9 million new entrants in 2005, and this number will peak at 3.1 million by 2020 before beginning to decline. These are the numbers of productive and decent jobs and livelihoods which will have to be created in these countries each year. If this is not achieved, the likelihood is that poverty and international emigration rates will rise.

Indeed, the relative slackness of the LDC labour market largely explains why the 2002–2008 boom had relatively weak effects on poverty reduction in the LDCs. Although the incidence of extreme poverty declined from 59 to 53 per cent between 2000 and 2007, a period when GDP growth approached an average 7 per cent per year, the impact of growth on the incidence of poverty has been slower than that experienced in other developing regions. The relatively poor performance of the agricultural sector in most LDCs has been particularly detrimental, given that the poverty elasticity of growth in agriculture is typically much higher than the corresponding elasticity of growth in other sectors of the economy.

In most LDCs, the main source of employment for the growing labour force is still agriculture, largely through people cultivating new land. However, LDCs have been facing persistent constraints on agricultural growth, such as shrinking investment in research and development, missing and imperfect factor markets, and limited access to producer-risk mitigation tools, as well as poor infrastructure. With rising population growth, declining agricultural farm sizes and low productivity, agricultural production is becoming a less viable livelihood for the rural poor. In addition, most LDC farmers cannot afford the means for sustainable intensification of agricultural production. More and more young people are seeking work outside agriculture, and urban centres are increasingly becoming the main attraction.

Therefore, the LDC population is not only growing rapidly but is also quickly urbanizing. More of the LDC population than ever before is entering the labour market. The convergence of these trends makes the current decade critical for these countries, particularly with regard to employment. There is thus a clear need to strengthen the link between employment and growth. During the period 2000–2012, LDC employment growth was 2.9 per cent per annum, a rate slightly above the population growth rate but well below their average GDP growth rates for the period (7 per cent). Employment growth in the African and island LDCs also outpaced the LDC average and will continue to do so until at least 2018.

Furthermore, the historic labour productivity divide between LDCs and ODCs remains substantial, although it has narrowed since 2000. LDC output per worker in 2012 (in constant 1990 international $) was just 22 per cent of the level in ODCs, 10 per cent of the European Union (EU) average and 7 per cent of the level in North America. The agricultural labour productivity gap between LDCs, ODCs and developed economies has also widened since 1985. Agricultural labour productivity fell in over a third of the LDCs (10 of the 27 for which there were comparable data) between 1985–1987 and 2009–2011.

Raising agricultural productivity is a *sine qua non* for LDC development and for the structural transformation of the sector. Increased agricultural labour productivity in these countries has the potential to both raise the real incomes of rural households and stimulate demand for rural non-farm goods and services. The employment-creating potential of investment in rural irrigation, drainage, provision of feeder channels, local land reclamation, forestation and so forth is considerable. This can be boosted if such investment, including through public work programmes, is embedded in a well-designed and well-targeted employment strategy.

The LDCs have a high labour force participation rate — an average 75 per cent, as compared to 68 per cent in ODCs. However, these figures should be interpreted with caution. The lack of a social security system, and limited family support due to low incomes, means that the poor in LDCs have no option but to seek work — no matter what kind of work. Generally low average earnings also mean that more members of a household need to enter the labour market in order to provide sufficient income to sustain the entire household. The LDCs' high labour force participation rate is thus largely a reflection of the desperate need of the poor to work for their survival, rather than an indicator of a well-functioning and effective labour market.

A breakdown of the labour force participation rate by gender and age group provides further insights into the distribution of the economically active population in LDCs. Although this distribution varies between different groups of LDCs, in general, women in the LDCs have a high propensity to work in the labour market. This is partly because women work predominantly in the informal sector (housekeeping, child-rearing, farming, etc.). Between 1990 and 2012, an estimated 290 million women entered the LDC labour force. During this period, women's labour force participation rates in LDCs rose by 3 percentage points, from 59 to 62 per cent on average.

An important source of income and employment for the poor in LDCs, and for women in particular, is rural non-farm economic activities. These activities are closely linked to farming, the food chain and the production of goods and services (often non-tradable) for local rural markets. With increasing urbanization and improvements in rural-urban transport networks, rural non-farm activities also produce goods and services (both non-tradable and tradable) for distant markets. There are no accurate data based on household surveys of full- or part-time employment in rural non-farm activities in LDCs. Based on estimates, however, the rural non-farm economy accounts for about 30 per cent of full-time rural employment in Asia, 45 per cent in Latin America, 20 per cent in West Asia and 40–45 per cent in Africa. In fact, as GDP per capita levels increase, the share of rural on-farm (agricultural) income typically falls as the share of rural non-agricultural income rises. But evidence from case studies suggests that although rural non-farm employment is increasingly important in LDCs, on-farm production and jobs remain the mainstay for most of these countries.

On the positive side, indicators for vulnerable employment and working poor have improved somewhat since 2000. Nonetheless, vulnerable employment still accounts for about 80 per cent of total employment in the LDCs. By 2017, African LDCs will have the highest share of working poor in the LDCs as a group. In addition, for the group as a whole, the gender gap in vulnerable employment is not only wide but has increased marginally, averaging 11 percentage points during the period 2000–2012. In 2012, 85 per cent of women and 73 per cent of men on average were in vulnerable employment.

In LDCs, vulnerability of jobs and the incidence of working poor are closely linked to unemployment, which in these countries has a disproportionate effect on young people joining the labour force. In most LDCs, the youth unemployment rate (i.e., for those aged 15–24 years) is higher than the average LDC rate for both men and women, and in most cases is almost twice that rate. LDC youths typically find work in the informal sector, but often these jobs do not pay reasonable wages, improve skills or offer much job security. More than 70 per cent of youths in the Democratic Republic of Congo, Ethiopia, Malawi, Mali, Rwanda, Senegal and Uganda are either self-employed or contributing to family work. If the growing LDC youth population could be provided with the necessary skills, education and decent jobs, it could become a major force of production for meeting global and domestic demand and a significant driver of local consumption and investment.

Sadly, the LDCs' record for generating decent jobs, even in times of growth, is far from impressive. To the contrary, the evidence shows that countries with faster GDP growth achieved this with relatively less employment creation. In addition, employment elasticity declined in about half of the LDCs in the period 2000–2008, and that elasticity tended to fall more frequently in precisely those LDCs that were growing faster. Although the reported LDC employment elasticities to growth have generally not been very low by international standards, given the demographic and economic challenges which these countries are likely to face, these elasticities will probably not be enough to reach the necessary employment levels.

This Report shows that during the period 2000–2010, the employment rate made a positive contribution to GDP per capita in only 3 of 11 LDCs surveyed: Cambodia (accounting for 9 per cent of the change in GDP per capita), Sierra Leone (6.3 per cent) and United Republic of Tanzania (4.7 per cent). This may reflect substantial positive changes for these economies in terms of the number of youths who continue their education for longer periods of time, which helps to build future productive capacities. But the Report also demonstrates that economic growth in the LDCs has tended over time to become less effective in terms of employment generation.

The available labour market and informal sector information for LDCs is sparse, however. There is an urgent need for more data collection and statistical analyses, which should figure prominently in the post-2015 debate on the Millennium Development Goals (MDGs).

Policy framework for linking employment creation and development of productive capacities in the LDCs

For the past three decades, LDCs were advised to focus on economic growth as a strategy for economic diversification, poverty reduction and economic development. In hindsight, this appears to have been sound policy advice, since it is highly unlikely that LDCs will achieve economic and social development and halve their poverty levels in line with internationally agreed goals without a sustained period of growth. In fact, in recognition of this likely scenario, the IPoA states (paragraph 28) that in order for LDCs to achieve "sustained, equitable and inclusive economic growth […] to at least the level of 7 per cent per annum", they should strengthen their productive capacity in all sectors through structural transformation and overcome their marginalization through effective integration into the global economy.

The market-based reforms and policies pursued by the LDCs in the past two decades were motivated by this advice and were based on the assumption that a combination of macroeconomic austerity, rapid liberalization, privatization and deregulation would attract investment in sufficient quantity to generate rapid output growth, which in turn would automatically create jobs of adequate quantity and quality. But it is now evident that economic growth, although necessary, by itself neither guarantees job creation nor automatically results in inclusive development. To the contrary, it may even lead in some cases to an intensification of social inequality, rising unemployment and an increased incidence of poverty. In short, if employment creation and inclusive growth are the ultimate objectives, then the type of growth matters. It is evident that growth resulting from labour-intensive activities or originating in areas where the poor live is more likely to create jobs and contribute to inclusiveness than growth based on capital-intensive investments.

This Report proposes a policy framework that links investment with growth and employment creation to generate inclusive and sustainable development. The framework is based on the assumption that maximizing the employment creation potential of growth will not happen without the development of productive capacities. While initiatives to provide jobs through government-sponsored or internationally sponsored programmes might be valuable sources of employment in the short term, they do not provide long-term, sustainable solutions to the LDC employment challenge.

The proposed framework builds on two sets of ideas and concepts developed through UNCTAD's analytical work on LDCs and other developing countries.

First, it hypothesizes that:

- Economic growth which does not create decent jobs in sufficient quantity is unsustainable; and
- Job creation without the development of productive capacities is equally unsustainable.

Second, it provides a definition of productive capacity that is broad enough to incorporate all the elements essential for a country to build the competencies needed to produce goods and services but that is also sufficiently focused to identify priority areas for policies.

What is meant by productive capacities? At UNCTAD, the development of the concept in the LDC context was linked to earlier efforts to understand how structurally weak and underdeveloped economies like LDCs promote economic growth and how they initiate and then accelerate the growth process. Such efforts also sought to understand what the key factors or capabilities are that enable such economies to produce goods they can consume or sell, and what kinds of productive activities create quality jobs that contribute to poverty reduction.

The analytical work carried out at UNCTAD in search of answers to these questions led to the identification of a number of basic elements of productive capacity. Productive capacities are the productive resources, entrepreneurial capabilities and production linkages which together determine a country's capacity to produce goods and services and enable it to grow and develop.

Productive resources are factors of production and include natural resources, human resources, financial capital and physical capital.

Entrepreneurial capabilities are the skills, technology, knowledge and information needed to mobilize resources in order to build domestic enterprises that transform inputs into outputs – outputs that can competitively meet present and future demand. They also include abilities to invest, innovate, upgrade and create goods and services. As such, they refer to the competencies and technological learning needed to induce economic change.

Production linkages are flows of goods and services in the form of backward and forward linkages, flows of information and knowledge and flows of productive resources among enterprises and sectors of activities.

These three elements together determine not only the overall capacity of a country to produce goods and services, but also which goods and services a country can produce and sell. In this respect, therefore, productive capacities are country-specific and differ enormously from one country to the other. They also determine the quantity and the quality of the goods and services which a country can produce at a given time. Such potential production is obviously limited in the short term, but could be expanded in the medium and long term.

Based on this notion of productive capacity, in effect, a country's productive capacities are developing when that country shows improvements or progress in all these areas — when, in other words, its productive resources are expanding, it is acquiring technological and entrepreneurial capabilities and it is also creating production linkages. All of these improvements will enable the country to produce a growing array of goods and services and to create jobs and integrate beneficially into the global economy on the basis of an internal growth momentum. If this type of development continues, then the country will have productive capacities which enable it to create jobs that pay higher wages and to acquire the capability needed to produce an increasing range of higher value added goods and services both efficiently and competitively.

The development of productive capacities occurs through three closely related core economic processes that all countries have to undergo if they are to achieve sustained development. These are: the investment necessary to build domestic capital stock (physical capital, human capital, and so forth), which economists refer to as capital accumulation; structural change (or structural transformation); and building the capabilities of the domestic enterprise sector.

Is it possible to conceive of a dynamic process that brings the different elements together in a virtuous circle? Such a process could, for example, use enterprise development to transform productive structures into higher value-added activities that involve more skilled and technology-intensive production, which in turn results in higher incomes that can fuel demand and stimulate new investment. Such capital accumulation in turn enables the development of new activities and further diversification of the economy away from traditional sectors, thereby intensifying the process of structural change. The question is how to integrate these synergies into a framework for optimizing employment, which also requires choosing policies that do not contradict one another.

The policy framework for maximizing employment creation proposed in this Report aims to achieve that objective. It does so by identifying the set of policies which Governments should implement if they wish to establish a strong link between growth, employment creation and the development of productive capacities. The policy framework is based on a pragmatic assessment of the challenges facing LDCs and on an explicit recognition that the key to inclusive development is not simply higher rates of economic growth but also a higher employment intensity of growth.

In terms of capital accumulation, the new element in the proposed framework is that it not only values policies for their potential to stimulate an investment-growth nexus but also adds employment as a third and integral element of the nexus. Thus, for LDC policymakers the primary goal of capital accumulation would be to promote growth *with employment*. This has implications for the manner in which resources are mobilized and investment decisions are taken. The critical entry point for creating a strong and sustainable investment-growth-employment nexus is investment. The aim would be — initially through public investment in priority areas (and particularly in infrastructure) — to set in motion a virtuous circle in which investment boosts growth and growth creates employment, which, in turn, entails increased income for workers, giving rise to consumption that supports the expansion of the aggregate demand. Import leakages apart, expanded aggregate demand ideally creates incentives for new or additional investment to meet the growing demand. This circle could then be reiterated at a higher level of investment, growth, employment and income.

Given that most LDCs are very open economies, they would not be able to put the nexus in motion in the whole economy. However, the non-tradable sector is still relatively insulated, and policy space there is larger than in other parts of the economy. Initially, therefore, the most pragmatic approach would be to start to stimulate the process of capital accumulation via that nexus in the non-tradable sector. Over time, and as domestic firms develop their technological and learning capabilities, it would be possible gradually to extend the nexus to modern services that have become tradable because of technological innovations, import substitution activities and exporting activities.

Given the relatively weak private sector in many LDCs, it is more likely and realistic that in the short to medium term, the investment push required to kick-start the growth process will originate in the public sector. The idea here is not to encourage public ownership, which would amount to returning to failed policies of the past. Rather, the idea is to ensure that the capital-mobilizing power of the State is used to provide the initial investment impulses needed to drive the virtuous cycle in the short term. In other words, while public investment is crucial for kick-starting the nexus, it should be limited to the short and medium term. In the long term, the private sector should have the primary role in the nexus, and the responsibility of the public sector would then be reduced to supporting the efficient functioning of the nexus through appropriate policies and incentives aimed at encouraging private-sector investment in priority areas.

While the sectors to which initial public investment should be directed will necessarily be country-specific, investment in infrastructure seems to be a natural starting point, since the lack of adequate infrastructure in most LDCs is a serious bottleneck to enterprise development and productive capacity-building. Both goals could be achieved using the factor of production that is abundant, namely, labour. The prerequisite for this is a reorientation of policies on infrastructure investment to ensure that technically viable, cost-effective and employment-intensive options are used instead of more capital-intensive ones. In other words, there is a need for adopting appropriate technology.

Social services are also strong candidates for initiating an investment-growth-employment nexus driven by public investment. Millions of LDC citizens still have very poor or inadequate access to the most basic requirements of decent life, such as nutrition, sanitation, electricity, water, transport and communication, health services and education. Other sectors that could be targeted because of their potential to create employment are construction, expansion of services in rural areas, textile and leather production, and food processing.

The policy framework also assigns greater importance to the upgrading of firms and farms of all sizes, in view of their potential role in contributing to growth, creating productive capacities and generating jobs for both unskilled and skilled workers. In most LDCs the distribution of enterprises by size is heavily skewed towards micro- and small enterprises, typically operating in the informal sector. At the other extreme are a small number of large firms, most of which are either State-owned enterprises or large private firms, frequently owned or controlled by foreigners. These large firms tend to be found in the most profitable sectors, such as extractive industries, air transport and modern financial activities, where a large size is needed to make capital-intensive investments. Medium-size firms are typically absent. This "missing middle" in the LDCs — as in many other developing countries — is a result of the inability of small firms to grow and attain minimum efficient production sizes. Thus, the most important task in the context of the LDCs is the creation of the missing middle.

Policies aimed specifically at helping enterprises to grow in size can be divided into four groups: policies for formalization of firms, policies for financing of firms, policies for strengthening the organizational and entrepreneurial capacities of firms, and policies for overcoming failures in information and cooperation (policies to encourage networking and clustering). If successful, these policies will enable micro- and small enterprises to grow and become medium-sized or even large enterprises. Their growth will hopefully create employment for large numbers of workers and will thus be employment-intensive. This is simply because, in order to reach the optimum size of production, these enterprises need to increase the scale of production with the existing technology and methods of production. The benefits associated with economies of scale will then induce these firms to grow further. At the same time, the creation of medium-sized enterprises will foster conditions for technological progress. Once medium-sized enterprises have increased the scale of production beyond the optimal point with the existing production processes, they will be forced to innovate in order to maintain their profitability.

The policy framework proposed here suggests that enterprise development should be accompanied by the adoption of active policies to influence technological choice in different types of activities. A differentiation of the types of technology choice and corresponding policies is required in order to accommodate the frequently conflicting policy goals of technological progress and employment creation. Two different strategies should thus be followed: one for the modern sectors, involving acquisition of advanced technologies from developed countries, and another for the rest, involving so-called "appropriate" technology.

In terms of structural change, the challenge for LDCs is not that their economic structure is static, but rather that in most cases it is changing in a manner not conducive to building productive capacities and creating quality jobs in sufficient quantity. In order to position the LDCs' economies on a job-rich growth and inclusive development path, the policy framework recommends a three-pronged approach to employment creation that focuses on the generation of foreign exchange through investment in both capital- and labour-intensive tradable activities; the expansion of the non-tradable sector and the concomitant creation of jobs; and productivity improvement in agriculture in general and subsistence agriculture in particular.

The three-pronged approach to employment creation recognizes that the process of structural change should ideally be led by the consolidation and expansion of the modernizing core of the economy, composed of high value added knowledge-intensive and competitive activities in manufacturing, mining, mechanized agriculture and modern services. In terms of labour, ideally this should be achieved through the transfer of workers from low-productivity, poorly paid work to more productive and better employment in other sectors (i.e., intersectoral transfer of labour).

However, the expansion of the modern sector needs to be complemented by an improvement in the quantity and quality of jobs in the remaining sectors of the economy. Given the prevalence of working poverty in LDCs, this implies raising productivity in traditional activities. All opportunities to improve livelihood opportunities and create employment in labour-intensive activities in these other sectors should be explored and promoted.

The logic behind the three-pronged approach to employment creation is that the increase in productivity in agriculture releases labour which should be absorbed by the rest of the economy, that is, tradable and non-tradable activities. Since the tradables are subject to intense competition, the extent to which they can absorb labour is limited. In other words, the choice of capital-labour ratio tends to be exogenously determined. As a consequence, non-tradable activities would have to provide the bulk of employment opportunities for new entrants and also for those released from subsistence activities. These sectors include infrastructure and housing; basic services (education, health, sanitation, communication, public administration); technical services, repair and maintenance, and most transportation services; insurance services, property and commercial brokerage; personal, social and community services; public administration; security and defence. Since these activities do not generally face international competition, the policy space to influence outcomes in these sectors is larger than in the tradable sector. This implies that there are much greater possibilities for increasing the employment intensity of growth in these activities.

However, it is important for policy to focus not only on employment generation, but also on productive transformation – in each of these sectors separately, and also in the economy as a whole. The three-pronged approach proposed here emphasizes that employment creation is crucial, but that it should be pursued simultaneously with modernization of economic activities and increase of productivity. The latter would ensure that not only the quantity of employment, but also the quality of jobs, improves.

The framework developed in this Report should not be viewed as a one-size-fits-all solution for the employment challenge faced by the LDCs. There is considerable room for diversity in applying the framework across LDCs, reflecting differences in resource endowments, size, geographical location, production structure and export structure. Such diversity implies different starting points and different policy choices. Policymakers in each country should carefully examine the specificities of their economies before deciding how to use the framework.

Policies for employment-rich growth

Policies for employment-rich growth in LDCs should have two complementary objectives: expanding the number of jobs so as to absorb the growing labour force and the youth bulge, and raising the incomes generated by these jobs (by means of productivity gains) so as to combat the generalized prevalence of poverty and underemployment. Reaching these objectives will involve implementing a range of mutually supportive policies aimed at building productive capacity and fostering structural transformation. Policy interventions should cover three broad areas: macroeconomic policies, enterprise development and technological learning, and public-sector investment and actions for job creation.

Macroeconomic policies

Inclusive development calls for a macroeconomic policy approach that goes beyond the narrower goal of macroeconomic stability. This broader approach calls for expanding the number of instruments and coordinating macroeconomic policies with other policies to stimulate the development of productive capacities. In this context, fiscal policy becomes more important than monetary policy. It should target financing public investment in physical and human capital by accelerating public investment in infrastructure and raising spending on education and training. To do so will require strengthening government capacity to mobilize and manage fiscal revenues, whether domestic or external. At the national level, this can be done initially through domestic resource mobilization, which entails changes in fiscal policy and tax administration. The measures most likely to raise fiscal revenues in the LDCs include the following: (i) introducing value added tax (VAT), reducing VAT exemptions and raising the VAT rate on luxury consumption; (ii) raising excise taxes on alcohol, tobacco and vehicles; (iii) reducing tax holidays and exemptions for corporations and high-income expatriates; (iv) increasing taxation on urban property (where the wealthiest live); (v) reforming the taxation of the financial sector; and (vi) refraining from further tariff cuts until alternative sources of revenue are put in place. Tax administration and collection, in turn, can be made more efficient, by streamlining information management, cross-checking statements and declarations and setting up a special unit for high-income taxpayers.

For resource-rich LDCs, fiscal revenue can be increased by modifying the extremely favourable terms currently offered to foreign investors in agriculture and mining. This may involve imposing a tax on land leased for large-scale investment projects, raising existing land taxes or revising the taxation of activities undertaken by those projects. Governments with mining resources can raise their revenues by adopting higher levies, royalties, income taxes or export taxes. LDC authorities should also strengthen the mobilization of external resources from both traditional and non-traditional aid donors and from multilateral and regional financial institutions.

Although fiscal policy may be more important than monetary policy in developing productive capacities, monetary policy is still critical. It should, however, be less fixated on attaining an inflation rate in the low single digits than on targeting full employment of productive resources and providing reasonable macroeconomic stability. Credit policy is of crucial importance in the LDCs, particularly for micro-, small- and medium-sized enterprises, which are typically credit-constrained in these countries. In that regard, public development banks can play an important role by providing credit when private financial institutions fail to do so.

LDCs are particularly vulnerable to external shocks. To protect themselves from such risks, they should also develop a capital account management system, including residence requirements on capital expatriation and stricter regulation of external borrowing. Large commodity-exporting countries may also consider setting up a stabilization fund to protect themselves against strong fluctuations in international commodity prices

Enterprise development

Private sector development is a *sine qua non* for large-scale employment generation in LDCs, since it generates the bulk of jobs, both today and tomorrow. The main policies for developing their private sector are industrial policy, enterprise policy, rural development policies, and education and training policies

Industrial policy is designed to steer the economy towards structural transformation, by moving to higher-productivity activities both among and within sectors. There are two types of strategies that LDCs can pursue to bolster the employment intensity of growth. The first is to build on activities of existing comparative advantage, by fostering backward and forward linkages and technological upgrading in these sectors. This typically means focusing on natural resource-based activities. Agriculture can be the basis for developing downstream industries, such as food processing, geared mainly to domestic and regional markets, but also global markets. It can also yield other types of products (e.g. agricultural raw materials) that can be further processed before exporting. To this end, such measures as the provision of industrial extension services, temporary export tariffs and support to firm clustering (see below) can be applied. Internationally, these actions should be complemented by enhanced regional cooperation on some agricultural commodity chains of production, processing and marketing (e.g. rice, maize, wheat, sugar, meat and dairy products) which have the potential to meet increasing regional demand through regional integration schemes. Governments should act simultaneously on transport, logistical, processing and market infrastructure to nurture regional value chains.

A second type of industrial policy strategy aims at changing the capital-labour ratio of the economy, by attracting investment in labour-intensive industries. Some LDCs will be able to take advantage of the window of opportunity opened by China's likely delocalization of the lower end of its manufacturing industry, through a combination of integrating domestic firms into manufacturing global value chains (GVCs) and attracting foreign direct investment (FDI). Domestically, this strategy should be complemented by policies on clustering, export promotion and labour costs. Clustering allows firms to benefit from technological and managerial economies of scale (externalities) and act collectively. Policymakers can support industrial clusters by ensuring a superior supply of infrastructure, logistical, customs, financial and legal services; providing preferential access to land; and facilitating easier administrative procedures. LDCs can promote exports (especially non-traditional exports) by means of export processing zones, export subsidies, public provision of trade finance, and trade promotion organizations. Labour costs can be kept competitive by ensuring an adequate supply of wage goods and services, particularly food (by means of agricultural policy – see below) and transport, housing and so forth.

International integration through global value chains (GVCs) and FDI will have a lasting developmental effect only if such undertakings are complemented by fostering continuous technological capacity-building on the part of participating domestic firms (so as to avoid being locked in to labour-intensive, lower-productivity activities). Policies should also target the creation of linkages with other domestic firms that can learn and upgrade through interactive learning. In some cases, authorities may have to negotiate with foreign investors in order to induce domestic linkages and technology transfer to local firms.

Effective *enterprise policy* measures for stimulating the development of urban-based micro- and small enterprises (MSEs) include facilitating their access to capital and helping them upgrade into formal status. Policymakers need to expand the financing made available to these firms through national development banks or commercial banks. The former should open special credit lines for MSEs. Authorities can counteract the risk aversion of commercial banks and encourage them to expand their lending to MSEs by: (a) subsidizing or providing loan guarantees for commercial bank credit to such firms; (b) enacting lower asset-based reserve requirements for this market segment than for other types of lending; and (c) linking formal and informal financial institutions (e.g. rotating savings and credit societies), which have more information on borrowers' risks and operate with lower transaction costs. Public and private financial institutions should select those MSEs with high growth potential, based on current profitability and entrepreneurs' profiles. In order to facilitate the entry of MSEs to the formal sector, LDC authorities can simplify procedures and requirements for registry and reporting operations, reduce the cost of registry, allow for gradual compliance of regulations and establish a department or semi-autonomous body to lend managerial support and advice to MSEs.

Rural development policy is a special challenge, given the dismally low level of productivity of rural areas, and requires action on infrastructure, technology and financing. The State needs to invest heavily in rural infrastructure, especially irrigation, electricity, transport, storage (warehousing) and communication (ICTs) in order to boost rural productivity and foster backward and forward linkages of farms. Rural extension services need to be established or rehabilitated to provide advice and training on cultivation techniques, water management, choice of seeds and/ or crops, warehousing, conditions of land quality and water access, avoiding soil degradation, and techniques for meeting market requirements. The technology content of such services should actively involve local communities and combine modern technology with traditional or indigenous knowledge systems. The services should focus on scale-neutral technologies that can be applied by smallholders. While typically provided by State institutions, the latter may also work with domestic and international non-governmental organizations (NGOs) and farmer associations in delivering extension services. The main upstream policy direction involves increased funding of national or regional agricultural research centres that deal with agro-ecological zones or strategic food products. To this end, funding by regional partners should be pooled and possibly backed by international donors.

Providing rural producers with access to capital and finance requires offering both seasonal and long-term finance to farmers and rural non-farm economic agents. This should be undertaken by agricultural development banks, State banks, post office financial services, community credit cooperatives (which have better knowledge of borrowers' creditworthiness) and, in some cases, commercial banks. Such institutions also have the capacity to mobilize rural savings and turn them into credit. Larger financial institutions may also set up specialized rural/microfinance units. State-sponsored credit provision, in turn, may entail establishing or rehabilitating rural development banks that can offer financial services not provided by commercial banks or other financial institutions. Using insurance and warehouse receipt schemes is one way of allowing farmers to turn their agricultural produce into collateral. Where mining is concerned, building linkages is more challenging, but this can be done by encouraging local firms to provide inputs like labour-intensive services (catering, cleaning, etc.).

Most of the above-mentioned instruments of industrial, enterprise and rural development policy are targeted policies. They need to be complemented by horizontal policy measures aimed at increasing the knowledge intensity of the LDC economies, so as to make them more adaptable and better prepared to meet the requirements of a modern economy. This leads us to *education and training policy*. In primary education, the priority is to improve quality. In secondary and tertiary education and in technical and vocational training, LDCs need to both expand the supply of services and improve the quality. This includes revising curricula and teaching methods in order to make the labour force more adaptable and innovative, and adjusting education policies to meet future domestic labour market requirements.

There are three other policy measures for raising the knowledge intensity of the economy. The first is to foster cooperation between academia (university and research institutions) and businesses (e.g. in the context of clusters). The second is to set up or strengthen standard-setting bodies (e.g. for quality and sanitary certification), either through government initiative or through partnerships between government and industry or sectoral associations. The third is to apply tax breaks or training levies in order to provide industry-specific training for the labour force.

Public sector-led job creation

But in addition to involving the private sector, the State itself must play a role in generating jobs, either directly or indirectly, especially in the earlier phases of development. Since infrastructure work is a non-tradable type of activity, and since it finances the bulk of projects, the State can influence the choice of technique so as to ensure the adoption of labour-intensive production processes. These have several advantages over capital-intensive technologies: they generate more jobs, have lower costs, can contribute to local enterprise development and capacity-building, provide more readily available maintenance and repair services, and can generate foreign exchange savings.

Dr. Mukhisa Kituyi
Secretary-General of UNCTAD

CHAPTER 1

RECENT TRENDS AND OUTLOOK FOR THE LDCs

A. Introduction

The performance of the least developed countries (LDCs) in terms of economic growth has been weaker by a full two percentage points in the past five years (2009–2013) than during the previous boom period (2002–2008). It has also been below the target rate of 7-per-cent annual growth established in the Istanbul Programme of Action (IPoA) for the Least Developed Countries for the Decade 2011–2020. This chapter analyses recent macroeconomic trends in the LDCs and assesses some of the factors behind their weaker performance.

The performance of the LDCs in terms of economic growth has been weaker by a full two percentage points in the past five years (2009–2013) than during the previous boom period (2002–2008).

The chapter shows that with the global economy still struggling to return to a strong and sustained growth path, the external environment faced by the LDCs has been less propitious in the past five years than in the previous period. The recent slowdown of world trade to a near standstill has weakened the demand for LDC imports, most notably in the case of developed countries, but also in emerging economies, which are affected by weak demand in developed countries as well. In addition to weaker demand for their exports, the LDCs have been faced with heightened volatility of commodity prices and capital flows. In particular, the international prices of many commodities have declined from their peaks of 2011, adversely affecting those LDCs which are characterized by high levels of commodity dependence. External financing has also been volatile recently, and less available than in the previous period.

Apart from the recent slower growth of their real GDP, the LDCs' investment and savings rates have continued to be insufficient for robust economic growth and rapid poverty reduction, and are also below the rates of other developing countries (ODCs). In addition, the process of structural change in most LDCs has advanced only very slowly, and in some cases has stalled. For the LDCs as a group, the share of agriculture and services in gross domestic product (GDP) declined somewhat during the first decade of the century, while the share of industry expanded. Within industry, however, manufacturing has stagnated, but non-manufacturing activities have expanded strongly. Critically, the share of the manufacturing sector in GDP has diminished in half of the LDCs over the period concerned. Thus, LDCs are still characterized by weak development of manufacturing industries, high levels of commodity dependence, heavy dependence on external financing and inadequate integration into the global economy.

Structural weaknesses of the LDCs are likely to remain unchanged, given that the prospects for the global economy continue to be fraught with uncertainties and risks and that slow growth is likely to persist at least through 2015.

These structural weaknesses of the LDCs are likely to remain unchanged, given that the prospects for the global economy continue to be fraught with uncertainties and risks and that slow growth is likely to persist at least through 2015. The outlook for the LDCs is accordingly not very good. Even if the downside risks do not materialize, the GDP growth rate in these countries will be lower than the IPoA target, and as such insufficient for substantial progress to be made in development and poverty reduction. Responding effectively to the employment challenge — the main topic of this Report — will be even more difficult for the LDCs given the current outlook.

This chapter is organized into three sections. Section B provides a brief analysis of recent trends in the global economy and their implications for the LDCs. Section C looks at recent economic performance in the LDCs. Where data are available, the section identifies the overall pattern for the LDCs as a group, regional differences between African, Asian and island LDCs, and variations among individual LDCs. Section D discusses the short-term outlook for the global economy and the LDCs.

B. Recent trends in the global economy and implications for the LDCs

1. GLOBAL GROWTH AND INTERNATIONAL TRADE

As pointed out in the *Trade and Development Report 2013* (UNCTAD, 2013a) of the United Nations Conference on Trade and Development (UNCTAD), the global economy is still struggling to return to a strong and sustained growth path. More than five years after the start of the global financial crisis the growth of the global economy has still not returned to pre-crisis levels. Economic activity in many countries, and particularly in developed economies, continues to suffer from the impacts of the financial and economic crisis that began in 2008, resulting from busts in the housing and financial markets of the major developed countries. Weak growth may also be due to the current macroeconomic policy stance, characterized by fiscal consolidation in many countries, both developed and developing.

More than five years after the start of the global financial crisis the growth of the global economy has still not returned to pre-crisis levels.

The growth rate of world output, at around 3.2 per cent in 2012 and 2013, was about one and a half percentage points lower than in the period 2002–2008 (table 1).[1] In addition, the global economy has been decelerating continuously since 2010. While the coordinated macroeconomic effort of policymakers in many countries to support growth in the wake of the financial crisis resulted in a vigorous rebound that year, the withdrawal of fiscal stimulus while the private sector was still very weak led to strong deceleration in 2011. Deceleration has continued since then in both developed and developing countries, although the growth rate in the former has been substantially lower than in the latter.

Slow growth in the United States and Japan, and recession in the European Union, means that developing countries continue to be the main growth drivers, accounting for about two thirds of global growth in 2011–2013. In several developing countries, growth has been driven more by domestic demand than by exports since external demand has been weak, especially in developed economies (UNCTAD, 2013a). The growth in LDCs, at an average 5 per cent since 2009, has been substantially lower than in the boom period of 2002–2008, when it reached 7.5 per cent. In per capita terms, real GDP growth rate in the LDCs has hovered at around 3 per cent from 2009 to date, or two percentage points lower than in the previous period.

Developing countries continue to be the main growth drivers, accounting for about two thirds of global growth in 2011–2013.

Economic activity in developed countries in 2013 has begun to show signs of divergence, and has been characterized by the *World Economic Outlook* of the International Monetary Fund (IMF) (International Monetary Fund, 2013) as a "three-speed" recovery. The continuing difficulties in the European Union of resolving the sovereign debt crisis while the private sector goes through

	Real GDP Growth						Real GDP per capita growth					
	2002–2008	2009	2010	2011	2012	2013	2002-2008	2009	2010	2011	2012	2013
LDCs	7.5	5.0	5.6	4.5	5.3	5.7	5.0	2.6	3.3	3.2	2.9	3.4
Advanced economies	2.5	-3.5	3.0	1.6	1.2	1.2	1.8	-4.1	2.5	1.1	0.8	0.8
Emerging and developing economies	7.6	2.7	7.6	6.4	5.1	5.3	6.1	1.3	6.2	5.5	3.7	4.0
World	4.7	-0.6	5.2	4.0	3.2	3.3	3.3	-1.8	4.0	3.0	1.9	2.1

Table 1. Real GDP and real GDP per capita growth rates for LDCs, advanced economies, emerging and developing economies and world, selected years

Source: UNCTAD secretariat calculations based on IMF, *World Economic Outlook* database, April 2013.
Notes: The LDCs' growth is calculated as the weighted average of each country's real growth (base year 2000); data for 2012 are preliminary and are forecasted for 2013.

the process of deleveraging have resulted in economic contraction for two consecutive years. The policy stance, characterized by expansionary monetary policy coupled with fiscal austerity, has not provided the necessary support in what has been termed a "balance-sheet recession". Some observers (Koo, 2011) find remarkable similarities between the Japanese experience of the past two decades and the recent problems faced by many advanced countries, particularly in Europe.

Experience shows that economies need a long time to recover from the balance-sheet recession caused by financial crisis, as the private sector must pay down its debt in the process of deleveraging (Reinhart and Rogoff, 2009). That process could go on for many years and could well induce a sort of "debt trauma", whereby the private sector remains reluctant to borrow money even after its balance sheet is fully repaired. Until the private sector is both willing and able to borrow again, the economy will operate at less than full potential. A clear policy direction which is suggested by this characterization is that fiscal support of the aggregate demand is needed to overcome the adverse effects of the balance-sheet recession.

In the United States, the economic situation has started to improve, slowly but steadily. Growth rates of around 2 per cent in the past couple of years have been the result of an accommodative monetary and fiscal policy. In contrast with the European insistence on early fiscal consolidation, the United States fiscal policy supported the process of private-sector deleveraging with fiscal deficits on the order of 10 per cent of GDP. Fiscal consolidation began only in the spring of 2013, when the fiscal drag on the economy had less chances of derailing the incipient recovery. Japan, in turn, has been radically changing the policy mix since early 2013, providing a strong fiscal stimulus in conjunction with monetary policy expansion aimed at reviving economic growth and curbing deflationary trends. While the full impact of these policies cannot be ascertained at the time of writing, early signs in terms of growth rebound are positive.

International trade in goods has not returned to the rapid growth rate of the pre-crisis years. Like the growth of real GDP, it rebounded strongly in 2010 and has been decelerating continuously since then. Trade in goods measured by volume expanded by 5.3 per cent in 2011 and by only 1.7 per cent in 2012. Most of that slowdown was due to lethargic economic activity in developed countries, particularly in Europe. As a result, exports from developing countries increased by 6.0 per cent in 2011 and just 3.6 per cent in 2012. This downward trend in international trade highlights the vulnerabilities of developing countries, and particularly of the LDCs, given their export-led strategy, at a time of lacklustre growth in developed countries. With a view to responding effectively to that adverse trend, *Trade and Development Report 2013* (UNCTAD, 2013a) explored the options for a gradual shift in the relative importance of sources of growth towards a greater emphasis on domestic sources.

2. RECENT TRENDS IN FINANCIAL FLOWS

As with international trade, private capital flows recovered quickly in 2010, helped by sharp cuts in interest rates and unorthodox monetary expansion (known as quantitative easing) in many developed countries. However, they have lost their pre-crisis momentum and have become unstable and uneven. In terms of magnitude, McKinsey Global Institute (Lund et al., 2013) reports that cross-border capital flows remain 60 per cent below their pre-crisis peak. Regarding instability, large capital inflows to many emerging economies in 2011 and 2012 turned into sudden outflows in the second quarter of 2013, as the first signs of a probable reversal of quantitative easing emerged in developed countries. This demonstrates how unstable these flows are and how easily they could

Economies need a long time to recover from the balance-sheet recession caused by financial crisis, as the private sector must pay down its debt in the process of deleveraging.

International trade in goods has not returned to the rapid growth rate of the pre-crisis years; measured by volume, it expanded by 5.3 per cent in 2011 and by only 1.7 per cent in 2012.

Private capital flows have become unstable and uneven; large inflows to many emerging economies in 2011 and 2012 turned into sudden outflows in the second quarter of 2013.

derail years of painstaking work to create stable macroeconomic conditions in developing countries.

The crisis in developed countries, however, did not have a sizeable impact on total flows of workers' remittances to developing countries. While the growth rate of remittances slowed down, the total amount continued to grow throughout the period 2009–2012. This points to their countercyclical nature, which is in contrast to other types of private capital flows. In the case of the LDCs, moreover, some two thirds of the total amount of remittances comes from other developing countries (UNCTAD, 2012a). Since their economies continued to grow at a reasonable pace, there is no reason for remittances to the LDCs to decelerate significantly.

Flows of foreign direct investment (FDI), in contrast, are proving to be less resilient than remittances. According to UNCTAD's *World Investment Report 2013* (UNCTAD, 2013b), global FDI fell 18 per cent in 2012; FDI recovery is on a bumpy road and may take longer than expected. In the case of the LDCs, however, FDI increased in 2011 and 2012, following two years of stagnation. Finally, flows of official development assistance (ODA) from member countries of the Development Assistance Committee (DAC) of the Organization for Economic Cooperation and Development (OECD) declined in both 2011 and 2012, reflecting a more conservative fiscal policy stance in developed countries.

As a result of these diverse trends, developing countries and economies in transition continue to make substantial net financial transfers to developed countries. In 2012, these net outflows were estimated at $845 billion, down from $1 trillion in 2011. The LDCs, however, received positive net transfers on the order of $17 billion in 2012 (United Nations, 2013).

3. RECENT TRENDS IN COMMODITY PRICES

Commodity prices are particularly important for many LDCs, given the predominance of commodities in these countries' total exports. After a precipitous fall in 2008 and early 2009, commodity prices have recovered strongly on the back of four different factors. First, the demand for many commodities remained buoyant, reflecting the shift from export- to investment-led growth in China in response to the global crisis (Akyüz, 2013). Second, accommodative monetary policy has flooded the developed economies with liquidity at a time when investment opportunities there have been scarce. In response, inflows of financial capital to commodity markets have intensified, driving up commodity prices. Third, the "Arab Spring" that began in 2011 resulted in disruptions of oil production in several producing countries, most notably in North Africa and the Middle East, driving up the price of oil despite increasing supply capacity in North America. Lastly, weather disruptions, including the worst drought in the United States in more than half a century, kept food prices high throughout the period (United Nations, 2013). For all these reasons, commodity prices have stayed high and have played a major role in supporting the growth of real GDP in the LDCs in the past four years. Recent commodity price trends, however, reflect a slight drop from the peaks of early 2011, possibly because of the slower growth of the world economy (table 2).

It is important to emphasize that most commodity prices are still substantially higher than the average prices during the commodity price boom of 2002–2008. This is particularly the case for food and oil prices, both of which have been fluctuating within a narrow band very close to their respective peaks of 2011 and 2012. Prices of other commodities, most notably some metals and ores, have been declining recently due to weaker demand, the uncertain outlook for global economic activity and improved supply prospects.

While the growth rate of remittances slowed down, the total amount continued to grow throughout the period 2009–2012.

Flows of foreign direct investment are proving to be less resilient than remittances.

Commodity prices have stayed high and have played a major role in supporting the growth of real GDP in the LDCs in the past four years.

Recent commodity price trends reflect a slight drop from the peaks of early 2011, possibly because of the slower growth of the world economy.

Table 2. Price indices for selected primary commodities of importance to LDCs, 2008–2013 (Price indices, 2000=100)									
	2008	2009	2010	2011	2012	2013 Q1	2013 Q2	Standard deviation 2000–2012	% change 2000–2012
All food	**236**	**216**	**232**	**273**	**269**	**260**	**253**	**66.8**	**169.0**
Wheat	288	197	204	276	275	280	272	67.3	175.5
Rice	344	289	256	271	285	280	270	91.0	184.7
Sugar	156	222	260	318	263	227	214	79.4	163.4
Fish meal	274	298	409	372	377	452	441	106.5	277.4
Coffee, Arabicas	163	166	228	321	220	182	174	73.4	120.4
Coffee, Robustas	252	183	200	275	263	260	246	75.4	162.6
Cocoa beans	291	325	353	336	269	249	260	81.5	169.5
Tea	109	127	125	140	141	129	107	24.2	40.6
Agricultural raw materials	**198**	**163**	**226**	**289**	**223**	**216**	**202**	**59.9**	**122.6**
Tobacco	120	142	144	150	144	147	146	23.4	44.0
Cotton	121	106	175	258	150	152	157	49.0	50.4
Non-coniferous woods	154	154	161	158	153	150	160	23.8	53.2
Minerals, ores and metals	**332**	**232**	**327**	**375**	**322**	**332**	**303**	**109.5**	**221.9**
Iron ore	83	100	184	210	161	186	157	..	..
Aluminium	166	107	140	155	130	129	118	30.5	30.4
Copper	384	283	416	487	438	437	410	152.1	338.5
Gold	312	349	440	562	598	584	507	174.2	498.1
Crude petroleum	**344**	**219**	**280**	**368**	**372**	**372**	**352**	**106.5**	**272.1**

Source: UNCTADstat, *Commodity Price Bulletin*, August 2013.

4. Recent developments in special and differential treatment of the LDCs

International support measures have been specifically designed and adopted by the international community to help the LDCs promote development and poverty reduction and reduce their marginalization and vulnerability in today's global economy. Some of these measures have been stipulated as provisions in multilateral agreements aimed at giving the LDCs flexibility in implementation or in meeting obligations. The preparatory negotiations for the Ninth Ministerial Conference of the World Trade Organization (WTO), to be held in December 2013 in Bali, have taken up several issues of interest to the LDCs, such as duty-free, quota-free access, services waivers, rules of origin and cotton-related issues. Although at the time of writing the outcome of the negotiations was not known, there has been progress in several of these areas.

The WTO Council on Trade-related Aspects of Intellectual Property Rights (TRIPS) adopted in June 2013 a decision to extend the time period allotted for the LDCs to implement the TRIPS Agreement.

One concrete result concerns the special and differential treatment of the LDCs in the area of intellectual property rights (IPRs). The WTO Council on Trade-related Aspects of Intellectual Property Rights (TRIPS) adopted in June 2013 a decision to extend the time period allotted for the LDCs to implement the TRIPS Agreement. This Agreement (art. 66.1) states that in view of the special needs and requirements of the LDCs, their economic, financial and administrative constraints, and their need for flexibility to create a viable technological base, the LDCs shall not be required to apply the provisions of the Agreement for a period that can be extended by the TRIPS Council. In practice, this means the LDCs are not obliged to implement many of the Agreement's provisions until 1 July 2021, or until they cease to be an LDC, whichever is earlier. The importance of the decision lies in the fact that the LDCs retain their policy space and continue to benefit from this international support measure in order to overcome their productive capacity constraints and develop their technological capabilities.

The importance of the decision lies in the fact that the LDCs retain their policy space and continue to benefit from this international support measure in order to overcome their productive capacity constraints and develop their technological capabilities.

On the negative side, it is important to emphasize that the world crossed a key threshold in relation to climate change in May 2013, when the concentration of carbon dioxide reached 400 parts per million (ppm) in two separate measurements, one at a Hawaii measurement station and the other in Switzerland. The global average is expected to exceed the 400 ppm mark within a year. Unfortunately, this event has not received due media coverage, despite the fact that the impacts of climate change are already being felt in the increased frequency of extreme weather events in many parts of the world. At the current rate of increase of carbon dioxide emissions into the atmosphere, the goal of staying below the 450-ppm threshold is unlikely to be achieved. Given the direct link between the carbon dioxide concentration in the atmosphere and the Earth's temperature, the average world temperature will likely rise by more than two degrees Celsius by the end of the century, causing irreversible changes in the global climate.

The world crossed a key threshold in relation to climate change in May 2013, when the concentration of carbon dioxide reached 400 parts per million.

Regrettably, the LDCs are more vulnerable to climate change than other countries, and are expected to bear the greatest burden of adjusting to its effects (UNCTAD, 2010). The recent crossing of the 400-ppm threshold should provide a wake-up call to the international community to change the course of events while the alterations to climate are still reversible. It should also be taken up by the LDCs themselves, which should renew their efforts to place the issue higher on the agenda of the international community and to devise national strategies to respond to this enormous challenge.[2]

C. Recent economic performance of the LDCs

1. TRENDS IN THE REAL ECONOMY

Despite the slow global recovery, real GDP growth in the LDCs has picked up somewhat, from 4.5 per cent in 2011 to 5.3 per cent in 2012. As was the case in other developing countries, more robust domestic demand in the LDCs partially compensated for feeble external demand (UNCTAD, 2013a). IMF forecasts for 2013 point to a similar growth rate for the LDCs, in the 5-to-6 per cent range. It is worth repeating that these growth rates, although much higher than in developed countries, are a full two percentage points lower than the LDCs' performance during the boom period, and are also below the target rate of 7-per-cent annual growth established in the IPoA (table 3).

Despite the slow global recovery, real GDP growth in the LDCs has picked up somewhat, from 4.5 per cent in 2011 to 5.3 per cent in 2012.

The real GDP growth rates of different groups of LDCs continued recent trends, with African LDCs lagging behind their Asian and island counterparts. These trends have now been in place for four consecutive years, unlike in the

Table 3. Real GDP and real GDP per capita growth rates for LDCs, by groups, selected years

	Real GDP Growth						Real GDP per capita growth					
	2002–2008	2009	2010	2011	2012	2013	2002–2008	2009	2010	2011	2012	2013
Total LDCs	**7.5**	**5.0**	**5.6**	**4.5**	**5.3**	**5.7**	**5.0**	**2.6**	**3.3**	**3.2**	**2.9**	**3.4**
African LDCs and Haiti	7.5	4.2	4.9	4.4	4.8	5.6	4.8	1.5	2.2	3.4	2.1	3.0
Asian LDCs	7.5	5.9	6.4	4.6	5.8	5.7	5.5	4.1	4.7	2.9	4.1	4.0
Island LDCs	4.9	2.7	5.5	6.8	5.7	5.8	2.7	0.6	2.9	4.5	3.5	3.6
Food and agriculture exporters	5.2	6.1	6.3	5.4	2.0	5.1	2.7	3.2	3.4	2.5	-0.8	2.2
Fuel exporters	9.2	3.0	4.0	-1.1	2.2	3.9	6.2	0.2	1.2	5.5	-0.5	1.1
Manufactures exporters	6.2	5.3	5.9	6.5	6.0	6.1	4.8	4.1	4.8	5.4	4.7	5.1
Mineral exporters	5.6	4.0	6.1	5.9	5.7	7.1	2.8	1.2	3.3	3.1	2.9	4.2
Services exporters	8.7	7.8	6.1	6.0	5.7	5.0	5.9	5.2	3.5	3.5	3.1	2.4
Mixed exporters	7.8	4.5	6.0	5.2	6.7	6.6	5.2	1.9	3.4	2.6	4.4	4.3

Source: UNCTAD secretariat calculations based on IMF, *World Economic Outlook* database, April 2013.
Notes: The LDCs' growth is calculated as the weighted average of each country's real growth (base year 2000); data for 2012 are preliminary and are forecasted for 2013.

previous period, when the African LDCs had been growing at the same pace as the Asian LDCs. In addition, the growth rates of African LDCs' real GDP per capita show a larger lag due to their higher population growth rate.

In terms of growth performance of groups based on export specialization, the fuel-exporting LDCs continued to record growth rates below those of other groups. One of the reasons is undoubtedly their extreme dependence on just one export product (ranging from 76.2 per cent of total exports in the case of Yemen to 96.6 per cent in the case of Angola), which means that any disruption of production and any price variation has a disproportionate influence on the performance of the economy as a whole. Food and agriculture exporters also registered low growth rates in 2012, in part because of erratic weather patterns. The performance of other groups of LDCs has been much more stable in the past four years, with only slight variations from one year to another.

There were 15 LDCs with growth rates exceeding 6 per cent, but also 10 with growth rates below 3 per cent.

The heterogeneous performance of LDC groups has been reflected not only in real GDP growth rates, but also in the growth rates of individual countries. In effect, there were 15 countries with growth rates exceeding 6 per cent, but also 10 countries with growth rates below 3 per cent. Given the high population growth rate, the latter countries had stagnant or negative growth in per capita terms. This has severe consequences for their poverty reduction, for their achievement of the Millennium Development Goals (MDGs), and more broadly for their human development. Three LDCs were in a recession in 2012, since they had negative growth rates of real GDP.

The heterogeneity in real GDP growth rates among the LDCs is a consequence of wide disparities in other macroeconomic indicators. Most notably, and most importantly for economic growth, the rates of gross capital formation differ widely across individual LDCs (annex table 4). The IPoA has identified a gross capital formation rate of 25 per cent of GDP as a prerequisite for attaining real GDP growth rates of 7 per cent. Seventeen LDCs managed to reach, or even exceed, that benchmark in 2011. However, 31 others had an investment rate below the 25-per-cent benchmark, and the rate in several LDCs was even below the 10-per-cent mark. Given the close relationship between investment and economic growth, these countries' growth prospects are not very bright.

31 LDCs had an investment rate below the 25-per-cent benchmark, and the rate in several LDCs was even below the 10-per-cent mark.

In addition, the gross domestic savings rate was lower than the gross capital formation rate in 40 of the 48 LDCs in 2011. In other words, these countries had a negative external resource gap, which means that they had to rely on external financing to close the gap between investment and domestic savings. This makes these LDCs not only dependent on external financing, but also vulnerable to fluctuations in different sources of external financing. Given that some such sources are less stable and predictable than others (see section 3 below on trends in external finance), the structure of external financing of individual countries is important for mitigating that vulnerability.

The gross domestic savings rate was lower than the gross capital formation rate in 40 of the 48 LDCs in 2011, which means that they had to rely on external financing to close the gap between investment and domestic savings.

While the average gross capital formation rate for LDCs was equivalent to 22 per cent of GDP in 2011, in developing countries excluding the LDCs it represented 32.8 per cent, almost 11 percentage points higher. The LDCs thus lag substantially behind other developing countries in creating potential for future growth.[3] Moreover, the gross domestic savings rate in other developing countries was 35.9 per cent of GDP, 15 percentage points higher than in the LDCs. As a consequence, other developing countries on average do not depend on external financing for investment and hence are much less vulnerable to external shocks than the LDCs.

The fact that most energy-exporting LDCs are located in Africa also explains the regional differences in gross domestic savings rates. African LDCs, mostly because of the energy exporters among them, had gross domestic savings rates equivalent to 23.8 per cent of GDP in 2011, in contrast to Asian LDCs, whose rate was only 15.1 per cent. Thus, African LDCs on average have higher gross domestic savings rates than gross capital formation rates. Within that group, however, there are pronounced differences. Asian LDCs, in turn, have a negative external resource gap equivalent to six percentage points of GDP. The data for island LDCs reveal a very high gross domestic savings rate of 38.6 per cent of GDP and a low gross capital formation rate of 15.4 per cent. These averages are due mostly to Timor-Leste, a large energy producer with characteristics atypical of small island developing States (SIDS).

Going beyond macroeconomic indicators to examine developments over a decade allows us to explore the extent and direction of the process of structural change in the LDCs (annex table 5). The evidence shows that the share of agriculture in GDP decreased in 33 LDCs and increased in 14 of them from 1999–2001 to 2009–2011.[4] During the same periods, the share of manufacturing increased in only 19 LDCs, stayed the same in 3, and decreased in 25. The share of non-manufacturing activities, in turn, increased in 32 LDCs, stayed the same in 1, and decreased in 14. Finally, the share of services in GDP increased in 28 LDCs, remained unchanged in 1, and declined in 18 of them in the same periods.

One of the most broadly confirmed stylized facts in economics is that the value added of agriculture in the national economy decreases in relative terms as the country develops. Thus, the fact that the share of agriculture in GDP increased in 14 LDCs over the past decade is a striking finding which reflects a lack of structural change towards higher value added activities, higher productivity, higher incomes and technologically more sophisticated activities in these economies. The data on manufacturing as a share of GDP point in a similar direction, namely, that in the recent past, this critical area of economic activity lost part of its previous share in GDP in more than half of the LDCs. Given that manufacturing played the main role in the industrialization and development of developed countries and in the first- and second-tier newly industrialized countries (NICs), economic growth that results in a decreasing share of manufacturing in the LDCs does not bode well for their development prospects.

The fact that non-manufacturing activities within industry (mining and quarrying, electricity, gas, water and sanitary services, and construction) now constitute a larger share in GDP in more than two thirds of the LDCs points to a process of greater specialization based on static comparative advantage. This apparent shift away from manufacturing towards activities based on the LDCs' existing comparative advantage is probably a result of the commodity price boom. Similarly, the falling share of services in the GDP of 18 LDCs is also a sign that there has been little structural change in many LDCs even at a time when their economic growth was higher than in any other decade.

For the LDCs as a group, the average share of agriculture declined from 31.4 per cent of GDP in 1999–2001 to 25.6 per cent in 2009–2011. The share of manufacturing stayed the same, at around 10 per cent of GDP. Once again, however, there are notable regional differences. While the share of manufacturing in African LDCs decreased slightly, from an already low value of 8.0 per cent of GDP to 7.5 per cent, its share in Asian LDCs increased from 12.7 per cent to 15.2 per cent. The data for non-manufacturing activities reflect exactly the opposite movement. In the African LDCs, the share went from 16.5 per cent to 27.3 per cent of GDP, while in the Asian LDCs it stayed the same, at 12.1 per cent. The data thus confirm the existence of two different strategies of economic development, one based mostly on extractive industries and the other on labour-

The share of agriculture in GDP decreased in 33 LDCs and increased in 14 of them between 1999–2001 and 2009–2011.

The share of manufacturing increased in only 19 LDCs, stayed the same in 3, and decreased in 25.

The share of services in GDP increased in 28 LDCs, remained unchanged in 1, and declined in 18 of them.

For the LDCs as a group, the average share of agriculture declined from 31.4 per cent of GDP in 1999–2001 to 25.6 per cent in 2009–2011 while the share of manufacturing stayed the same, at around 10 per cent of GDP.

intensive manufacturing. On average, the share of services declined somewhat in the African LDCs and increased in the Asian LDCs.

More generally, the trends suggest that for the LDCs as a group, over the period between 1999–2001 and 2009–2011 — which was characterized by the most rapid economic growth in decades — there was little structural change of the type that results in strong increases in productivity, incomes, technological intensity and high value added. Overall, the share of both agriculture and services has been declining slowly in these countries, while that of industry is expanding. Within industry, however, manufacturing stagnated, while non-manufacturing activities expanded vigorously over the 10-year period. Much of the increase of industrial value added is concentrated in mining industries and in the exploitation of crude oil, gas and hydroelectric power, rather than in manufacturing. The overall lack of a dynamic process of structural change is characteristic mainly of the African LDCs. The Asian LDCs, in turn, are following the path of other successful East and South-East Asian economies, although at a slower pace.

2. TRENDS IN CURRENT ACCOUNT AND INTERNATIONAL TRADE

According to available preliminary data, the current account deficit for the LDCs as a group widened substantially, from $10.5 billion in 2011 to $28.8 billion in 2012. Most of the increase was due to the African LDCs and Haiti, where the deficit rose from $9.2 billion to $26.1 billion over the same two years. In terms of GDP, the current account deficit of the African LDCs widened from 5.0 per cent in 2011 to 13.2 per cent in 2012. Asian LDCs also recorded a larger deficit, expanding from $3.2 billion to $4.3 billion in the same period. The surplus of island LDCs, by contrast, shrunk from $1.9 billion to $1.6 billion, although this is due entirely to the surplus of Timor-Leste. Excluding the data from that country, this group of LDCs registered a deficit of some $300 million in 2012. Only seven LDCs, mostly energy exporters, recorded a current account surplus in 2012.

The deterioration of the LDCs' current account was mainly due to a strong worsening of the merchandise trade balance, which expanded from a $3.7-billion deficit in 2011 to a much larger one of $18.5 billion in 2012 for the LDCs as a group. The surplus of African LDCs plummeted from $22.2 billion to $11.9 billion, while the deficit of Asian LDCs widened from $24.5 billion to $29.0 billion in the same period.

The terms of trade for the LDCs as a group continued to improve in the three years since their sharp deterioration of 2009 (chart 1). In 2011 and 2012 they reached a higher level than during the previous peak of 2008, just before the adverse impact of the crisis was felt. However, the terms of trade for regional groups reveal pronounced differences. The African LDCs have benefited from an unprecedented improvement in their terms of trade with the rest of the world. High commodity prices are the most important factor in these positive developments. However, despite their favourable terms of trade, their real GDP growth rate has been lower than that of the Asian and island LDCs.

The terms of trade for the Asian LDCs also improved somewhat in 2012, although both that year and during the boom period of 2002–2008 they were below the levels of 2000. A similar evolution can be seen in the terms of trade of the island LDCs, which have worsened since 2000 and deteriorated somewhat in 2012 from the previous year's levels. Comparing the LDCs as a group with other developing countries, we see that the terms of trade improved significantly in the former from 2000 to 2012 but improved only slightly in the latter.

For the LDCs as a group, over the period between 1999–2001 and 2009–2011 — characterized by the most rapid economic growth in decades — there was little structural change of the type that results in strong increases in productivity, incomes, technological intensity and high value added.

The current account deficit for the LDCs as a group widened substantially, from $10.5 billion in 2011 to $28.8 billion in 2012.

The deterioration of the LDCs' current account was mainly due to a strong worsening of the merchandise trade balance, from a $3.7-billion deficit in 2011 to a much larger one of $18.5 billion in 2012.

The terms of trade for the LDCs as a group continued to improve in the three years since their sharp deterioration of 2009.

Box 1. Graduation of Samoa from LDC status

The IPoA adopted at the Fourth United Nations Conference on the Least Developed Countries (LDC-IV) in Istanbul, Turkey, in 2011 is the international community's main document on the LDCs for the decade 2011–2020. Its overarching goal is to overcome the structural challenges faced by LDCs in order to eradicate poverty, achieve internationally agreed development goals and enable graduation from the LDC category. More specifically, national policies and international support measures should focus on enabling half the number of LDCs to meet the criteria for graduation by 2020 (United Nations, 2011, paras. 27-28).

The LDC category is a United Nations grouping of countries based on three criteria: a) income; b) human assets; and c) economic vulnerability. Each country needs to meet graduation thresholds in at least two criteria in order to graduate.[1] The decision on graduation is made by the United Nations Economic and Social Council based on recommendations from the Committee for Development Policy (CDP). The main novelty of the IPoA is its explicit inclusion of targets for graduation. A prospect of graduation can be a powerful motivating force for pursuing more rapid structural change and development of productive capacities in the LDCs, as well as an opportunity for addressing the employment challenge analysed in this Report.

Within that context, the news that Samoa will graduate from LDC status is indeed cause for celebration. It also constitutes recognition of the progress made by LDCs over the past decade and should motivate other LDCs to focus their efforts on reaching graduation thresholds. Samoa was among the 25 countries included in the first group of LDCs when the category was formally established by the United Nations in 1971. By 2012, Samoa stood at 242 per cent of the graduation threshold for per capita income, with an estimated per capita GNI of $3,220 that year, when the threshold was $1,190. Economic progress was steady in the first decade of the twenty-first century, albeit without spectacular growth: real GDP growth rates were negative in 2008 and 2009, and the years that followed the tragic tsunami of September 2009 were ones of slow recovery. The two main factors in Samoa's rise above the graduation line were: (a) the successful specialization of the economy in international services, notably tourism; and (b) the multiplier impact of a steady flow of remittances (equivalent to 82 per cent of total exports in 2011) and ODA inflows.

The steady progress with respect to the human asset criterion over the past 20 years has been the other main factor in the country's graduation. At 141 per cent of the graduation threshold in 2012, the country is the LDC with the highest human capital status. Samoa's situation with respect to the economic vulnerability criterion is of a different nature: at 63 per cent of the graduation threshold in 2012, the economy is among the 30 per cent most vulnerable LDCs. As indicated by the disaster victim ratio — a new component of the Economic Vulnerability Index (EVI) — Samoa was much affected by natural disasters in the past two decades, twice more than comparable small island developing States. According to another new component of the EVI, the ratio of low-lying areas, Samoans are 72 per cent more exposed to sea-related risks than other LDCs. Despite the increased vulnerability to natural shocks overall, 2012 was a year of slightly improved performance under this indicator: the country was seen as having scored points in resilience-building, as evidenced by the limited instability in overall exports in the long run.

By virtue of the graduation rule under which a country that has stood above two graduation thresholds in at least two consecutive reviews of the list will qualify for graduation, CDP in March 2006 recommended Samoa's graduation from LDC status. The Economic and Social Council endorsed this recommendation in July 2007, and the General Assembly confirmed that decision through resolution 62/97 of 17 December 2007. In another resolution in September 2010 (64/295), the Assembly decided to defer Samoa's graduation to 1 January 2014, owing to the "unique disruption" caused by the 2009 tsunami. The year 2013 is the third and last year of the country's normal grace period before graduation. Samoa has been actively engaged, with its development partners, in preparing a "smooth transition" to post-LDC life.

Samoa's relative economic prosperity owes little to LDC-specific benefits, however, as the latter do not involve concessions in the area of trade in services. International tourism and business-related services in 2011 accounted for 78 per cent of the country's total export earnings. Also in 2011, tuna, its largest merchandise export, ranked only fifth among the sources of export earnings, with 2.5 per cent of relevant total receipts. (Exports of wiring sets to Australia and New Zealand for the automobile industry are counted as re-exports, although some value addition does take place in Samoa in the single factory making up this sector.)

As a service-dominated economy, Samoa is not likely to be harmed by its upcoming loss of LDC status. Preferential access to the Australian and New Zealand markets will not be affected either by this change of status or by the possible advent of reciprocal free trade arrangements between South Pacific States and the region's two large preference givers. At the same time, Samoa's exports to the EU are very small, and the EU's smooth transition policy on market access would automatically benefit Samoa for at least three years. Trade-related technical assistance under the Enhanced Integrated Framework (EIF) for LDCs will continue to be received by the country for a number of years after graduation, as will United Nations budget support for Samoan delegations to major United Nations events.

As we celebrate the graduation of Samoa from the LDC category, however, one more country has been added to the list. The latest official addition to the category was South Sudan, which was admitted on 18 December 2012 when the General Assembly endorsed with immediate effect CDP's March 2012 recommendation to add that newly independent country to the list. This is a potent reminder that there are countries and populations in need of special attention from the international community in supporting their development strategies to address their development needs and specific challenges and overcome their structural vulnerabilities.

[1] According to the graduation rule established by the United Nations, a first-time performance above two graduation thresholds makes the country "pre-eligible" for graduation, while "full eligibility" will take place after a second observation of the same performance has been made in the subsequent consecutive triennial review of the list of LDCs.

Chart 1. Terms of trade indices of LDCs, regional groups of LDCs and ODCs, 2000–2012
(Index, 2000=100)

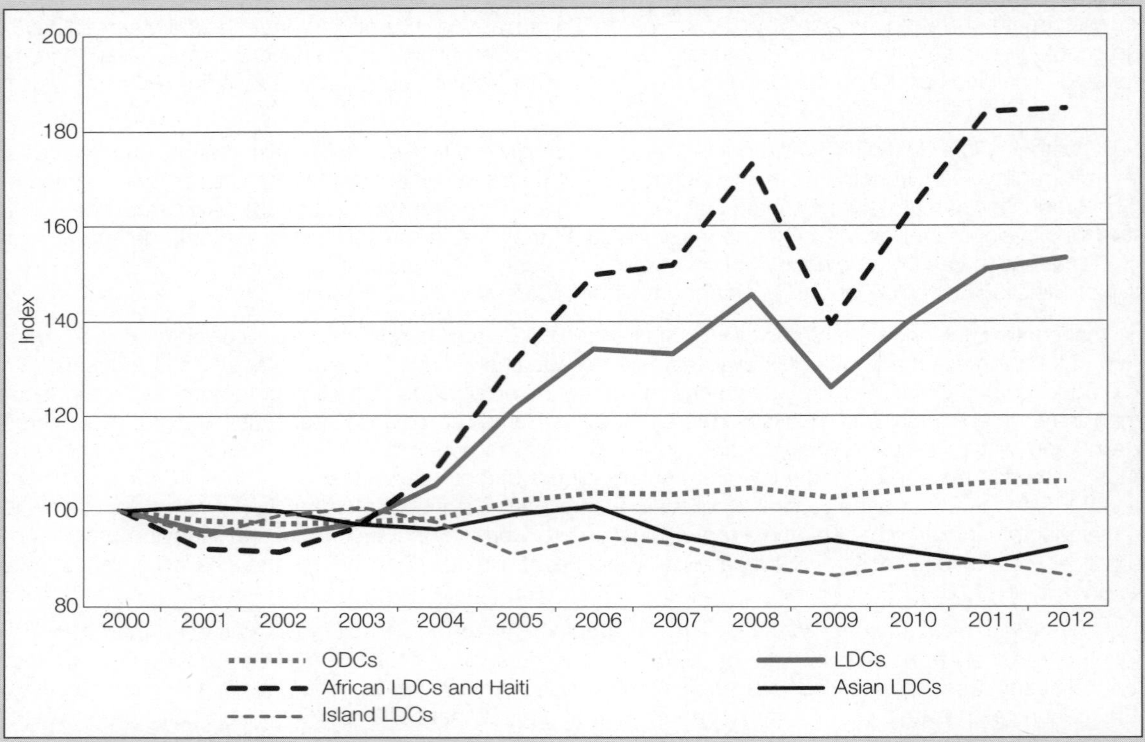

Source: UNCTAD secretariat calculations, based on UNCTADstat database.

Table 4. Exports and imports of merchandise and services in LDCs								
	Country groups	2008	2009	2010	2011	2012	Change 2011	Change 2012
Merchandise trade								
Merchandise exports	LDCs total	167'907.6	127'672.3	162'436.8	203'004.4	204'310.8	25.0	0.6
	African LDCs and Haiti	129'832.7	92'392.6	117'021.8	146'797.3	148'138.5	25.4	0.9
	Asian LDCs	37'690.7	34'974.1	45'030.6	55'613.1	55'512.9	23.5	-0.2
	Island LDCs	384.1	305.6	384.4	594.0	659.4	54.5	11.0
Merchandise imports	LDCs total	162'074.1	153'444.1	169'565.8	206'736.0	222'777.2	21.9	7.8
	African LDCs and Haiti	106'739.0	101'054.3	106'005.5	124'573.6	136'149.6	17.5	9.3
	Asian LDCs	53'758.9	50'907.3	61'828.9	80'180.9	84'552.1	29.7	5.5
	Island LDCs	1'576.3	1'482.6	1'731.4	1'981.5	2'075.5	14.4	4.7
Merchandise trade balance	LDCs total	5'833.46	-25'771.85	-7'128.96	-3'731.63	-18'466.42	47.7	-394.9
	African LDCs and Haiti	23'093.80	-8'661.74	11'016.31	22'223.65	11'988.90	101.7	-46.1
	Asian LDCs	-16'068.21	-15'933.17	-16'798.25	-24'567.76	-29'039.20	-46.3	-18.2
	Island LDCs	-1'192.13	-1'176.94	-1'347.03	-1'387.51	-1'416.11	-3.0	-2.1
		2008	2009	2010	2011	2012	change 2011	change 2012
Services trade								
Service exports	LDCs total	20'706.6	21'534.9	25'002.2	29'744.1	30'373.3	19.0	2.1
	African LDCs and Haiti	13'719.4	12'834.8	13'839.6	17'443.8	17'756.1	26.0	1.8
	Asian LDCs	6'435.5	8'105.7	10'463.5	11'537.2	11'795.8	10.3	2.2
	Island LDCs	551.7	594.4	699.2	763.0	821.3	9.1	7.6
Service imports	LDCs total	58'895.7	54'536.0	60'550.4	71'904.7	74'847.8	18.8	4.1
	African LDCs and Haiti	49'099.4	44'298.4	47'905.4	57'091.7	59'228.1	19.2	3.7
	Asian LDCs	8'804.6	8'941.1	11'018.9	12'672.0	13'398.7	15.0	5.7
	Island LDCs	991.7	1296.5	1626.1	2141.0	2221.0	31.7	3.7
Service trade balance	LDCs total	-38'189.2	-33'001.1	-35'548.2	-42'160.5	-44'474.6	-18.6	-5.5
	African LDCs and Haiti	-35'380.1	-31'463.5	-34'065.8	-39'647.9	-41'472.1	-16.4	-4.6
	Asian LDCs	-2'369.1	-835.5	-555.4	-1'134.8	-1'602.8	-104.3	-41.2
	Island LDCs	-440.0	-702.1	-927.0	-1'377.9	-1'399.7	-48.6	-1.6

Source: UNCTAD secretariat calculations, based on UNCTADstat database, July 2013.

The widening of the merchandise trade deficit was driven by developments on both export and import fronts (table 4). With respect to exports, the strong growth of about 25 per cent in both 2010 and 2011 stalled to a mere 0.6 per cent in 2012 for the LDCs as a group. This is in line with the worldwide deceleration of trade in goods mentioned earlier. Exports of goods from the Asian LDCs actually declined in 2012, although by only 0.2 per cent. Those from island LDCs, by contrast, grew by 11 per cent. Imports to the LDCs as a group also slowed, but not as much as exports. While imports expanded 21.9 per cent in 2011, one year later their growth had slowed to 7.8 per cent. Nonetheless, that was enough to worsen the LDCs' merchandise trade deficit substantially.

Trends in the trade balance of services were broadly the same. The deficit increased from $42.1 billion in 2011 to $44.5 billion in 2012. Exports of services, which expanded by 19 per cent in 2011, had barely advanced one year later (2.1 per cent). The change in the growth rate of services imports was almost as significant, from a robust expansion of 18.8 per cent in 2011 to only a 4.1-percent increase in 2012.

The composition of LDCs' merchandise exports reflects the dominant position of fuels, which account for more than half of the total (table 5). However, their predominance is the result of merchandise exports from the African LDCs, whose share is around 65 per cent. In the case of the Asian LDCs, fuels account for only one fifth of the total, whereas manufactured goods, at around 57 per cent of the total, are the main export item. In particular, textile fibres, yarn, fabrics and clothing amount to about half of all merchandise exports from the Asian LDCs.

Exports of ores and metals, at 17.4 per cent, are the second largest export item from the African LDCs, followed by food (8.5 per cent) and manufactured goods (6.1 per cent). The export structure of the island LDCs is dominated by agricultural raw materials (44 per cent) and food (29.5 per cent). Manufactured goods are in third place, with 13.4 per cent.

The largest items in the import structure of the LDCs as a group are food (36.9 per cent) and agricultural raw materials (22 per cent). The fact that their combined imports account for 60 per cent of all LDC imports reflects the neglect of agriculture, a topic which is more broadly discussed in chapters 4 and 5 of this Report. Fuels account for 18 per cent of imports of goods, while the share of manufactured goods is around 15 per cent of the total. Imports of manufactured goods in the LDCs are composed primarily of machinery and transport equipment.

With respect to exports, the strong growth of about 25 per cent in both 2010 and 2011 stalled to a mere 0.6 per cent in 2012.

The composition of LDCs' merchandise exports reflects the dominant position of fuels, which account for more than half of the total.

The largest items in the import structure of the LDCs as a group are food (36.9 per cent) and agricultural raw materials (22 per cent).

Table 5. Composition of merchandise exports and imports in LDCs, average 2010–2012 (Percentage of total exports and imports)								
	Exports				**Imports**			
	LDCs	African LDCs and Haiti	Asian LDCs	Island LDCs	LDCs	African LDCs and Haiti	Asian LDCs	Island LDCs
All food	8.5	8.5	8.3	29.5	36.9	34.7	40.3	40.2
Agricultural raw materials	3.3	2.7	4.5	44.0	22.0	20.8	23.7	25.4
Fuels	52.8	64.8	22.7	2.0	18.0	17.5	18.6	23.2
Ores and metals	14.3	17.4	6.4	7.7	1.9	1.2	3.1	1.5
Manufactured goods	20.3	6.1	56.9	13.4	14.9	13.9	16.5	14.8
Chemical products	1.4	1.4	1.3	0.9	2.5	2.2	3.1	0.7
Machinery and transport equipment	1.6	1.6	1.4	10.2	61.3	64.0	57.2	53.5
Other manufactured goods	17.4	3.1	54.2	2.2	10.2	10.2	10.2	5.0
Memo item: Textile fibres, yarn, fabrics and clothing	15.9	2.9	49.5	0.3	24.9	23.9	26.8	18.8
Source: UNCTAD secretariat calculations, based on UNCTADstat database, July 2013.								

Chart 2. Food, meat and cereal price indices, January 2005-June 2013
(Index, 2002–2004=100)

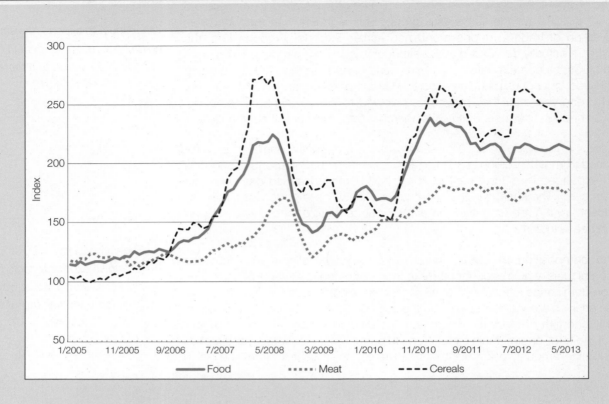

Source: UNCTAD secretariat calculations, based on FAO *Food Price Index*, July 2013.

The persistence of high food prices and the strong dependence of the LDCs on food imports point to a need to reverse the long-standing neglect of agriculture. High prices of food, especially of cereals, remain a major problem for poor people everywhere, and particularly in the LDCs.

The increasing share of food in total LDC imports points to the impact of changes in international food prices on the LDCs' trade balance. As shown in chart 2, food prices increased sharply in 2007 and 2008, before experiencing a downward correction in 2009 and 2010. Since then, however, they have rebounded rapidly, and in 2011 reached a level higher than in the previous peak during the so-called triple crisis (food, fuel and financial). Unlike other commodity prices, international food prices have not fallen substantially from that peak, and are still more than double those of the 2002–2004 average. In the composite food price index, the price index of cereals is more important for the LDCs than indices of other types of food, given that cereals predominate in LDC food consumption. As shown in chart 2, cereal prices are almost one and a half times higher today than their 2002–2004 average. The persistence of high food prices and the strong dependence of the LDCs on food imports[5] point to a need to reverse the long-standing neglect of agriculture. High prices of food, especially of cereals, remain a major problem for poor people everywhere, and particularly in the LDCs.

An analysis of concentration indices of LDC exports (chart 3) shows that the long-lasting trend towards higher concentration has recently been reversed. In effect, the concentration index of exports of the LDCs as a group followed a strong upward trend from 1995 to 2008, when it reached a value of 0.54.[6] However, since the onset of the crisis, the concentration of exports as measured by the concentration index for the LDCs as a group has gone down to 0.41. When considered by regional groupings, the African LDCs have the highest concentration index, followed by island LDCs, while that of the Asian LDCs is the lowest of all LDC groups. The index has recently decreased in both African and Asian LDCs, while it has increased in island LDCs.

It is not immediately clear why the concentration of exports from the LDCs as a group has declined in recent years. Commodity prices have remained high, in

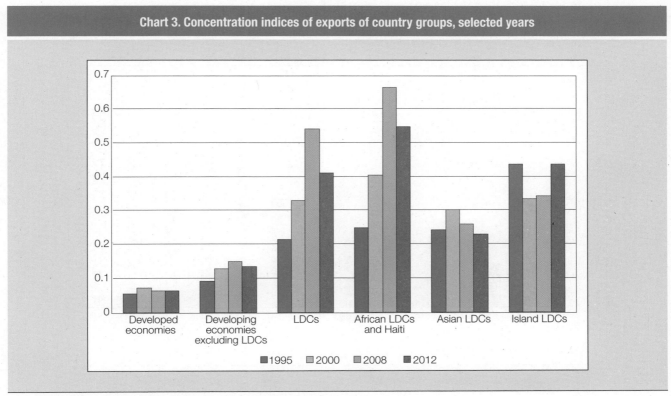

Chart 3. Concentration indices of exports of country groups, selected years

Source: UNCTAD secretariat calculations, based on UNCTADstat database.

many cases even higher than in the boom period of 2002–2008, and are thus an unlikely factor of change. In any case, the falling concentration index of exports is a welcome development, as it suggests that the LDCs today have a more diversified export structure than before the crisis.

3. TRENDS IN EXTERNAL FINANCE

External finance is of particular importance to the LDCs given their low level of domestic savings relative to investment. In the absence of external finance, that gap would have to be closed by a reduction in investment. Availability of external finance, however, makes possible a higher level of investment than could be financed solely by domestic savings. Both the level and the composition of external finance are important, as some forms are more volatile than others. Portfolio investment, for example, is generally much more volatile and more unpredictable than FDI.

Recent private capital flows to the LDCs have followed the same pattern as those to developing countries in general. The abundance of liquidity in developed countries caused by expansionary monetary policy, coupled with a dearth of opportunities to invest in developed countries where the private sector is undergoing a painful deleveraging process, resulted in a recomposition of investor portfolios, which up to the spring of 2013 had been favouring assets in developing economies. That search for higher yields has also benefited the LDCs. As shown in chart 4, private financial flows to the LDCs have been increasing steadily, reaching $56.3 billion in 2012, a 16-per-cent increase over the previous year.

FDI inflows to LDCs hit a record high of almost $26 billion in 2012, which is about 20 per cent more than in 2011 (annex table 6). Inflows to African LDCs and Haiti rose from $16.9 billion in 2011 to $19.8 billion last year. Asian LDCs

Private financial flows to the LDCs have been increasing steadily, reaching $56.3 billion in 2012, a 16-per-cent increase over the previous year.

FDI inflows to LDCs hit a record high of almost $26 billion in 2012, which is about 20 per cent more than in 2011.

Chart 4. Private financial flows to the LDCs, 2000–2012
(Millions of current dollars)

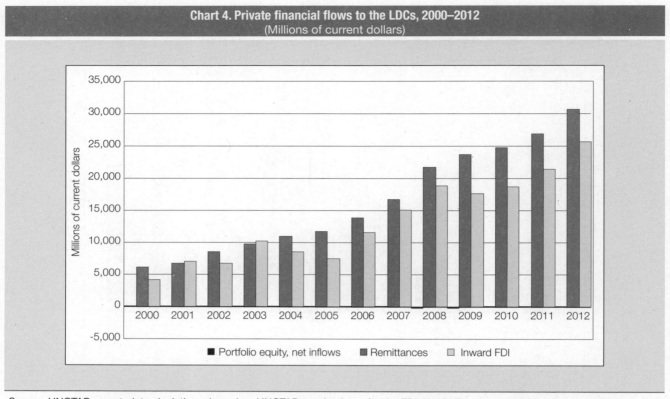

Source: UNCTAD secretariat calculations, based on UNCTADstat database for the FDI, *World Development Indicators* for portfolio investment and World Bank for remittances.

also saw an increase, from $4.2 billion to $5.6 billion, while the island LDCs suffered a reversal, from $320 million to $235 million. FDI outflows from LDCs increased at a much higher rate of around 66 per cent, to $5 billion in 2012. As a result, net FDI inflows to more than 20 LDCs were negative. These negative net flows were particularly high in Angola, where they totalled $6.9 billion.

The share of investments in extractive industries and related processing activities in total greenfield investments in the LDCs has been declining, from over 80 per cent of the total in 2003–2005 to around 30 per cent in 2012.

The share of LDCs in global FDI inflows grew from 1.3 per cent in 2011 to 1.9 per cent in 2012. A long-standing feature of those inflows is their high concentration in just a few countries. In 2012, five countries had inflows of over $2.0 billion each, namely, Mozambique, Democratic Republic of the Congo, Sudan, Myanmar and Equatorial Guinea. Also on the negative side, the estimated value of greenfield investment projects in LDCs amounted to only $22 billion, the lowest level in six years, due to a pronounced contraction of announced projects in the primary sector and related processing industries. Since the estimated value of greenfield investment projects is indicative of future trends, this does not bode well for the value of FDI inflows in the future.[7]

The share of investments in extractive industries and related processing activities in total greenfield investments in the LDCs has been declining, from over 80 per cent of the total in 2003–2005 to around 30 per cent in 2012 (UNCTAD, 2013b). As a result, manufacturing and services are gaining ground. Investment in transport and logistics includes oil pipelines, petroleum bulk stations and terminals, which are support services for the extractive activities. Financial services represented one fourth of all greenfield projects in the LDCs in 2012, concentrated primarily in retail banking.

The flow of workers' remittances to the LDCs continued to expand in 2012, reaching a new record of $30.5 billion.

The flow of workers' remittances to the LDCs continued to expand in 2012, reaching a new record of $30.5 billion. Remittances to these countries are much more stable than FDI inflows (chart 4), and have risen even during the worst stage of the crisis. With respect to regional distribution, remittances are mostly a feature of Asian LDCs, where they increased from $16.3 billion in 2010 to $17.8

billion a year later (annex table 7). The figures for the Asian LDCs are heavily dominated by flows to Bangladesh, which receives around 40 per cent of all remittance flows to the LDCs. In 2011, Bangladesh took in almost $12 billion in remittances, and some preliminary estimates place the 2012 figure at over $14 billion. Remittances to the African LDCs grew by some $800 million in 2012 over the $8.1 billion received in 2010.

Remittances are especially important for smaller countries, where they account for a large share of gross national income (GNI). In Samoa, for example, their share of GNI was 23.9 per cent; in Lesotho and Haiti, 23.7 per cent. Workers' remittances also represent a large share of GNI in Nepal, Gambia and Senegal (more than 10 per cent), and in Togo, Guinea-Bissau and Kiribati (between 5 and 10 per cent). For the LDCs as a group, remittances account for 4.4 per cent of GNI. In the African LDCs, the figure is 2.5 per cent, and in the Asian LDCs, 7.4 per cent.

After playing an important countercyclical role during the financial crisis, ODA to the LDCs began to decline.

After playing an important countercyclical role during the financial crisis, ODA to the LDCs began to decline in 2011 (chart 5). According to DAC data, the net ODA disbursement from all donors to LDCs, excluding debt relief, fell slightly, from $41.7 billion in 2010 to $41.6 billion in 2011. Preliminary data for 2012 show that bilateral net ODA to the LDCs fell by 12.8% in real terms. If these estimates are confirmed, they would mark the largest decline of ODA to the LDCs since 1997.

The net ODA disbursement from all donors to LDCs, excluding debt relief, fell slightly, from $41.7 billion in 2010 to $41.6 billion in 2011.

Moreover, 2012 was the first time since 1996–1997 that ODA to all developing countries declined for two consecutive years. According to OECD, the decline is part of a broader set of recent austerity measures adopted by policymakers in traditional donor countries. The aid provided by DAC members amounted to 0.29 per cent of their combined GNI, way below the 0.7-per-cent target.

The total external debt of the LDCs expanded in 2012 to an estimated $183 billion, up 6.7 per cent in nominal terms from 2011. The debt-to-GDP ratio grew

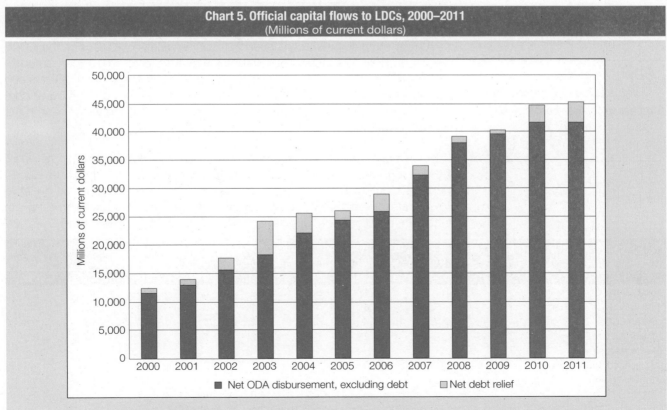

Chart 5. Official capital flows to LDCs, 2000–2011
(Millions of current dollars)

Legend: ■ Net ODA disbursement, excluding debt   ▫ Net debt relief

Source: UNCTAD secretariat calculations, based on OECD-DAC, *International Development Statistics*, online, August 2013.

slightly, from 26.6 per cent in 2011 to 26.7 per cent in 2012, while the ratio of total debt to exports increased from 78.7 per cent to 82.5 per cent. Both ratios were higher than those in other developing countries. However, average debt service as a percentage of GDP and exports remained lower than for ODCs, since most (more than 80 per cent) of LDC external debt is long-term, on highly concessional terms. The stock of short-term debt was up by $2.5 billion in 2012, an increase of 14 per cent.

The total external debt of the LDCs expanded in 2012 to an estimated $183 billion, up 6.7 per cent in nominal terms from 2011. The debt-to-GDP ratio grew slightly, from 26.6 per cent in 2011 to 26.7 per cent in 2012.

As of mid-2013, there were 2 LDCs in debt distress (Myanmar and Sudan) and 10 at high risk of debt distress.[8] Meanwhile, both Comoros and Guinea have reached the completion point under the Heavily Indebted Poor Countries Initiative (HIPC). As a result of debt cancellation obtained from the Paris Club, the latter two countries are no longer considered to be in debt distress. While a combination of relatively strong growth, prudent macroeconomic management, and debt relief has brought down the debt burden of many LDCs, public debt ratios have been rising in many post-HIPC and Multilateral Debt Relief Initiative (MDRI) countries. The increase in debt-to-GDP ratios following MDRI has been quite significant in Benin, Ghana, Senegal and Malawi, where it is more a reflection of a sharp exchange rate depreciation in 2012 than of new borrowing.

As of mid-2013, there were 2 LDCs in debt distress (Myanmar and Sudan) and 10 at high risk of debt distress.

In general, the LDCs have fewer opportunities and less sources of financing than other developing countries. With few exceptions, their domestic debt markets are not sufficiently developed, especially in the long maturity segment, and funds that can be mobilized domestically for investment are constrained by the limited amount of savings. Developing a domestic debt market is costly in terms of financial and human resources and in most cases takes many years. In the meantime, current account imbalances suggest that external capital will continue to play a key role in financing development for the LDCs.

D. Outlook for the LDCs

According to IMF forecasts, real GDP worldwide will expand by 3.3 per cent in 2013, a slight improvement over the 3.2 per cent of 2012. For the LDCs as a group, IMF forecasts a 5.7-per-cent growth rate for 2013, compared to 5.3 per cent for emerging and developing economies. The growth of the world economy should increase to 4.0 per cent in 2014 and to around 4.5 per cent in the subsequent four years. LDC growth should be around 6 per cent in the medium term (table 6).

For the LDCs as a group, IMF forecasts a 5.7-per-cent growth rate for 2013.

However, these forecasts may be overly optimistic. Five years after the onset of the global crisis, economic conditions remain precarious in most developed countries, with high sovereign debt, high unemployment, a low or negative growth rate of real GDP, and an ongoing deleveraging process in the private sector. In addition, the adjustments currently being implemented in many

Table 6. Real GDP growth rates for LDCs, developing and advanced economies, selected years and forecasts (Annual weighted averages, percentages)								
	2002–2008	2009–2012	2013	2014	2015	2016	2017	2018
Total LDCs	**7.5**	**5.1**	**5.7**	**6.2**	**6.4**	**6.4**	**6.1**	**6.4**
African LDCs and Haiti	7.5	4.6	5.6	6.1	6.3	6.0	5.6	6.0
Asian LDCs	7.5	5.7	5.7	6.2	6.6	6.7	6.8	6.8
Island LDCs	4.9	5.2	5.8	6.2	7.7	8.7	6.3	5.5
Memo Items:								
Advanced economies	2.5	0.6	1.2	2.2	2.6	2.6	2.6	2.5
Emerging and developing economies	7.6	5.4	5.3	5.7	6.0	6.1	6.1	6.2
World	4.7	2.9	3.3	4.0	4.4	4.5	4.5	4.5

Source: UNCTAD secretariat calculations based on IMF, *World Economic Outlook* database, April 2013.
Notes: The LDCs' growth is calculated as the weighted average of each country's real growth (base year 2000); data for 2012 are preliminary and are forecasted for 2013-2018.

developed countries are deflationary in nature. Debtor countries are forced to reduce expenditure, while there is no obligation on the part of creditor countries to expand. The result is a shortfall in demand at the global level. It is not clear when the crisis in the developed countries will be over or how the LDCs will fare if these weaknesses are sustained for several years.

It is not clear when the crisis in the developed countries will be over or how the LDCs will fare if these weaknesses are sustained for several years.

Another problem, which is structural in nature, is the changing share of labour and capital in total income. Over the past three decades, labour income in the world economy has been rising slower than growth of world output. As a result, the wage share has been declining relative to profits. However, wage income represents a large part of total income, particularly in developed countries (around two thirds of the total), and is therefore the biggest source of demand for goods and services. A reduction of wage share has negative effects on household consumption. To the extent that investment in new capacities is driven by expectations of future demand, lower consumption acts as a disincentive for new investment. Income inequality issues are thus bound to have an impact on the pace of future economic growth, not only in developed but also in developing economies (UNCTAD, 2012c).

For the LDCs, international trade has been the single most important channel of transmission of the recessionary impulses from the developed countries since the start of the crisis. The recent slowdown of world trade will thus have further negative impacts on the prospects of the LDCs. While the demand for imported goods in developed countries has been weak at best, the LDCs have avoided a sharp deceleration of growth by relying more on their domestic demand and on South-South trade. Both will be necessary in the future, but the recent deceleration of economic growth in the large emerging economies means that further possibilities for such reorientation are currently limited. In addition, changes in the growth model of China will have repercussions that will differ among individual LDCs according to their specialization pattern (see box 2 below).

For the LDCs, international trade has been the single most important channel of transmission of the recessionary impulses from the developed countries since the start of the crisis. The recent slowdown of world trade will thus have further negative impacts on the prospects of the LDCs.

The availability of external financing is another precondition for strong growth of real GDP in the LDCs. As the analysis throughout this chapter has suggested, external financing has been subject to strong fluctuations since the beginning of the crisis. Moreover, the prospect of a tighter monetary policy in developed countries over the course of 2014 and 2015 will change the relative profitability of investments between developed and developing countries' assets. This has already begun to provoke some pull-out from the emerging and developing countries as of the second quarter of 2013. Reduction in the interest rate differential between developed and developing countries will make financing the current account deficits more difficult. LDCs with large such deficits should start now to prepare for these future developments. Moreover, countries that peg their exchange rate to the United States dollar can expect their currency to appreciate, making imports cheaper and exporting more difficult.

Reduction in the interest rate differential between developed and developing countries will make financing the current account deficits more difficult. LDCs with large such deficits should start now to prepare for these future developments.

The third major factor affecting the external conditions for the LDCs is movements in international commodity prices. Changing international prices have long been recognized as a major external source of a country's vulnerability. IMF projections in WEO 2013 (International Monetary Fund, 2013) suggest continued declines for prices of both oil and non-fuel primary commodities. But the short-term outlook for commodity prices is highly uncertain, not only because of possible supply-side disruptions (energy, food), but also because of demand uncertainties.

The short-term outlook for commodity prices is highly uncertain, not only because of possible supply-side disruptions (energy, food), but also because of demand uncertainties.

Moving beyond the short term, three main scenarios are possible for the "commodity supercycle" (for details and references see discussion in UNCTAD, 2013a, chapter 2). The most optimistic is that the expansionary phase of the supercycle still has many years to run. A less optimistic scenario is that commodity prices have entered a calmer and more stable phase of growth, but will nevertheless remain at their relatively high recent levels. The most pessimistic scenario is that the supercycle has come to an end and that international commodity prices will decrease substantially in the midterm.

Of crucial importance is the fact that North America is forecast to become self-sufficient in energy production by the end of the decade...

While it is impossible to know what the future holds, two unrelated developments will certainly influence the course of international commodity prices. One is the changing growth model in China (see box 2 below), and the other is the new method based on hydraulic fracturing for extracting oil and gas that is remaking world energy markets. Regarding the latter, crude production in the United States increased 14 per cent in 2012 (British Petroleum, 2013). This was a major factor in keeping oil prices from rising sharply, despite a second consecutive year of large oil supply disruptions in many parts of the world, but most notably in North Africa and the Middle East.

... this will have a significant impact on the fuel-exporting LDCs, whose income from oil could be substantially reduced.

Of crucial importance is the fact that North America is forecast to become self-sufficient in energy production by the end of the decade (Citigroup, 2013). As a result, oil prices in the medium term should decrease and are likely to fluctuate within a range that is significantly below recent movements in the vicinity of $100 per barrel. This will have a significant impact on the fuel-exporting LDCs, whose income from oil could be substantially reduced. Preparing for such a scenario should start now and should provide buffers for a time of lower

---

Box 2. Changing growth model in China and possible consequences for the LDCs

Chinese growth over the past 30 years has been investment- and export-led. Given that the country possessed surplus labour characteristic of the Lewis model[1], heavy investment in new factories, construction and infrastructure has been possible without incurring diminishing returns. Wages have been kept low thanks to competition from this reserve army of surplus labour even as the economy has grown richer. Exports have increased at rates even higher than GDP growth rates.

However, much of the contribution to growth from shifting resources from agriculture to industry has already occurred in China. Some analysts (for example, Schellekens, 2013) suggest that China has already passed the Lewis turning point at which it is no longer possible to tap into a surplus pool of low-wage labour without raising wages. This suggests that the recent slowdown in growth from more than 10 per cent to 7 per cent is structural in nature.

In addition, in November 2012 the Government announced at the 18th National Congress of the Communist Party of China that it will seek to alter the pattern of growth in the next five years. Domestic sources of growth, particularly consumption, will be emphasized, while exports and investment will receive lower priority. China will also try to move up the value chain. As a result, the structure of production and exports will progressively shift from resource- and labour-intensive activities to more sophisticated and technologically more advanced products.

One of the factors relevant for LDCs is the expected lower resource intensity of future Chinese production. The pattern of Chinese import demand may change, moving away from commodities, which would have major consequences for international commodity prices. In effect, just as Chinese demand for commodities caused an upsurge of prices in the previous decade, weaker demand is likely to have the opposite effect on prices (Akyüz, 2010).

A second factor is that the income elasticity of China's imports is expected to rise as the country becomes richer (Schellekens, 2013), which will open up new opportunities for exporters from other countries. In particular, the demand for protein-based food will continue to grow, offering the potential for LDCs to increase their livestock production and exports.

A third factor is the increase in China's labour costs and its intention to move towards more sophisticated and technologically advanced goods, which will create opportunities for LDCs in many tradable sectors where Chinese producers previously dominated international markets. Thus, labour-intensive manufacturing industries in the LDCs could become competitive internationally, and could even supply such goods to the Chinese domestic market.

In short, China's rebalancing towards more consumer-led growth and away from investment- and export-led growth will produce both winners and losers. For the LDCs, this presents opportunities but also potential risks. As to which countries would be able to benefit from that shift, this is a matter not only of endowments and the current structure of economic activities but also of policies.

[1] The Lewis model is a dual-sector model in development economics, named after Sir W. Arthur Lewis, winner of the Nobel Memorial Prize in Economics, who first analysed it. The model explains the growth in developing economies in terms of a labour transition from the subsistence (agriculture) sector to the capitalist (modern) sector. Its main characteristic is the existence of surplus labour in the subsistence sector. Hence, when the capitalist sector expands, labourers move from the subsistence sector to the capitalist sector, holding down wages. This makes it possible to earn extra profits in the capitalist sector and reinvest them in capital stock until the surplus labour from the subsistence sector has been completely absorbed.

prices. In addition, resources from oil exports should be used for diversification of economic activities so as to decrease vulnerability to and dependence on oil-related shocks.

In addition to longer-term shifts related to changes in the Chinese growth model, the outlook for the global economy is also clouded by the prospect of downside risks linked to current trends in emerging economies. Some analysts fear that because of the credit and property bubbles created by the response to the global crisis in 2008, some major emerging economies, in particular China, are now displaying symptoms similar to those of the sub-prime crisis in the United States five years ago (Akyüz, 2013). If there is a crisis in the Chinese banking system, for example, the country's growth could decelerate substantially at a time when there are no other countries or regions to support world demand. Even if the banking crisis hypothesis is less likely in China because of its ownership structure, a slowdown in emerging economies in general and in China's growth in particular could have adverse consequences for the global economy.

Finally, the policy mix in many countries has been turning towards fiscal austerity. This is the case not only in developed countries but in developing countries as well. One of the key findings of a review of public expenditures and adjustment measures in 181 countries (Ortiz and Cummins, 2013) is that fiscal contraction is most severe in the developing world. Overall, 68 developing countries are projected to cut public spending by an average 3.7 per cent of GDP during the period 2013–2015. Moreover, one fourth of them will reduce such expenditure to below pre-crisis levels. These authors accordingly characterize the current global conjuncture as the "age of austerity".

Against this background, the outlook for the LDCs in the short to medium term is not very good. Even if none of the downside risks materialize and the IMF growth rate forecasts prove accurate, the growth of the LDCs as a group will be below the 7-per-cent IPoA target. In that scenario, responding effectively to the employment challenge, whose future magnitude is analysed in chapters 2 and 3, will be even more difficult in the LDCs.

The policy mix in many countries has been turning towards fiscal austerity...

... overall, 68 developing countries are projected to cut public spending by an average 3.7 per cent of GDP during the period 2013–2015.

Against this background, the outlook for the LDCs in the short to medium term is not very good.

Notes

1   The growth rates reported in tables 1, 3 and 6, as well as annex tables 2 and 3, are from the International Monetary Fund. As such, they may differ, at times even substantially, from those reported by individual LDCs. The IMF data have been used instead of the data reported by countries themselves in order to ensure consistency and to present forecasts for individual LDCs and different groups of countries.

2   For the Agenda for Action and concrete proposals on the financing of climate change adaptation and mitigation in the LDCs, see UNCTAD (2010), chapter 7.

3   The data for ODCs are heavily biased by China's very high capital formation rate. When that country is excluded, the difference between ODCs and LDCs is closer to five percentage points of GDP. A similar caveat applies to the savings rate.

4   The data for Timor-Leste for 1999–2001 are not available, so it is not possible to determine whether there was a change in the structure or not.

5   For data on food security and dependency on commodities in general in developing countries, see UNCTAD's *The State of Commodity Dependence 2012* (UNCTAD, 2012b).

6   The concentration index of exports is also called the Herfindahl-Hirschmann index. It normalizes the values to a range, from 0 (the most diversified exports) to 1 (the most concentrated exports).

7   Owing to the data collection method applied in the greenfield project database, the announced values of projects tend to overestimate the actual, realized investment values, since not all announced projects are realized.

8   A borrower in debt distress is one that is already experiencing repayment difficulties.

References

Akyüz Y (2010). Export Dependence and Sustainability of Growth in China and the East Asian Production Network. South Centre Research Paper No. 27.South Centre. Geneva.

Akyüz Y (2013). Waving or Drowning: Developing Countries after the Financial Crisis. South Centre Research Paper No. 48.South Centre. Geneva.

British Petroleum (2013). BP statistical review of world energy 2013. London.

Citigroup (2013). Energy 2020: independence day. Citi Global Perspectives & Solutions.

International Monetary Fund (2013). *World Economic Outlook 2013: Hopes, Realities, Risks*. International Monetary Fund. Washington, DC.

Koo R (2011). The world in balance sheet recession: causes, cure, and politics. *Real-world economics review.* (58):19–37.

Lund S et al. (2013). Financial globalization: retreat or reset? McKinsey Global Institute.

Ortiz I and Cummins M (2013). The Age of Austerity: A Review of Public Expenditures and Adjustment Measures in 181 Countries. Initiative for Policy Dialogue and the South Centre. New York and Geneva.

Reinhart CM and Rogoff KS (2009). *This Time Is Different: Eight Centuries of Financial Folly*. Princeton University Press. Princeton.

Schellekens P (2013). A Changing China: Implications for Developing Countries. *Economic Premise, 118*. Poverty Reduction and Economic Management Network. World Bank. Washington DC.

UNCTAD (2010). *The Least Developed Countries Report 2010: Towards a New International Development Architecture for LDCs*. United Nations publication. Sales No. E.10.II.D.5. New York and Geneva.

UNCTAD (2012a). *The Least Developed Countries Report 2012: Harnessing Remittances and Diaspora Knowledge to Build Productive Capacities*. United Nations publication. Sales No. E.12.II.D.18. New York and Geneva.

UNCTAD (2012b). The state of commodity dependence 2012. United Nations. Geneva.

UNCTAD (2012c). *Trade and Development Report, 2012: Policies for Inclusive and Balanced Growth*. United Nations. New York and Geneva.

UNCTAD (2013a). *Trade and Development Report 2013: Adjusting to the Changing Dynamics of the World Economy*. United Nations publication. Sales No. E .13.II .D.3. New York and Geneva.

UNCTAD (2013b). *World Investment Report 2013: Global Value Chains: Investment and Trade for Development*. United Nations Conference on Trade and Development (UNCTAD). New York and Geneva.

United Nations (2011). Programme of action for the least developed countries for the decade 2011–2020. No. A/CONF.219/3/Rev.1. United Nations. New York.

United Nations (2013). *World Economic Situation and Prospects 2013*. United Nations publication. Sales No. E .13.II.C.2. New York.

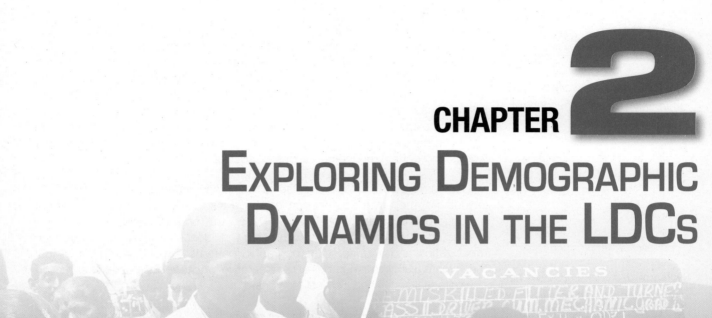

CHAPTER 2

EXPLORING DEMOGRAPHIC DYNAMICS IN THE LDCs

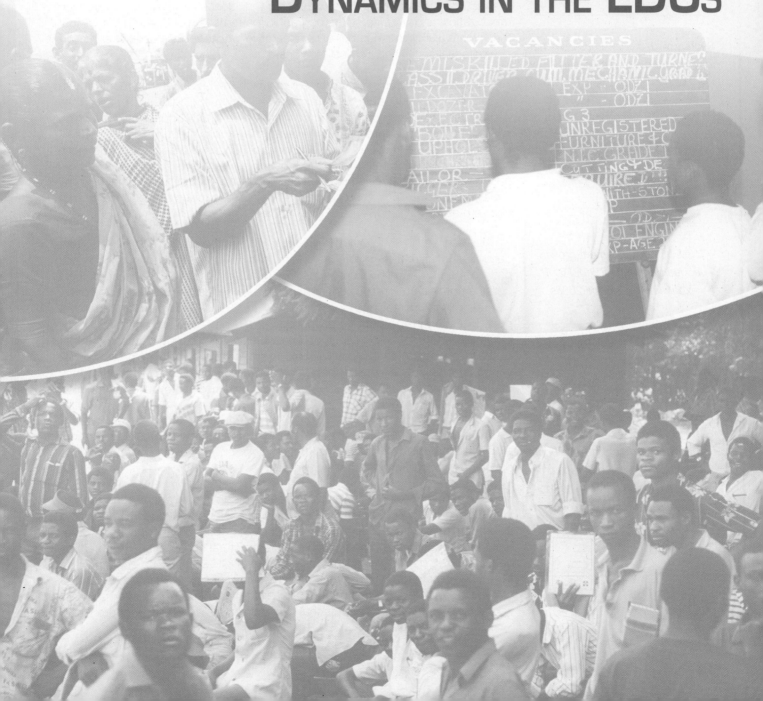

A. Rationale for addressing growth with employment for inclusive and sustainable development in the LDCs

As explained in chapter 1, despite recently sluggish economic performance, the LDCs have generally enjoyed more than 10 years of economic growth. Per capita income for the group as a whole has been steadily expanding, raising hopes that some of them may even be able to graduate from the category within the decade. There are, however, worrying signs that this growth trend has not been inclusive and that its contribution to poverty reduction has been limited. The main explanation for the lack of inclusiveness is that such growth as there has been has not generated enough "quality" jobs – that is, jobs offering higher wages and better working conditions – especially for the young.

The LDCs have generally enjoyed more than 10 years of economic growth.

Jobless growth is not unique to LDCs. Many other developing countries, including some advanced economies, have also experienced growth without a concomitant creation of jobs. However, the special conditions of LDCs – structurally weak economies with a high incidence of poverty, accelerating urbanization and worrisome demographic patterns – make it imperative that they create a sufficient number of remunerative jobs to reduce poverty and avert any potential social and political tensions.

Such growth as there has been has not generated enough "quality" jobs, especially for the young.

This chapter documents the extent to which the LDCs' employment growth lagged behind their rapid GDP expansion during the 2000s. That lag has understandably generated serious concerns among LDC policymakers, which is why the Report addresses the growth and employment nexus. Periods of relatively rapid GDP growth, such as that experienced in the past decade, have apparently failed not only to provide jobs for new entrants to the labour force, but also to clear the backlog of open and disguised unemployment that typically prevails in most LDCs. The question is: What will happen if economic growth decelerates?

The LDCs' employment growth lagged behind their rapid GDP expansion during the 2000s.

As discussed in chapter 1, the growth of GDP in the LDCs, both in the current decade and in mid-term forecasts, points clearly to a less dynamic growth pattern than in the previous decade. There are thus compelling reasons for a policy emphasis on employment generation as a central development objective. Indeed, this is increasingly recognized by LDCs as an urgent development goal, including in the context of the post-2015 development agenda. Not all LDCs are rich in mineral resources and other natural endowments. For most of these countries, their most valuable asset is their people, in particular the young. It is only by engaging their people in productive employment that they can ensure that growth is inclusive and that it contributes to poverty reduction and sustainable development.

For most LDCs, their most valuable asset is their people, in particular the young. It is only by engaging their people in productive employment that they can ensure that growth is inclusive.

What explains the failure to translate high output growth in LDCs into rapid employment growth, and why is the employment issue such an immediate development challenge for these countries?

There are well-known structural impediments to employment generation in LDCs and other low-income countries, which have been well documented in the development literature. They mainly concern the absence of capital and other features of underdevelopment, such as infrastructural bottlenecks, which act as constraints on development. As was noted in LDCR 2006: "One consequence of the combination of a deficiency of domestic demand on the one hand, and of weak capabilities, infrastructure and institutions for being internationally competitive on the other hand, is that productive resources and entrepreneurial capabilities are underutilized within the LDCs owing to lack of demand and structural weaknesses. There is surplus labour, latent entrepreneurship, untapped traditional knowledge, a vent-for-surplus through exporting and unsurveyed natural resources. Policy thus needs to be geared to mobilizing these underutilized potentials."

In addition, the policy discussion of the past decade on national development in LDCs has tended to focus on growth, changes in per capita incomes and the structure of output, rather than on the development of productive capacity and the level and composition of employment. This has been based on two assumptions.

First, if GDP growth is sufficiently rapid, it will lead to productive transformation and will generate increases in aggregate employment, even if at a somewhat slower rate because of rising labour productivity.

It has become evident across many developing countries that rapid and sustained output growth will not necessarily generate increases in aggregate employment or shifts towards more desirable forms of employment.

Second, changes in the structure of output will be associated with changes in the structure of the labour force in the classic manner described by Kuznets (1973) and Kaldor (1966), so that growth through industrialization will generate shifts in the structure of the workforce as well.

Neither of these assumptions, however, can be readily accepted today, since it has become evident across many developing countries, including those described as dynamic and successful, that rapid and sustained output growth will not necessarily generate increases in aggregate employment or shifts towards more desirable forms of employment. In rethinking their development policy agenda, then, LDCs will need to pay closer attention to the employment dimension, which has so far been missing from the policy discussion on growth and economic development.

In many LDCs, public expenditure contraction after the global recession has been directed not only at such employment-intensive social sectors as health and education, but also at spending which directly affects agriculture.

The slow growth of employment in LDCs in recent years was also a result of the choice of sectors that were the main drivers of economic growth and the technologies associated with the emerging production process. GDP growth in many LDCs was primarily the product of exceptionally buoyant international conditions during the 2000s (LDCR, 2010). The steep increase in commodity prices which some authors termed a commodity supercycle (Kaplinsky, 2010; Erten and Ocampo, 2012) boosted LDC exports and GDP growth. The boom not only reinforced their existing specialization in primary commodities, but also encouraged investment inflows and the transfer of a capital-intensive production system. The result has been a weakened relationship between output and employment growth.

Furthermore, macroeconomic policies aimed at restricting domestic demand for stabilization purposes – policies that were applauded for the macroeconomic prudence they advocated – have also had adverse effects. Restrictive monetary policy regimes that target very low rates of inflation and reduce the credit access of small producers, and fiscal policies that emphasize fiscal discipline through reduced government spending, all tend to inhibit the possibilities of local employment generation. In many LDCs, public expenditure contraction after the global recession has been directed not only at such employment-intensive social sectors as health and education (Ortiz et al., 2011), but also at spending which directly affects agriculture, and which is typically a major source of livelihood. This leads to less direct job creation by government and also has a less direct impact through multiplier effects. These employment effects operate in addition to other redistributive effects of public expenditure and monetary and credit policies.

For LDCs, the employment dimension is even more pressing today because of the demographic challenges they face.

For LDCs, the employment dimension is even more pressing today because of the demographic challenges they face, as explained in the rest of this chapter.

Given these challenges and the predominantly youthful demographic structure of most LDCs, there are additional reasons for the urgency of creating jobs that meet the aspirations and requirements of the young. Improving livelihoods and the quality of life for this growing population will require substantial investments in education to create a more skilled labour force. It will also necessitate the development of productive capacities through job creation to employ the growing labour force, and the development of infrastructure and housing to accommodate the service and amenity needs of new firms and households. In addition, unemployment and underemployment amount to a huge waste of national resources. If productive employment opportunities do not expand sufficiently for the growing LDC labour force, there may also be rising pressures for international migration from these countries, as documented and analysed in LDCR 2012 (UNCTAD, 2012). Therefore, a central challenge for LDC economic policymakers is to spur the creation of jobs for their rapidly expanding working-age population and at the same time improve the quality of those jobs.

A central challenge for LDC policymakers is to spur the creation of jobs for their rapidly expanding working-age population and at the same time improve the quality of those jobs.

Providing decent employment for all is a major economic goal in and of itself, since putting people to work increases current and future income, consumption and investment for countries and for their citizens. But decent employment has even broader non-economic benefits. The LDCs are characterized by all-pervasive and persistent poverty. Moreover, a substantial majority of the population suffers from income poverty, which means that even when they do have jobs — most of which are in subsistence sectors — many people cannot escape poverty. Reducing poverty under these conditions requires inclusive development strategies that can generate productive employment. Creating more jobs and better jobs — which is what decent employment is all about — is thus the only sustainable way to alleviate poverty.

Creating more jobs and better jobs is the only sustainable way to alleviate poverty.

Social and political stability is another area where the benefits of high levels of productive employment are evident. It is perhaps no coincidence that high youth unemployment rates have become a structural characteristic of the countries in North Africa where the so-called "Arab Spring" movements began in 2011 (Groth and Sousa-Poza, 2012; ILO, 2011). Decent employment, by contrast, enables individuals to live the kind of lives they have reason to value. This premise reflects the view of development as a process of enhancing individual freedoms and of mobilizing the social commitment required to attain them (Sen, 1999).

For all these reasons, the issue of how to respond effectively to the LDC employment challenge should be high on the agenda of policymakers in the near future. But this Report posits that policies to address that challenge should be different from those pursued in previous decades. They should be part of a new development agenda and should be integrally associated with strategies for developing productive capacities and encouraging structural transformation.

Social and political stability is another area where the benefits of high levels of productive employment are evident.

The central premise of the Report is that since the lack of productive employment in the LDCs is a consequence of the lack of productive capacities, employment creation on a large scale is intrinsically linked to the development of productive capacities. Indeed, economic development is ultimately about the transformation of productive structures — and more specifically, as discussed here, about shifting the majority of the labour force from low-productivity, low-technology and poorly remunerated activities to ones with higher productivity and higher value added. It also entails a process of diversification from a relatively small number of traditional activities to a much larger number of modern activities. The criteria used to define the category of least developed countries (low income, weak human assets and economic vulnerability) all stem from this fundamental lack of economic transformation and diversification into more productive activities. By definition, the LDCs are countries that are still in the early or incipient stages of the process.

While this aggregate movement from productive activities with lower technology and lower value to ones with higher technology and higher value is essential to development, it is by no means inevitable or even unidirectional. Reinert (2008) has shown how throughout history, and even in relatively recent times, countries have moved in varying trajectories that do not always show progress but that can involve slipping back even after achieving some degree of diversification. One example is the recent pattern of growth in Africa, where 34 of the 49 LDCs are located. That growth pattern has been accompanied by deindustrialization, as evidenced by the fact that the share of manufacturing in Africa's GDP shrunk from 15 per cent in 1990 to 10 per cent in 2008. The most significant decline was observed in western Africa, where it fell from 13 per cent to 5 per cent over the same period. So the notion of stages of development that presumes necessary movement from one stage to the next may be too optimistic: History, context and policies all matter critically. The increase in the number of LDCs over the past four decades, and the slow rate of graduation from LDC status, suggests that the forces which prevent or constrain productive transformation and employment generation are significant and often self-reinforcing. Nevertheless, they can be and have been overcome, as testified by the histories of today's developed countries and by the recent performance of some newly industrializing countries.

Bearing these historical patterns in mind, the rest of this Report sets itself four main tasks:

- First, it addresses the policy dimension of the employment challenge faced by the LDCs, as highlighted in the IPoA (see appendix 1), through an analysis of the potential opportunities and challenges of the demographic projections.

- Second, it provides a baseline assessment of the LDCs' recent labour market performance and of their future job creation needs.

- Third, it develops a policy framework with employment creation as a central objective of economic policy, linking investment, growth and employment creation with the development of productive capacities.

- Fourth, it makes specific policy proposals for generating employment-rich growth and development in the LDCs.

The rest of the chapter focuses on the demographic transition as a critical dimension of the future employment challenges for the LDCs. The trend should sound a wake-up call to LDC Governments and to the entire international community.

Chapter 3 considers the quantity of employment (labour demand and supply trends) and quality of employment (working poor and vulnerable employment) in LDCs since 1990. It concludes with a brief discussion of the interaction between employment and growth in these countries.

Chapter 4 suggests a policy framework that links employment creation and the development of productive capacities in the LDCs. It builds on the ideas developed in UNCTAD's Trade and Development Report 2010, which proposed a strategy for rapid employment generation in developing countries. The strategy focused on investment dynamics coupled with policies to ensure that productivity gains are distributed equally between labour and capital (UNCTAD, 2010a). The objective of the policy framework in this Report is to identify the set of policies LDC Governments should implement if they wish to establish a strong link between growth, employment creation and the development of productive capacities. The framework is designed to provide a logical structure and to explain the rationale for choosing or preferring certain policies or policy approaches to others in order to meet the specific objective of increasing the employment intensity of growth. The framework also elucidates the sequences

The central premise of the Report is that employment creation on a large scale is intrinsically linked to the development of productive capacities. Indeed, economic development is ultimately about the transformation of productive structures.

History, context and policies all matter critically. The forces which prevent or constrain productive transformation and employment generation are significant and often self-reinforcing. Nevertheless, they can be overcome.

This Report suggests a policy framework that links employment creation and the development of productive capacities in the LDCs.

in which policies should be implemented and the conditions (institutional or otherwise) under which the preferred policies may be successfully executed. Finally, it illustrates the desired coherence and complementarity among the policies to be implemented.

Chapter 5 then formulates a coherent set of policies for employment-rich growth and development reflecting the key elements of the conceptual framework, which brings together growth, development of productive capacities and employment.

The LDCs are in the early stages of what has been termed a "demographic transition".

B. Exploring demographic dynamics in the LDCs

The LDCs are in the early stages of what has been termed a "demographic transition" (Bloom et al., 2001), which refers to the transition of countries from high birth and death rates to low birth and death rates. In developed countries, this transition began in the eighteenth century, while for LDCs it began much later, in the twentieth century.[1] In most LDCs, life expectancy is rising due to improvements in food supply, education and sanitation, and in the absence of a corresponding fall in birth rates, most of these countries are experiencing high rates of population growth. The LDC population is forecast to grow from 858 million in 2011 to 1 billion by 2020 and 1.7 billion by 2050.[2] By 2050, the LDCs should have a working-age population of 1.1 billion, compared to 469.9 million in 2010. However, large future increases in population may hinder the creation of employment opportunities on the required scale. This could entrench unemployment and underemployment[3] while making poverty alleviation less likely.

The LDC population is forecast to grow from 858 million in 2011 to 1 billion by 2020 and 1.7 billion by 2050.

The LDC youth population (aged 15–24 years) is becoming better educated and is growing fast, as it is set to rise to from 168 million in 2010 to 300 million by 2050, an increase of 131.7 million. The African LDCs accounted for 63 per cent of the total in 2010, a proportion that will reach 78 per cent by 2050. Of the 46 LDCs for which data are available, only Bangladesh, Bhutan, Cambodia, Laos, Lesotho and Myanmar are likely to experience a reduction in the youth population during the same period. Nonetheless, overall the youth share of the LDC working-age population will decline from 36 per cent in 2010 to 27 per cent by 2050.

The LDC youth population is set to rise to from 168 million in 2010 to 300 million by 2050, an increase of 131.7 million.

The analysis in this section of the Report focuses on the demographic dimension of the employment challenges faced by LDCs. The section highlights key baseline demographic trends in LDC life expectancy, fertility rates, dependency ratios, population growth and working-age population. Although treated here only briefly, educational enrolment, outcomes and investment are other important elements of the demography and employment discourse, and are discussed extensively in chapter 5. Women's participation in the labour force and other relevant gender issues are covered in chapter 3. This section concludes with a discussion of the potential employment implications of rising population densities, urbanization and migration in the LDCs.

1. Key demographic trends in the LDCs

The LDCs have the world's highest population growth rate, at 2.2 per cent per annum — almost twice the 1.2 per cent of other developing countries.

Although the LDCs have the world's highest population growth rate, at 2.2 per cent per annum — almost twice the 1.2 per cent of other developing countries (ODCs) — this rate is slowly declining. The LDC population doubled between 1980 and 2010 and should do so again by 2050 (see chart 6). As of 2011, the total LDC population was 858 million, approximately 12 per cent of the world population. Some 64 per cent of that population lives in Africa (548

Chart 6. LDC population, 1970–2050
(Absolute value, millions)

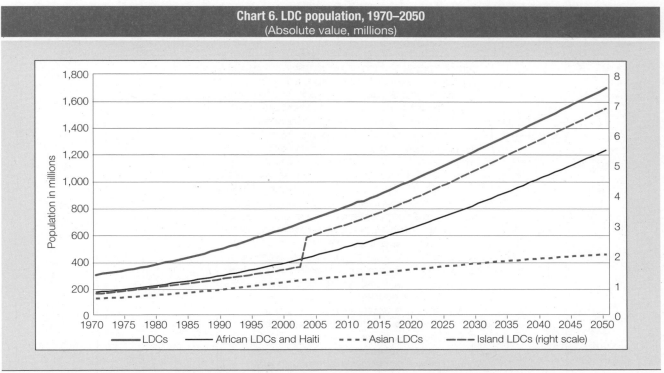

Source: UNCTAD secretariat calculations, based on UNCTADstat database.
Note: Timor-Leste was included in the LDC category in 2003, hence the sharp rise in the Island LDCs trend that year.

million), 36 per cent in Asia (306 million) and 0.4 per cent in island LDCs (3.1 million).[4] The world population was 7.0 billion in 2012 and is projected to reach 9 billion by 2050, of which the LDC population will account for 19 per cent.

Within the LDC group, during the period 1970–2012, African LDCs had the highest population growth rate at 2.8 per cent per annum, which is above the overall LDC average of 2.5 per cent. The rates for island LDCs and Asian LDCs were lower, at 2.4 and 2.2 per cent, respectively. Chart 7 shows the countries with the highest population growth rates during the period 1970–2012: Djibouti (4.1 per cent), Gambia (3.5 per cent), Uganda (3.3 per cent), Niger (3.2 per cent) and Equatorial Guinea (3.1 per cent). Of these, the highest fertility rates were in Uganda and Niger (6.1 and 7.0 births per woman, respectively.). During the period 1950–2010, all five of the above-mentioned countries experienced a six-fold population increase, as compared to a four-fold increase for the LDCs as a group.

Between 2010 and 2050, the LDC working-age population is expected to increase by an average 15.7 million people per year.

As mentioned earlier, between 2010 and 2050, the LDC working-age population (i.e., those between 15 and 64 years of age) is expected to increase by 630 million people, or an average 15.7 million people per year. By 2050, the least developed countries will account for 19 per cent of the global working-age population. Chart 8 shows that over the same period, in 11 LDCs that population is likely to rise by at least 0.5 million a year. The projected increases are highest in African LDCs: Democratic Republic of the Congo, Ethiopia, United Republic of Tanzania and Uganda, for example, will each increase their working-age population by more than 1 million people per annum. Of the Asian LDCs, Bangladesh will probably have the greatest such increase (935,000 people per annum). Whether these countries can exploit the potential "demographic dividend",[5] however, will depend on their economies' capacity to absorb and productively employ new labour market entrants.

Whether these countries can exploit the potential "demographic dividend", however, will depend on their economies' capacity to absorb and productively employ new labour market entrants.

The data presented in table 7 suggest that the LDC demographic transition is still in its early stages and is progressing at a relatively slow pace. Nonetheless, as was the case in China, this does not mean it cannot accelerate (Feng, 2011). Although since 1980 the LDC fertility rate has declined sharply, it remains above

The LDC fertility rate is nearly twice the world average.

Chart 7. Average annual population growth rate in the LDCs, 1970–2012

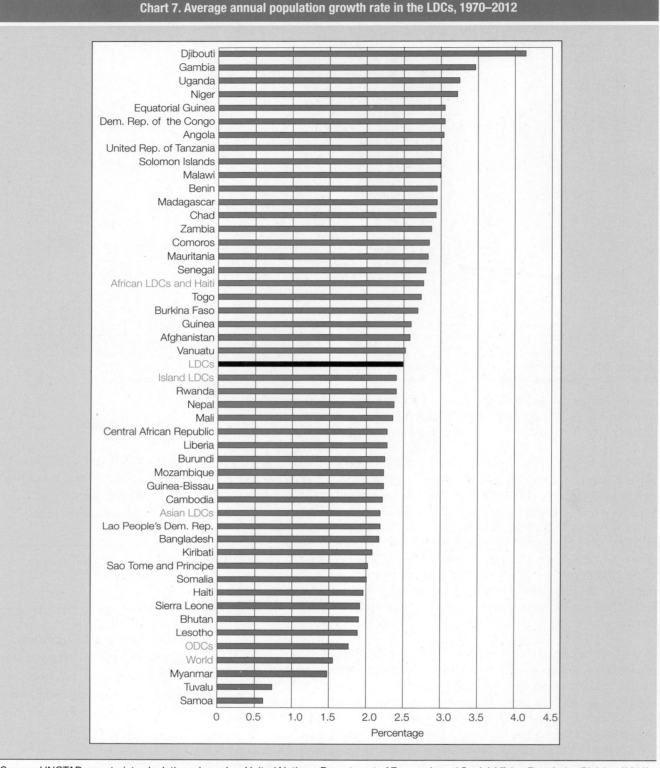

Source: UNCTAD secretariat calculations, based on United Nations, Department of Economic and Social Affairs, Population Division (2012). *World Population Prospects: The 2012 Revision*, CD-ROM.

LDCs have the world's highest infant, child and maternal mortality rates.

four children per woman, nearly twice the world average. Alongside these high fertility rates, however, LDCs have the world's highest infant, child and maternal mortality rates. Since 1980, efforts to improve the outreach of health-care systems across these countries have lengthened life expectancy by 10 years; in 2011, the average was 58 years. Life expectancy in ODCs (68 years) and developed countries (77 years), however, is still considerably higher.

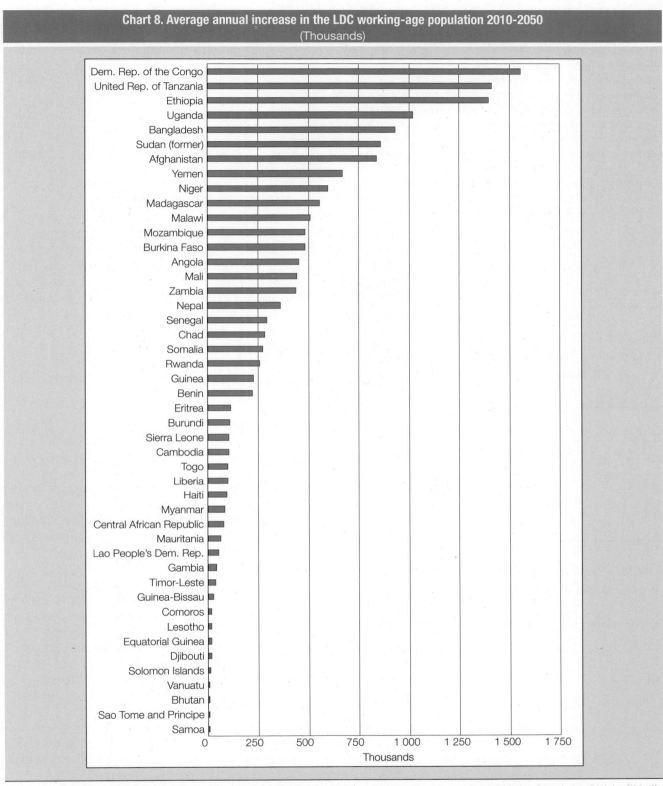

Chart 8. Average annual increase in the LDC working-age population 2010-2050
(Thousands)

Source: UNCTAD secretariat calculations, based on United Nations, Department of Economic and Social Affairs, Population Division (2012). *World Population Prospects: The 2012 Revision*, CD-ROM.

The overall result of these trends has been a slight deceleration in the LDC population growth rate, which remains and will likely continue to be above 2 per cent per annum until 2020. That decline was particularly evident in the Asian LDCs, where it fell from an average 2.5 per cent in 1990–1999 to 1.6 per cent in 2000–2012 (see annex table 12 for data on individual LDCs).

Table 7. Broad demographic trends in the LDCs, 1980–2011				
	1980	1990	2000	2011
Population, (millions)	389.9	510.1	658.4	843.7
Population growth (annual percentage)	2.7	2.7	2.4	2.2
Life expectancy at birth, total (years)	48.5	51.1	53.2	58.4
Fertility rate, total (births per woman)	6.5	6.0	5.3	4.5
Age dependency ratio (percentage of working-age population)	92.0	91.4	86.7	78.1
Labour force participation rate, total (percentage of total population ages 15+)		74.2	73.2	73.9
Adjusted net enrolment rate, primary (percentage of primary school age children)	52.9	52.7	59.1	79.8
Primary completion rate, total (percentage of relevant age group)	36.1	40.8	45.8	63.7
School enrolment, secondary (percentage net)	12.8	14.7	23.0	32.3
Literacy rate, youth total (percentage of people ages 15-24)		56.7	65.2	72.4

Source: UNCTAD secretariat calculations, based on UNTADstat and *World Development Indicators* online databases.
Note: 2011 is the most recent year for available data.

By 2030, some 46 per cent of the LDC population will be under 20 years of age.

The relatively slow pace of the LDCs' demographic transition is clear when we consider population structure by age group, as represented in the "population pyramid" of chart 9. Throughout the period 1990–2020, approximately half of the people in LDCs are expected to be under 20 years of age and about 5 per cent over 60. This is a young demographic structure, which explains the high age dependency ratio[6] reported in table 7. However, there will also be a 6-percentage-point decline in the share of people under 10 years of age, and a corresponding increase in the three age groups between 20 and 49 years. By 2030, some 46 per cent of the LDC population will be under 20 years of age and about 6.5 per cent will be over 60 — a proportion that will almost double (to 10 per cent) between 1990 and 2050.

As stated above, change has come slowly, since 38 per cent of the LDC population in 2015 will be under 15 years of age, 20 per cent will be between 15 and 24 years of age and 38 per cent between 25 and 64 years of age. By 2050, 29 per cent will be under 15 years of age, which is still above the projected proportion for ODCs (see chart 12). The number of LDCs where over 40 per cent of the population is under 15 years of age has declined, from 44 countries in 1990 to 33 in 2010. That number should shrink further to 26 (24 of them in Africa) by 2015 and to 4 by 2050. Despite these changes, however, there is both a "youth bulge" and a growing working-age population in LDCs.

By 2050, one in four 15–24-year-olds worldwide will live in an LDC.

The data presented in chart 10 show the declining LDC dependency ratios between 2010 (77 per cent of the working-age population) and those forecast for 2050 (57 per cent), a trend evident since 1980. African LDCs have the highest dependency ratios — 80 per cent in 2010 — which will shrink to around 60 per cent by 2050. Asian LDCs are consistently below the LDC averages, accounting for 63 per cent in 2010 and a projected 48 per cent by 2050. However, they will remain above the ODC average for both 2010 and 2050. For Asian LDCs, forecasts suggest a rising share of old-age dependants, who will account for 17 per cent of the total population by 2050.

The LDC youth population could potentially drive growth in new and innovative directions.

As we see in chart 11, LDCs as a group will continue to experience strong growth in the number of young people aged 10–24, which is expected to increase sharply between 2010 and 2050. In the developed countries, by contrast, the youth population peaked in 1980 and has been declining ever since. The situation is similar in ODCs, whose youth population peaked in 2010 and should decline thereafter. By 2050, one in four 15–24-year-olds worldwide will live in an LDC (see chart 12). A burgeoning youth population could have major implications for labour markets, with a relatively low absorption rate of new entrants, rapid urbanization and concomitant pressure on the health and sanitation infrastructure in urban centres, which in many LDCs is already at breaking point. Economic growth and political stability could suffer as well in many LDCs (World Bank, 2013). On the other hand, the LDC youth population could potentially drive growth in new and innovative directions through a rise in

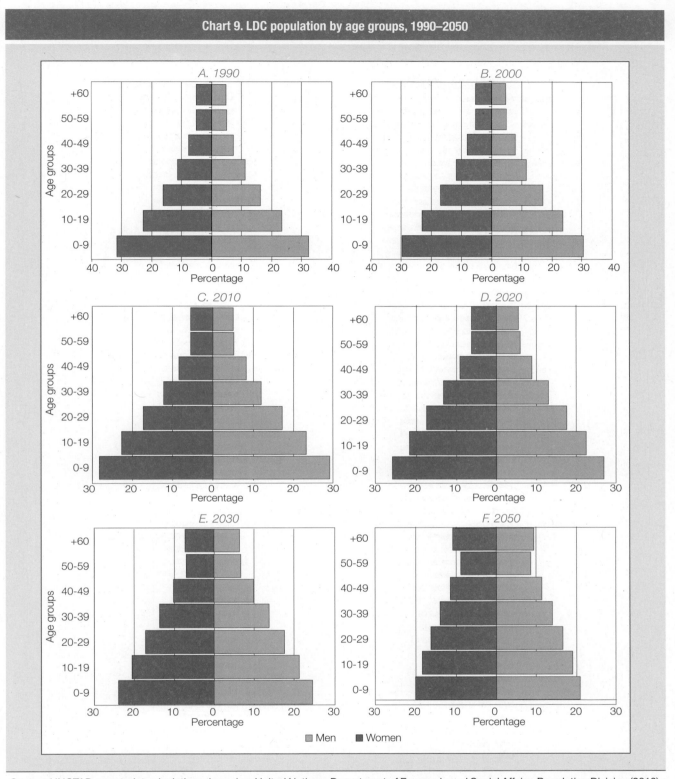

Chart 9. LDC population by age groups, 1990–2050

Source: UNCTAD secretariat calculations, based on United Nations, Department of Economic and Social Affairs, Population Division (2012). *World Population Prospects: The 2012 Revision*, CD-ROM.

information and communication technology (ICT) and enterprise development and through higher levels of education, creativity, and talent, which will be crucial to future prosperity.

As shown in chart 12, the Asian LDCs are forecast to have the lowest share of youths in the LDC group (51 per cent of the total population in 2015 and 34 per cent in 2050). These countries are strongly influenced by drivers of change in Bangladesh, the most populous member of the group. However, although they

The Asian LDCs are forecast to have the lowest share of youths in the LDC group (51 per cent of the Asian LDC population in 2015 and 34 per cent in 2050).

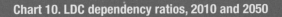

Chart 10. LDC dependency ratios, 2010 and 2050

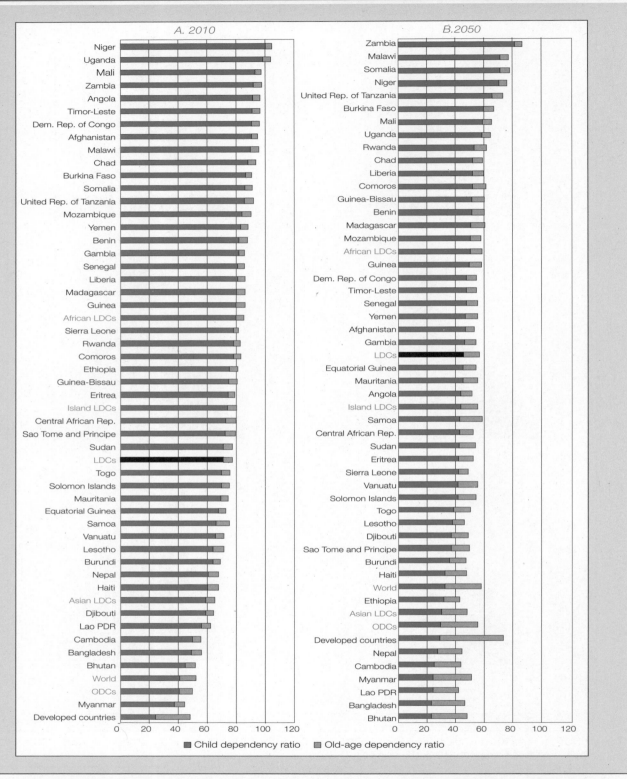

Source: UNCTAD secretariat calculations, based on United Nations, Department of Economic and Social Affairs, Population Division (2012). *World Population Prospects: The 2012 Revision*, CD-ROM.

started from a relatively low base, the Asian LDCs have a growing and significant share of old-age dependants. The share of youths in the total population of island LDCs, like their African counterparts, is above the LDC average (61 per cent in 2015 and a projected 48 per cent in 2050). In LDCs where mortality levels at young ages remain high compared to ODCs, over the next 40 years life expectancy is still expected to be higher at birth than at older ages (UNICEF,

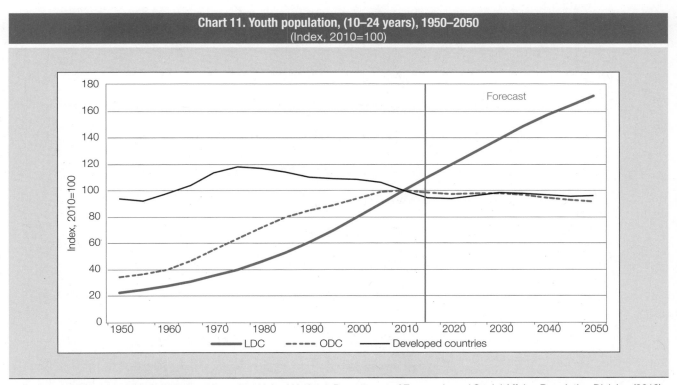

Chart 11. Youth population, (10–24 years), 1950–2050
(Index, 2010=100)

Source: UNCTAD secretariat calculations, based on United Nations, Department of Economic and Social Affairs, Population Division (2012). *World Population Prospects: The 2012 Revision*, CD-ROM.

2013. In Asian LDCs, on the other hand, decreasing fertility, along with greater life expectancy, is reshaping the population age structure by shifting the relative weight from younger to older groups. At this point it is difficult to determine the extent to which rising international migration contributes to the changing age distribution, or whether it has a more significant impact than fertility and mortality rate changes (UNCTAD, 2012).

Although the proportion of African LDC youths in the total population is expected to decline from 60 to 50 per cent by 2050, it will remain above the LDC average. The demographic transition will probably be slower in African LDCs than other least developed countries. In Asian LDCs, there is already an increasing downward trend in both the number and share of youths in the total population, due largely to declining fertility rates. For example, in Bangladesh a sharp drop in the fertility rate from seven children per woman during the 1970s to three in the 1990s has slowed population growth and gradually changed the age structure. Because of population ageing, the number of children and young people under 15 years of age (approximately 47 million) is unlikely to rise significantly, which should help Government in planning the education and health systems.

A declining dependency ratio, together with a growing working-age population, should in theory provide a demographic dividend and development opportunity for LDCs. Bloom et al. (2003) maintain that a decline in the number of dependants can enable households to increase investments in human capital (particularly education and health), and that a rise in the working-age population can potentially expand a country's productive output. The Asian LDCs will face the challenge of exploiting the demographic dividend earlier than other LDCs because their socio-economic and health indicators (e.g. fertility rates) are improving more quickly, resulting in a faster decline in the share of dependants and an increase in the share of the working-age population.

It is clear from the foregoing that the youth bulge is set to persist in the medium term. This will put greater pressure on the labour market, as numerous

A declining dependency ratio, together with a growing working-age population, should in theory provide a demographic dividend and development opportunity for LDCs.

The youth bulge is set to persist in the medium term. This will put greater pressure on the labour market.

While investment in education is rising, employment prospects remain uncertain.

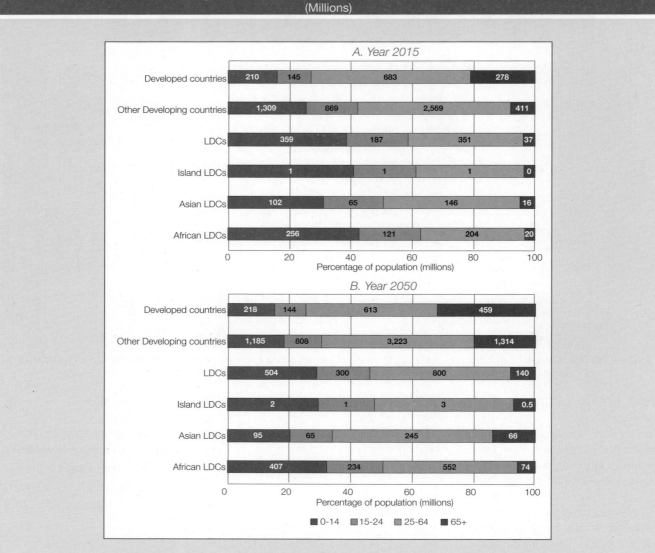

Chart 12. Age distribution of LDC and ODC populations, 2015 and 2050
(Millions)

A. Year 2015

B. Year 2050

■ 0-14   ■ 15-24   ■ 25-64   ■ 65+

Source: UNCTAD secretariat calculations, based on United Nations, Department of Economic and Social Affairs, Population Division (2012). *World Population Prospects: The 2012 Revision*, CD-ROM.

cohorts of new entrants will seek employment in the near future. The promise of a demographic dividend requires investment in youths, their training and their employment. Critically, over the past 20 years LDCs have made significant investments in education, and remain on track to achieve universal primary education and gender equality (MDGs 2 and 3, respectively). In addition, the net primary enrolment ratio increased by more than 25 per cent over the past two decades, reaching 80 per cent in 2011, and the secondary school enrolment ratio rose to 32 per cent (table 7). Thus, while investment in education is rising, employment prospects remain uncertain (see chapter 3).

Around two thirds of the LDCs' population live in rural areas.

2. URBANIZATION AND RURAL–URBAN LABOUR MIGRATION

Despite strong LDC growth during the period 2002–2008, very little structural change has occurred, and progress in reducing vulnerable employment has been limited (McKinley and Martins, 2010 and UNECA, 2010). The relationship between demographics and employment in the LDCs is perhaps most clearly articulated through the following drivers of change: rising urbanization, rural–urban migration, growing pressure on natural resources and gender equality.

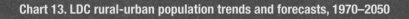

Chart 13. LDC rural-urban population trends and forecasts, 1970–2050

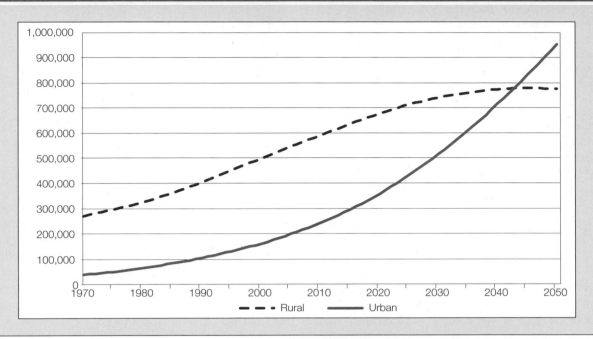

Source: UNCTAD secretariat calculations, based on FAO, FAOSTAT, online, 30 May 2013.

Most LDCs have a large rural population, although there are some exceptions (such as Angola, Djibouti, Gambia, Liberia and Sao Tome and Principe, all of whose rural populations account for less than 50 per cent of the total population). Around two thirds of the LDCs' population live in rural areas, and these zones will probably continue to host the majority of the population until 2040 (see chart 13).

As shown in table 8, the current level of urbanization in LDCs is 28 per cent, which is about 20 percentage points below the world average (50.5 per cent). That level should reach 39 per cent by 2020, largely because of rising rural–urban migration, high fertility rates and population growth. Based on the average annual urban population growth rate of 4 per cent during 2010–2020, the LDC urban population should expand by 116 million, with the rural population rising by 87 million. If these demographic trends (e.g. rural–urban migration, high fertility rates, etc.) persist, the rural population should start declining by 2035 (see chart 13).

Nevertheless, the urban population growth rate has been nearly three times higher than that of the rural population since 1980 (see table 9). Concerns about the pace of urbanization and its impact on living conditions in large conurbations (especially basic infrastructure) are thus well placed, especially because such conurbations host over 60 per cent of the urban population in sub-Saharan

The urban population growth rate has been nearly three times higher than that of the rural population since 1980.

Since most people in LDCs reside in rural areas, greater urban drift will support higher rates of emigration, unless major LDC urban centres can generate higher levels of employment.

Table 8. LDC distribution of population and labour, 2000–2020								
		Distribution of population *(percentage)*			Absolute numbers *(thousands)*			Average annual change *(percentage)*	
		2000	*2010*	*2020*	*2000*	*2010*	*2020*	*2000-2010*	*2011-2020*
African LDCs	Rural	69.9	65.9	61.4	298 454	367 570	438 878	2.1	1.8
	Urban	30.1	34.1	38.6	103 279	158 524	240 371	4.4	4.3
Asian LDCs	Rural	77.9	72.6	67.1	198 831	219 793	235 145	1.0	0.7
	Urban	22.1	27.4	32.9	59 034	83 352	117 101	3.5	3.5
Island LDCs	Rural	68.2	65.4	62.5	1 757	2 185	2 626	2.2	1.9
	Urban	31.8	34.6	37.5	640	909	1 322	3.6	3.8
Total LDCs	Rural	75.7	71.9	67.3	499 042	589 548	676 649	1.7	1.4
	Urban	24.3	28.1	32.7	162 953	242 785	358 794	4.1	4.0

Source: UNCTAD secretariat calculations, based on FAO, FAOSTAT, online, 30 May 2013.

Table 9. Urbanization and pressure on land in the LDCs, 1980–2011				
	1980	1990	2000	2011
Population density (people per sq. km of land area)	19.2	25.2	32.6	42.6
Urban population (percentage of total)	17.3	20.9	24.3	28.3
Urban population growth (annual percentage)	5.7	4.6	3.8	3.8
Rural population (percentage of total population)	82.7	79.1	75.7	71.3
Rural population growth (annual percentage)	2.1	2.2	2.0	1.6
Agricultural land (percentage of land area)	37.1	38.1	38.6	38.3
Arable land (percentage of land area)	6.2	6.5	7.0	8.1
Arable land (hectares per person)	0.3	0.3	0.2	0.2
Forest area (percentage of land area)	-	32.8	31.1	29.7
Renewable internal freshwater resources per capita (cubic metres)	12'131[a]	9'320[b]	6'685[c]	5'465

Source: UNCTAD secretariat calculations based on UNTADstat and World Development Indicators online databases.
Note: a 1982 data; b 1992 data; c 2002 data.

With a population density already twice that of the 1980s, the availability in LDCs of arable land per person may continue to decline.

An immediate priority for most LDCs is to foster environmentally sustainable socio-economic development and employment in those rural areas that host the majority of their population.

Most LDCs have not been able to generate sufficient productive off-farm jobs to absorb the growing labour force seeking work outside agriculture.

Africa (SSA) and 35 per cent in southern Asia. The rate of LDC rural–urban migration is mounting and will continue to do so until at least 2050. It is therefore likely that — as previously mentioned — since most people in LDCs reside in rural areas (an average 71 per cent of the population in 2011), greater urban drift will support higher rates of emigration, unless major LDC urban centres can generate higher levels of employment (UNCTAD, 2012; Lewis, 1954).[7] If — as in China, India and Brazil — LDC urbanization and GDP growth rates rise, and the outflow of resources from the rural (agricultural) sector to urban areas is exacerbated, demand for food will grow as well. This will increase the pressure to raise agricultural productivity in LDCs and may also encourage policymakers to look more closely at the role played by rural–urban migration in economic development. The urgency of this policy challenge is dramatically illustrated in table 9, which documents the mounting pressure on natural resources.

With a population density already twice that of the 1980s, and with only marginal expansion of the agricultural frontier (mostly in SSA), the availability in LDCs of arable land per person may continue to decline (see table 9). In per capita terms, renewable internal freshwater resources have also fallen by more than one third in the space of 20 years. Furthermore, the problems posed by the declining size of farms in terms of poverty and food security — not to mention distributional issues — are likely to be aggravated by the potentially disruptive effects of climate change on land productivity, especially in marginal areas (see also chapter 3 of UNCTAD, 2009). The critical nature of this additional policy challenge was clearly reflected in the negotiations at the United Nations Conference on Sustainable Development (Rio+20).[8] The immediate priority for most LDCs, however, is to foster environmentally sustainable socio-economic development and employment in those rural areas that host the majority of their population.

The LDC rural population as a share of the total population has also declined steadily since 1980. In the African LDCs' urban population, the percentage change is 4.4 per cent; in the rural population, 2.1 per cent. In Asian LDCs, the figures are 3.5 per cent and 1.0 per cent, respectively (see table 8). In 2012, Burkina Faso, Eritrea and Uganda reported the highest urban population growth rates in all the least developed countries (see annex table 12 for data on individual LDCs).

As the population grows, agricultural farms decline in size and new farms are increasingly located on marginal land.[9] Mass poverty means that many people cannot afford the means for the sustainable intensification of agricultural production. More and more people are thus seeking work outside agriculture, and urbanization is accelerating. Most LDCs have not been able to generate sufficient productive off-farm jobs to absorb the growing labour force seeking work outside agriculture. Both agricultural and non-agricultural enterprises have been severely challenged to compete following the widespread and deep unilateral trade liberalization and regional trade agreements that began in the 1990s.

As previously stated, rural–urban migration in LDCs is on the rise. The rural underemployed tend to move to urban centres or other rural areas where there is demand for labour to work as unskilled labourers. They often earn low wages and incur extra costs for travel and accommodations. Their remittances are often small — for example, in African LDCs whose citizens mainly migrate within their home country or to neighbouring countries — but again, this depends on where they move and on the prevailing wage differentials. The other qualification is that migration can be highly uneven between regions, between villages and within communities (UNCTAD, 2012).

Policymakers in the LDCs are hence confronted with an imperative need both to increase agricultural productivity and to foster the creation of greater income opportunities in high value added rural activities. In this respect, UNEP/ILO (2012) estimates that over the next decade, the shift to sustainable agriculture in developing countries could increase global employment by 4 per cent, while also helping to preserve the quality of the soil and of the natural environment. In any event, support for sustainable agricultural practices should be complemented by more effective development of rural non-farming activities. Such activities provide a broad range of opportunities to promote economic diversification, employment and potential spillovers, thereby encouraging further transformation in the agricultural sector. A similar strategy, which necessarily hinges on a better and more widespread provision of key infrastructure (such as irrigation, roads and electricity), would intrinsically dampen the push factors that lead to rapid urbanization and informalization in the LDCs and relieve some of the pressure on agricultural land.

LDCs are confronted with an imperative need both to increase agricultural productivity and to foster the creation of greater income opportunities in high value added rural activities.

If, as expected, an additional 630 million people enter the LDC labour market between 2010 and 2050, these countries will be confronted with even greater employment and development problems.

3. CONCLUSIONS

If the recent patterns of growth and structural change explain the LDC "employment challenge" with respect to labour demand and sectoral reallocation, demographic developments complement them on the labour supply side. This chapter has highlighted the importance of the demographic dynamics underlying LDC efforts to achieve poverty reduction, decent employment and social development. Given their limited progress towards the Millennium Development Goals (MDGs) (UNCTAD, 2010) and their demographic situation, the scale of the employment challenge facing LDC policymakers cannot be overestimated.

The chapter has also highlighted the scale of the demographic challenge faced by the LDCs: As previously mentioned, their population, about 60 per cent of which is currently under 25 years of age, is projected to double to 1.7 billion by 2050. If, as expected, an additional 630 million people enter the LDC labour market between 2010 and 2050, these countries will be confronted with even greater employment and development problems. In addition, although the proportion of people in the LDCs living on less than $1.25 per day (i.e., in situations of extreme poverty) has fallen, the number has continued to rise due to high population growth.

For most LDCs, the realization of a potential demographic dividend — one where the dependency ratio is at its lowest — will depend upon the policy mix adopted to encourage future job creation and growth. If the right socio-economic policies are formulated — such as increased investment in health, gender equality, training, education and employment — the LDCs will have an opportunity to realize the demographic dividend. But despite the fact that many LDCs have experienced high levels of economic growth since 2002,

If the right socio-economic policies are formulated — such as increased investment in health, gender equality, training, education and employment — the LDCs will have an opportunity to realize the demographic dividend.

However, high fertility rates and population growth have tended to slow the demographic transition in LDCs, potentially delaying the demographic dividend.

the persistence of relatively high rates of population growth, poverty and low human development indicators means that such growth has not translated into improved living standards and decent employment for most people. As a consequence, high fertility rates and population growth have tended to slow the demographic transition in LDCs, potentially delaying the demographic dividend.

Rising educational levels and youth bulge will be crucial for future growth, innovation and employment in the LDCs.

This chapter has also stressed the importance of human development (e.g. access to sexual and reproductive health care, education and health services) as part of a more balanced approach to development in LDCs. Such an approach would stress the potential complementarities required to promote inclusive growth and employment in LDCs. For example, although the LDCs' primary and secondary education enrolment and youth literacy rates have improved since 1990, they are still below the levels in ODCs and developed countries (United Nations, 2013). In any event, the rising educational levels and youth bulge will be crucial for future growth, innovation and employment in the LDCs.

In short, many LDCs are now at a critical stage of development, one with rapid population growth and a changing rural employment challenge. As population densities rise, farms decline in size and farmers increasingly cultivate more ecologically fragile land, agricultural productivity is likely to remain perilously low. Because of these factors, and as already noted, the rates of LDC urbanization and emigration are expected to remain high.

Many LDCs are now at a critical stage of development, one with rapid population growth and a changing rural employment challenge.

Given the clear demographic challenges discussed in this chapter, the LDCs will need to make significant efforts to generate a sufficient volume of jobs to provide decent employment in the medium term. The benefits of the potential demographic dividend arising from this substantial rise in population growth are not unconditional. Successful exploitation of that dividend will depend on the ability of the LDC economies to absorb and productively employ not just new labour market entrants, but those who are presently unemployed or underemployed. The sustained creation of productive employment and the development of productive capacities will be particularly important in countries where extreme poverty affects the majority of the population and where the Government is unable to address the problem through redistribution (UNCTAD, 2010a; McKinley and Martins, 2010; Ravallion, 2009).

Appendix 1

This Report highlights the following key employment-related provisions of the IPoA (United Nations, 2011):

[Principles guiding the implementation of the Programme of Action:]

- Balanced role of the State and market considerations, where the Government in least developed countries commits to design policies and institutions with a view to achieving sustainable and inclusive economic growth that translates into full employment, decent work opportunities and sustainable development. The State also plays a significant role in stimulating the private sector towards the achievement of national development objectives and creates an appropriate enabling stable, transparent and rules-based economic environment for the effective functioning of markets (para. 29(h)).

- Partnerships with the private sector play an important role for promoting entrepreneurship, generating employment and investment, increasing the revenue potential, developing new technologies and enabling high, sustained, inclusive and equitable economic growth in least developed countries (para. 38).

- Building a critical mass of viable and competitive productive capacity in agriculture, manufacturing and services is essential if least developed countries are to benefit from greater integration into the global economy, increase resilience to shocks, sustain inclusive and equitable growth as well as poverty eradication, achieve structural transformation, and generate full and productive employment and decent work for all (para. 44).

[Action by least developed countries:]

- Strengthen the capacity of domestic financial institutions to reach out to those who have no access to banking, insurance and other financial services, including through leveraging the contribution of, among others, micro-finance, micro-insurance, and mutual funds, in creating and expanding financial services targeted to poor and low-income populations, as well as small and medium-sized enterprises (para. 45.1(d)).

- Promote women's entrepreneurship to make better use of untapped economic potential in least developed countries (para. 55.1(d)).

- Strengthen institutions, including cooperatives, to boost smallholder farmer food production, agricultural productivity and sustainable agricultural practices (para. 60.2(a)).

- Promote the empowerment of rural women as critical agents for enhancing agricultural and rural development and food and nutritional security and ensuring their equal access to productive resources, land, financing, technologies, training and markets (para. 60.2(k)).

[Policy measures on education and training ... will be pursued in line with the following goals and targets:]

- Ensure universal access to free primary education in least developed countries by increasing the enrolment and retention rates, and also increase access to secondary, tertiary and vocational education and skill development training (para. 73(a)).

[Action by least developed countries:]

• Ensure that formal and informal education systems provide the skills training required by the labour market, particularly for the youth to achieve full and productive employment and decent work (para. 74.1(d)).

• Social protection has both short- and long-term benefits to sustainable economic growth, poverty eradication and social stability. Social protection systems, including cash transfers, public works programmes, and unemployment benefits, protect the poor and support growth, employment and broader economic resilience. These systems act as stabilizers for the economy, bolster the resilience of the poor and help prevent people from falling into poverty (para. 91).

[Action by development partners:]

• Strengthen support for least developed countries affected by conflict to address country-specific needs and situations, including broad-based, inclusive and rapid socio-economic development with a special focus on rebuilding national institutions and capacity, rebuilding critical infrastructure and generating productive employment and decent work for all (para. 130.2(l)).

Notes

1 The demographic transition comprises the following four stages, with the LDCs currently situated between stages 2 and 3:
   1. Both death and birth rates are high and approximately in balance.
   2. Death rates fall rapidly due to improvements in food supply and sanitation, which increases life expectancy. Without a corresponding fall in birth rates, countries in this stage experience high rates of population growth.
   3. Birth rates decline due to improved access to contraception, urbanization, better wages, greater gender equality and access to education. Population growth begins to level off. This may produce a "demographic dividend".
   4. Birth rates and death rates are both low.

2 See United Nations Department of Economic and Social Affairs, Population Division (2012). World Population Prospects: The 2012 Revision, CD-ROM.

3 Underemployment reflects underutilization of the productive capacity of the employed population.

4 Based on data from UNCTADstat online database, September 2013.

5 A demographic transition produces a "demographic dividend". Many developing countries have reached the point in their demographic transition where the largest segment of the population is of productive working age and where the dependency ratio declines dramatically, leading to a demographic dividend. The ratio also shrinks significantly at the point where fertility rates continue falling and older generations have shorter life expectancies. When combined with effective public policies, the demographic dividend can help facilitate economic growth, reduce family pressures and encourage women to enter the labour force.

6 The dependency ratio reflects the number of people of non-working age compared to the number of those of working age (15–64 years old). The dependency ratio shows the proportion of dependents per 100 members of the working-age population. A high ratio means that those of working age — and the economy in general — face a greater burden in supporting an ageing or youthful population. The youth dependency ratio includes only under-15s, while the old-age pensioner dependency ratio focuses on those over 64. The dependency ratio does not account for people aged 65+, an increasing proportion of whom work (and are therefore not dependent), or those of working age who are unemployed.

7 Lewis (1954) maintained that surplus labour from the traditional agricultural sector is transferred to the modern industrial sector, whose growth over time absorbs the surplus labour, promotes industrialization and stimulates sustained development. Rural–urban migration is accordingly the means by which surplus labour in the

traditional (agricultural) sector is re-deployed to fill rising modern (urban) sector labour demands. Migration is demand- or employment-driven rather than being driven by wages, which are assumed to be fixed. However, the Harris-Todaro model (1970) identified the decision to migrate as a function of wage differentials, moderated by the availability of job opportunities. In theory, formal sector urban earnings exceed the rural wage rate (or the marginal return to own-account farming), and potential migrants armed with this information assess the probability of attaining urban employment (i.e., the rate of urban employment).

8 See United Nations, The Future We Want, Rio + 20, http://www.uncsd2012.org/rio20/about.html (10 January 2012).

9 When arable land per farmer is declining, that land is used with an increasing intensity of inputs (especially labour and capital) per hectare, but diminishing marginal returns lead to a fall in per capita income and living standards (Jayne et al., 2003; Jayne and Muyanga, 2012). In addition, growing pressure on land tends to induce the development of marginal low-quality arable land (UNCTAD, 2009).

References

Bloom DE, Canning D and Sevilla J (2001). Economic growth and the demographic transition. Working Paper No. 8685. National Bureau of Economic Research. Cambridge (MA).

Erten B and Ocampo JA (2012). *Super-cycles of Commodity Prices Since the Mid-nineteenth Century.* DESA Working Paper No.110. United Nations, Dep. of Economic and Social Affairs. New York.

Feng W (2011). The Future of a Demographic Overachiever: Long-Term Implications of the Demographic Transition in China. *Population and Development Review.* 37: 173–190.

Groth H and Sousa-Poza A (2012). *Population Dynamics in Muslim Countries: Assembling the Jigsaw.* Springer.

International Labour Office (2011). *The Global Crisis: Causes, Responses and Challenges.* International Labour Office. Geneva.

Jayne T and Muyanga M (2012). Land Constraints in Kenya's Densely Po pulated Rural Areas: Implications for Food Policy and Institutional Reform. Presented at the 86th Annual Conference of the UK Agricultural Economics Society. University of Warwick, United Kingdom. 16 April. Available at http://ageconsearch.umn.edu/bitstream/134723/2/Milu_Muyanga_Jayne-Muyanga-Land%2520Constraints%2520in%2520Kenya%27s%2520Densely%2520Populated%2520Areas.pdf.

Jayne TS et al. (2003). Smallholder income and land distribution in Africa: implications for poverty reduction strategies. *Food Policy.* 28(3):253–275.

Kaldor N (1966). *Causes of the Slow Rate of Economic Growth of the United Kingdom: An Inaugural Lecture.* Cambridge University Press.

Kaplinsky R (2010). Asian Drivers, Commodities and the Terms of Trade. In: Nissanke M and Mavrotas G, eds. *Commodities, Governance and Economic Development Under Globalization.* Palgrave Macmillan. Basingstoke and New York: 117–138.

Kuznets S (1973). Modern Economic Growth: Findings and Reflections. *American Economic Review.* 63(3):247–58.

Lewis WA (1954). Economic Development with Unlimited Supplies of Labour. *The Manchester School.* 22(2):139–191.

McKinley T and Martins P (2010). "Empowering MDG Strategies Through Inclusive Economic Development." Paper prepared for UNCTAD Geneva.

Ortiz I, Chai J and Cummins M (2011). Identifying fiscal space: options for social and economic development for children and poor households in 184 countries. Social and Economic Policy Working Paper. United Nations Childern's Fund (UNICEF). New York.

Ravallion M (2009). Do poorer countries have less capacity for redistribution? One Pager No. 97. International Policy Centre for Inclusive Growth. Brasilia.

Reinert ES (2008). *How Rich Countries Got Rich and Why Poor Countries Stay Poor.* Public Affairs. New York.

Sen A (1999). *Development as Freedom.* Oxford University Press. Oxford.

UNCTAD (2006). *The Least Developed Countries Report 2006: Developing Productive Capacities.* United Nations publication. Sales No. E.06.II.D.9. New York and Geneva.

UNCTAD (2009). *The Least Developed Countries Report 2009: The State and Development Governance.* United Nations publication. Sales No. E.09.II.D.9. New York and Geneva.

UNCTAD (2010a). *Trade and Development Report 2010: Employment, Globalization and Development.* United Nations publication. Sales No. E.10.II.D.3. New York and Geneva.

UNCTAD (2010b). *The Least Developed Countries Report 2010: Towards a New International Development Architecture for LDCs.* United Nations publication. Sales No. E.10.II.D.5. New York and Geneva.

UNCTAD (2012). *The Least Developed Countries Report 2012: Harnessing Remittances and Diaspora Knowledge to Build Productive Capacities.* United Nations publication. Sales No. E.12.II.D.18. New York and Geneva.

UNEP and ILO (2012). *Working Towards Sustainable Development: Opportunities for Decent Work and Social Inclusion in a Green Economy.* United Nations Environment Programme (UNEP) and International Labour Office (ILO), Geneva.

UNICEF (2013). *The State of the World's Children 2013: Children with Disabilities.* UNICEF. New York.

United Nations (2011). Programme of Action for the Least Developed Countries for the Decade 2011–2020. Fourth United Nations Conference on the Least Developed Countries Istanbul, 9-13 may 2011. No. A/CONF.219/3/Rev.1. United Nations. New York.

United Nations (2013). *The Millennium Development Goals Report 2013.* United Nations. New York.

World Bank (2013). *World Development Report 2013: Jobs.* World Bank. Washington (DC).

World Population Prospects, the 2010 Revision (n/d). United Nations Department of Economic and Social Affairs (UN/DESA). See http://esa.un.org/wpp/.

CHAPTER 3

EMPLOYMENT TRENDS IN LDCs

A. The quantity of employment in the LDCs

1. Introduction

Since the 2009 global recession, LDCs have undergone a slowdown in GDP growth (see chapter 1). While recent growth patterns may have exacerbated these countries' employment challenge with respect to labour demand and sectoral reallocation, as shown in chapter 2, socio-demographic developments have also had a major impact from the labour supply side. This chapter considers the quantity of employment (labour demand and supply trends) and quality of employment (working poor and vulnerable employment) in LDCs since 1990. The chapter concludes with a brief discussion of the interaction between employment and growth in LDCs.

2. The LDC employment challenge

The central employment challenge in the LDCs is to create productive jobs and livelihoods for the millions of people who are entering the labour force each year. The scale of this challenge will be even greater in the coming years. It is useful to illustrate what this increasing trend actually means for individual LDCs. In 45 of the 48 LDCs for which data are available, there are rising numbers of new entrants[1] to the labour market, and those numbers will not even have peaked by 2050. A few examples illustrate how dramatic the trend is. In Niger there were 224,000 new entrants in 2005, a number expected to increase five-fold (1.4 million) by 2050. In Ethiopia, there were 1.4 million new entrants in 2005, which should rise to 2.7 million by 2030 and 3.2 million by 2050 (see annex table 13). It was estimated that in Nepal, for example, new entrants to the labour force numbered 465,000 in 2005, a figure that is expected to peak at 633,000 by 2020. After that, the annual number will start to decline. Similarly, in Bangladesh, there were 2.9 million new entrants in 2005; this figure will peak at 3.1 million by 2020 and decline thereafter. These are the numbers of productive and decent jobs that will have to be created in these countries each year. If this does not happen, the likelihood is that poverty and international emigration rates will rise.

It is also clear that the magnitude of the employment challenge is not only growing, but becoming increasingly complex to address. As previously noted, the main source of employment for the growing LDC labour force has been agriculture, largely through people cultivating new land. However, LDCs face persistent constraints on agricultural growth — declining research and development investment, missing and imperfect factor markets, limited access to producer-risk mitigation tools and poor infrastructure (UNCTAD, 2013). With rising population growth, declining agricultural farm sizes and low productivity, agricultural production is becoming a less viable livelihood for the rural poor. In addition, most LDC farmers cannot afford the means for sustainable intensification of agricultural production. More people are thus seeking work outside agriculture, and urbanization is forecast to accelerate in coming decades.

Unfortunately, the least developed countries have not been able to generate sufficient productive off-farm jobs to absorb the growing labour force seeking work outside agriculture. Most of these people find work in survival urban informal activities. As shown in chart 14, LDC employment growth during the period 2000–2012 was 2.9 per cent per annum, slightly above population growth for the period. Employment growth in the African and island LDCs also outpaced the LDC average and will continue to do so until at least 2018. ILO

The central employment challenge in the LDCs is to create productive jobs and livelihoods for the millions of people who are entering the labour force each year.

In 45 of the 48 LDCs for which data are available, there are rising numbers of new entrants to the labour market, and those numbers will not even have peaked by 2050.

It is also clear that the magnitude of the employment challenge is not only growing, but becoming increasingly complex to address.

(2011) notes that employment growth for adults in LDCs during 2000–2009 was 3.2 per cent per annum, and for youths only 2.1 per cent, far below the period's average GDP growth levels of 7 per cent. Chart 14 also shows that average employment growth lagged behind real GDP growth in the LDCs during the period 2000–2012.

Existing labour market data on the LDCs are incomplete,[2] which makes a detailed empirical evaluation of labour conditions difficult. The broad description outlined in this section is based on data from ILO, the United Nations Population Fund (UNFPA) and the Food and Agriculture Organization of the United Nations (FAO). First, we consider the economically active population (EAP) and break down the LDC labour force[3] into agricultural and non-agricultural sectors. Next, we consider labour force participation, employment-to-population dynamics, labour productivity and rural non-farm (RNF) employment. The chapter concludes with a discussion of the quality of employment in LDCs, employment growth and estimated net job creation in LDCs.

Average employment growth lagged behind real GDP growth in the LDCs during the period 2000–2012.

3. Gross employment trends in the LDCs

This outline of gross employment trends in the LDCs is based largely on FAO estimates of the EAP. These estimates provide a labour force classification of the agricultural and non-agricultural sectors of the economy, the latter encompassing all economic activities outside agriculture (mining, construction,

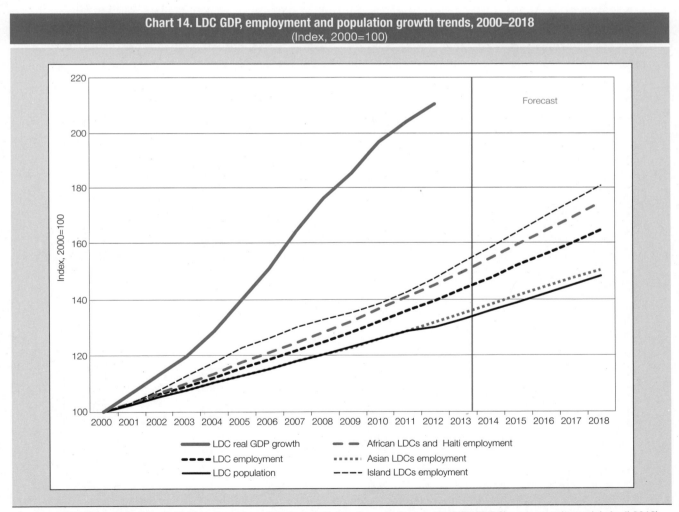

Chart 14. LDC GDP, employment and population growth trends, 2000–2018
(Index, 2000=100)

Legend:
— LDC real GDP growth
■■■■ LDC employment
— LDC population
— — African LDCs and Haiti employment
····· Asian LDCs employment
---- Island LDCs employment

Source: UNCTAD secretariat calculations, based on data from ILO, Employment Trends (EMP/TRENDS) econometric model, April 2013).
Note: Data series 2013 to 2018 are preliminary projections. Real GDP data series covers the period 2000 to 2012 ($ at constant prices, 2005 and constant exchange rates, 2005).

utilities, manufactures and various kinds of services). The EAP is defined as those who furnish the supply of labour for the production of goods and services during a specified reference period. This includes employers, self-employed workers, salaried employees, wage earners, casual day workers, unpaid workers assisting in a family farm or business operation, members of producers' cooperatives and members of the armed forces (International Labour Office, 2009).[4] The terms "EAP" and "labour force" will be used interchangeably throughout this chapter.

The total LDC labour force comprised 364 million people in 2010. Between 2000 and 2010, it increased by 86.9 million, and between 2010 and 2020 it is expected to grow by a further 109 million.

According to FAO estimates, the total LDC labour force comprised 364 million people in 2010. Between 2000 and 2010, it increased by 86.9 million, and between 2010 and 2020 it is expected to grow by a further 109 million (equivalent to 30 per cent of the 2010 labour force) to reach 474 million (chart 15). A significant share of the 30 per cent increment in the total labour force between 2010 and 2020 will occur in Ethiopia (accounting for 12 per cent), Bangladesh (11 per cent) and United Republic of Tanzania (9 per cent). However, all LDCs will experience substantial growth in their labour force during the same period. In 36 of the 48 LDCs for which data are available, the labour force should increase by over 25 per cent. The LDCs that will experience the most rapid growth in labour force are all African: Madagascar, Malawi, Niger, United Republic of Tanzania and Zambia.

In 36 of the 48 LDCs for which data are available, the labour force should increase by over 25 per cent.

Chart 15 also depicts past trends and future projections for the share of the labour force in non-agricultural activities and the distribution of the population between urban and rural areas. In 2010, 65 per cent was engaged in agriculture and 71 per cent lived in rural areas, both down from 2000 levels. The urbanization

Chart 15. Labour force dynamics in the LDCs, 1990–2020

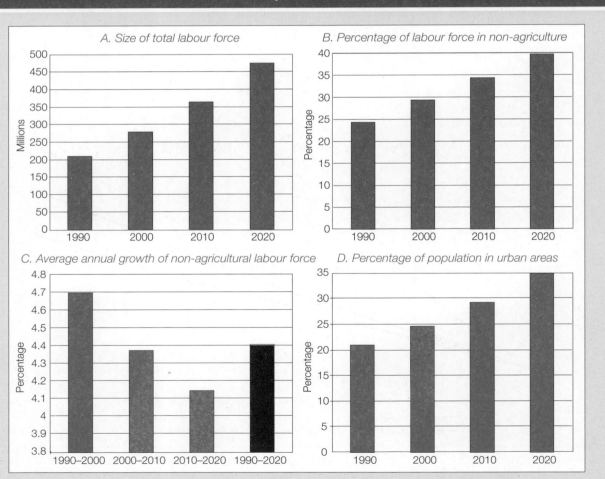

Source: UNCTAD secretariat estimates based on FAO, FAOStat, June 2013.

rate has increased as well, from 20 per cent in 1990 to 29 per cent in 2010, while the share of the population engaged in non-agricultural activities rose from 24 per cent in 1990 to 34 per cent in 2010. The annual growth rate of the non-agricultural labour force, however, has slowed marginally since 1990–2000, to 4.1 per cent per annum in 2010–2020 (chart 15c).

Table 10 summarizes the projected shift between 1990 and 2020 in individual countries. In 1990, two thirds of the LDCs had less than one third of their population living in urban areas and less than one third of their EAP engaged outside agriculture. By 2020, however, this situation will have reversed, with the majority of countries having over a third of their population living in urban areas and engaged (economically active) outside agriculture. During the period 1990–2020, some LDCs — namely, Bangladesh, Chad, Democratic Republic of the Congo, Equatorial Guinea, Haiti, Myanmar, Sao Tome and Principe, and Yemen — will experience a very substantial shift in both the location of their population (largely urbanized) and the increased share of their non-agricultural labour force in the total labour force. As previously noted, the population is not only growing rapidly but also urbanizing quickly. More of the LDC population than ever before is entering the labour market, and a growing proportion of the labour force is working or seeking work outside agriculture. The convergence of these trends makes the current decade critical for these countries, particularly with regard to employment.

Nonetheless, agriculture will remain the major source of livelihood in the LDCs until at least 2020. The EAP in agriculture should also continue to rise until at least that year, when it is projected to increase to 285 million people, as against 187 million in non-agricultural activities. Moreover, according to recent projections of the EAP for 2010–2020, 62 million of the 109-million increase will be outside agriculture and 47 million in agriculture (chart 16).

African LDCs and Bangladesh (as the most populous LDC) are driving the overall pattern of change for the LDCs as a group. In African LDCs, 63 per cent of the increase in the total EAP is expected to be outside agriculture during 2010–2020 (as against 46 per cent during 2000–2010), and in Asian LDCs (excluding Bangladesh), 13 per cent in the 2010–2020 EAP (vs. 45 per cent in 2000–2010). When Bangladesh is included, the projected Asian LDC proportion rises to 37 per cent of the EAP (chart 16). Bangladesh has made significant progress in diversifying its economy and in improving health, fertility and educational outcomes. In addition, as the country has enjoyed a relatively prolonged and constant inward flow of remittances since 1980, families have increasingly reduced their reliance on cultivation and diversified into various non-farm activities (see box 3). African LDCs, by contrast — and despite a rise in the EAP outside agriculture — have not yet managed a sound economic diversification. Island LDCs account for 0.4 per cent of the increase in the total LDC EAP outside agriculture. That EAP is projected to grow faster than the EAP in agriculture during the decade 2010–2020 in all LDCs for which data are available (48 countries). The countries with the fastest expected growth in the non-agricultural labour force during 2010–2020 are Chad, Malawi, Mali, Uganda and United Republic of Tanzania in Africa; Afghanistan, Bangladesh and Yemen in Asia; and Comoros, Sao Tome and Principe and Timor-Leste among the island LDCs.

4. SECTORAL DISTRIBUTION OF EMPLOYMENT BY STATUS

A further decomposition of the non-agricultural labour force provides a better picture of job creation across sectors.[5] As shown in chart 17A, the agricultural sector in 2000 accounted for 71 per cent of total employment in both LDCs and ODCs; by 2018, it is expected to represent 63 per cent in LDCs but only 29 per cent in ODCs. However, the industrial and services sectors are rising significantly

In 2010, 65 per cent was engaged in agriculture and 71 per cent lived in rural areas.

In 1990, two thirds of the LDCs had less than one third of their population living in urban areas and less than one third of their EAP engaged outside agriculture. By 2020, however, this situation will have reversed.

The population is not only growing rapidly but also urbanizing quickly.

According to recent projections of the EAP for 2010–2020, 62 million of the 109-million increase will be outside agriculture and 47 million in agriculture.

Table 10. Changing locus of the labour force in LDCs 1990–2020

Population in urban areas as percentage of total population

1990 — Labour Force in non-agriculture, % total labour force in 1990

Non-agriculture band	Urban 0-33%	Urban 34-66%	Urban 67-100%
0-33%	Afghanistan, Bhutan, Burkina Faso, Burundi, Cambodia, Chad, Comoros, Dem. Rep. of the Congo, Ethiopia, Guinea, Guinea-Bissau, Haiti, Lao People's Dem. Rep., Madagascar, Malawi, Mali, Mozambique, Myanmar, Nepal, Niger, Rwanda, Solomon Islands, Somalia, Sudan (former), Uganda, United Rep. of Tanzania	Angola, Central African Rep., Equatorial Guinea, Gambia, Liberia, Sao Tome & Principe, Senegal, Sierra Leone, Timor-Leste, Zambia	Djibouti
34-66%	Samoa, Vanuatu, Lesotho, Yemen, Bangladesh, Togo	Benin, Mauritania	
67-100%	Kiribati, Tuvalu		

2000 — Labour Force in non-agriculture, % total labour force in 2000

Non-agriculture band	Urban 0-33%	Urban 34-66%	Urban 67-100%
0-33%	Bhutan, Burkina Faso, Burundi, Cambodia, Chad, Comoros, Eritrea, Ethiopia, Guinea, Guinea-Bissau, Lao People's Dem. Rep., Madagascar, Malawi, Mali, Mozambique, Myanmar, Nepal, Niger, Rwanda, Solomon Islands, Uganda, United Rep. of Tanzania	Angola, Central African Rep., Equatorial Guinea, Gambia, Liberia, Senegal, Somalia, Zambia	Djibouti
34-66%	Afghanistan, Lesotho, Samoa, Vanuatu, Bangladesh, Yemen, Dem. Rep. of the Congo	Sudan, Haiti, Sierra Leone, Benin, Mauritania, Togo, Sao Tome & Principe	
67-100%	Kiribati, Tuvalu		

2010 — Labour Force in non-agriculture, % total labour force in 2010

Non-agriculture band	Urban 0-33%	Urban 34-66%	Urban 67-100%
0-33%	Burkina Faso, Burundi, Eritrea, Ethiopia, Guinea-Bissau, Malawi, Mali, Nepal, Niger, Rwanda, Timor-Leste, Uganda, United Rep. of Tanzania	Bhutan, Gambia, Guinea, Lao People's Dem. Rep., Mozambique	Djibouti
34-66%	Afghanistan, Bangladesh, Cambodia, Chad, Comoros, Lesotho, Madagascar, Solomon Islands, Yemen	Angola, Benin, Central African Rep., Dem. Rep. of the Congo, Equatorial Guinea, Haiti, Liberia, Mauritania, Myanmar, Sao Tome and Principe, Senegal, Sierra Leone, Somalia, Sudan, Togo, Zambia	
67-100%	Samoa, Vanuatu	Kiribati, Tuvalu	

2020 — Labour Force in non-agriculture, % total labour force in 2020

Non-agriculture band	Urban 0-33%	Urban 34-66%	Urban 67-100%
0-33%	Burundi, Eritrea, Ethiopia, Malawi, Nepal, Niger, Rwanda, Uganda, United Rep. of Tanzania	Bhutan, Burkina Faso, Gambia, Guinea, Guinea-Bissau, Lao People's Dem. Rep., Mali, Mozambique, Timor-Leste	Djibouti, Sao Tome & Principe
34-66%	Afghanistan, Cambodia, Comoros, Lesotho, Madagascar, Solomon Islands	Angola, Bangladesh, Benin, Central African Rep., Chad, Dem. Rep. of the Congo, Equatorial Guinea, Liberia, Mauritania, Myanmar, Senegal, Sierra Leone, Somalia, Sudan, Togo, Zambia	Haiti
67-100%	Samoa, Vanuatu	Kiribati, Tuvalu, Yemen	

Source: UNCTAD secretariat estimates based on 'Food and Agriculture Organization of the United Nations: Statistics'.

Chart 16. Growth of agricultural and non-agricultural labour force in LDCs, 1990–2020

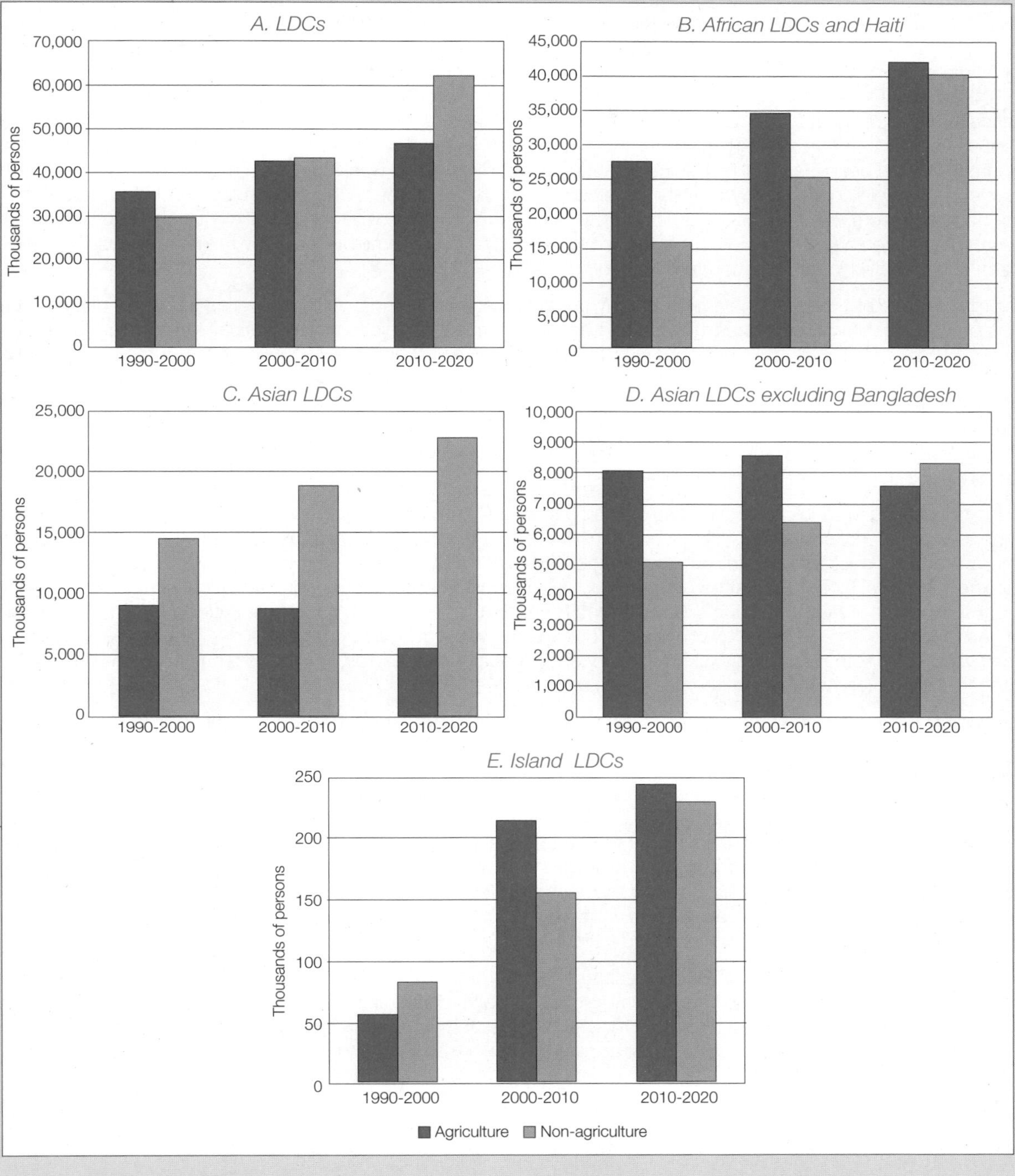

A. LDCs

B. African LDCs and Haiti

C. Asian LDCs

D. Asian LDCs excluding Bangladesh

E. Island LDCs

■ Agriculture ■ Non-agriculture

Source: UNCTAD secretariat estimates based on FAO, FAOStat, June 2013.

as a share of the LDC labour force. Industry accounted for 7 per cent of total LDC employment in 2000 and, based on recent trends, will reach 10 per cent by 2018. Services accounted for 22 per cent of LDC employment in 2000, a proportion likely to increase to 27 per cent by 2018. African LDCs will still have the least diversified economies in terms of employment share, retaining above-average levels of agricultural employment (67 per cent) and below-average levels of industry (8 per cent) and services (25 per cent) as a share of total employment by 2018 (chart 17B). Relatively high GDP growth rates in the LDCs have not translated into concomitant levels of employment growth in industry; only in the services sector has employment growth risen substantially. This reflects a shift

Relatively high GDP growth rates in the LDCs have not translated into concomitant levels of employment growth in industry; only in the services sector has employment growth risen substantially.

Box 3. Observations on rural non-farm employment in Bangladesh

The challenge for Bangladesh, as for other LDCs, is to create a dynamic rural economy that both attracts investment and provides productive employment for the population. During the period 2000–2012, Bangladesh enjoyed a per capita economic growth rate of around 4.6 per cent a year. Although exports of textiles and garments are its principal source of foreign exchange earnings, and the industry has about 4 million employees, the agricultural sector is the largest sector in terms of employment. Some 71 per cent of the population is rural, 46 per cent of them employed in agriculture and the remainder in the RNF sector. The agricultural sector accounts for 21 per cent of GDP, and the RNF sector, which is driven largely by the agricultural sector, for a further 33 per cent (World Bank, 2011). At present around 53 per cent of the rural population is classified as poor, and the average rate of poverty reduction has been only 1 percentage point per annum, which means that some 50 million people are still below the absolute poverty line (World Bank, 2011a). Employment creation as a means of reducing poverty is consequently a major development challenge. Despite the preponderant role of agriculture in rural employment, the sector cannot fully absorb the growing rural labour force or generate sufficient income to reduce poverty.[1] Rural–urban migration has created job opportunities for many, but overall employment growth in rural areas since the 1990s has been concentrated in the rural non-farm economy.

The main drivers of change in the rural economy of Bangladesh are technological innovation within agriculture, increased linkages between rural and urban areas (improved transportation, communications, electrification), growing market linkages and access (demand/supply), skills development, availability of financial services and rising migrant remittances (UNCTAD, 2012). Bangladesh has also undergone a continuous transformation of agricultural production since 1990 with the rising use of high-yield varieties of rice and other cereals, the increased use of chemical fertilizers and pesticides and a rapid increase in irrigation through both deep and shallow tube wells. While much of the supply system is privatized,[2] the new technology and market systems are widespread, and double cropping has become commonplace in many areas of the country (Toufique and Turton, 2002; Hossain, 2004).

Rising agricultural production (involving several crop seasons) has helped to reduce seasonal vulnerability and household dependency on one major crop per year. In addition, the steady decline in average farm size has been somewhat offset by a rise in average production gains for rural households (Mendola, 2007; Bäckman et al., 2011). Increased production has also affected the local labour market as demand for labour has increased, resulting in real wage increases for the landless poor and seasonal migration within the country (World Bank, 2011a; Howes, 2002). At the national level, Bangladesh has in recent years become self-sufficient in food grain. However, the value added of crop types and processing is often very low and the availability of other foodstuffs (such as dairy and wheat), with the exception of rice, has not increased, which may have negatively affected nutritional outcomes (Hossain et al., 2005).

The rural non-farm economy has emerged as a potential source of productive employment and consequently poverty reduction in Bangladesh since the 1990s. As shown in chart 26, this economy is primarily composed of rural manufacturing, agribusiness, livestock, fisheries, cottage industries, trade and marketing services, rural construction, transport, infrastructure and various other services. It also comprises a highly productive dynamic sector that caters mainly to urban demand and a low-productivity, mainly traditional sector that encompasses many of the rural poor. The latter sector is essential to many households' livelihoods and acts as a safety net for the poorest rural dwellers. The dynamic rural economy is composed of specialist firms run by entrepreneurs with relatively high skill levels. These businesses tend to be small and medium-sized enterprises (SMEs) that are larger in scope and scale than traditional household or microenterprises (World Bank, 2007). The case of Bangladesh is important because it highlights the role of supportive technological innovation, investment and rural infrastructure policies in promoting rural non-farm employment and diversification.

Nonetheless, the rural economy in Bangladesh still has the potential for substantial improvements, whether in the local labour market, physical capital, land, agricultural production and distribution or marketing linkages. However, a lack of investment in public goods, especially in remote rural areas; high barriers of entry for the poor or vulnerable groups to various dynamic RNF markets; high transaction costs for access to existing markets; and a general asymmetry of market information may limit this potential.

[1] During the period 2000–2012, the labour force grew by an average 1.5 million people a year due to overall population growth and other demographic changes.

[2] Irrigated boro rice has become more important than traditional amon rice as the primary crop.

of labour out of low-productivity activities — mainly in agriculture — to low-productivity activities in the services (largely non-tradable) sector. The services sector has accounted for a greater share of the LDC labour force over time, and that share is probably under-reported, since much of the sector is composed of informal activities. Employment in the LDC services and industrial sectors is rising fastest in the Asian LDCs.

Similarly, if we consider the share of employment by export specialization, mineral exporters have the highest forecast share of agriculture in the total labour force (74 per cent in 2013) and fuel exporters the lowest (45 per cent). In general, fuel-exporting countries are the least diversified in the LDC group, with among the highest export concentration ratios (UNCTAD, 2013). This

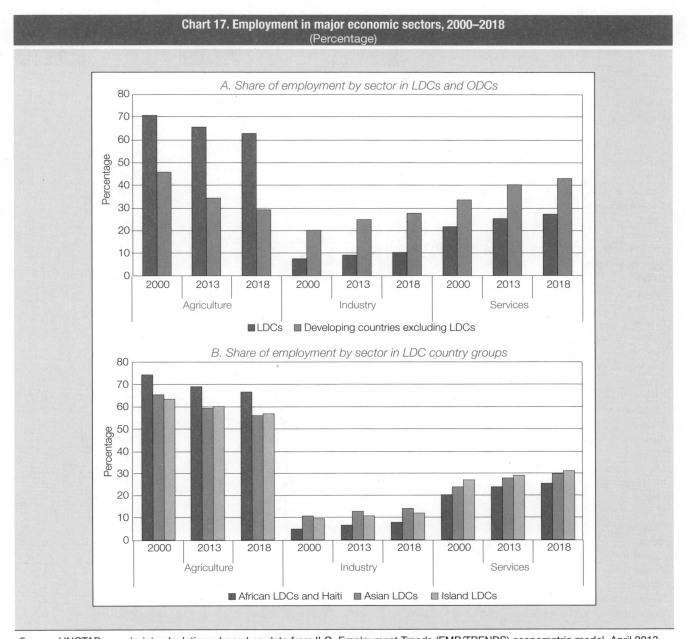

Chart 17. Employment in major economic sectors, 2000–2018
(Percentage)

Source: UNCTAD secretariat calculations, based on data from ILO, Employment Trends (EMP/TRENDS) econometric model, April 2013.
Note: Forecast data presented is from 2013 to 2018. There was no data series available beyond 2018 at the time of writing.

excessive dependence on fuel exports can cause capital to migrate to the sector, leading to exchange rate appreciation. This may in turn result in reduced competitiveness for domestically produced goods and services, crowding out previously productive sectors, such as agriculture.

Clearly, the agricultural sector still accounts for the dominant share of LDC employment. However, there is some evidence of structural change in employment, although not to the same extent as in ODCs, where the share should fall by 17 percentage points during the period 2000–2018. By comparison, it is likely that both African and Asian LDCs will experience less structural change in employment — around 8 percentage points of total employment change — over the same period. Island LDCs should undergo the least structural change in employment in the LDC group, with around 6 percentage points of total employment change over the period. We return to these issues later in this chapter in the context of a broader decomposition of GDP growth in the LDCs.

Table 11 provides a further breakdown of the sectoral share of employment for 42 LDCs. It shows that during the period 2000–2018, only one LDC

During the period 2000–2018, only one LDC of the 42 will have experienced a higher share of agricultural employment in total employment; in the 41 other countries, that share will have declined.

Table 11. Sectoral share of total employment for selected LDCs, various years											
	Agriculture			Percentage point change 2000–2018	Industry			Percentage point change 2000–2018	Services			Percentage point change 2000–2018
	2000	2013	2018		2000	2013	2018		2000	2013	2018	
Total LDCs	71	65	63	-8	7	9	10	3	22	26	27	5
Afghanistan	61	54	51	-9	9	13	14	5	30	33	35	5
Angola	54	38	34	-20	7	10	12	5	39	51	54	15
Bangladesh	65	56	53	-12	11	13	15	4	25	31	33	8
Benin	45	42	39	-6	10	9	9	-1	45	50	52	7
Bhutan	80	57	47	-33	3	10	17	14	17	33	36	19
Burkina Faso	87	84	82	-5	3	3	4	1	10	13	14	4
Burundi	92	91	90	-2	2	2	3	1	6	6	7	1
Cambodia	74	72	68	-5	8	8	11	2	18	20	21	3
Central African Republic	74	74	72	-2	4	4	4	0	22	22	23	1
Chad	83	77	76	-7	2	4	5	2	15	19	20	5
Comoros	70	71	70	0	8	7	8	0	22	22	22	0
Dem. Rep. of the Congo	85	82	80	-5	2	2	3	1	13	16	17	4
Equatorial Guinea	49	38	47	-1	14	18	10	-4	38	43	43	5
Eritrea	79	79	78	-1	6	5	5	-1	15	16	17	1
Ethiopia	86	78	76	-10	4	9	10	6	10	13	14	4
Gambia	64	59	56	-8	5	5	6	1	31	36	37	7
Guinea	74	68	64	-10	7	8	10	3	19	24	27	7
Guinea-Bissau	69	68	65	-4	6	4	5	-1	25	28	30	5
Haiti	50	45	41	-9	11	11	13	2	39	43	46	7
Lao People's Dem. Republic	83	74	68	-15	4	7	10	6	13	19	22	10
Lesotho	72	66	63	-9	9	10	11	2	18	25	26	8
Liberia	55	47	45	-11	8	10	11	3	37	43	45	8
Madagascar	77	80	78	1	8	3	4	-5	15	17	18	3
Malawi	77	75	73	-4	7	8	9	2	15	17	18	2
Mali	69	65	62	-7	6	6	7	1	25	29	31	6
Mauritania	62	57	52	-10	9	10	13	4	29	33	35	6
Mozambique	82	75	73	-9	3	5	6	3	15	20	21	6
Myanmar	61	60	56	-6	13	14	16	3	26	26	28	3
Nepal	75	71	69	-6	10	12	13	2	15	17	19	4
Niger	56	54	51	-5	11	12	13	2	32	34	36	4
Rwanda	83	75	73	-10	3	5	6	3	14	20	21	7
Senegal	50	37	35	-15	13	16	17	4	37	47	48	10
Sierra Leone	72	60	57	-15	4	8	9	5	24	33	34	10
Solomon Islands	60	56	53	-7	11	13	14	3	29	31	33	4
Somalia	78	76	74	-4	4	4	4	1	18	20	22	4
Sudan (former)	41	38	36	-5	9	9	10	1	50	53	54	4
Timor-Leste	61	55	51	-10	10	12	14	4	29	33	35	6
Togo	55	53	50	-5	8	7	8	0	37	40	42	5
Uganda	71	64	60	-11	5	8	9	4	23	28	31	7
United Republic of Tanzania	82	73	70	-12	3	5	6	4	15	21	23	8
Yemen	52	50	47	-4	12	13	13	2	36	38	39	3
Zambia	72	71	68	-4	6	10	11	6	22	20	21	-2

Source: UNCTAD secretariat calculations, based on ILO *Key Indicators of the Labour Market (KILM)*, Seventh Edition, 2013.
Note: Sample of 42 LDCs.

(Madagascar) of the 42 will have experienced a higher share of agricultural employment in total employment; in the 41 other countries, that share will have declined. Angola, Bhutan, and Senegal are expected to see the largest declines in the agricultural labour force. Bhutan, Chad, Ethiopia, Laos and United Republic of Tanzania should have the largest increases in the share of industrial sector employment, but this share will shrink in five other countries (Benin, Comoros, Guinea-Bissau, Madagascar and Togo). With the exception of Comoros and Zambia, the services sector's share of employment is likely to rise in the LDCs. Some countries — Bangladesh, Bhutan, Haiti, Liberia and Senegal — should enjoy a more balanced portfolio of jobs across the different sectors, although like most other LDCs, their industrial sector will still account for the smallest share of total employment.

The estimates presented in charts 15, 16 and 17 are projections that may not prove accurate, as they rely on international data, and national estimates may vary. They nonetheless capture the basic dimensions of the employment and poverty reduction challenges faced by the LDCs. Certainly, poverty reduction requires employment creation in both the agricultural and non-agricultural sectors. As Gurrieri and Sainz (2003) note, productive labour absorption may occur when there are "employment changes in the economically active population that increase the average productivity of those in work, without increasing open unemployment and without average productivity falling in major production branches or groupings".

Poverty reduction requires employment creation in both the agricultural and non-agricultural sectors.

5. LDC LABOUR PRODUCTIVITY

The present section identifies trends in labour productivity using data from various sources, including ILO, World Bank, the United Nations Statistical Division and FAO. However, it is difficult to acquire detailed, internationally comparable data on what LDCs produce and how people in these countries earn a living. The following analysis is accordingly limited to the relatively broad level of sectoral disaggregation allowed by the data, namely, agriculture, industry, manufacturing and services. The information available on LDC wage data is similarly sparse, and there is an urgent need for more data collection and statistical analyses, which should figure prominently in the post-2015 MDG debate. Improved data collection and labour market statistics should help improve government policy analysis and planning. In any case, we show here that wage employment in LDCs is a small share of total employment, which means that average wage data may create a misleading impression of the labour market. Accordingly, the focus here is more on productivity, on the assumption that productivity drives wage adjustment (in a perfectly competitive labour market).

The labour productivity divide between LDCs and ODCs remains substantial, but has narrowed since 2000.

a. Shifts in production structure

As previously noted, there has been little structural transformation in the LDCs as a group over the past 30 years, as most of these countries continue to be dominated by agriculture and minor (largely informal) services activities. Nonetheless, manufacturing and industrial activities and services have become more important for the group as a whole. Since 2000, in the wake of the commodity boom of 2002–2008, the types of industrial activities that have expanded are mining and the exploitation of crude oil. Petty trade and commercial services have grown, among services; and particularly in the Asian LDCs, the manufacturing sector has gained quite significantly as a share of GDP (see annex table 5).

b. Labour productivity: output per worker

LDC output per worker in 2012 was just 22 per cent that of ODCs, 10 per cent that of the EU average and 7 per cent that of North America.

Labour productivity is a key measure of economic performance, as it highlights some of the underlying drivers of growth, particularly improvements in human capital (e.g. skills, education and health), technological accumulation, innovation, organization, and physical and institutional infrastructures. All of these are critical for formulating policies to promote economic growth and develop productive capacities.

As shown in chart 18A, the labour productivity divide between LDCs and ODCs remains substantial, but has narrowed since 2000. Average output per worker in the ODCs was $30,000 in 2012 (constant 2005 international $), as compared with $5,372 in the LDCs. Thus, the average LDC worker can be said to produce 18 per cent of the output of the average ODC worker. LDCs are not, however, a homogeneous group, since during the period 2003–2012 African labour productivity grew steadily[6] and has been higher than levels in the Asian and island LDCs. The oil and metals exporters in the African group may at least partly have driven this phenomenon. The trend is even more apparent if we consider labour productivity by export orientation. Chart 18B shows that during the period 2000–2012 the fuel-exporting LDCs had the highest labour productivity of the group (an average $19,800 in 2012).

Chart 18. LDC labour productivity, by country groups and by export specialization, 2000–2012
(Constant 2005 international dollars)

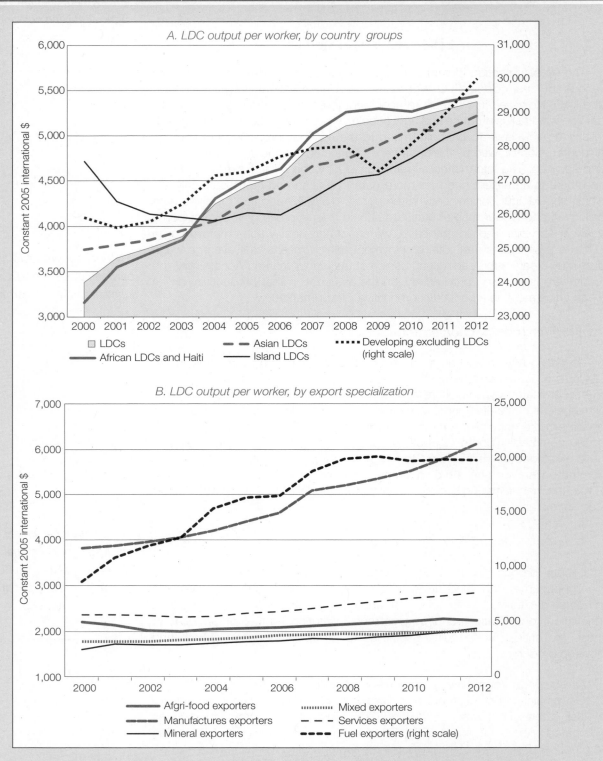

A. LDC output per worker, by country groups

- LDCs
- African LDCs and Haiti
- Asian LDCs
- Island LDCs
- Developing excluding LDCs (right scale)

B. LDC output per worker, by export specialization

- Afgri-food exporters
- Manufactures exporters
- Mineral exporters
- Mixed exporters
- Services exporters
- Fuel exporters (right scale)

Source: UNCTAD secretariat calculations, based on data from ILO, Employment Trends (EMP/TRENDS) econometric model, April 2013.

There is also evidence of steady growth in output per worker in the manufacturing and mixed exporter groups (an average $6,000 in 2012). For the Asian LDCs — such as Bangladesh, Cambodia and Laos, which, together with Haiti, account for the bulk of LDC exports in this sector — the garment industry is a leading driver of growth and employment.

Using an alternate ILO KILM dataset, chart 19 shows that LDC output per worker in 2012 (constant 1990 international $) was just 22 per cent that of ODCs, 10 per cent that of the EU average and 7 per cent that of North America (comprising Canada and the United States). Although the LDC sample covers only 18 countries, it would appear that their average productivity levels have increased only marginally compared to other developing economies, the EU and North America.

Given the importance of the agricultural sector as a share of both GDP and employment in the LDCs, we specifically consider agricultural labour productivity in these countries. The agricultural labour productivity gap between LDCs, ODCs and developed economies has widened since 1985. Agricultural labour productivity fell in over a third of the LDCs (in 10 of the 27 countries for which there were comparable data) between 1985–1987 and 2009–2011. As shown in chart 20A, during the period 2009–2011, average labour productivity was just 7 per cent that of ODCs and 3 per cent that of developed countries. Chart 20B shows that between 1985 and 2011, value added per worker in agriculture[7] in the LDCs increased 17 per cent.[8] The equivalent rise in agricultural labour productivity in ODCs was 152 per cent, and in developed countries, 194 per cent. In the LDC group, value added per worker is higher in Asian LDCs ($338) than in African LDCs ($276) (see chart 20C). However, during the period 1993–2011, what is particularly striking is the rapid rise in agricultural labour productivity in Asian LDCs (up around 79 per cent). In African LDCs, by contrast, productivity levels have been stagnant (up only 1 per cent), and in island LDCs these levels actually declined by 5 per cent over the same period.

Raising agricultural productivity in the LDCs is a *sine qua non* for their development and the structural transformation of the sector. The introduction of

The agricultural labour productivity gap between LDCs, ODCs and developed economies has widened since 1985.

During the period 2009–2011, average agricultural labour productivity was just 7 per cent that of ODCs and 3 per cent that of developed countries.

Raising agricultural productivity in the LDCs is a sine qua non for their development and the structural transformation of the sector.

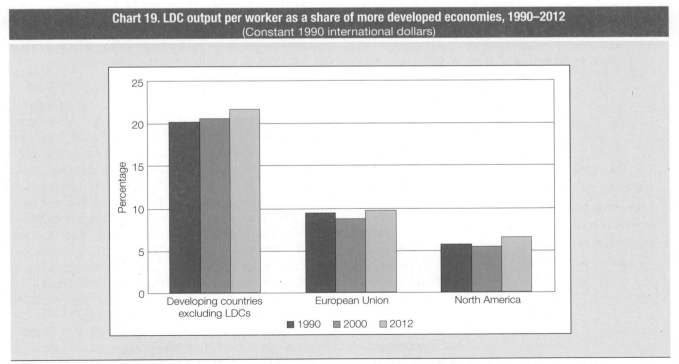

Chart 19. LDC output per worker as a share of more developed economies, 1990–2012
(Constant 1990 international dollars)

Source: UNCTAD secretariat calculations, based on ILO, *Key Indicators of the Labour Market (KILM)*, Seventh Edition, 2013..
Note: LDC sample includes 18 countries due to limited available data.

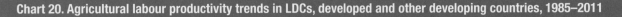

Chart 20. Agricultural labour productivity trends in LDCs, developed and other developing countries, 1985–2011

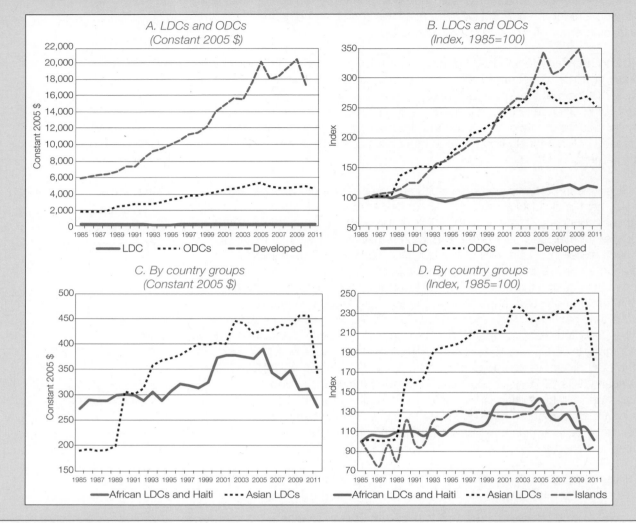

Source: UNCTAD secretariat calculations, based on UNCTADstat and *World Development Indicators* online databases.

Notes: The LDC group sample in A and B includes 41 countries; the ODC group sample, 65 countries; and the developed countries' group sample, 30 countries. Labour per worker data are based on constant 2005 dollars. Indices are based on data in constant 2005 dollars. The data series for developed countries covers the period 1985–2010. All other data cover the period 1985–2011.

> *Greater agricultural labour productivity in LDCs has the potential to both raise the real incomes of rural households and stimulate demand for rural non-farm goods and services.*

innovations and technology in order to increase output per worker in the sector could also be critical for improved food availability per capita and food security. If LDCs can raise their relatively low levels of agricultural labour productivity, this could lower food prices relative to agricultural incomes, thereby reducing food expenditures and potentially increasing household budget surpluses. Such surpluses could then be used to increase demand for rural-non-farm goods and services. Increases in farm-based income are closely linked with increases in non-farm income, such as from vending, petty trading and transport services. Non-farm income is especially pronounced in broad-based smallholder-led agricultural growth, because as local labour is hired, income is typically spent locally (Deichmann et al., 2009; Haggblade et al., 2007; Davis, 2005). This could have major employment generation benefits for the rural non-farm economy. In addition, with higher agricultural labour productivity over time (following Lewis, 1954), less on-farm labour will be required to raise output levels, thus releasing labour resources for other sectors of the economy. Greater agricultural labour productivity in LDCs therefore has the potential to both raise the real incomes of rural households and stimulate demand for rural non-farm goods and services. Curiously, these factors are often overlooked by policymakers intervening in the sector.

6. LABOUR FORCE PARTICIPATION RATES

LDCs have a high labour force participation rate (LFPR)[9] of 75 per cent on average (table 12), as compared to 68 per cent in ODCs. With limited or no social security in many least developed countries, the poor have no option but to seek work, since they would starve without engaging in some sort of work, no matter how poorly paid. To some extent, this is also a result of the significant share of economic activity accounted for by subsistence farming in these countries. Moreover, with earnings from work being low, more household members need to enter the labour market to ensure that family earnings are sufficient to provide the household with a subsistence income. One consequence is that a high labour force participation rate is by no means indicative of a comfortable labour market situation. Unemployment rates, however, do not reveal much, since the poor cannot afford the luxury of choosing open unemployment when only extremely low-paid employment is available.

LDCs have a LFPR of 75 per cent on average. With limited or no social security in many LDCs, the poor have no option but to seek work, since they would starve without engaging in some sort of work

A breakdown of the LFPR by gender and age group provides further insights into the distribution of the EAP in LDCs. Women in these countries have a high propensity to work in the labour market, especially in the informal sector (housekeeping, child-rearing, farming and so forth). In chart 21A, the LDC labour force participation rate in 2012 by gender and age group is an inverted-U shape, more pronounced for men than for women. The fact that the male curve is above the female curve reflects the higher LFPR of men in all age groups. As to the gender dimension, the curve increases at low ages as youths leave school and enter the labour market, and peaks in the 35–39-year age group for men and the 40–49-year group for women. Thereafter, it decreases gradually for women and more sharply for men as they retire from the labour market.

Women in these countries have a high propensity to work in the labour market, especially in the informal sector.

Chart 21B–D illustrates the extent to which the LFPR varies between LDCs by gender and age group. In the African LDCs, the rate for both men and women follows patterns similar to the LDC average, and gender differences are much less accentuated than for other LDCs. Indeed, the female rate is almost equal to the male rate for the 15–24-year age group. In African LDCs it appears that most 15-to-24-year-olds of both genders are in the labour force, where women remain until they reach 60–64 years of age. This pattern may reflect a lack of social security for elderly Africans and a preponderance of agricultural sector employment in Africa, which relies heavily on female labour. The Asian LDCs have a much wider gender gap in labour participation rates (around 24 percentage points) for people aged 35–54 years. The difference is particularly acute in the island LDCs (38 percentage points) (chart 21D).

The overwhelming majority of women in LDCs work in the informal sector with few employment rights, such as maternity leave. The age at which most LDC youths enter the labour force is between 15 and 24 years for both genders, whereas in high-income OECD countries the equivalent is 20–24 years.

If we consider the world average, we see that most men leave the labour force between 60 and 64 years of age; most women, between 50 and 54 years. In contrast to the LFPR for women in high-income OECD countries, in LDCs there are no discernible peaks reflecting the age at which women leave the labour market due to marriage and childbearing (25–29 years) or at which they return to the labour market (45–49 years) (OECD, 2012). The overwhelming majority of women in LDCs work in the informal sector with few employment

Table 12. Labour force participation rates, 1980–2009				
(Percentage of working-age population, aged 15-64 years)[a]				
	1980	1990	2000	2009
Total LDCs	75.6	75.8	74.8	75.1
LDCs African LDCs and Haiti	77.3	76.6	77.0	77.5
Asian LDCs	73.4	74.9	71.9	71.7
Island LDCs	68.5	66.8	66.4	68.4
ODCs	70.2	70.5	69.5	68.4
Source: UNCTAD secretariat calculations, based on ILO *Key Indicators of the Labour Market (KILM)*, Seventh Edition, 2013. *a* Weighted averages.				

Chart 21. LDC labour force participation rates by gender and region, 2012

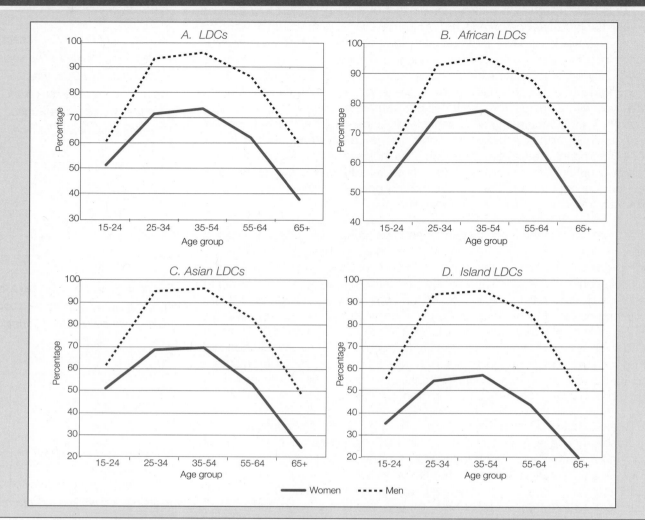

Source: UNCTAD secretariat calculations, based on ILO, *Key Indicators of the Labour Market (KILM)*, Seventh Edition, 2013.

rights, such as maternity leave. The age at which most LDC youths enter the labour force is between 15 and 24 years for both genders, whereas in high-income OECD countries the equivalent is 20–24 years (OECD, 2012).

As shown in chart 22A, the LFPR has risen most for people aged between 25 and 54 years. For the LDC working-age population (15–64 years) as a whole, however, the rate barely declined between 1990 and 2009 (by 0.7 percentage points). Similarly, the youth rate has fallen quite sharply since 1990 for the LDC group, by an average 4.7 percentage points, compared to a 10.9-percentage-point decline in the ODC rate. At the LDC regional level, this drop was driven largely by the Asian LDC group, which recorded an 11-percentage-point decline (chart 22C). As previously noted, this may be a function of the higher rates of primary, secondary and tertiary education enrolment and completion rates in the LDCs (see chapter 5). There was a modest (1.5-percentage-point) rise in youth employment in the island LDCs (chart 22D), and a modest (1-percentage-point) decline in the African LDCs.

Between 1990 and 2012, around 290 million women entered the LDC labour force.

Between 1990 and 2012, around 290 million women entered the LDC labour force. During this period, the labour force participation rates for women in LDCs rose by 3 percentage points, from 59 to 62 per cent on average (chart 23). Within the LDC group as a whole, the LFPRs are highest, and have risen the most, in Africa and Asia (by 3 percentage points), and are the lowest in the island LDCs (by 0.1 percentage point).

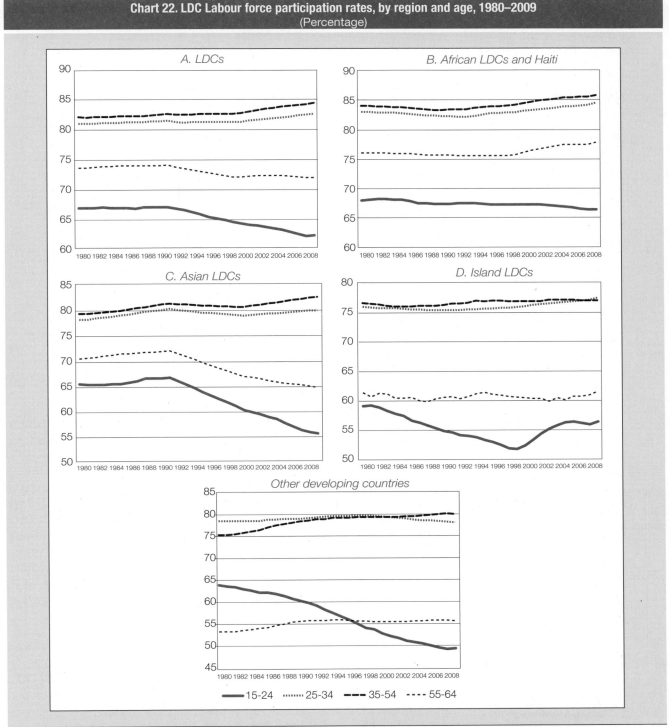

Chart 22. LDC Labour force participation rates, by region and age, 1980–2009
(Percentage)

Source: UNCTAD secretariat calculations, based on ILO, *Key Indicators of the Labour Market (KILM)*, Seventh Edition, 2013.
Note: Weighted averages.

7. LDC EMPLOYMENT-TO-POPULATION RATIOS

The employment-to-population ratio is an indicator of the availability of jobs.[10] When considered jointly with the employment level, it enables us to evaluate the magnitude of job growth. Fluctuations in the employment level reflect net changes in the number of people employed, while movements in the ratio are net changes in the number of people employed relative to changes in the size of the population. As the LDC population is growing rapidly, a rise in employment may or may not appear as an increase in the employment-to-population ratio, while a fall in employment is usually reflected as a decline in the ratio. In a developing-

Chart 23. Labour force participation rates for women in LDCs, 1990–2012

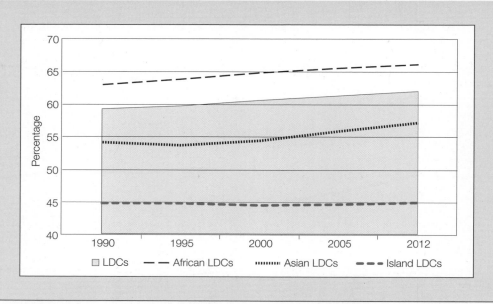

Source: UNCTAD secretariat calculations based on ILO, *Key Indicators of the Labour Market (KILM)*, Seventh Edition, 2013.
Note: Sample of 46 LDCs.

country context, a high employment-to-population ratio is often correlated with high levels of working poverty.[11]

Employment-to-population ratios for the LDCs range from 54 per cent in island LDCs to 65 per cent in African LDCs. Chart 24 shows simple averages of available employment-to-population ratios in 2012 by region. For the LDCs as a group, the average ratio is 65 per cent, which is much higher than the 53 per cent average for ODCs. Most ODCs and developed countries are within the range of 50 to 60 per cent. Countries whose average ratio is above 70 per cent tend to have a high share of the population in poverty, relying on their labour as a means of survival. In fact, 16 of the 42 LDCs for which data are available had employment-to-population ratios of above 70 per cent during the period 2000–2012. The following countries had both high employment-to-population ratios (above 80 per cent) and a relatively high share of the population (above 75 per cent)[12] living below the $2-per-day poverty line: Burkina Faso, Madagascar, Nepal, Rwanda and United Republic of Tanzania.

> *For the LDCs as a group, the average employment-to-population ratio is 65 per cent, which is much higher than the 53 per cent average for ODCs.*

The average female employment-to-population ratio is highest in African LDCs, at 60.1 per cent, and lowest in island LDCs, at 38.7 per cent, which have the lowest such ratio in the group. In Asian LDCs and some island LDCs, women's economic contribution may be constrained by social institutions and cultural norms. For example, in Afghanistan and Bangladesh the difference between the male and female employment-to-population ratio was 57 and 24 percentage points, respectively, in 2012. By contrast, men and women in African LDCs are involved almost equally in the labour market. In some African LDCs — namely, Burundi, Malawi, Mozambique and Rwanda — the female ratio is higher than the male ratio. During the period 2000–2012, most LDCs experienced an overall rise in the employment-to-population ratio. In 26 LDCs, that ratio increased more for women than for men, and was greatest (although starting from a relatively low base) in Afghanistan, Bhutan, Comoros, Mauritania and Yemen. The increased female ratio may in part reflect the wider introduction of equality legislation and increased educational and employment opportunities for women in LDCs.

> *In some African LDCs — namely, Burundi, Malawi, Mozambique and Rwanda — the female ratio is higher than the male ratio.*

Youths in most LDCs experienced a decline in employment-to-population ratios relative to adults between 2000 and 2012, as shown in chart 25. The only

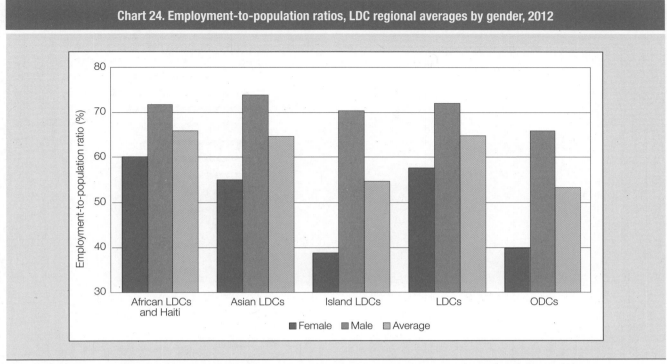

Chart 24. Employment-to-population ratios, LDC regional averages by gender, 2012

Source: UNCTAD secretariat calculations, based on ILO, *Key Indicators of the Labour Market (KILM)*, Seventh Edition, 2013.
Note: Sample of 46 LDCs.

exceptions were Angola, Burundi, Myanmar, Timor-Leste, Uganda and Zambia, where both youth and adult ratios declined. A falling youth employment-to-population ratio may be positive if the change is due to youths staying on at school or moving into tertiary-level education, rather than becoming unemployed. However, it is difficult to determine whether this is the case.

8. RURAL NON-FARM EMPLOYMENT: PANACEA, OR PANDORA'S BOX?

The rural non-farm economy (RNFE) may be defined as comprising all those non-agricultural activities that generate income for rural households (including income in kind), either through waged work or through self-employment. In some contexts, rural non-farm activities are also major sources of local economic growth (e.g. tourism, mining and timber processing). The RNFE is of great importance to the rural economy because of its production linkages and employment effects, and the income it provides to rural households represents a substantial and sometimes growing share of rural incomes. Often this share is particularly high for the rural poor. There is evidence that these contributions are becoming increasingly significant for food security, poverty alleviation and farm sector competitiveness and productivity (Dirven, 2011; World Bank, 2005; Balcombe et al., 2005).

Youths in most LDCs experienced a decline in employment-to-population ratios relative to adults between 2000 and 2012.

The RNFE can also be defined or classified according to many dimensions, such as on-farm/off-farm, wage/self-employment and agriculturally related/other. An ideal classification of the RNFE should capture some or all of the following distinctions:

(i) Activities closely linked to farming and the food chain, and those not part of that chain, since agricultural linkages are often important determinants of the RNFE's potential for employment and income generation;

(ii) Activities producing goods and services for the local market (often non-tradables);

(iii) Activities producing for distant markets (tradables), since the latter have the potential to create employment and incomes independently of the rural economy;

Chart 25. Youth and adult employment-to-population ratios in selected LDCs, 2000 to 2012
(Percentage change)

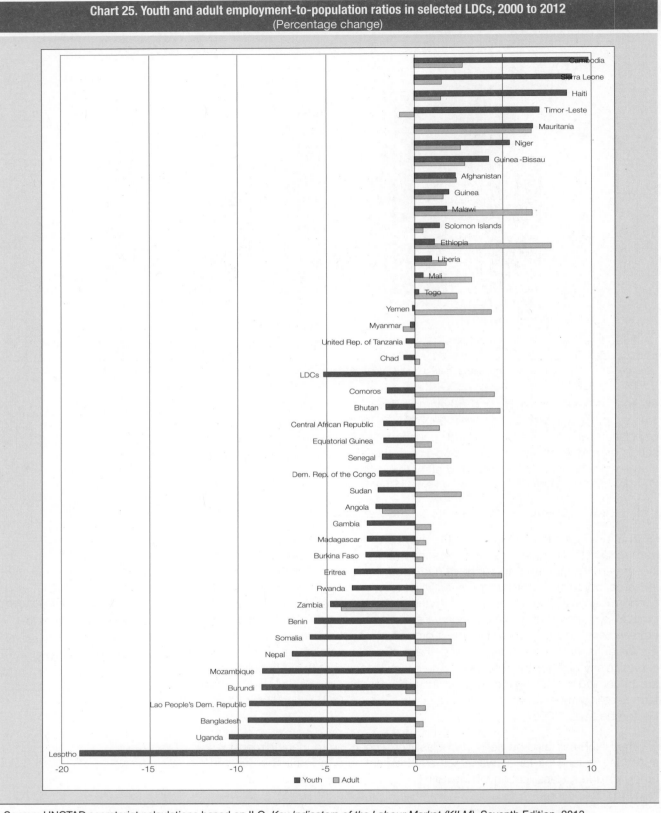

Source: UNCTAD secretariat calculations based on ILO, *Key Indicators of the Labour Market (KILM)*, Seventh Edition, 2013.

(iv) Activities that are on a sufficiently large scale, are sufficiently productive and have enough capital to generate incomes above returns obtainable from farming; and

(v) Activities that offer only marginal returns, since this reflects the RNFE's capacity to generate local economic growth. Although low-return activities can keep households above the poverty line, they usually do not foster growth.

The RNFE accounts for about 30 per cent of full-time rural employment in Asia, 45 per cent in Latin America (Dirven, 2011), 20 per cent in West Asia and 40–45 per cent in Africa (Haggblade et al., 2007; Davis, 2005; Stifel, 2010; Hossain, 2004). Surveys covering part-time employment in the RNFE are relatively scarce, but would suggest that as most rural households in Asia and Africa are increasingly pluriactive, the share of non-farm employment may be even higher than these estimates suggest, due in part to the under-reporting of female part-time labour activities (Stifel, 2010). The RNFE is largely composed of a highly heterogeneous collection of trading, agro-processing, manufacturing, commercial and service activities, which results in its widely varying productivity and profitability (Haggblade et al., 2007). It may be further broken down into at least three categories: the activities undertaken; employment and the use of labour time; and incomes generated. These clearly overlap, particularly for incomes, since most rural income arises from payments to factors used in activities and from employment.

The fact that most of the poor live in rural areas is as much an argument for social welfare as for economic development. Nonetheless, the data highlight the importance of RNF employment in providing sustainable livelihoods for many rural LDC households. Moreover, as Haggblade et al. (2010) note, poverty-reducing rural non-farm growth requires an aggregate increase in rural non-farm income coupled with growing income per worker, which in turn depends on the development of productive capacities and improved productivity of rural tradables (e.g. agriculture, mining and tourism).

The data in chart 26 on non-agricultural income are disaggregated first into non-farm wage and self-employment components and then by sector, indicating which activities are more important in the LDC rural non-farm economy. Following Davis et al. (2010), eight sectors in wage employment are identified (mining, manufacturing, utilities, construction, commerce, transport, finance, services and other), and nine sectors in self-employment, with the addition of agriculture and fish processing.

As GDP per capita levels increase, the share of rural on-farm (agricultural) income typically falls and the share of rural non-agricultural income rises (Haggblade et al., 1989; Davis et al., 2007). Chart 26A shows that agricultural sources of income account for significant shares (between 45 and 78 per cent) of total household income in selected LDCs (Bangladesh, Madagascar, Malawi and Nepal) for which we have detailed data, drawn from Davis et al. (2010) (see annex table 15).[13] On-farm sources of income tend to be more important for African LDCs, as they typically have a less diversified economy than most Asian LDCs (UNCTAD, 2009). If income from agricultural labour, livestock and crop production is combined, all the LDCs in this dataset derive the majority of household income from agricultural sources (chart 26B). Although RNF employment is increasingly important in LDCs, on-farm production and jobs remain the mainstay for most of them. However, as depicted in chart 26C for Bangladesh, Malawi and Nepal, whose non-farm activity participation rates are in excess of 45 per cent, the RNFE is a vital source of employment (see box 3).

Further examination shows that for these countries, the range of participation in RNF wage and self-employment is quite diverse. RNF employment income from the commerce and manufacturing sectors features very prominently, although the services and construction sectors are also important (chart 26D). Chart 26E shows that Bangladesh has the most diversified RNF self-employment income by sector, whereas the commerce sector dominates in the other countries. Agricultural processing in Bangladesh accounts for a relatively large share of RNF self-employment income (21 per cent), in contrast to the more dominant manufacturing sector, which represents 31 per cent of RNF wage employment income (chart 26F). The services sector holds the dominant share in the other

The RNFE accounts for about 30 per cent of full-time rural employment in Asia, 45 per cent in Latin America, 20 per cent in West Asia and 40–45 per cent in Africa.

Although RNF employment is increasingly important in LDCs, on-farm production and jobs remain the mainstay for most of them.

Chart 26. Household participation and shares in rural non-farm income-generating activities in four selected LDCs

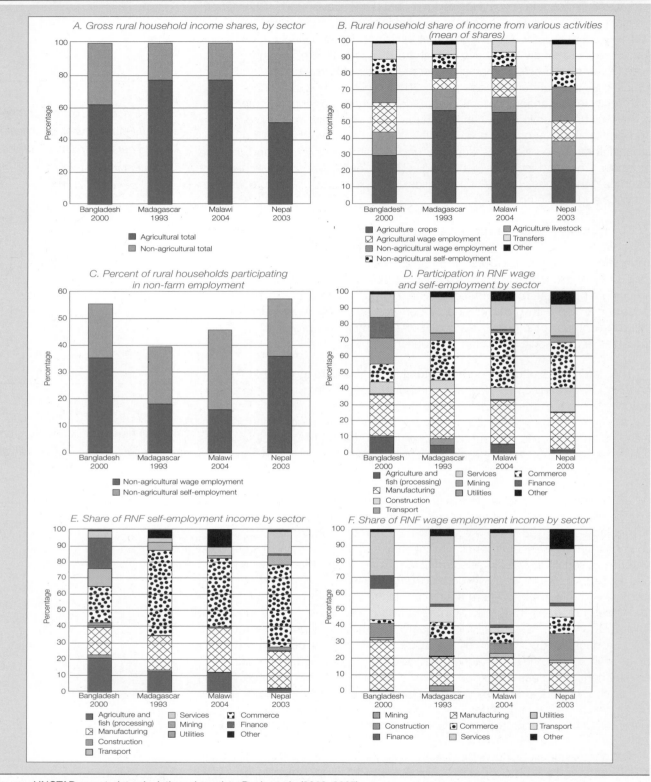

Source: UNCTAD secretariat calculations, based on Davis et al., (2010, 2007).

Note: The data presented in B. Davis et al., (2010, 2009) utilize the Rural Income Generating Activities (RIGA) database, which is constructed from a pool of several dozen Living Standards Measurement Study (LSMS) and other multi-purpose household surveys made available by the World Bank through a joint project with the FAO. The authors identify rurality via the domicile of the household, and not the location of the job. Participation is defined as the receipt of any household income (negative or positive) by any household member from that income-generating activity. All the charts are based on the mean of shares which is defined as the income shares calculated for each household, and then the mean of the household shares of each type of income is calculated. The mean of shares reflects the household-level diversification strategy, regardless of the magnitude of income (Davis et al., 2010).

LDCs, especially Malawi, where it provides 57 per cent of such income. Country-specific cultural and labour market institutions play a key role in determining both access to non-farm employment and the associated remuneration (Barrett et al., 2001; Davis, 2005; Hossain, 2004). In Malawi, for example, 50 per cent of the households surveyed earned an agricultural wage, which is much higher than the rate observed in the other LDCs because casual *ganyu*[14] labour on non-own farms is much more prevalent (Davis et al., 2010). There appears to be a high rate of labour force participation in both agricultural and non-agricultural activities, which suggests a relatively high diversity of non-farm income-earning opportunities in rural areas. Most RNF labour market opportunities in LDCs will initially be agriculture-linked and will often involve elements of seasonal non-own farm labour migration. Rural construction businesses, processing mills, manufacturing and assembly market networks are other significant sources of non-farm wage employment. There are also many government and private-sector opportunities for RNF employment for both unskilled and professional workers.

There appears to be a high rate of labour force participation in both agricultural and non-agricultural activities.

When considering the importance of the RNFE for employment and development in the LDCs, two key factors should be stressed: the potential multiplier effects (demand-led growth linkages between the RNFE and farming), and the integration of farming into national and international value chains, shifting value addition to rural areas (UNCTAD, 2009). These factors should help rural areas to take advantage of the potential benefits of trade and improve incomes and employment opportunities.

Most RNF labour market opportunities in LDCs will initially be agriculture-linked and will often involve elements of seasonal non-own farm labour migration.

The process of structural transformation is not identical in all LDCs and regions, and is shaped in part by such factors as a region's comparative advantage in the production of tradable products (especially agriculture), population density, infrastructure, location, and government policies. Regions with significant recreational, mineral or trade advantages (e.g. ports or highways) may be less dependent on agriculture as an engine of growth, and hence may expand and diversify their RNFE much earlier in the development process. Growth of the RNFE can also be delinked from agriculture to varying degrees by market and trade liberalization policies that enhance non-agricultural opportunities. Moreover, an engine of growth does not even have to be local, as long as the local economy is open, in the sense that workers can commute and local farm and non-farm firms can sell to the area where the engine is providing job opportunities and generating growth (Dirven, 2011; UNCTAD, 2009; Stifel, 2010).

When considering the importance of the RNFE for employment and development in the LDCs, two key factors should be stressed: the potential multiplier effects, and the integration of farming into national and international value chains, shifting value addition to rural areas.

9. Unemployment and inactivity

a. Unemployment trends

Registered unemployment in LDCs did not fall significantly during the boom period of 2002–2008. Chart 27A shows a remarkably stable unemployment rate during the period 2000–2012, at around 5.5 per cent. Even in 2009–2010, with the onset of the global financial and economic crisis, the rate barely changed from the 2000–2012 average. In 2012, island LDCs had the highest rate of unemployment (7.3 per cent on average), followed by African LDCs at 6.1 per cent and Asian LDCs at 4.7 per cent.

Registered unemployment in LDCs did not fall significantly during the boom period of 2002–2008.

Female unemployment was an average 1 percentage point higher than male unemployment in LDCs during the period 2000–2012, which suggests that it was largely unaffected by the relatively high rates of real GDP growth of 2002–2008 (chart 27B). Also in 2000–2012, the gender gap in unemployment was above 1 per cent on average in African LDCs, less than 1 per cent in Asian LDCs and around 2 per cent in island LDCs.

Generally speaking, it is the LDC youth labour force (aged 15–24 years) that is most affected by unemployment, in disproportionate numbers, as that rate is almost invariably higher than that of adults. In most LDCs, it is higher than the average LDC unemployment rate for both men and women, and in most cases is almost twice the rate (chart 27C). The relative prevalence of youth unemployment is evident particularly in the island LDCs (16 per cent in 2011) and Asian LDCs (10.5 per cent in 2012).

Generally speaking, it is the LDC youth labour force that is most affected by unemployment, in disproportionate numbers, as that rate is almost invariably higher than that of adults.

The causes of LDC youth unemployment are numerous and include the following: (i) a skills mismatch on entering the labour market; (ii) low levels of entrepreneurial, education and technical skills among youths (World Bank, 2013); (iii) a low absorptive capacity of the labour market for new entrants; (iv) limited access to adequate finance, technology and markets (UNCTAD, 2010); and (v) a lack of structural change and diversification, which reinforces the concentration of growth in traditional capital-intensive and urban-based sectors like mining and oil extraction (UNCTAD, 2013). These sectors typically generate limited labour-intensive growth multipliers.

b. Inactivity rates

The inactivity rate is the proportion of the working-age population that is not in the labour force. Inactive people are those who are outside the labour force

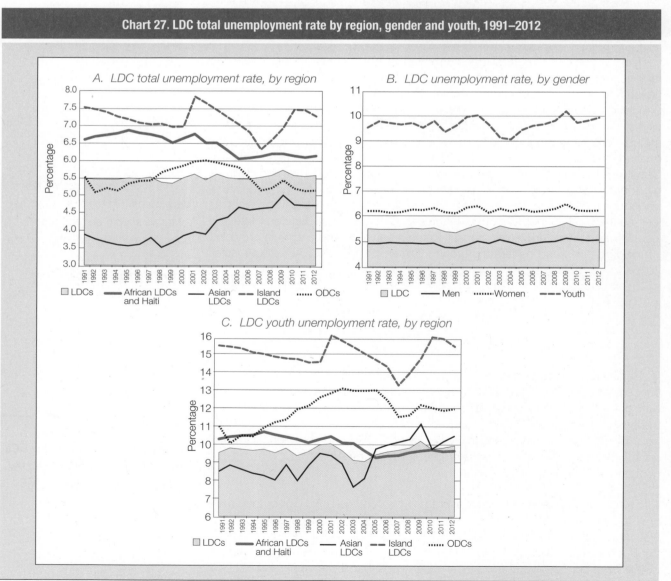

Chart 27. LDC total unemployment rate by region, gender and youth, 1991–2012

Source: UNCTAD secretariat calculations, based on data from ILO, Employment Trends (EMP/TRENDS) econometric model, April 2013.

if they are neither employed nor unemployed or are not actively seeking work. Inactive people may include the early retired; women who leave the labour force to raise a family and provide childcare; school or university students; the sick or disabled, or discouraged workers. [15] Table 13 shows that although LDC inactivity rates have been increasing since 1980, they remain lower on average (24.9 per cent) than in ODCs (30 per cent). The 2010 rate in developed economies and the EU was 52 per cent (ILO, *Key Indicators of the Labour Market (KILM), Seventh Edition*, 2013). The reason why inactivity rates are lower in LDCs and other low-income countries than in developed countries is probably that the option of being unemployed or inactive is unavailable to the poor.

Chart 28 compares the inactivity rates for the LDC working-age and youth (aged 15–24 years) populations. With the exception of the island LDCs, these rates climbed during the period 2000–2009, especially in Asian LDCs. Nonetheless, at 38 per cent for all LDCs in 2009, the rates were well below the ODC levels of 52 per cent, and above the working-age inactivity rates. Typically, rising youth inactivity rates are due to the following: higher rates of young people enrolling in education than entering the labour market; and higher rates of discouraged workers, which is untypical of most LDCs. It is often assumed that LDC youths do not have the option of continuing their education due to a lack of educational infrastructure and high tuition fees. In addition, the opportunity cost for youths — particularly from the poorest households — of continuing their

Although LDC inactivity rates have been increasing since 1980, they remain lower on average (24.9 per cent) than in ODCs (30 per cent).

Table 13. LDC Inactivity rates, 1980–2009				
(Percentage of working age population, aged 15-64 years)[a]				
	1980	**1990**	**2000**	**2009**
Total LDCs	24.4	24.2	25.2	24.9
LDCs African LDCs and Haiti	22.7	23.4	23.0	22.4
Asian LDCs	26.6	25.1	28.1	28.3
Island LDCs	31.5	33.2	33.6	31.6
ODCs	29.8	29.5	30.5	31.6

Source: UNCTAD secretariat calculations, based on ILO *Key Indicators of the Labour Market (KILM)*, Seventh Edition, 2013.
  a Weighted averages.

Chart 28. LDC inactivity rates for youths and working-age population, 2009

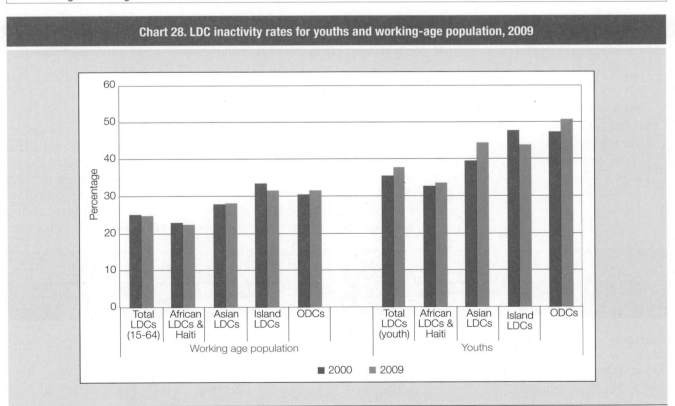

Source: UNCTAD secretariat calculations, based on data from ILO, *Key Indicators of the Labour Market (KILM)*, Seventh Edition, 2013.
Note: Weighted averages.

education, as opposed to entering the labour market, is often high (World Bank, 2008). As previously noted, however, education enrolment and completion rates have steadily risen in LDCs since 1990 (see chapter 2, table 7). Inactivity rates increased by an average 2 percentage points between 2000 and 2009, and rose the most (4 percentage points) in the Asian LDCs. For LDC policymakers tackling a burgeoning youth labour force, it may be preferable to focus less on rising inactivity rates (or declining participation rates) and more on the type of activities in which youths can productively engage, given appropriate public- and private-sector support.

For LDC policymakers tackling a burgeoning youth labour force, it may be preferable to focus less on rising inactivity rates and more on the type of activities in which youths can productively engage, given appropriate public- and private-sector support.

LDCs will need comprehensive job creation programmes to address youth unemployment and underemployment.[16] Typically, their youths find work in the informal sector, but often such jobs do not pay reasonable wages, improve skills or offer much job security. More than 70 per cent of youths in Democratic Republic of the Congo, Ethiopia, Malawi, Mali, Rwanda, Senegal and Uganda are either self-employed or contributing to family work (Brookings Institute, 2012). LDC job strategies will need to encourage investment in the agricultural sector, promote rural development and help prepare youths for employment opportunities in urban areas.

B. The quality of employment in the LDCs

More than 70 per cent of youths in Democratic Republic of the Congo, Ethiopia, Malawi, Mali, Rwanda, Senegal and Uganda are either self-employed or contributing to family work.

Having examined the quantity of jobs available to LDC citizens in the previous section, we now look at the quality of those jobs, and more specifically at what ILO has termed "decent employment", the "working poor" and "vulnerable employment". Vulnerable employment is defined as the sum of contributing family workers (unpaid work) and own-account workers as a share of total employment. It represents around 80 per cent of total employment in LDCs and is therefore very important for these countries (International Labour Office, 2011). Table 14 provides a detailed summary of vulnerable employment and working-poor dynamics in the LDCs for the period 2000–2018. Each of these indicators has improved since 2000, but from a relatively weak base, especially in African and Asian LDCs. We explore these trends in greater detail below.

1. THE LDC WORKING POOR

The percentage of the working poor living on less than $1.25 per day is declining as a share of total employment.

The working poor are broadly defined as working persons who are unable to earn enough to maintain either their own welfare or that of their families. More specifically, they are persons who are working and living in households with income below the poverty line. They comprise two distinct categories: working people living as unrelated (non-own-family) individuals with income below the poverty level; and working people living in families with total income below the poverty level. As shown in chart 29, the percentage of the working poor living on

Table 14. Employment and poverty dynamics in the LDCs, 2000–2018 (Percentage)													
	Vulnerable employment as a share of total employment *(percentage)*					Share of extremely poor (less than $1.25 in PPPs) in total employment *(percentage)*					Total unemployment rate *(percentage)*		
	2000	*2005*	*2010*	*2015*	*2018*	*2000*	*2005*	*2010*	*2015*	*2018*	*2000*	*2005*	*2010*	*2012*
Total LDCs	86	84	82	80	79	61	50	41	33	29	5.5	5.5	5.6	5.6
ODCs	61	59	56	53	52	30	20	13	9	7	5.9	5.8	5.2	5.2
African LDCs and Haiti	86	84	82	80	79	65	55	46	38	35	6.7	6.1	6.1	6.1
Asian LDCs	85	84	81	80	79	56	43	33	24	20	3.9	4.7	4.7	4.7
Island LDCs	75	78	77	75	74	36	36	29	22	20	7.0	7.0	7.5	7.3

Source: UNCTAD secretariat calculations, based on ILO *Key Indicators of the Labour Market (KILM)*, Seventh Edition, 2013.
Note: Data series 2013 to 2018 are preliminary projections.

| Chart 29. Share of the working poor in LDCs living on less than $1.25 per day in total employment, 2000–2017 |

Source: UNCTAD secretariat calculations, based on data from ILO, Employment Trends (EMP/TRENDS) econometric model, April 2013.
Note: Data series 2013 to 2017 are preliminary projections.

less than $1.25 per day is declining as a share of total employment, from 61 per cent in 2000 to a projected 29 per cent by 2017. However, that percentage is still substantially above levels prevalent in ODCs, where it is expected to shrink from 30 per cent in 2000 to 7 per cent by 2017.

African LDCs are forecast to have the highest share of working poor in the LDC group by 2017. Among that group, Liberia and Madagascar experienced no overall change in the share of the working poor living on less than $1.25 per day during the period 2000–2012. The share fell the most in Sierra Leone (down by 49 percentage points), Ethiopia (40) and Mozambique (32). Using actual and forecast data, chart 29 shows that Asian and island LDC levels of the working poor are likely to be below the LDC average for the period 2000–2017 and to begin to converge by 2015. During this period, the Asian LDCs' share of working poor in total employment declined by 36 percentage points; the island LDCs' share, by 16 percentage points. Of the Asian LDCs, only Yemen witnessed an increase in the share of working poor (up 4 percentage points); Myanmar is expected to have the largest decline in the group (down by 50 percentage points). Among the island LDCs, the share should remain high in Comoros (at around 43 per cent) and decline sharply in Solomon Islands and Timor-Leste during 2000–2017.

African LDCs are forecast to have the highest share of working poor in the LDC group by 2017.

Asian and island LDC levels of the working poor are likely to be below the LDC average for the period 2000–2017.

2. EMPLOYMENT STATUS AND VULNERABLE WORK IN THE LDCs

Vulnerable employment is often characterized by inadequate earnings, low productivity and difficult working conditions. Since 2009 the number of workers in vulnerable employment worldwide has increased by around 100 million, and with it global poverty (ILO, 2013). Such workers are less likely to have formal employment arrangements and also tend to lack adequate social security and effective representation by labour organizations (e.g. trade unions).

During the period 2000–2018, the share of vulnerable employment will have declined by 7 percentage points in LDCs and 9 percentage points in ODCs. However, the level of vulnerable employment is on average 25 percentage points higher in the former than in the latter.

For the group as a whole, the gender gap in vulnerable employment is not only wide but has increased marginally, averaging 11 percentage points during the period 2000–2012.

As indicated in chart 30, during the period 2000–2018, the share of vulnerable employment will have declined by 7 percentage points in LDCs and 9 percentage points in ODCs. However, the level of vulnerable employment is on average 25 percentage points higher in the former than in the latter. Further data disaggregation by export specialization shows that LDC fuel exporters have experienced the largest reduction (11 percentage points) in vulnerable employment. On a country group basis, the island LDCs have seen the smallest decline (1-percentage-point change on average), and the African LDCs the largest (7 percentage points on average). In addition, for the group as a whole, the gender gap in vulnerable employment is not only wide but has increased marginally, averaging 11 percentage points during the period 2000–2012. In 2012, 85 per cent of women and 73 per cent of men on average were vulnerably employed.

ILO data on LDC employment status distinguish between two categories of the employed: wage and salaried workers; and the self-employed. These two groups are presented in table 15 and chart 31 as percentages of the total employed. The self-employed are the most prevalent group in LDCs and comprise: (i) self-employed workers with employees (employers); (ii) self-employed workers without employees (own account-workers); and (iii) contributing family workers (usually unpaid family workers) and members of producers' cooperatives. The distribution of employment by status is an important indicator for describing and comparing LDC conditions of work, vulnerability, the informal sector and levels of economic development.

Table 15 presents data for 2012 on the distribution of employment by status in LDCs, ODCs and country groups, and by gender. As previously noted, women in LDCs are concentrated primarily in the most vulnerable job categories: own-account (44 per cent) and contributing family workers (40 per cent). Only 20 per cent of LDC men were employed as contributing family workers. The island

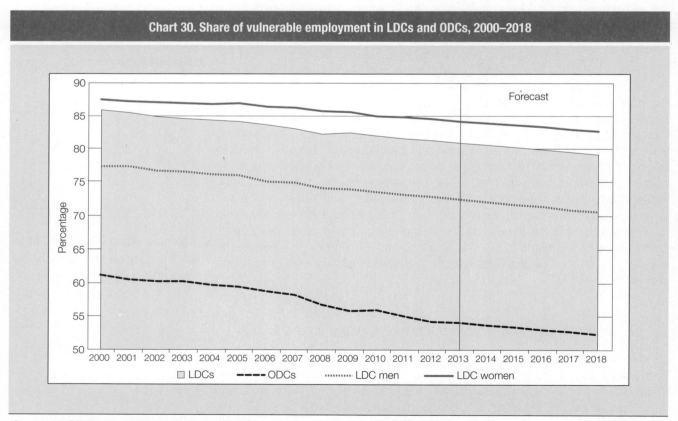

Chart 30. Share of vulnerable employment in LDCs and ODCs, 2000–2018

Source: UNCTAD secretariat calculations based on data from International Labour Organisation, Employment Trends (EMP/TRENDS) econometric model, April 2013.

Note: Data series 2013 to 2018 are preliminary projections.

Table 15. Distribution of employment by status, 2012 (Percentage of total employment)								
	Waged and salaried workers		Employers		Own-account workers		Contributing family workers	
	Women	*Men*	*Women*	*Men*	*Women*	*Men*	*Women*	*Men*
Total LDCs	15	26	1	2	44	52	40	20
ODCs	61	63	2	5	24	27	13	5
African LDCs and Haiti	14	25	1	2	48	53	37	20
Asian LDCs	17	30	1	1	35	53	47	16
Island LDCs	19	25	0	1	27	46	54	28

Source: UNCTAD secretariat calculations, based on data from ILO Employment Trends (EMP/TRENDS): ILO Trends econometric models, April 2013.

LDCs have the highest concentration of women in the contributing family workers category (54 per cent), 14 percentage points above the LDC average. African LDC women are found mainly in the own-account worker category (48 per cent), and Asian women in the contributing family workers category (47 per cent). There is also a clear gender disparity in employment in the waged/salaried worker and employer categories, which boast the most secure jobs and the best employment conditions. LDC men are employed at almost twice the rate of women in these sectors, whereas in ODCs there is a greater gender balance in employment (61 per cent of women and 63 per cent of men are employed as waged or salaried workers).

Women in LDCs are concentrated primarily in the most vulnerable job categories: own-account (44 per cent) and contributing family workers (40 per cent).

Despite the relatively high rates of GDP growth in 2002–2008, and despite a small rise in the share of waged and salaried workers, the level of vulnerable employment in LDCs has not declined significantly because of the high share of own-account and unpaid family workers in total employment.

Chart 31 shows the distribution of employment by status in nine LDCs in 2012. Based on this small sample, most LDCs had a relatively low proportion of waged and salaried workers (22 per cent on average) and employers (1 per

The level of vulnerable employment in LDCs has not declined significantly because of the high share of own-account and unpaid family workers in total employment.

Chart 31. Distribution of employment by status in selected LDCs, 2012
(As a percentage of total employment)

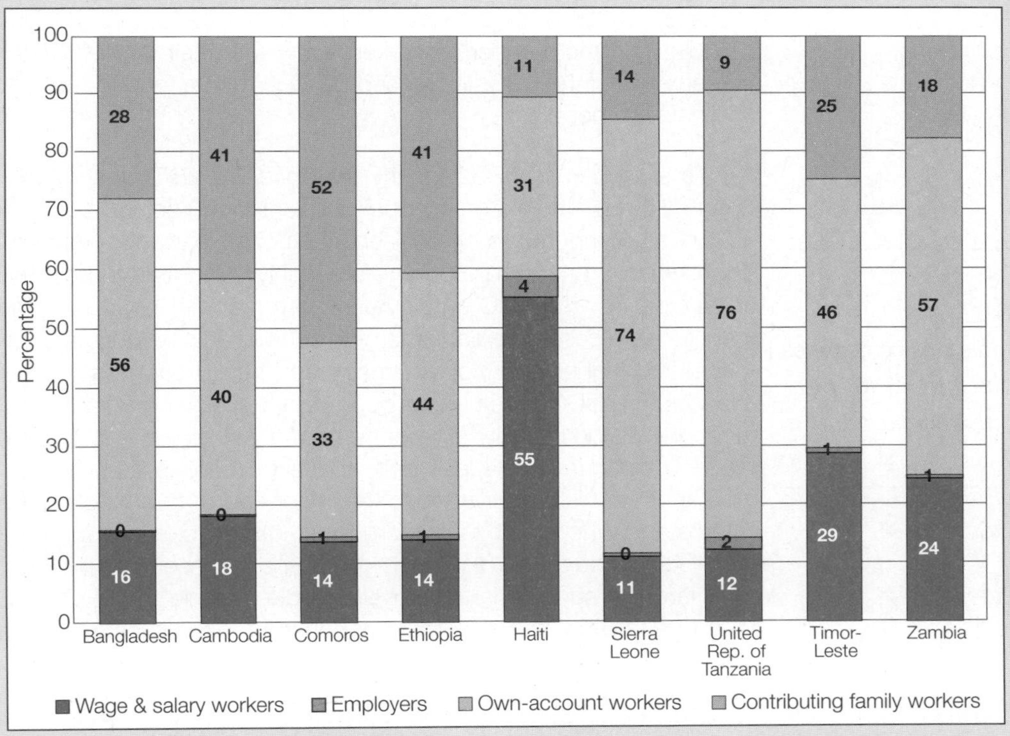

Source: UNCTAD secretariat calculations, based on data from ILO, Employment Trends (EMP/TRENDS) econometric model, April 2013.

cent); only in Haiti does that share exceed 30 per cent of total employment. The proportion of own-account workers (50 per cent on average) and contributing family workers, by contrast, is much higher (26 per cent). The predominance of these employment categories in LDCs may reflect the importance of the agricultural sector (which accounted for an average 65 per cent of the labour force and 26 per cent of GDP in 2010), widespread informality and low growth in the formal sector. Own-account workers (the self-employed) and vulnerable employment are the main categories of the informally employed. Emigration from rural to urban areas due to low-productivity agriculture is largely responsible for the observed informality in these countries. The majority of workers in LDCs with a high share of contributing family workers are doing unpaid work, often supporting agricultural production for the market, and most of this unpaid work is undertaken by women (International Labour Office, 2011).

Own-account workers (the self-employed) and vulnerable employment are the main categories of the informally employed.

In the LDC group as a whole, based on a sample of 42 countries, Somalia (96 per cent), Guinea-Bissau (95 per cent), Central African Republic (94 per cent), Malawi and Togo (both 90 per cent) have the highest shares of vulnerable employment in total employment, most of it concentrated in the informal sector. Again, it is useful to illustrate what this meant for individual LDCs in 2012: in Bangladesh, there were 62 million in vulnerable employment; in Ethiopia, 36 million; in Myanmar, 24 million; and in United Republic of Tanzania, 19 million.

Nearly two thirds of LDC workers are living on less than $2 a day. The extremely poor account for 50 per cent of those employed in LDCs, as compared to 14 per cent in ODCs.

It is often argued that growth in a developing country's middle class is an important driver of economic and social development, with positive effects on labour markets.[17] But if this is so, is there much evidence of the trend in the LDCs? While the assertion is beyond the scope of this Report, we discuss the question below. Following Kapsos and Bourmpoula's (2013) study of the working poor, in which they introduce a model for generating national estimates and projections of the distribution of the employed across five economic classes for 142 developing countries over the period 1991–2017, we derive aggregate estimates of employment by economic class for 20 LDCs from that dataset (see chart 32). They put the developing world's workforce into five classes, for the first time. Those classes are defined as: the extreme working poor (< $1.25 a day), moderate working poor (< $2 a day), near poor ($2–4 a day), middle class ($4–13 a day) and above middle class (> $13 a day).[18] During the period 2000–2012, the number of workers living with their families below the $2-a-day poverty line in the LDCs increased by 27.3 million, and by 2012 there were 246 million such people.[19]

As shown in chart 32, nearly two thirds of LDC workers are living on less than $2 a day. The extremely poor account for 50 per cent of those employed in LDCs, as compared to 14 per cent in ODCs. Near poor workers are defined as those who are not poor but who are highly vulnerable to poverty; they account for 17 per cent of LDC employment. Workers in the developing middle class category are considered an emerging consumer class and are more likely to have access to higher levels of education and health care than the aforementioned classes. In ODCs, the near poor and developing middle class categories account for the majority (61 per cent) of those employed. The group described as developed middle class and above encompasses workers in developing countries who are equivalent to the lower end of the middle class in the United States and who are able to afford most international consumer goods (Kapsos and Bourmpoula, 2013). Based on the data presented, there is little evidence of a large or substantial employed middle class in the LDCs, which may have negative implications for wider economic growth, investment and employment generation. However, other evidence suggests that in sub-Saharan Africa and Asia, over the past 20 years the middle class has been growing quite rapidly (African Development Bank, 2011; Ravallion, 2009a).

In ODCs, the near poor and developing middle class categories account for the majority (61 per cent) of those employed.

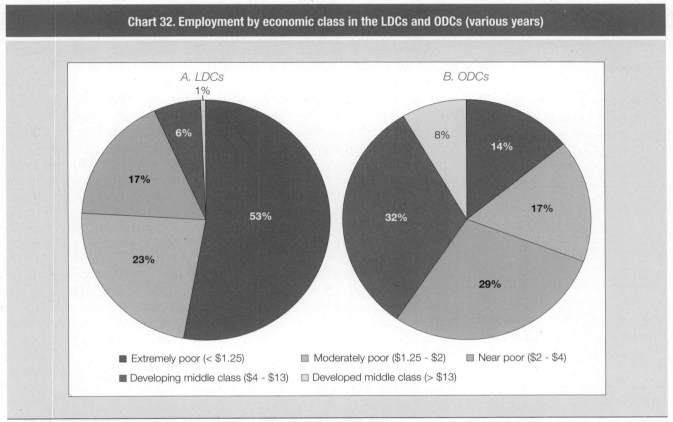

Chart 32. Employment by economic class in the LDCs and ODCs (various years)

A. LDCs
B. ODCs

- Extremely poor (< $1.25)
- Moderately poor ($1.25 - $2)
- Near poor ($2 - $4)
- Developing middle class ($4 - $13)
- Developed middle class (> $13)

Source: UNCTAD secretariat calculations, based on Kapsos and Bourmpoula (2013).
Note: The LDC sample comprises 20 LDCs: Benin, Bhutan, Burkina Faso, Burundi, Cambodia, Democratic Republic of the Congo, Guinea, Lesotho, Liberia, Madagascar, Malawi, Mali, Mozambique, Nepal, Niger, Senegal, Sierra Leone, Timor-Leste, Togo and Uganda. The ODC sample comprises 32 developing countries. The dataset includes several household and enterprise panel surveys and databases for each individual country conducted during the period 2000–2011 (see Kapsos and Bourmpoula, 2013).

3. INFORMAL SECTOR EMPLOYMENT

The informal sector may be defined as consisting of units engaged in the production of goods or services with the primary objective of generating employment and incomes for the persons concerned. It covers a wide range of labour market activities that combine two main groups of activities. The first group is made up of coping strategies (survival activities, such as casual jobs, temporary jobs, unpaid jobs, subsistence agriculture and multiple job holding) of individuals and families in an economic environment where alternative income generation opportunities are scarce. The second group comprises activities that are a product of frequently rational behaviour and unofficial earning strategies of entrepreneurs seeking to avoid State regulations; such strategies may include tax evasion and the avoidance of labour regulation and other government or institutional regulations. In the informal sector, labour relations are based more on casual employment, kinship or personal and social relations than on contractual arrangements. In the LDCs, the informal sector is typically characterized by the following:

- Labour-intensive low-technology activities (ILO, 2012);

- Limited (if any) social protection schemes;

- A predominance of microenterprises (employing a maximum of five people);

- A prevalence of unskilled labour, although in some LDCs this is changing (e.g. Ethiopia, Uganda and Zambia, where more graduates are entering the informal labour market because of few formal-sector employment opportunities) (World Bank, 2012a);

- Production mainly for urban or peri-urban markets using local raw materials; and

- Heterogeneity of scope, scale, activities and employees (e.g. children, women, etc.).

Employment in the informal economy compares the estimated number of people in informal employment to the total number of employed persons in the non-agricultural sector. Table 16 presents available data on the importance of informal sector firms in LDC employment. The number of persons employed in the informal sector greatly exceeds those in informal employment outside the informal sector. If both components of informal sector employment in informal firms and informal (wage) employment outside informal firms as a share of non-agricultural employment are considered, employment in the informal sector accounts for between 40 and 82 per cent of non-agricultural employment. For example, in Mali, employment in informal firms is especially significant, comprising 72 per cent of non-agricultural employment, while informal employment outside informal firms is estimated at 11 per cent of non-agricultural employment. Some 83 per cent of all non-agricultural employment in Mali is in the informal sector.

The share of women employed in the informal sector in total non-agricultural employment is much higher than for men in all LDCs except Uganda. This is primarily because the non-agricultural informal sector there is dominated by traditionally male occupations (such as carpentry, handicrafts and transportation services), and gender norms continue to dictate what women are allowed to do and whether they can work outside the marital home. In 2008, 40 per cent of Ugandan women were unpaid family workers, mainly in agriculture (Kasirye, 2011).

Table 16 also presents cross-country data suggesting that informal employment is associated with low income per capita and relatively high rates of poverty. As previously noted, significant sections of the LDC population struggle to survive and face extreme poverty with no option other than to work in the informal sector, with little legal, employment or social welfare protection.

Employment opportunities in the formal sector are apparently not expanding quickly enough to absorb the growing non-agricultural labour force, and consequently the proportion of employment in the informal sector as a share of non-agricultural employment is rising. The informal economy plays a significant role in the LDCs' socio-economic and political life in terms of both size and growth. As discussed earlier, in those LDCs characterized by high rates of population growth and/or urbanization, the informal sector tends to absorb much of the labour force.

C. Employment growth and estimated net job creation

As we have previously stressed, sustainable and inclusive economic growth in the LDCs will critically depend on the creation of productive and decent employment, which paves the way for broader social and economic advancement. But the pattern of economic growth also matters for both job creation and poverty reduction. Where growth is largely driven by capital-intensive industries (e.g. mining), employment multipliers and poverty reduction are often low. Although the LDCs' growth performance of the past decade has been impressive, it has failed to generate sufficient productive employment. A broad vindication of this assertion is provided by the evolution of employment elasticities to GDP growth, which measure the relative change in employment associated with each percentage point of economic growth. Employment elasticities also furnish useful information about employment and labour productivity trends. LDCs with a fast-growing working-age population and high

---

Employment in the informal sector accounts for between 40 and 82 per cent of non-agricultural employment.

Informal employment is associated with low income per capita and relatively high rates of poverty.

Employment opportunities in the formal sector are not expanding quickly enough to absorb the growing non-agricultural labour force.

In those LDCs characterized by high rates of population growth and/or urbanization, the informal sector tends to absorb much of the labour force.

Table 16. Contribution of informal sector to total non-agricultural employment in selected LDCs

Countries	Year of estimate	A+B Persons employed in the informal sector ('000)	Share of persons employed in the informal sector (percentage)			C Persons in informal employment outside the informal sector ('000)	Share of persons in informal employment outside the informal sector (percentage)			A+C Persons in informal employment as a share of total non-agricultural employment (percentage)			Labour force participation rate as a share of working age population (percentage)	Poverty share of population living below national poverty line (various years) (percentage)	GDP per capita (in current 2012 dollars) (dollars)
			F	M	Average		F	M	Average	F	M	Average	(percentage)	(percentage)	(dollars)
Ethiopia*	2004	1,089	48	36	42	-	-	-	-	-	-	-	46	39	474
Lesotho	2008	225	48	49	49	99	24	20	22	36	34	35	42	57	1067
Liberia	2010	342	65	33	49	62	7	15	11	72	47	60	63	64	305
Madagascar	2005	1,271	64	41	53	378	17	26	22	81	67	74	87	69	456
Mali	2004	1,180	80	63	72	163	10	13	11	89	74	82	49	47	612
Rwanda	2005	659	-	-	73	-	-	-	-	-	-	-	-	-	643
Uganda	2010	2,720	62	58	60	512	12	15	13	71	65	68	38	25	662
United Rep. of Tanzania	2005/06	3,467	50	53	52	-	-	11	-	-	-	-	-	33	604
Zambia	2008	920	70	61	66	155	12	11	12	80	63	72	56	59	1453

Source: Based on data from (Key Indicators of the Labour Market (KILM), Seventh Edition, 2013).

Notes: A+C = Persons in informal employment (excluding employees with formal jobs in informal enterprises);

A+B = Persons employed in the informal sector (including formal employment (where relevant) in the informal sector, i.e. employees holding formal jobs in informal enterprises);

B = Formal employment in the informal sector: comprising employees who, even though they work in an informal sector unit, have basic social or legal protection, and employment benefits.

C = Informal employment outside the informal sector (i.e. employees holding informal jobs in formal enterprises including government units and non-profit-institutions, and/or holding informal jobs as paid domestic workers employed by households, or as contributing family workers in formal enterprises).

A+B+C = Total employment in the informal economy

* = Informal sector data for Ethiopia cover urban areas only.

rates of labour force participation need relatively high employment elasticities because their population relies primarily on its own labour for survival. The provision of sufficient employment opportunities for the working poor and youths is thus a crucial government policy objective. It is worth noting that during the "Arab Spring" of 2011 and other anti-government protests in Africa, joblessness was a key issue in bringing youths onto the streets. Similarly, a World Bank (2011) report notes that half of the young people who join a dissident movement cite unemployment as the main reason for doing so.

Following Martins (2013), the elasticities[20] presented in chart 33 and chart 34 should be interpreted as follows: During periods of positive economic and employment growth, elasticities below unity suggest that employment growth is dominated more by labour productivity growth than by broad-based employment generation. For developing countries, employment elasticities should be around 0.7, and for some African countries even higher, given the rapid rise in labour force growth (Martins, 2013; Khan, 2007). In chart 33, employment elasticities to GDP for 2004–2008 indicate that some LDCs have been able to translate modest GDP growth into higher employment. The data further suggest that some of the LDCs with the lowest average GDP growth per annum during the period enjoyed the highest growth elasticities of employment. This is the case, for example, in Burundi (1.18), Chad (1.02), Comoros (1.49), Haiti (1.31) and Yemen (1.05). Conversely, the LDCs with the highest average GDP growth per annum during the same period had some of the lowest growth

The pattern of economic growth also matters for both job creation and poverty reduction. Where growth is largely driven by capital-intensive industries (e.g. mining), employment multipliers and poverty reduction are often low.

Chart 33. Growth elasticity of employment in LDCs, 2004–2008

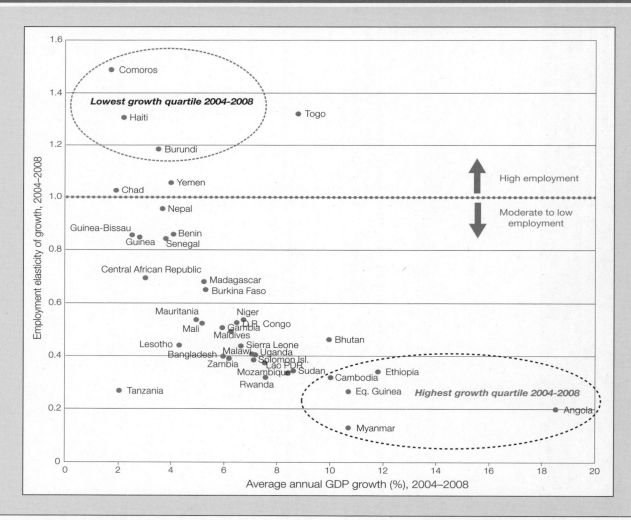

Source: UNCTAD secretariat calculations, based on ILO, *Key Indicators of the Labour Market (KILM)*, Sixth Edition, 2009.

elasticities of employment: Angola (0.20), Myanmar (0.13), Equatorial Guinea (0.27), Mozambique (0.30) and United Republic of Tanzania (0.27). Each of these countries averaged GDP growth rates in excess of 8 per cent per annum (above the 2001 Brussels Programme of Action target of 7 per cent) during the period 2004–2008. The relatively low elasticities for countries like Angola, Equatorial Guinea, Ethiopia, Mozambique and United Republic of Tanzania indicate that their economic growth has been primarily capital-intensive — since some of these countries are mainly energy and minerals exporters — with relatively limited employment generation.

Nonetheless, the data suggest that some countries, such as Bhutan, Togo and Uganda, have been better able to translate high rates of GDP growth into employment increases, especially during the 2000s. Their elasticities for 2004–2008 were considerably higher than those for Angola, Equatorial Guinea, Mozambique and United Republic of Tanzania.

Chart 34 shows employment elasticities to GDP covering two periods (2004–2008 and 2000–2008) for a sample of 39 LDCs. For Bhutan (0.73), Ethiopia (0.66), Rwanda (0.40) and Uganda (0.47), the 2000–2008 elasticities are much higher than the 2004–2008 iteration.

Although employment elasticities to GDP are often unstable, and to some extent depend on the pattern of growth and related policy frameworks, it is nonetheless clear that in most LDCs those elasticities have declined over the past decade; hence, the average 2004–2008 elasticity tends to be lower than that for 2000–2008 (for 17 of the 39 LDCs in the sample). During the past decade, employment elasticities to growth have declined in at least half of the LDCs (see chart 34). When elasticity estimates are compared for the periods 1996–2000 and 2004–2008, 21 of the 39 LDCs experienced a decline in employment elasticities to growth. This is a concern, given the high rates of labour force growth in the LDCs (see chart 16).

Only two LDCs have negative employment elasticities to GDP: Guinea Bissau and Mauritania. Negative elasticity, together with positive rates of economic growth, suggests that employment decreased over the period, while labour productivity grew faster than overall GDP. Eritrea is clearly a statistical outlier, given its exceptionally high elasticity of employment to GDP growth (exceeding 2.0) during the period 2000–2008. This may be due to contentious government policies, such as the National Service Programme and its concomitant Warsai-Yikaalo Development Campaign, which are based on compulsory labour schemes (Kibreab, 2009, World Report 2013: Eritrea, 2013).

In summary, the negative relationship depicted in chart 33 demonstrates that those countries with faster GDP expansion grew with relatively lower employment creation. Moreover, as Valensisi and Davis (2011a) have shown, elasticity tended to fall more frequently precisely in those LDCs that were growing faster. Considering the elasticities in conjunction with growth data provides useful complementary information about productivity change. As previously noted, McMillan and Rodrik (2011) argued that a pattern of sectoral labour reallocation has emerged in African developing countries, with perverse effects on aggregate labour productivity, which they term *"productivity-reducing structural change"*. This is where labour has moved towards less productive activities, such as urban services, in the informal sector, rather than towards higher-productivity activities, which enhance growth and structural change. However, Martins (2013) notes that in Ethiopia, although agricultural productivity is low, much of the services sector is modern (primarily financial, business and real estate services) and has the highest productivity levels.

Some of the LDCs with the lowest average GDP growth per annum during the period 2004–2008 enjoyed the highest growth elasticities of employment.

The LDCs with the highest average GDP growth per annum during the same period had some of the lowest growth elasticities of employment.

During the past decade, employment elasticities to growth have declined in at least half of the LDCs. This is a concern, given the high rates of labour force growth in the LDCs.

Chart 34. Elasticity of total employment to total GDP in the LDCs, 2000–2008

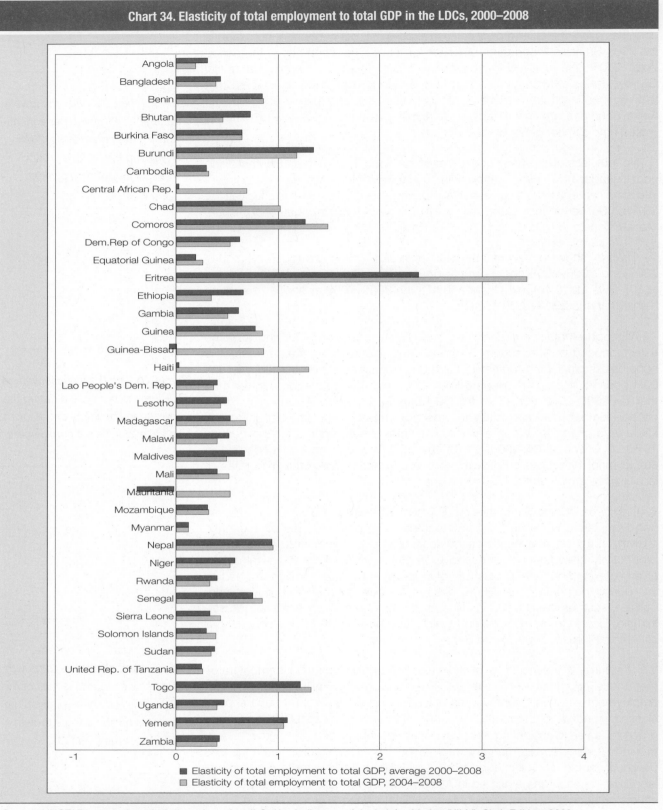

■ Elasticity of total employment to total GDP, average 2000–2008
■ Elasticity of total employment to total GDP, 2004–2008

Source: UNCTAD secretariat calculations, based on ILO, *Key Indicators of the Labour Market (KILM)*, Sixth Edition, 2009.

A useful conceptual experiment involves computing the counterfactual effect that growth could have had on employment if the elasticities had remained the same as during 1996–2000. In this respect, the estimates suggest that, ceteris paribus, nearly 25 million additional jobs could have been created in the LDCs had all elasticities remained at their 1996–2000 levels (Valensisi and Davis, 2011). Although the question is beyond the scope of this chapter, given that the LDCs apparently failed to translate growth adequately into employment during the boom of 2002–2008, what are the key impediments to their doing so? Valensisi and Gauchi (2013) combine secondary labour force data with different growth scenarios based on historical employment elasticities of growth to assess whether achieving the IPoA target of a 7-per-cent growth rate by 2020 would actually be enough to generate sufficient employment. They show that, even if the IPoA target is achieved, a number of LDCs will not be in a position productively to employ all the new labour market entrants unless their pattern of growth shifts towards more diversified employment-intensive sectors.

The estimates suggest that, ceteris paribus, nearly 25 million additional jobs could have been created in the LDCs had all elasticities remained at their 1996–2000 levels.

For the LDCs, improved labour productivity growth, especially through structural change, may have consequences for several elements of the labour market since intersectoral shifts of labour require different sets of skills and mobility. If, due to a lack of appropriate training and skills and to limited geographical mobility, LDC citizens cannot avail themselves of these job opportunities, the process may be impeded, creating barriers to successful job-hunting.

Table 17 presents the main data used for a decomposition of GDP growth per capita for 11 LDCs (listed in the following paragraph) in order to explore whether growth has translated into increased productivity and employment at the aggregate level and by sector. Following the World Bank (2012b), to begin the decomposition we use the equation $Y/N = A/N * Y/E$ – where Y is total GDP, N the total population, A the working-age population (i.e., the labour force), and E is total employment. This approach allows us to assess the contribution of the following factors to GDP growth: the employment rate (i.e., the employment-to-population ratio);[21] output per worker (i.e., labour productivity); and demographic change.

LDCs will not be in a position productively to employ all the new labour market entrants unless their pattern of growth shifts towards more diversified employment-intensive sectors.

This chapter began by outlining the main employment trends in the quantity and quality of jobs in the LDCs. Most LDCs have the potential to benefit from a demographic dividend (fewer dependants per working-age adult), given the rising and relatively high share of working-age population in the total population. For this section of the chapter, we have selected 11 LDCs that are broadly representative of the group (Angola, Bangladesh, Cambodia, Comoros, Ethiopia, Haiti, Mozambique, Nepal, Sierra Leone, United Republic of Tanzania and Zambia) in terms of export orientation, employment structure and data availability, (see table 17). The results of the decomposition are quite interesting.

		Percentage change 2000–2010					Decomposition of growth in per capita value added, percentage contribution, 2000–2010		
Sectoral classification	**LDC**	Total Growth in per capita GDP (value added, 2000 $) Δ(Y/N)	Total number of employed	Total population of working age	Output per worker	Employment rate	Growth linked to output per worker Δ(Y/E)	Growth linked to changes employment rate Δ(E/A)	Growth linked to changes in the share of population of working age Δ(A/N)
Manufactures	Bangladesh	54.7	24.6	25.4	42.5	-0.6	81.0	-1.5	20.5
	Cambodia	84.3	39.3	31.8	50.3	5.6	66.3	9.1	24.6
	Haiti	-6.6	27.1	23.6	-15.0	2.8	239.4	-41.1	-98.3
Agriculture	Ethiopia	80.3	36.4	36.6	67.2	-0.2	87.0	-0.3	13.3
	United Rep.of Tanzania	48.7	33.7	31.2	46.6	1.9	96.3	4.7	-1.0
Mining and minerals	Angola	91.9	36.7	40.0	92.3	-2.3	100.3	-3.7	3.4
	Zambia	52.7	24.3	25.4	57.6	-0.9	107.7	-2.1	-5.6
Mixed	Mozambique	71.5	27.2	27.6	73.3	-0.4	102.0	-0.7	-1.3
	Sierra Leone	61.8	44.9	40.6	58.2	3.0	95.2	6.3	-1.5
Services	Comoros	-3.2	35.8	28.0	-6.9	6.1	219.7	-182.4	62.7
	Nepal	18.8	29.9	32.2	12.3	-1.7	67.2	-10.0	42.8

Table 17. Decomposition of GDP per capita in selected LDCs, 2000–2010

Source: UNCTAD secretariat calculations, from UNCTADstat and *World Development Indicators* data using World Bank JoGGs (2012).
Note: Δ(Y/N): Total Growth in per capita GDP (value added, 2000 $). (Y= total GDP and N= the total population).
Δ(Y/E): Growth linked to output per worker. (E is total employment).
Δ(E/A): Growth linked to changes in the employment rate. (A is the working-age population).
Δ(A/N): Growth linked to changes in the share of population of working-age.

During the period 2000–2010, the LDC extractive industry economies registered a fall in employment rates and a strong rise in output per worker. The manufactures exporters had a mixed growth and employment performance.

For the whole period 2000–2010, Angola — the only oil exporter in the sample — had the highest per capita GDP growth rate (91.9 per cent). This growth was accompanied by a rise in output per worker (92.3 per cent), an increase in the working-age population (40 per cent) and a decline in employment rates (-2.3 per cent).

Cambodia (84.3 per cent), Ethiopia (80.3 per cent), Mozambique (71.5 per cent) and Sierra Leone (61.8 per cent) all had high per capita GDP growth rates for the decade. Only the island and services-oriented LDCs in the sample had relatively low or negative growth rates: Comoros (-3.2 per cent) and Haiti (-6.6 per cent).

Over the period concerned, the extractive industry economies of Angola, Mozambique and Zambia all registered a fall in employment rates and a strong rise in output per worker. The manufactures exporters — namely, Bangladesh, Cambodia and Haiti — had a mixed growth and employment performance. The employment rate declined in Bangladesh (-0.6 per cent) but grew in Cambodia (5.6 per cent). Haiti not only registered a negative per capita GDP growth rate, it also had a decline in output per worker (i.e., labour productivity fell), in part due to the disastrous economic impact of the 2010 earthquake. Nonetheless, the country's employment rate rose by 2.8 per cent.

If we consider the contribution of demographic change ($\Delta(A/N)$), the employment rate ($\Delta(E/A)$) and output per worker ($\Delta(Y/E)$), it is clear that for all 11 countries the bulk of the growth per capita was accounted for by productivity growth (output per worker), with minor changes in the demographic structure and employment rate. Growth linked to changes in the share of population of working age (demographic structure) was significant only in Nepal and to a lesser extent in Bangladesh, Cambodia and Ethiopia. Nepal appears to be successfully exploiting its demographic dividend, since its working-age population as a share of the total population is rising (i.e., fewer dependants per working-age adult) and accounted for about 42 per cent of the change in GDP per capita during 2000–2010. Ceteris paribus, the demographic transition would thus have generated per capita growth equivalent to 42 per cent of the actual observed growth (table 17).

The bulk of the growth per capita was accounted for by productivity growth (output per worker), with minor changes in the demographic structure and employment rate.

The only countries in the sample where the employment rate made a positive contribution to GDP were Cambodia (where it accounted for 9 per cent of the change in GDP per capita), Sierra Leone (6.3 per cent) and United Republic of Tanzania (4.7 per cent). This may reflect important positive changes for these economies, such as youths continuing their education for longer periods of time, which helps build future productive capacities. A negative contribution of the employment rate implies that had the rate not declined, then GDP per capita would have been higher. The decomposition does not provide information about the quality of work.

In order tentatively to explore employment, growth and structural change, productivity growth should be decomposed into two parts: within sectors, and across sectors (McMillan and Rodrik, 2011b). Table 18 summarizes the results of a sectoral disaggregation of GDP and employment for three broad sectors: agriculture, industry and services. Unfortunately, further disaggregation was not possible because of insufficient sectoral-level employment data for the LDCs. Where such data from household or other micro-level surveys exist (for example, a World Bank Living Standards Measurement Study), they are often not internationally comparable due to different sampling, data collection and collation methodologies. For the 11 selected LDCs, we decompose growth, changes in employment and intersectoral shifts to highlight the sectors with potentially high employment intensity and productivity growth.

Table 18. Growth decomposition, percentage contribution to total growth in GDP (value added) per capita, 2000–2010
(Percentages)

LDC	Sectoral contributions	Contribution of within sector changes in output per worker	Contribution of changes in employment	Contributions of inter-sectoral shifts	Total
Bangladesh	Agriculture, hunting, forestry, fishing	12.8	-22.0	13.8	4.7
	Industry	19.1	5.1	6.6	30.8
	Services	15.1	15.4	13.5	44.1
	Subtotals	47.1	-1.5	33.9	79.5
	Demographic component	-	-		20.5
	Total				100.0
	Total percentage change in value added per capita 2000–2010				*54.7*
Cambodia	Agriculture, hunting, forestry, fishing	10.1	4.8	1.0	15.9
	Industry	26.1	0.3	-1.0	25.4
	Services	27.4	.4.0	2.7	34.1
	Subtotals	63.6	9.1	2.7	75.4
	Demographic component	-	-		24.6
	Total				100.0
	Total percentage change in value added per capita 2000–2010				*84.3*
Ethiopia	Agriculture, hunting, forestry, fishing	27.0	-3.5	1.5	25.0
	Industry	10.9	0.1	0.5	11.5
	Services	40.4	3.1	6.7	50.2
	Subtotals	78.3	-0.3	8.7	86.7
	Demographic component				13.3
	Total				100.0
	Total percentage change in value added per capita 2000–2010				*80.3*
United Rep.of Tanzania	Agriculture, hunting, forestry, fishing	18.5	-16.8	12.4	14.2
	Industry	0.0	5.7	26.5	32.3
	Services	14.6	15.7	24.2	54.5
	Subtotals	33.1	4.7	63.2	101.0
	Demographic component				-1.0
	Total				100.0
	Total percentage change in value added per capita 2000–2010				*48.7*
Angola	Agriculture, hunting, forestry, fishing	14.0	-24.0	18.0	8.0
	Industry	31.2	3.9	28.5	63.6
	Services	17.9	16.5	-9.3	25.1
	Subtotals	63.1	-3.7	37.2	96.6
	Demographic component				3.4
	Total				100.0
	Total percentage change in value added per capita 2000–2010				*91.9*
Zambia	Agriculture, hunting, forestry, fishing	15.9	-3.4	1.1	13.6
	Industry	8.1	8.5	17.2	33.8
	Services	74.1	-7.2	-8.8	58.1
	Subtotals	98.2	-2.1	9.5	105.6
	Demographic component				-5.6
	Total				100.0
	Total percentage change in value added per capita 2000–2010				*52.7*
Mozambique	Agriculture, hunting, forestry, fishing	28.2	-10.0	6.2	24.4
	Industry	9.7	2.5	12.0	24.2
	Services	32.2	6.8	13.6	52.6
	Subtotals	70.2	-0.7	31.8	101.3
	Demographic component				-1.3
	Total				100.0
	Total percentage change in value added per capita 2000–2010				*71.5*
Sierra Leone	Agriculture, hunting, forestry, fishing	79.7	-13.3	3.7	70.1
	Industry	-3.6	4.6	4.3	5.3
	Services	6.2	15.0	4.9	26.1
	Subtotals	82.3	6.3	12.9	101.5
	Demographic component	-	-		-1.5
	Total				100.0
	Total percentage change in value added per capita 2000–2010				*61.8*

Table 18 (contd.)

LDC	Sectoral contributions	Contribution of within sector changes in output per worker	Contribution of changes in employment	Contributions of inter-sectoral shifts	Total
Comoros	Agriculture, hunting, forestry, fishing	104.1	-162.2	10.7	-47.4
	Industry	30.0	0.6	5.9	36.5
	Services	52.4	-20.9	16.6	48.1
	Subtotals	186.5	-182.4	33.3	37.3
	Demographic component	-	-		62.7
	Total				100.0
	Total percentage change in value added per capita 2000–2010				*-3.2*
Haiti	Agriculture, hunting, forestry, fishing	71.1	23.6	-23.5	71.2
	Industry	62.2	-6.8	-4.4	51.0
	Services	138.6	-57.9	-4.6	76.1
	Subtotals	271.9	-41.1	-32.5	198.3
	Demographic component	-	-		-98.3
	Total				100.0
	Total percentage change in value added per capita 2000–2010				*-6.6*
Nepal	Agriculture, hunting, forestry, fishing	21.1	-24.3	9.3	6.0
	Industry	-9.2	4.5	3.2	-1.4
	Services	17.8	9.8	25.0	52.6
	Subtotals	29.6	-10.0	37.5	57.2
	Demographic component	-	-		42.8
	Total				100.0
	Total percentage change in value added per capita 2000–2010				*18.8*

Source: Secretariat calculations based on UNCTADstat and *World Development Indicators* data using World Bank JoGGs (2012).

Within-sector productivity growth contributions to GDP per capita growth during the period 2000–2010 were large for most of the selected LDCs.

The data suggest that demographic change made a relatively small contribution to per capita GDP growth in most of the selected LDCs.

Within-sector productivity growth contributions to GDP per capita growth during the period 2000–2010 were large (70 to 98 per cent) for most of the selected LDCs. The main exceptions are United Republic of Tanzania and Nepal, where the respective 63-per-cent and 37.5-per-cent contributions of intersectoral shifts (i.e., structural change) are the largest such contributions. In terms of within-sector contributions to GDP growth, the services sector plays a prominent role in 6 of the 11 countries. The contribution of agriculture is still predominant in three LDCs: United Republic of Tanzania, Sierra Leone and Comoros. The industrial sector plays a key role in Angola and to a lesser extent in Cambodia. Nonetheless, gains in labour productivity within sectors (especially industry and services) are often the main driver of aggregate economic growth. Finally, the data suggest that demographic change made a relatively small contribution to per capita GDP growth in most of the selected LDCs, with the exception of Comoros (62.7 per cent) and Nepal (42.8 per cent). These trends in turn indicate that economic growth tended to become less effective in terms of employment generation.

While these estimates represent simple orders of magnitude, the nature of the problem can clearly not be overlooked: Relatively high rates of economic growth in the LDCs had limited employment intensity. On the other hand, if technological change, macroeconomic conditions and labour supply issues are also considered, there is little doubt that the "employment challenge" faced by LDCs is, at least to some extent, a consequence of the prevailing pattern of structural change.

D. Conclusions

Following the path to full, decent employment is a challenge in any country, let alone in those with special needs. It requires that per capita GDP is adequate to ensure reasonable compensation and to leave a surplus for financing investment, social security and other human development needs, while also delivering a satisfactory profit in economies driven predominantly by private initiative. However, per capita GDP depends, *inter alia*, on productivity, and the higher the productivity, the lower the employment delivered by every unit increment in GDP. Ensuring adequate decent work thus entails combining a reasonably high average productivity with a rejuvenation of some traditionally important employment-intensive areas of activity, such as agriculture, and a fast enough rate of growth in the volume of economic activity to foster conditions for realizing both employment expansion and reasonable compensation.

This chapter shows that relatively high rates of GDP growth in the LDCs have not translated into concomitant levels of employment growth in industry. Instead, the services sector has seen employment rise more vigorously. This reflects a shift of labour from low-productivity activities (mainly in agriculture) to low-productivity activities in the services (largely non-tradable) sector. Over time, the services sector is thus accounting for a greater share of the LDC labour force. Furthermore, the historic labour productivity divide between LDCs and ODCs remains substantial, although it has narrowed since 2000. The agricultural labour productivity gap between LDCs, ODCs and developed economies has also widened since 1985. Increased agricultural labour productivity in LDCs has the potential to both raise the real incomes of rural households and stimulate demand for rural non-farm goods and services. The employment-creating potential of investment in rural irrigation, drainage, provision of feeder channels, local land reclamation, afforestation and so forth is considerable. This can be strengthened if such investment is embedded in well-designed and well-targeted employment programmes (see chapter 5).

Although RNF employment is increasingly important in LDCs, on-farm production and jobs are still the mainstay for most LDCs. As the Report shows, the rural non-farm economy is a vital source of employment for Bangladesh, Malawi and Nepal, with non-farm activity participation rates in excess of 45 per cent.

The LDCs have a high labour force participation rate because with limited or no social security in many of these countries, the poor have no option but to seek work. More women than ever before are part of the LDC labour force, but this has not translated into better jobs or less gender discrimination. Similarly, the rise in women's employment has in most LDCs failed to generate a significant improvement in their standard of living. A disproportionate number of women are "contributing family workers" in vulnerable employment.

This chapter also documents the fact that indicators of vulnerable employment and working poor have improved since 2000, but from a relatively weak starting point. Vulnerable employment still accounts for about 80 per cent of total employment in the LDCs.

Generally speaking, unemployment in the LDCs disproportionately affects the youth labour force. In most LDCs, the youth unemployment rate (i.e., the unemployment rate for those aged 15–24 years) is higher than the average LDC unemployment rate for both men and women, and in most cases is almost twice that rate. LDC youths typically find work in the informal sector, but often these jobs do not pay reasonable wages, improve skills or offer much job security. If,

This chapter shows that relatively high rates of GDP growth in the LDCs have not translated into concomitant levels of employment growth in industry.

More women than ever before are part of the LDC labour force, but this has not translated into better jobs or less gender discrimination.

Vulnerable employment still accounts for about 80 per cent of total employment in the LDCs.

however, LDCs can provide the burgeoning youth population with the necessary skills, education and decent jobs, their youth can potentially become a major source of global and domestic consumption.

The chapter has further shown that countries with faster GDP growth achieved this with relatively lower employment creation. Employment elasticities declined in about half of the LDCs in the period 2000–2008, and tended to fall more frequently in precisely those LDCs that were growing faster. Although the reported LDC employment elasticities to growth have generally not been very low by international standards, given the demographic and economic challenges these countries are likely to face, these elasticities will probably not be high enough to reach the necessary employment levels.

It is clear from the chapter's consideration of the contribution of demographic change, the employment rate and output per worker to per capita GDP growth that for all of the selected LDCs, the bulk of the growth per capita was accounted for by productivity growth (output per worker), with minor changes in the demographic structure and employment rate. There were only three countries in the sample where the employment rate made a positive contribution to GDP. But the chapter also argues that economic growth has tended over time to become less effective in terms of creating jobs.

Although the reported LDC employment elasticities to growth have generally not been very low by international standards, given the demographic and economic challenges these countries are likely to face, these elasticities will probably not be high enough to reach the necessary employment levels.

This fact has been recognized to some extent at the multilateral level by the inclusion of "full and productive employment" among the targets for MDG 1, especially as the functioning of the labour market is also critical to human development and poverty reduction. But the available labour market and informal sector information for LDCs is sparse. There is an urgent need for more data collection and statistical analyses, which should figure prominently in the post-2015 MDG debate. Further poverty reduction will, however, require the sustained creation of productive employment, especially in countries where extreme poverty affects the majority of the population and where government is unable to address the problem through redistribution (McKinley and Martins, 2010; Ravallion, 2009b; UNCTAD, 2010).

The bulk of urban workers in LDCs have accordingly sought employment in services or remain underemployed in the informal sector.

During the 2002–2008 commodity boom, mining and quarrying thrived as relatively capital-intensive industries, although with limited multiplier effects on other sectors of the economy. The agricultural sector, by contrast, performed poorly, further entrenching subsistence living standards in rural areas. Certainly, the relatively poor performance of the agricultural sector in most LDCs has been particularly detrimental, given that the poverty elasticity of growth in agriculture is typically much higher than the corresponding elasticity of growth in other sectors of the economy (Warr, 2002; Ravallion and Chen, 2004). While the manufacturing and services sectors also grew during this period, that growth was too weak to absorb large segments of the labour force. The bulk of urban workers in LDCs have accordingly sought employment in services or remain underemployed in the informal sector. McMillan and Rodrik (2011) maintain that this pattern of sectoral labour reallocation has perverse effects on aggregate labour productivity, which they term "productivity-reducing structural change". In most LDCs, rather than moving from low-productive to highly productive sectors, thereby enhancing the GDP per person employed, this labour reallocation tends to perpetuate the dual nature[22] of their economies, which could potentially keep large sections of the labour force underemployed or unemployed.

In most LDCs, rather than moving from low-productive to highly productive sectors, thereby enhancing the GDP per person employed, this labour reallocation tends to perpetuate the dual nature of their economies.

Thus, much of the relatively strong economic growth performance of the LDCs during the 2000s may have represented a lost opportunity to stimulate employment generation and foster stronger demand for "human capital deepening" by encouraging a shift towards more knowledge-intensive activities. Since 1990, these countries have made significant improvements in primary school completion rates and literacy rates for people aged 15–24 years (see chapter 5). However, the critical issue for LDCs is whether their economies will be able productively to employ new labour market entrants, thereby seizing the window of opportunity created by the "youth bulge" and realizing the potential benefits arising from significant long-term investments in education.

Notes

1 These data reflect the group (cohort) of workers (aged 15–24 years) entering the LDC labour market, or reaching the age when they seek an income-generating activity, which is considered to represent 1/10 of the 15–24 year age group (Losch et al., 2012). The annual group (cohort) of new workers highlights the weight of youth in the labour market. The estimate also makes it possible to avoid statistical uncertainties about whether people in developing countries actually leave the workforce after age 64 (the working-age population is usually defined as 15–64 years). This is because in most LDCs, the labour markets include many people who continue to work after age 64, notably in the agricultural and urban informal sectors.

2 Labour market data for Sudan also include South Sudan. In the ILO *Key Indicators of the Labour Market (KILM)* series, there are no available data for Djibouti, Liberia, Sao Tome and Principe, and Somalia.

3 The labour force is the sum of the employed and the unemployed. The population not economically active is generally classified by the reason for inactivity.

4 FAO estimates of the economically active population and the agricultural/non-agricultural population segments are obtained by systematically applying to the total population the series of relevant ratios, such as the proportion of economically active population by age. The time series of estimates for the total population are provided by the United Nations Population Division.

5 Most of the data presented here on LDC employment by sector are from ILO and cover only the period 2000–2012. Other ILO employment forecasts cover the period 2013–2018 (International Labour Organisation, Employment Trends (EMP/TRENDS) econometric model, April 2013).

6 During the 1990s many African LDCs introduced microeconomic reforms (such as strengthening legal and regulatory systems and privatization) and policies to improve their business and investment climate. These internal reforms (or structural changes) helped spur productivity growth. In addition, urbanization is rising rapidly in African LDCs and may in turn be boosting labour productivity (which tends to rise as workers move from farm production to urban jobs) and investment.

7 Agriculture value added per worker is a measure of agricultural productivity. Value added in agriculture measures the output of the agricultural sector (divisions 1–5 of the International Standard Industrial Classification (ISIC)) less the value of intermediate inputs. Agriculture comprises value added from forestry, hunting and fishing as well as from the cultivation of crops and livestock production (World Development Indicators, 2013).

8 On the face of it, this outcome is somewhat surprising. However, there is growing evidence that the adoption of technology (mainly in Asian LDCs) and expanding land holdings (mainly in African LDCs) of small farmers result in changes in factor ratios that in turn lead to productivity gains (Dercon and Zeitlin, 2009; Salami et al., 2010; World Bank, 2007). However, the type of technology adopted, and the extent of access to land, can affect productivity in different ways. For example, increased access to land tends to lift labour productivity at the expense of land productivity, while technology adoption tends to improve the productivity of all factors of production (Thirtle et al., 2003; Dercon and Zeitlin, 2009; Salami et al., 2010).

9 The labour force participation rate is an indicator of the level of labour market activity. It reflects the extent to which a country's working-age population is economically active and is defined as the ratio of the labour force to the working-age population, expressed in percentage terms.

10 Additional indicators would be required in order to assess such issues as income, working hours, informal sector employment, and underemployment, but they are not available.

11 The term "working poverty" refers to those working persons with income below the poverty line.

12 According to Karshenas' (2010) LDC poverty estimates, in 2007, 53 per cent of the population was living on less than $1.25 a day, and 78 per cent on less than $2 a day. This means that 421 million people were living in extreme poverty in LDCs in 2007. The incidence of extreme poverty ($1.25 a day) was significantly higher in African LDCs, at 59 per cent, than in Asian LDCs, at 41 per cent. For the $2-a-day poverty line, however, the difference was less marked: 80 per cent in African LDCs and 72 per cent in Asian LDCs.

13 The agricultural total is the sum of the mean of shares for the following income sources: agricultural crops, livestock and agricultural wage employment.

14 In Malawi the term *ganyu* describes various short-term rural labour relationships, such as casual non-own-farm work (e.g. weeding, tillage) for other smallholders or plantations.

15 Discouraged workers are defined as persons not in the labour force who are available for work but do not seek work because they think they will not find a job.

16 Underemployment reflects underutilization of the productive capacity of the employed population.

17 See, for example, Birdsall (2010) and Banerjee and Dufflo (2008), who maintain that because the middle class tend to have greater levels of human, financial and physical capital, growth in this group tends to lead to widespread gains in living standards due to a higher propensity to invest in productive capacities.

18 All the dollar figures are calculated at purchasing power parity (PPP), a conversion rate that eliminates differences between countries in the cost of goods and services. National poverty rates are taken from the World Bank's PovcalNet database of internationally comparable poverty data.

19 UNCTAD secretariat calculations, based on data from ILO, Employment Trends (EMP/TRENDS) econometric model, April 2013. This group now accounts for 62 per cent of the LDCs' workforce.

20 The employment elasticities presented here are derived from KILM (2004–2008 and 2000–2008) averages. No post-crisis (after 2009) elasticities have been utilized, as they may be subject to errors and bias.

21 For a full explanation of the empirical relationship between the employment elasticity of growth and the contribution of the employment rate methodology, see World Bank (2012b), Job Generation and Growth Decomposition Tool (JoGGs).

22 An economy is considered to be dual when there are two distinct economic sectors within a country that can be classified by different levels of development (for example, the modern industrial sector and the traditional agriculture sector) and technology.

References

African Development Bank (2011). The middle of the pyramid: dynamics of the middle class in Africa. Market Brief, 04/2011. Tunis.

African Development Bank and Organisation for Economic Co-operation and Development (2012). *African Economic Outlook 2012*. African Development Bank and Development Centre of the Organisation for Economic Co-operation and Development. Paris.

Bäckman S, Islam KMZ and Sumelius J (2011). Determinants of technical efficiency of rice farms in north-central and north-western regions in Bangladesh. *The Journal of Developing Areas*.

Banerjee AV and Duflo E (2008). What is Middle Class about the Middle Classes around the World? *Journal of Economic Perspectives*. 22(2):3–28.

Barrett CB, Reardon T and Webb P (2001). Nonfarm income diversification and household livelihood strategies in rural Africa: concepts, dynamics, and policy implications. *Food Policy*. 26(4):315–331.

Bezemer D, Balcombe K, Davis J and Fraser I (2005). Livelihoods and farm efficiency in rural Georgia. *Applied Economics*. 37(15):1737–1745.

Birdsall N (2010). The (Indispensable) Middle Class in Developing Countries; or, The Rich and the Rest, Not the Poor and the Rest. In: Kanbur S M R and Spence M, eds. *Equity and Growth in a Globalizing World*. Commission on Growth and Development/ World Bank. Washington, DC.

Brookings Institute (2013). Foresight Africa: top priorities for the continent in 2013. Brookings Institute. Washington.

Davis B et al. (2007). Rural income generating activities; a cross country comparison. Working Paper No. 07-16. Agricultural and Development Economics Division of the Food and Agriculture Organization of the United Nations (FAO - ESA). Rome

Davis B et al. (2010). A Cross-Country Comparison of Rural Income Generating Activities. *World Development*. 38(1):48–63.

Davis B, Winters P, Reardon T and Stamoulis K (2009). Rural nonfarm employment and farming: household-level linkages. *Agricultural Economics*. 40(2):119–123.

Davis J (2004). The rural non-farm economy, livelihoods and their diversification: issues and options. Development and Comp Systems No. 2753. EconWPA.

Davis J (2006). Rural non-farm livelihoods in transition economies: emerging issues and policies. *Journal of Agricultural and Development Economics*. 3(2):180–224.

Davis J, Bezemer D, Janowski M and Wandschneider T (2005). The rural non-farm economy and poverty alleviation in Armenia, Georgia and Romania: a synthesis of findings. Development and Comp Systems. EconWPA.

Deichmann U, Shilpi F and Vakis R (2009). Urban Proximity, Agricultural Potential and Rural Non-farm Employment: Evidence from Bangladesh. *World Development*. 37(3):645–660.

Dercon S and Zeitlin A (2009). Rethinking agriculture and growth in Ethiopia: a conceptual discussion. Unpublished mimeo. United Kingdom.

Dirven M (2011). Non-farm rural employment and rural poverty reduction: What we know in Latin America in 2010. IFAD Conference on New Directions for Smallholder Agriculture, Rome.

Gurrieri A and Sainz P (2003). CEPAL - Employment and structural mobility. Revisiting a Prebischian theme. *CEPAL Review*. 80:135–158.

Haggblade S, Hazell P and Brown J (1989). Farm-nonfarm linkages in rural sub-Saharan Africa. *World Development*. 17(8):1173–1201.

Haggblade S, Hazell P and Reardon T (2010). The Rural Non-farm Economy: Prospects for Growth and Poverty Reduction. *World Development*. 38(10):1429–1441.

Haggblade S, Hazell PBR and Reardon TA (2007). *Transforming the Rural Nonfarm Economy: Opportunities and Threats in the Developing World.* Johns Hopkins University Press. Baltimore (MD).

Hossain M (2004). Rural non-farm economy in Bangladesh: a view from household surveys. CPD Working Paper No. 40. Centre for Policy Dialogue (CPD), Dhaka.

Hossain M, Naher F and Shahabuddin Q (2005). Food Security and Nutrition in Bangladesh: Progress and Determinants. *Journal of Agricultural and Development Economics.* 2(2):103–132.

Howes M (2002). *Extension for Sustainable Livelihoods in Bangladesh. Ebook.*

Human Rights Watch (2013). World Report 2013: Eritrea. Available at http://www.hrw.org/world-report/2013/country-chapters/eritrea (accessed 31 July 2013).

International Labour Office (2009). *Yearbook of Labour Statistics*. International Labour Office. Geneva.

International Labour Office (2011). *Growth, Employment and Decent Work in the Least Developed Countries: Report of the International Labour Office for the Fourth Conference on the Least Developed Countries*, Istanbul, 9-13 May 2011. International Labour Office. Geneva.

International Labour Office (2012). Statistical update on employment in the informal economy June. Available at http://laborsta.ilo.org/applv8/data/INFORMAL_ECONOMY/2012-06-Statistical%20update%20-%20v2.pdf.

International Labour Office (2013). Global employment trends 2013: recovering from a second jobs dip. International Labour Office. Geneva.

Kapsos S and Bourmpoula E (2013). Employment and economic class in the developing world. ILO Research Paper No. 6. International Labour Office (ILO). Geneva.

Karshenas M (2010). Global poverty: new national accounts consistent estimates based on 2005 purchasing power parity exchange rates, with extension to the least developed countries poverty trends. The Least Developed Country Report 2010, background paper No. Background Paper No. 8. 43.

Kasirye I (2011). Addressing Gender Gaps in the Ugandan Labour Market. *Economic Policy Research Centre Policy Brief*. Economic Policy Research Centre Policy Brief. (12):4.

Khan AR (2007). Growth, employment and poverty. In: Ocampo J A and Sundaram J K, eds. *Full and Decent Employment*. Orient Longman, Zed Books and Third World Network. Hyderabad, London and New York, and Penang: 123–157.

Kibreab G (2009). Forced labour in Eritrea. *The Journal of Modern African Studies*. 47(01):41.

Losch B, Fréguin-Gresh S and White ET (2012). *Structural Transformation and Rural Change Revisited: Challenges for Late Developing Countries in a Globalizing World*. World Bank. Washington (DC).

Martins P (2013). Growth, employment and poverty in Africa: tales of lions and cheetahs. Background paper prepared for the World Development Report 2013. World Bank. Washington (DC).

McKinley T and Martins P (2010). "Empowering MDG Strategies Through Inclusive Economic Development." Paper prepared for UNCTAD Geneva.

McMillan M and Rodrik D (2011a). Globalization, Structural Change and Productivity Growth June. Available at http://www.nber.org/papers/w17143.

Mendola M (2007). Agricultural technology adoption and poverty reduction: A propensity-score matching analysis for rural Bangladesh. *Food Policy*. 32(3):372–393.

OECD (2012). *OECD Employment Outlook 2012*. Organisation for Economic Co-operation and Development (OECD). Paris.

Ravallion M (2009a). The developing world's bulging (but vulnerable) "middle class." Policy Research Working Paper Series No. 4816. World Bank. Washington (DC).

Ravallion M (2009b). Do poorer countries have less capacity for redistribution? One Pager No. 97. International Policy Centre for Inclusive Growth. Brasilia.

Ravallion M and Chen S (2004). China's (uneven) progress against poverty. SSRN Scholarly Paper No. ID 625285. Social Science Research Network. Rochester (NY).

Salami A, Kamara A and Brixova Z (2010). Smallholder agriculture in east Africa: trends, constraints and opportunities. Working Papers Series No. 105. African Development Bank. Tunis.

Stifel D (2010). The rural non-farm economy, livelihood strategies and household welfare. *African Journal of Agricultural and Resource Economics*. 4(1):82–109.

Thirtle C, Lin L and Piesse J (2003). The Impact of Research-Led Agricultural Productivity Growth on Poverty Reduction in Africa, Asia and Latin America. *World Development*. 31(12):1959–1975.

Toufique KA and Turton C (2002). *Hands Not Land: How Livelihoods Are Changing in Rural Bangladesh*. Bangladesh Institute of Development Studies.

UNCTAD (2009). *The Least Developed Countries Report 2009: The State and Development Governance*. United Nations publication. Sales No. E.09.II.D.9. New York and Geneva.

UNCTAD (2010). *The Least Developed Countries Report 2010: Towards a New International Development Architecture for LDCs*. United Nations publication. Sales No. E.10.II.D.5. New York and Geneva.

UNCTAD (2012). *The Least Developed Countries Report 2012: Harnessing Remittances and Diaspora Knowledge to Build Productive Capacities*. United Nations publication. Sales No. E.12.II.D.18. New York and Geneva.

UNCTAD (2013). *Commodities and Development Report: Perennial Problems, New Challenges and Evolving Perspectives*. United Nations Conference on Trade and Development. New York and Geneva.

Valensisi G and Davis J (2011). Least Developed Countries and the Green Transition: Towards a renewed political economy agenda. November. Available at http://ideas.repec.org/p/msm/wpaper/2011-27.html (accessed 21 May 2013).

Valensisi G and Gauci A (2013). Graduated without passing? The employment dimension and LDCs prospects under the Istanbul Programme of Action. Presented at the Conference on Structural Change, Dynamics, and Economic Growth. Livorno, Italy. 12 September. Available at https://editorialexpress.com/cgi-bin/conference/download.cgi?db_name=STCHANGE&paper_id=79.

Warr PG (2002). Poverty incidence and sectoral growth: evidence from Southeast Asia. Working Paper No. UNU-WIDER Research Paper DP2002/20. World Institute for Development Economic Research (UNU-WIDER). Helsinki.

World Bank (2005). Pro-poor growth in the 1990s: lessons and insights from 14 countries. World Bank. Washington (DC).

World Bank (2007a). *Agriculture for Development*. World Bank. Washington, D.C.

World Bank (2007b). Bangladesh Data - World Bank Enterprise Survey of Business Managers - World Bank Group. Available at http://www.enterprisesurveys.org/Data/ExploreEconomies/2007/bangladesh#performance--size (accessed 15 July 2013).

World Bank (2008). *Youth in Africa's Labor Market*. Directions in development. Human development. United Nations publication. Sales No. HD6276.A32 Y685 2008. Washington (DC).

World Bank (2011a). Agriculture - Bangladesh: priorities for agriculture and rural development. Washington (DC).

World Bank (2011b). *World Development Report 2011: Conflict, Security, and Development*. World Bank. Washington (DC).

World Bank (2012a). *World Development Report 2013: Jobs*. World Bank. Washington (DC).

World Bank (2012b). *Job Generation and Growth Decomposition Tool: Understanding the Sectoral Pattern of Growth and Its Employment and Productivity Intensity Reference Manual and User's Guide Version 1.0*. World Bank Publications.

World Bank (2013). *World Development Report 2013: Jobs*. World Bank. Washington (DC).

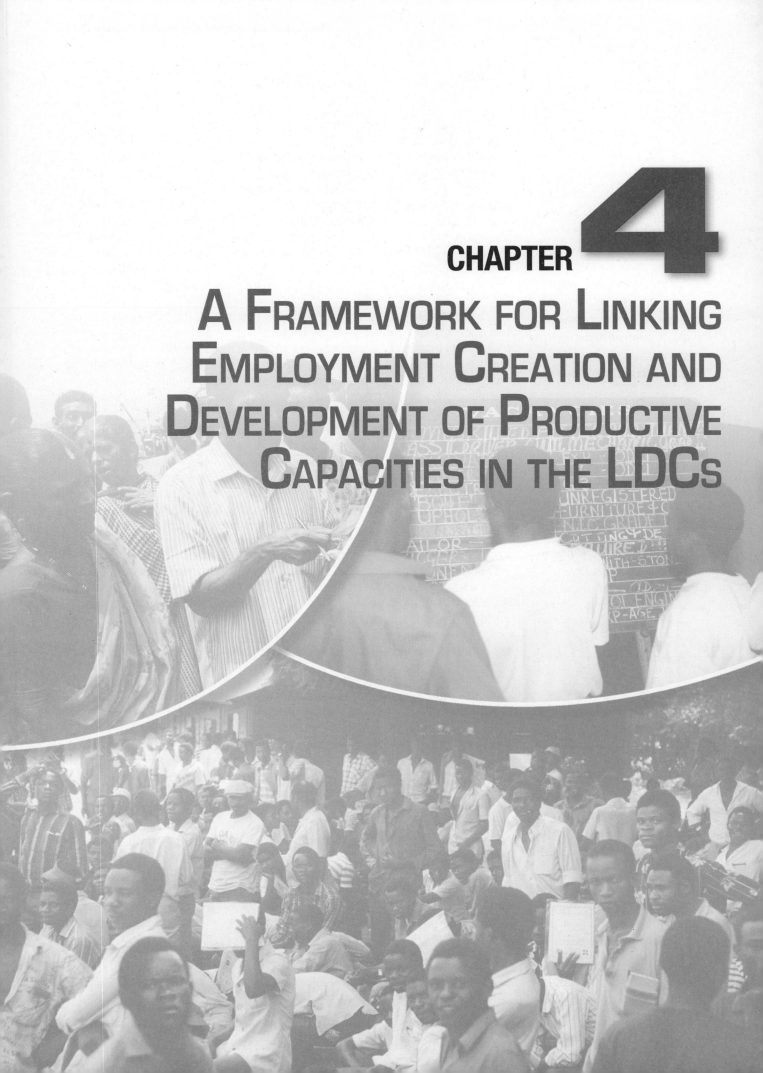

CHAPTER **4**

A Framework for Linking Employment Creation and Development of Productive Capacities in the LDCs

A. Introduction

For the past three decades, LDCs have been advised to focus on economic growth as a strategy for economic diversification, poverty reduction and economic development. In hindsight, this appears to have been sound policy advice, since it is highly unlikely that LDCs will achieve economic and social development and halve their poverty levels in line with internationally agreed goals without a sustained period of growth. In fact, in recognition of this likely scenario, the IPoA states (United Nations, 2011,para. 28) that in order for LDCs to achieve "sustained, equitable and inclusive economic growth [...] to at least the level of 7 per cent per annum", they should strengthen their productive capacity in all sectors through structural transformation and overcome their marginalization through effective integration into the global economy.

The market-based reforms and policies pursued by the LDCs over the past two decades were motivated by this advice and were based on the assumption that a combination of macroeconomic austerity, rapid liberalization, privatization and deregulation would attract investment in sufficient quantity to generate rapid output growth, which in turn would automatically create jobs of adequate quantity and quality. As explained in chapter 3, however, it is now evident that economic growth, although necessary, by itself neither guarantees job creation nor automatically results in inclusive development. To the contrary, it may even lead in some cases to an intensification of social inequality, rising unemployment and an increased incidence of poverty. In short, if employment creation and inclusive growth are the ultimate objectives, then the type of growth matters. It is further evident that growth resulting from labour-intensive activities or originating in areas where the poor live is more likely to create jobs and contribute to inclusiveness than growth based on capital-intensive investments.

This chapter proposes a policy framework that links investment with growth and employment creation to generate inclusive and sustainable development. The framework is based on the premise that the employment creation potential of growth will not be maximized without the development of productive capacities. While initiatives to provide jobs through government- or internationally sponsored programmes might be valuable sources of employment in the short term, they do not provide long-term, sustainable solutions to the LDC employment challenge.

The proposed framework builds on three sets of ideas and concepts developed through UNCTAD's analytical work on LDCs and other developing countries.

First, it hypothesizes that economic growth which does not create decent jobs in sufficient quantity is unsustainable, and that job creation without the development of productive capacities is equally unsustainable.

Second, it acknowledges that private sector development is critical for economic growth and for creating employment and building productive capacity. However, given the relatively weak private sector in many LDCs, it also recognizes that in the short to medium term, the investment push required to kick-start the growth process will likely originate in the public sector. The idea here is not to encourage public ownership, which would amount to returning to failed policies of the past. Rather, the idea is to ensure that the capital-mobilizing power of the State is used to provide the initial investment impulses needed to generate growth with employment.

Third, the policy framework provides a definition of productive capacity that is broad enough to incorporate all the elements essential for a country to

---

The policies pursued by the LDCs over the past two decades were based on the assumption that a combination of macroeconomic austerity, rapid liberalization, privatization and deregulation would attract investment in sufficient quantity to generate rapid output growth, which in turn would automatically create jobs of adequate quantity and quality.

It is now evident that economic growth, although necessary, by itself neither guarantees job creation nor automatically results in inclusive development.

This chapter proposes a policy framework that links investment with growth and employment creation to generate inclusive and sustainable development. The framework is based on the premise that the employment creation potential of growth will not be maximized without the development of productive capacities.

build the competencies needed to produce goods and services but that is also sufficiently focused to identify priority areas for policies.

What is meant by productive capacities? At UNCTAD, the development of the concept in the LDC context was linked to earlier efforts to understand how structurally weak and underdeveloped economies like LDCs should promote economic growth and how they should initiate and then accelerate the growth process. Such efforts also sought to understand what are the key factors or capabilities that enable such economies to produce goods they can consume or sell, and what kinds of productive activities create quality jobs that contribute to poverty reduction.

The analytical work carried out at UNCTAD in search of answers to these questions led to the identification of a number of basic elements of productive capacity (LDCR 2006). Productive capacities are the productive resources, entrepreneurial capabilities and production linkages which together determine a country's capacity to produce goods and services and enable it to grow and develop.

Productive resources are factors of production and include natural resources, human resources, financial capital and physical capital.

Entrepreneurial capabilities are the skills, technology, knowledge and information needed to mobilize resources in order to build domestic enterprises that transform inputs into outputs — outputs that can competitively meet present and future demand. They also include abilities to invest, innovate, upgrade and create goods and services. As such, they refer to the competencies and technological learning needed to induce economic change.

Production linkages are flows of goods and services in the form of backward and forward linkages, flows of information and knowledge and flows of productive resources among enterprises and sectors or activities.

These three elements together determine not only the overall capacity of a country to produce goods and services, but also which goods and services a country can produce and sell. In this respect, productive capacities are country-specific and differ enormously from one country to the other. They also determine the quantity and the quality of the goods and services which a country can produce at a given time. Such potential production is obviously limited in the short term, but could be expanded in the medium and long term.

Based on this notion of productive capacity, a country's productive capacities are developing when that country shows improvements or progress in all these areas — when, in other words, its productive resources are expanding, it is acquiring technological and entrepreneurial capabilities and it is also creating production linkages. All of these improvements will enable the country to produce a growing array of goods and services and to create jobs and integrate beneficially into the global economy on the basis of an internal growth momentum. If this type of development continues, then the country will have productive capacities which enable it to create jobs that pay higher wages and to acquire the capability needed to produce an increasing range of higher value added goods and services both efficiently and competitively.

The development of productive capacities occurs through three closely related core economic processes that all countries have to undergo if they are to achieve sustained development. These are: the investment necessary to build domestic capital stock (physical capital, human capital, and so forth), which economists refer to as capital accumulation; structural change (or structural transformation); and building the capabilities of the domestic enterprise sector.

Economic growth which does not create decent jobs in sufficient quantity is unsustainable, and job creation without the development of productive capacities is equally unsustainable.

Productive capacities are the productive resources, entrepreneurial capabilities and production linkages which together determine a country's capacity to produce goods and services and enable it to grow and develop.

The development of productive capacities occurs through three closely related core economic processes: the investment necessary to build domestic capital stock (physical capital, human capital, and so forth), which economists refer to as capital accumulation; structural change (or structural transformation); and building the capabilities of the domestic enterprise sector.

Efforts to meet the employment challenge in the LDCs will have to involve finding concrete ways to link the development of productive capacities with employment creation. The policy framework proposed here is intended to contribute to thinking about how this might be done, given the specific conditions of a typical LDC. The main novelty in the framework is that it explicitly links employment creation with the three processes through which productive capacities develop. It also links capital accumulation to employment through the investment-growth-employment nexus, links technological progress to employment through enterprise development and links structural change to employment through the three-pronged approach to employment creation (chart 35).

The main novelty in the framework is that it explicitly links employment creation with the three processes through which productive capacities develop.

This new policy orientation puts employment creation at the heart of economic policies at the macro, meso and micro levels. It also involves going beyond recent efforts to improve investment climate in the LDCs and proposes a more active role for the State, including, but not limited to, public investment.

This new policy orientation puts employment creation at the heart of economic policies at the macro, meso and micro levels.

As concerns capital accumulation, the new element is that policies are understood not only in terms of stimulating investment-growth nexus but also as adding employment as a third and integral element of the nexus. Thus, for policymakers in LDCs, the primary goal of capital accumulation is to promote growth with employment. This has implications for the manner in which resources are mobilized and investment decisions are taken. The critical entry point in creating a strong and sustainable investment-growth-employment nexus is investment. The aim — initially through public investment in priority areas (in particular infrastructure) — is to set in motion a virtuous circle where investment boosts growth and growth creates employment. The latter in turn generates increased income for workers, giving rise to consumption that supports the expansion of aggregate demand. Import leakages apart, employment-creating growth also creates incentives for new or additional investment to meet the growing demand, and this cycle can be repeated at a higher level of investment, growth, employment and income.

Chart 35. Policy framework for linking development of productive capacities with employment creation in LDCs

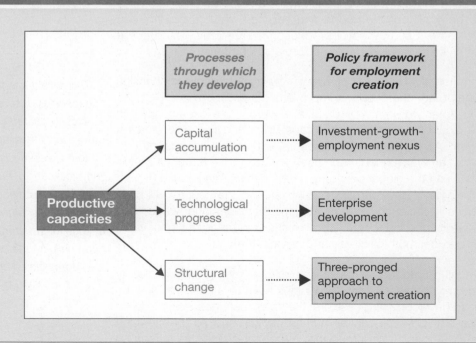

Source: UNCTAD secretariat, adapted from UNCTAD (2006), chart 8 (p.63).

The policy framework also assigns greater importance to development of firms and farms of all sizes, thanks to their potential role in contributing to growth, creating productive capacities and generating jobs for both unskilled and skilled workers. According to the policy framework, policies to encourage micro and small firms to upgrade their production capacity and to grow in scale are needed. Moreover, it proposes the adoption of active policies to influence technological choice in different types of activities. The differentiation of the types of technology choice and corresponding policies is required in order to accommodate the frequently conflicting policy goals of technological progress and employment creation.

In terms of structural change, the challenge for LDCs is not that their economic structure is static, but rather that in most cases it is changing in a manner not conducive to building productive capacities and creating quality jobs in sufficient quantity. In order to position the LDCs' economies on a job-rich inclusive development path, the policy framework recommends a three-pronged approach to employment creation that focuses on the generation of foreign exchange through investment in both capital- and labour-intensive tradable activities; the expansion of non-tradables sector and the concomitant creation of jobs; and productivity improvement in agriculture in general, and subsistence agriculture in particular.

Given that processes of capital accumulation, technological progress and structural change are closely interrelated (UNCTAD, 2006), different aspects of the framework for maximizing employment are also interrelated. For example, a transformation of productive structures into more skilled and technology-intensive production systems consistent with higher value added activities will also result in higher incomes, thus fuelling demand and stimulating new investment. Capital accumulation, in turn, will help develop new activities and diversify the economy away from traditional sectors, further stimulating the process of structural change. A framework for maximizing employment might use that insight in order to intensify these synergies and to adopt a set of policies that do not contradict one another. For example, if the policies that are part of the three-pronged approach to employment creation succeed in making wage goods cheap, that would have a very beneficial impact on the investment-growth-employment nexus.

The next three sections of this chapter explain each element of the framework in more detail.

B. Investing to develop productive capacities: capital accumulation

1. Capital accumulation and the role of the investment-growth-employment nexus

Capital accumulation is the process whereby investment increases various kinds of capital stock: physical capital, human resources, financial capital and natural resources. The patterns and sources of investment mobilization, and the policies applied to guide the investment process, have a direct impact on the type of growth achieved and its impact on employment. Capital accumulation is often seen as a function of private agents in an economy, and in fact the private sector accounts for the bulk of capital accumulation, except for human capital accumulation. However, historically and even in today's developed economies, the State has played and continues to play significant roles, both in creating

The policy framework also assigns greater importance to development of firms and farms of all sizes, thanks to their potential role in contributing to growth, creating productive capacities and generating jobs for both unskilled and skilled workers.

In order to position the LDCs' economies on a job-rich inclusive development path, the policy framework recommends a three-pronged approach to employment creation.

Capital accumulation is the process whereby investment increases various kinds of capital stock: physical capital, human resources, financial capital and natural resources.

A strong investment-growth-employment nexus in LDCs requires the involvement of a developmental State.

The successful cases of long-term economic growth have invariably been associated with investment rates of 25 per cent or more.

an enabling environment for capital accumulation in the private sector and in directly engaging in capital accumulation. The need for a substantial State role is even more evident in LDCs, since the institutions which facilitate and foster active private corporate involvement tend to be less developed and since private agents themselves often do not operate on the scale required for large investments. This means that a strong investment-growth-employment nexus in LDCs requires the involvement of a developmental State.[1]

As has already been noted, the policies pursued by the LDCs in the past two decades were based on the assumption that a market-friendly environment would attract private investment in sufficient quantity to generate rapid output growth, which, in turn, would automatically create sufficient jobs of adequate quality. Exceptionally buoyant external conditions for LDC exports — in the form of the global commodity boom, strong external demand and ample external financing – did result in higher GDP growth in the 2000s. That, in turn, led to some increased investment, including, and in some cases mainly, by foreign firms. The investment ratio of LDCs (i.e., gross fixed capital formation as a share of GDP) rose from 18.5 per cent to 21.8 per cent between 2000–2001 and 2010–2011[2] — the highest level in over 40 years. As a result, LDCs managed to narrow the gap between their investment ratio and that of other developing countries, where the ratio stood at 23.5 per cent at the end of the period (chart 36).[3]

Although these are very positive developments, two aspects give rise to concern. First, the increase in the LDCs' investment ratio still falls short of the level typically required for developing countries to sustain high growth rates over long periods. The successful cases of long-term economic growth (i.e., growth sustained over 30 years or more) since the mid-twentieth century have invariably been associated with investment rates of 25 per cent or more (Spence, 2011). In other words, even during the boom period the LDCs as a group did not attain the desired rate of investment. This means that reaching these levels may prove even more challenging in the coming period, when growth will likely be slower than during the boom period of 2002–2008.

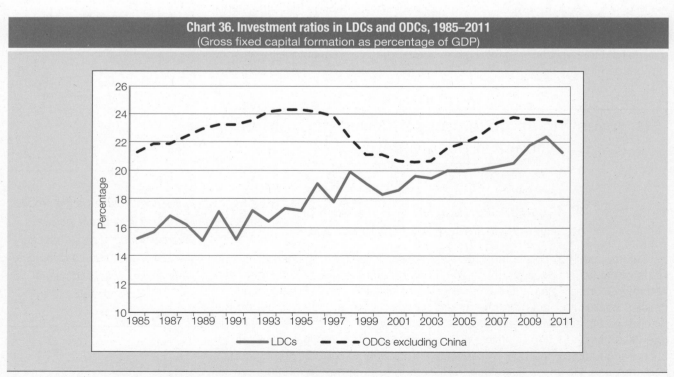

Chart 36. Investment ratios in LDCs and ODCs, 1985–2011
(Gross fixed capital formation as percentage of GDP)

Source: UNCTAD secretariat calculations, based on UNCTADstat database, June 2013.

The second and equally important cause for concern about the LDCs' investment patterns is the type of capital formation that took place. The pursuit of export-led growth, coupled with policies to attract FDI, resulted in a type of investment that primarily targeted their extractive industries. As the data presented in chapter 1 demonstrate, the share of non-manufacturing industrial activities in GDP (mining and quarrying, electricity, gas, water and sanitary services, and construction) in the LDCs as a group rose from 14.5 per cent of GDP in 1999–2001 to 22 per cent in 2009–2011. The problem is that those investments were mostly capital-intensive, with small employment effects. So the relatively high rates of economic growth were not accompanied by the expected employment creation. The boom was thus characterized by jobless growth in many LDCs.

This experience underlines the need for a policy framework in which the primary goal of capital accumulation in the LDCs is to promote growth with employment. This can be achieved by establishing an investment-growth-employment nexus as a virtuous cycle in which investment boosts growth, growth creates productive employment, productive employment generates an expansion of aggregate demand, and the expansion of aggregate demand creates incentives for new investment (chart 37). Obviously, supportive public policies are required both to set this virtuous cycle in motion and to ensure that it becomes self-sustaining. If these policies are successful, the process feeds new rounds at higher and higher levels of GDP per capita, simultaneously providing employment and accelerated capital accumulation.

The emphasis in this approach is on both aggregate supply and aggregate demand, as well as on their interplay. Both of them are needed in order to achieve a dynamic economic growth that increases the level of employment. This is due to the close interconnectedness of aggregate supply and aggregate demand. For example, rapid growth in aggregate demand can have positive supply-side effects due to productivity gains generated by dynamic economies

The primary goal of capital accumulation in the LDCs is to promote growth with employment by establishing an investment-growth-employment nexus as a virtuous cycle in which investment boosts growth, growth creates productive employment, productive employment generates an expansion of aggregate demand, and the expansion of aggregate demand creates incentives for new investment.

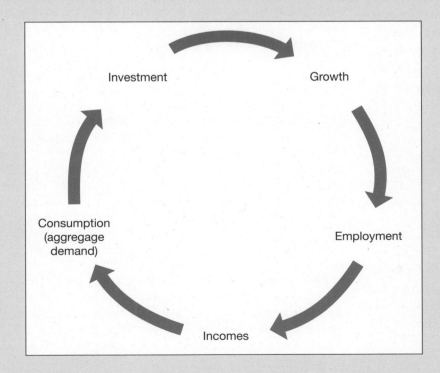

Chart 37. The investment-growth-employment nexus in a closed economy

Investment

Growth

Employment

Incomes

Consumption (aggregage demand)

Source: UNCTAD secretariat.

of scale and the increased use of underutilized resources. Since underutilization of labour is one of the main characteristics of LDC economies, there are ample possibilities to put such a nexus in motion. Rapid growth of employment, in turn, increases incomes and fuels consumption, boosting aggregate demand.

The nexus depicted in chart 37 can work in a perfect manner only in a closed economy where there are no transactions with the rest of the world. In an open economy, however, the functioning of the nexus is weakened. Import leakages reduce the domestic demand effects of income growth. The problem of import leakage is usually acute in LDCs, where local manufacturing production is often poorly developed and where most activities do not operate at scales that ensure some degree of international competitiveness. It is clear that if incomes are spent mainly on imported goods, the incentive to invest in production for the domestic market diminishes or disappears. Similarly, intermediate goods industries are unlikely to emerge or expand if the production process itself requires components that at present cannot be produced locally. Broadly speaking, the best strategy for reducing import leakage is to develop productive capacities, but considerable time is needed for that process to produce results. There are, however, short-term policies for reducing leakages and making the nexus more effective. Some of these are discussed in the following chapter.

> *The most pragmatic approach would be to start to stimulate the process of capital accumulation via that nexus in the non-tradables sector.*

Given that most LDCs are very open economies, they will be unable to put the nexus in motion in the whole economy. However, the non-tradables sector is still relatively insulated, and policy space there is larger than in other parts of the economy. Initially, therefore, the most pragmatic approach would be to start to stimulate the process of capital accumulation via that nexus in the non-tradables sector. Over time, and as domestic firms develop their technological and learning capabilities, the nexus can be extended to modern services that have become tradable because of technological innovations, import substitution activities and exporting activities.

> *The critical links in this nexus are not only those which involve jump-starting investment, but also those which ensure that the resulting production process is associated with higher employment.*

While the nexus in chart 37 is the desired process, it is evident from recent experience that not all investment (even investment that results in higher growth) generates higher employment levels. The critical links in this chain are not only those which involve jump-starting investment, but also those which ensure that the resulting production process is associated with higher employment. A major challenge, therefore, is how to promote and encourage the kind of investment that spurs employment-intensive growth.

Two factors are crucial in that regard.

> *Different types of economic activities are associated with diverse levels of employment intensity. A major policy implication is that policy interventions have to be designed to encourage investment in activities with the strongest employment effects.*

First, policymakers should be aware that different types of economic activities are associated with diverse levels of employment intensity. For example, services are generally more intensive in their use of the labour force than are activities in the extractive industries. Thus, if investment in activities which are more employment-intensive is promoted, the resulting GDP growth will also be more employment-intensive. If, on the other hand, the investment is directed primarily into extractive industries, it is highly likely that the intensity of employment will be low. A major policy implication is that policy interventions have to be designed to encourage investment in activities with the strongest employment effects.

Second, technology choices can increase or reduce the employment intensity of production. The choice of technology often creates a conflict between the objective of achieving competitiveness by acquiring advanced technology (which invariably tends to be capital-intensive) and the objective of creating decent jobs in sufficient quantity. These issues are discussed further in section C.

> *An additional policy challenge is to ensure that the virtuous cycle, once it is on track, remains in motion and becomes sustainable.*

An additional policy challenge is to ensure that the virtuous cycle, once it is on track, remains in motion and becomes sustainable. This issue is closely related to policies of distribution in the national economy. As emphasized in UNCTAD (2010, page 87), "the ability to achieve sustained growth of income and employment on the basis of productivity growth depends critically on how the resulting gains are distributed within the economy, how much additional wage income is spent for the consumption of domestically produced goods and services, and whether higher profits are used for investment in activities that simultaneously create more employment, including in some service sectors, such as the delivery of health and education".

In a typical LDC context, a continuous increase in domestic demand for wage goods is a major precondition for the nexus to work and to become sustainable. This will provide incentives for domestic food production, for local provision of basic services and for engaging in import-substituting activities. If local producers can count on a steady demand for their goods and services, they will be induced to increase supply, which will in turn encourage further investment and facilitate the growth of domestic enterprises.

There are accordingly two key requirements for a sustainable virtuous cycle: employment-intensive activities must be sufficiently profitable, and improvements in labour productivity must be translated into increases in wages. Adequate profitability is necessary for further investment and increased supply, while a growth of wages is a prerequisite for buoyant demand.

Other equally important elements essential for the nexus to work in the long term include an enabling policy and regulatory environment and appropriate macroeconomic policies, as follows.

First, enabling conditions (a business-friendly environment) are needed to encourage private sector development, which is essential for generating decent employment in sufficient quantity. The specific policies for promoting private sector development in both the short and the long term are discussed in chapter 5.

As already noted, in view of the weak private sector in LDCs, in the short term the State will have to play a more prominent role in mobilizing and initiating the investment needed to kick-start the virtuous cycle. While its role in the current "good governance" agenda is to support markets rather than to promote economic development directly, UNCTAD has long advocated injecting a much stronger and more direct development dimension into governance reforms so as to enable a more active role of the State in promoting LDC development (UNCTAD, 2009).

Second, macroeconomic policies should be appropriate to the task at hand. The prevailing policy framework in the LDCs of the past 20 years did not consider employment as an important macroeconomic objective. Rather, it focused on such intermediate variables as price stability, fiscal balance and, sometimes, external balance. These were seen as having an intrinsic value in their own right and were considered to be principal targets of macroeconomic policies. The instruments that were deemed sufficient for achieving these goals were monetary and fiscal policy.

The policy framework proposed in this chapter argues that the focus should instead be on "real macroeconomics".[4] It considers the development of productive capacity and the deployment of labour and capital at their highest potential level to be the paramount goals for policymakers in LDCs. The focus of development policies in these countries should accordingly be on the long-term sustainability and inclusiveness of growth, rather than on intermediate goals, such as price stability. The point here is not to deny the importance of price stability. To the contrary, controlling the rate of inflation is as critical for LDCs

In a typical LDC context, a continuous increase in domestic demand for wage goods is a major precondition for the nexus to work and to become sustainable. This will provide incentives for domestic food production, for local provision of basic services and for engaging in import-substituting activities.

There are two key requirements for a sustainable virtuous cycle: employment-intensive activities must be sufficiently profitable, and improvements in labour productivity must be translated into increases in wages.

Macroeconomic policies should be appropriate to the task at hand.

The focus should be on the development of productive capacity and the deployment of labour and capital at their highest potential level.

as it is for developed economies. It is, however, important not to confuse the means with the ends, and not to forget that poverty reduction and a higher standard of living for the population are the immediate and also the ultimate goals of economic policymaking for the LDCs. In short, all policy choices involve tradeoffs, and policymakers must be aware of them and carefully weigh the benefits and costs in implementing each policy. As discussed in chapter 5, LDCs may need to consider a mix of policies that go beyond the traditional monetary and fiscal policy focus. It is clear, however, that if the broader goal of LDCs is to create more quality jobs than they have done in the past two decades, then fiscal policy will have to play a central role in driving the public investment-led growth process (McKinley and Martins, 2010).

A further relevant factor is the difference in the objectives and role of macroeconomic policies between developed countries and the LDCs. The main challenge in the former is the underutilization of existing resources, which is often influenced by business cycles. In developing countries, by contrast, the problem is the deficiency of productive capacities. Supply constraints in the LDCs are much greater than in developed countries. The LDCs often face two serious constraints on growth: a shortage of domestic savings, and a lack of foreign exchange. The resulting dependence on foreign sources of financing produces a much more pronounced economic volatility than is generally found in developed countries. Moreover, the nature of growth is different. In developed countries it is primarily the result of technological progress and its introduction into the broader economy. In many developing countries, and the LDCs in particular, growth is more often than not the result of a shift of resources from less productive activities like subsistence agriculture to more productive ones like manufacturing; of investing in physical capital; and of introducing activities and technologies that were previously developed in more advanced economies (Stiglitz et al., 2006). For all these reasons, when LDC policymakers consider the range of macroeconomic policies that they deem appropriate for their circumstances, they need to bear in mind these systematic differences between developed economies and their own countries, and choose policies that will help them tackle their specific problems.

2. The nexus in the short term: the primary role of the public sector

The starting point of the nexus should be policies that promote the types of investment which spur employment-intensive growth. Investment can come from both domestic and foreign sources. In many LDCs, foreign investment has been largely concentrated in extractive industries, which are mostly capital-intensive with limited potential for job creation and which typically have few linkages to other local sectors that could generate more jobs. Relying on foreign investment to provide employment-intensive growth is thus not the best option.

Domestic investment can be either private or public. Given the relatively weak development of the private sector in many LDCs, the primary investment push should come from the public sector in the short to medium term. In these countries, which usually have small domestic markets, the private sector may lack the incentive to invest unless the State expands its expenditure through public capital formation. This is especially true of public investment in infrastructure. An expanded supply of infrastructure services tends to create externalities for the private sector that can make its investment profitable.

From the standpoint of long-term economic growth, public investment in infrastructure has the effect of raising living standards and inducing higher-productivity growth (Rodríguez, 2007). In the short term, public investment

---

It is important not to confuse the means with the ends, and not to forget that poverty reduction and a higher standard of living for the population are the immediate and also the ultimate goals of economic policymaking for the LDCs.

When LDC policymakers consider the range of macroeconomic policies that they deem appropriate for their circumstances, they need to bear in mind systematic differences between developed economies and their own countries, and choose policies that will help them tackle their specific problems.

The starting point of the nexus should be policies that promote the types of investment which spur employment-intensive growth.

Given the relatively weak development of the private sector in many LDCs, the primary investment push should come from the public sector.

also directly increases the demand for private sector products, because of the purchases made by the State. In addition, it generates indirect demand because of the employment created by public expenditure and the multiplier effects of such expenditure. Public spending also generates more employment and domestic demand, thereby kick-starting macroeconomic processes that can eventually create enhanced supply as well.

Public investment can play a major role in increasing growth and domestic employment, both over the cycle and in the medium term, by increasing demand in the short term and enlarging the capital base of the economy. The nature, direction and efficacy of such investment are important, as the multiplier effects and long-term growth implications will differ accordingly. Nonetheless, it is still important to be attentive to other structural features, such as technology choice and institutional conditions, and to create incentives within the economy for more productive employment generation.

Public investment can be designed to encourage certain types of private investment, not to crowd them out. By providing key infrastructure, public investment can turn previously uneconomical private investments into profitable ones. Public investment in rail transport, roads, and airport and port facilities can lower the cost of private sector involvement in almost all economic activities. As energy and water become available thanks to public investment, private businesses can count on a steady supply of these vital inputs and expand their operations as well as upgrading technologically. Better infrastructure is also crucial for attracting foreign investors, increasing a country's chances of becoming a market for FDI.

As to the duration of strong public sector involvement, it is important to ensure that public sector investment plays the crucial role of providing an impulse to the virtuous cycle in the short term. In the long term, private sector should have the primary role in the nexus. The public sector can then influence the process of capital accumulation within the nexus indirectly by creating incentives for investment in certain types of activities.

Apart from the theoretical considerations, the critical role of public investment is confirmed by the empirical evidence from successful developing and developed economies that have had sustained catch-up growth over the long term. All these countries invariably had public investment rates on the order of 7 per cent of GDP or higher (Spence, 2011).

The evidence for Africa[5] suggests that investment in infrastructure should be scaled up significantly. The World Bank estimates the cost for redressing Africa's infrastructure deficit at $38 billion worth of investment per year. An additional $37 billion per year would be needed for operations and maintenance activities. Hence, the overall price tag would be on the order of $75 billion per annum. The total required spending translates into some 12 per cent of Africa's GDP. There is currently a funding gap of $35 billion per year. Since most LDCs are in Africa, it is evident that the LDCs lag far behind other developing countries in terms of infrastructure and that their investment needs are of a similar order of magnitude.

While the theoretical discussion on the crowding-in and crowding-out effects of public investment in infrastructure may continue for many years, the simple fact that the LDCs have a huge gap in infrastructure suggests that pragmatic solutions are needed. Since the private sector has been unable to fill that gap after more than two decades of market-friendly policies to facilitate private sector involvement, there is clearly a role for the public sector in filling the gap. In other words, crowding out the private sector will not happen if the public sector undertakes investment which the private sector itself is reluctant to make. Given

Public investment can play a major role in increasing growth and domestic employment, both over the cycle and in the medium term, by increasing demand and enlarging the capital base of the economy.

Public investment can be designed to encourage certain types of private investment, not to crowd them out. By providing key infrastructure, public investment can turn previously uneconomical private investments into profitable ones.

It is important to ensure that public sector investment plays the crucial role of providing an impulse to the virtuous cycle in the short term. In the long term, private sector should have the primary role in the nexus.

The simple fact that the LDCs have a huge gap in infrastructure suggests that pragmatic solutions are needed.

these unmet needs, it seems that only the State has the capacity to mobilize capital and increase the investment in infrastructure in the LDCs.

Indeed, recent trends suggest that this shift may already be under way in many LDCs. The World Bank data show that public gross fixed capital formation (public investment) for the group of 38 LDCs[6] on average stood at 7.2 per cent of GDP over the period 1999–2001. Ten years later (2009–2011), public investment reached on average 8.8 per cent of GDP. The boom period thus resulted not only in higher GDP growth in the LDCs, but also in an increase of the share of public investment in GDP. Given that both the share of public investment in GDP and GDP itself increased during that period, the absolute value of public investment is now substantially higher than in the early 2000s. The commodity boom of the past decade was very likely the main source of the increase in public revenue, which, in turn, made possible the increase of public investment.

Public gross fixed capital formation (public investment) for the group of 38 LDCs on average stood at 7.2 per cent of GDP over the period 1999–2001. Ten years later (2009–2011), it reached on average 8.8 per cent of GDP.

While the sectors to which public investment should be directed will necessarily be country-specific, investment in infrastructure seems to be a natural starting point since the lack of adequate infrastructure in most LDCs represents a serious supply-side bottleneck. Government policies should try to remove that bottleneck and at the same time create jobs. Both goals can be achieved using the factor of production that is more abundant, namely labour. This will depend on reorienting policies on infrastructure investment to ensure that technically viable and cost-effective, employment-intensive options are used instead of more capital-intensive ones. In other words, there is a need for adopting appropriate technology.

While the sectors to which public investment should be directed will necessarily be country-specific, investment in infrastructure seems to be a natural starting point since the lack of adequate infrastructure represents a serious supply-side bottleneck.

Social services are another strong candidate for public involvement aimed at increasing employment by kick-starting the investment-growth-employment nexus. Millions of LDC citizens still have very poor or inadequate access to the most basic conditions of decent life, such as nutrition, sanitation, electricity, water, transport and communication, health services and education. The role of the State is to provide minimally acceptable standards of living for everyone in the LDCs. Social policy is important and desirable not only in its own right, but also because it contributes to employment creation. To meet the basic needs of the majority of the population, there are ample opportunities for public sector to influence the urbanization process and help provide urban services. These are mostly labour-intensive and can generate numerous jobs. They can also increase the disposable income of households, which tends to reduce the precautionary savings of the lower- and middle-income groups, thus boosting their purchasing power (UNCTAD, 2013). Other sectors that can be targeted because of their potential to create employment are construction, expansion of services in rural areas, textile and leather production, and food processing.

Social services are another strong candidate for public involvement aimed at increasing employment by kick-starting the investment-growth-employment nexus.

In view of the recent increase of public investment in the LDCs, the proposals in this chapter may be interpreted as advocating the redirection of such investment into sectors and activities with greater employment creation, rather than proposing a large increase in public investment. In that sense, for some LDCs, the issue of financing may not be daunting. However, the LDCs are not a homogenous group. For some of them, public finances have been invigorated by rents from extractive industries, but for others the financing of public investment may pose a major problem. For many of these countries, fiscal space constraints will continue to make it difficult to finance the desired level of public investment, which underscores the importance of efforts to mobilize additional fiscal resources. Given the relatively low share of public revenue in GDP in most LDCs, improving domestic resource mobilization may be the best way to place the financing of public investment on sounder footing. This can be done by strengthening fiscal revenues through tax reforms and by making tax collection and administration more efficient.

In view of the recent increase of public investment in the LDCs, the proposals in this chapter may be interpreted as advocating the redirection of such investment into sectors and activities with greater employment creation, rather than proposing a large increase in public investment.

Going beyond the budgetary sources for financing public investment involves some sort of borrowing. Many LDCs receive ODA in the form of grants and conditional lending, which enables them to finance significant public investments. Despite recent decrease in aid disbursements from OECD-DAC countries, ODA will continue to be a key source for financing for most LDCs. Innovative sources of financing based on a steady flow of workers' remittances could also be explored. UNCTAD (2012) considered using remittances as collateral for long-term syndicated loans, issuing bonds securitized by future flows of remittances and issuing so-called "diaspora" bonds. Thus, there are options for financing public investment; the issue is which option or combination of options is the best at any given moment for a particular country.

3. THE NEXUS IN THE LONG TERM: THE PRIMARY ROLE OF THE PRIVATE SECTOR

Making the process sustainable in the long term will entail reducing the heavy involvement of the public sector over time and stimulating the private sector to assume a steadily greater role in the process of capital accumulation. It follows that the role of the developmental State should be not only to provide investment that spurs employment-intensive growth, but also to help create a vibrant and strong private sector.[7] This should ultimately be the target of LDC policymakers with regard to capital accumulation.

The efforts of the developmental State to steer the economy towards a jobs-rich path should aim at creating and managing rents in line with the objectives of inclusive growth. When designing policies to spur employment-intensive growth, policymakers should bear in mind the dual functions of both profits and wages in a capitalist economy. Profits are a major incentive for investment (since investment results in profits) and a main source of investment. For that reason a strong investment-profits nexus in which businesses constantly reinvest their profits would accelerate the process of capital accumulation. Policies that reinforce the nexus therefore promote and accelerate capital accumulation, and with it the development of productive capacities. A key determinant of the willingness of entrepreneurs to invest in real productive capacity is the expected profitability of a potential investment. This in turn depends on estimates as to whether future demand will be sufficient to permit the full utilization of additional capacity (UNCTAD, 2013).

However, not all activities result in capital accumulation that enables net job creation. Government policies should accordingly try to reduce the possibilities for wealth accumulation through large landholdings, moneylending and real estate speculation, since they have very limited job-creating effects. Instead, they should promote wealth accumulation through investment in employment-intensive productive sectors. High profit in these sectors will simultaneously increase both the incentives for enterprises to invest and their capacity to finance new investment from profits. High profitability of targeted activities can be created with such policy instruments as selective and time-bound protection, close monitoring of interest rates and credit allocation, and fiscal instruments. Policymakers could, for example, use such fiscal instruments as tax breaks and special depreciation allowances to create incentives for reinvestment of profits.

Similarly, wages are a major determinant of both production costs and consumption, and thus of aggregate demand. Government policies should accordingly ensure that wage increases keep pace with increases in labour productivity and that the income share of labour in GDP does not fall. If this does not happen, the stimulus for wage-driven consumption and aggregate demand may weaken over time, eventually diminishing the incentive to reinvest profits. Policymakers should also try to lower the prices of wage goods, as explained

Making the process sustainable in the long term will entail reducing the heavy involvement of the public sector over time and stimulating the private sector to assume a steadily greater role in the process of capital accumulation.

The role of the developmental State should be not only to provide investment that spurs employment-intensive growth, but also to help create a vibrant and strong private sector.

The efforts of the developmental State to steer the economy towards a jobs-rich path should aim at creating and managing rents in line with the objectives of inclusive growth.

A strong investment-profits nexus in which businesses constantly reinvest their profits would accelerate the process of capital accumulation.

in section D of this chapter. That would on the one hand keep wage costs for enterprises low, thereby ensuring high profits, and on the other hand provide workers with sufficient income to increase consumption and thus stimulate aggregate demand. Ultimately, more jobs will be created in the nexus where new jobs and higher real wages boost the purchasing power of households and push up domestic demand.

More jobs will be created in the nexus where new jobs and higher real wages boost the purchasing power of households and push up domestic demand.

Whether or not aggregate demand rises sufficiently to create net employment depends crucially on the distribution of gains from productivity growth, which in turn is greatly influenced by policy choices (UNCTAD, 2010). Profits and wages, in other words, determine domestic consumption and domestic investment. They, like government expenditure, are all sources of domestic demand, and there is a marked interdependence among the three. While the interdependence of consumption and investment has already been explained, it should be added that higher public spending has a positive impact on both private consumption and private investment by creating additional income for consumers and by improving the conditions for private investment (UNCTAD, 2013). Since the last component of aggregate demand — net exports — is mainly determined exogenously in the short term, policymakers can influence only the endogenous factors, namely, domestic consumption, domestic investment and government expenditure. Policies that influence distributional outcomes in the economy are thus an important component of making the investment-growth-employment nexus work. They are endogenous to the growth process and are one of the determinants of how capital accumulation takes place and how productive capacities develop.

Policies that influence distributional outcomes in the economy are an important component of making the investment-growth-employment nexus work.

Whether or not the investment-growth-employment nexus can be put in motion will depend primarily on the extent to which the sectoral structure of domestic production is linked to that of domestic demand. In larger, more closed economies, the two are relatively closely linked. In smaller, open economies, on the other hand — as in primary commodity exporters — domestic production is largely delinked from that of domestic demand (UNCTAD, 2013). In other words, there is a big gap between what these countries produce and what they consume. Thus, creating the nexus will be easier or more complicated, depending, inter alia, on the structure of domestic production vis-à-vis the structure of domestic demand. This is one of the reasons why it is important to consider how this framework can be adapted to the specific conditions of different LDCs, as examined in Section E of this chapter.

4. FORMATION OF HUMAN CAPITAL

Capital accumulation also encompasses the formation of human capital, which is achieved mainly through formal education (at the primary, secondary and tertiary levels), technical and vocational training, and on-the-job training. The bulk of formal and vocational training is financed by the State in both developed and developing countries. Education, vocational training and upgrading of workers' skills are thus key elements of government policies.

Capital accumulation also encompasses the formation of human capital, which is achieved mainly through formal education (at the primary, secondary and tertiary levels), technical and vocational training, and on-the-job training.

Human capital formation has received increasing attention since the 1990s as the development community has become more aware of the importance of human capital for long-term growth and development in developing countries. Consequently, greater focus has been placed on expanding spending on health and education in these countries, including the LDCs. This has been reinforced by the prominence given to education and health in the human development discourse (reflected inter alia in the Human Development Index of the United Nations Development Programme (UNDP)) and the MDGs. A critical consequence of this focus on human capital in developing countries has been the consistent increase in donor financing of health and education. Total ODA commitments to the two areas in the LDCs soared from $2 billion in 1995–1996 to $7.8 billion in 2010–2011.[8] This has been accompanied by a growing allocation of national budgets to these areas, financed mainly by domestically mobilized resources.

Increased spending on education has led to continuous improvements in the LDCs' educational progress, which has allowed them to narrow the gap with other developing countries, particularly in primary education. The school enrolment ratio improved substantially between 1995 and 2010 at the primary, secondary and tertiary levels in the LDCs. Primary school enrolment has become almost universal, and the gap between LDCs and ODCs has virtually been closed (table 19).

Increased spending on education has led to continuous improvements in the LDCs' educational progress, which has allowed them to narrow the gap with other developing countries, particularly in primary education.

Although these positive quantitative developments have to be weighed against the quality of schooling and education, the result is that human capital accumulation has been accelerating in the LDCs. In principle this means that LDC populations are gradually becoming more prepared for the requirements of a modern production process, i.e., better skilled and more adaptable. A more educated labour force is more productive, learns more easily, is more open to new ideas and technologies and adapts more easily to new conditions. It also involves the presence of much better conditions than before for implementing the proposed policy framework. Since the ultimate goal is to create decent employment in sufficient numbers for all, the development of a dynamic private sector that can meet that goal will be greatly facilitated by the availability of a better educated and more adaptable labour force.

Despite these positive developments in education and training in LDCs, the issue of matching education and skills with available jobs — or what is often described as the "employability" of the labour force — is emerging as a key concern. The recent increase in LDCs' tertiary enrolment is certainly to be welcomed, but a significant part of that increase has occurred in private institutions with much higher user fees. Many students, including those from relatively poor families, invest a great deal of their own and their families' resources in order to acquire an education that holds out the promise of a better life.

LDC populations are gradually becoming more prepared for the requirements of a modern production process, i.e., better skilled and more adaptable.

There are, however, two problems: an absolute shortage of formal sector jobs relative to demand, and a skills mismatch resulting in severe labour shortages for some kinds of workers and a massive oversupply of others. Often this is not in spite of, but because of, market forces, since both markets and

Table 19. Indicators of human capital formation in LDCs and ODCs, 1995 and 2011						
	Education level					
	Primary		Secondary		Tertiary	
	1995	2011	1995	2011	1995	2011
Gross enrolment ratio by education level (per cent)[a]						
LDCs	68.8	104.2	17.6	40.4	2.4	8.4
African LDCs and Haiti	62.8	103.1	14.0	34.4	1.6	5.8
Asian LDCs	93.0	108.7	30.6	50.7	4.6	12.5
Island LDCs	97.4	112.6	32.4	58.7	0.8	13.2
Other developing countries	104.8	109.0	50.9	71.1	8.4	23.5
Average years of schooling by education level[b]						
	1995	2010	1995	2010	1995	2010
LDCs	2.38	3.20	0.65	1.09	0.05	0.10
African LDCs and Haiti	2.46	3.24	0.62	1.01	0.03	0.08
Asian LDCs	2.15	3.07	0.75	1.34	0.09	0.17
Other developing countries	4.30	4.89	2.08	2.72	0.23	0.35

Source: UNCTAD Secretariat computations, based on data from World Bank, *World Development Indicators* online database (downloaded in August 2013), and data from the Barro-Lee dataset (Barro and Lee, 2013).

Notes: *a* Averages weighted according to school age population. Data refer to the inidcated year or to the closest year for which data are available; *b* Averages weighted by population. No data are available for island LDCs.

higher educational institutions tend to lag in their response to the demands of employers for some skills, and then to oversupply others. One result is that many young people are forced to take jobs that require less skills and training than they have actually received, and that are at lower levels than they might otherwise expect. This situation can create resentment and other forms of alienation, with adverse consequences for social stability. Another result is the emigration of qualified people — the so-called "brain drain" (UNCTAD, 2012). A special focus on employment policies for younger people and first-time job holders is therefore essential, as are labour market policies designed specifically to address these issues.

Looking ahead, the main principle behind educational policies for developing productive capacities should be to achieve some consistency with the future labour needs of the economy. Given that the educational process encompasses several years, today's students will be seeking jobs in 3, 5, or even 7 to 10 years' time. Some idea of where the economy as a whole is headed for the next five to ten years will thus be needed to guide the educational system on the future needs of the labour market. This would minimize the mismatch between the skills and the knowledge of labour market entrants and the needs of that market. It would also significantly aid the process of capital accumulation in the LDCs by providing domestic enterprises with adequately skilled labour market entrants.

C. Enterprise development and technological change

Enterprise development and technological progress are the second element of the policy framework for employment creation. As discussed earlier, enterprise development involves the development of productive capacities through entrepreneurial capabilities and technological progress. It is argued here that successful enterprise development will enable the LDCs to improve both the quantity and quality of employment creation and also embark on a technological catch-up with more developed countries. This was recognized in the IPoA (United Nations, 2011, para. 53), which emphasized that the private sector "is a key to sustained, inclusive and equitable economic growth and sustainable development in least developed countries".

Enterprise development is the process of building domestic production capacity through investment in new enterprises and technological progress and the introduction of new or improved goods and services; new or improved machinery, equipment and skills for production; and new or improved forms of organizing production. Ultimately, wealth is created by entrepreneurs who take the risk of borrowing capital in order to bring labour and technology together to produce goods or services for local and/or external markets. Whether countries succeed in developing dynamic and competitive enterprises depends to a large extent on the effectiveness of policies for mobilizing capital, creating virtuous supply and demand linkages, building the skills base of the economy, encouraging technological learning and the transfer of appropriate technology, and strengthening linkages.

The weakness of entrepreneurial capabilities has been identified as a major obstacle to the development of productive capacities (UNCTAD, 2006).[9] This weakness refers to the two main types of entrepreneurial capabilities. The first consists of core competencies, which are the routine knowledge, skills and information required to operate established facilities or use existing agricultural land, including production management, quality control, repair

---

A special focus on employment policies for younger people and first-time job holders is essential, as are labour market policies designed specifically to address these issues.

Some idea of where the economy as a whole is headed for the next five to ten years will be needed to guide the educational system on the future needs of the labour market.

The weakness of entrepreneurial capabilities has been identified as a major obstacle to the development of productive capacities.

Successful enterprise development will enable the LDCs to improve both the quantity and quality of employment creation and also embark on a technological catch-up with more developed countries.

and maintenance of physical capital, and marketing. The second comprises technological capabilities (or dynamic capabilities), which refer to the ability to build and reconfigure competencies to increase productivity, competitiveness and profitability, and to address the conditions of supply and demand in a changing external environment (UNCTAD, 2006: 64).[10] While enterprises are the locus of innovation and technological learning, they are embedded in a broader set of institutions that play a major role in these processes. These institutions are referred to as "domestic knowledge systems" that enable or constrain the creation, accumulation, use and sharing of knowledge (UNCTAD, 2007).

1. Enterprise development and the employment challenge: Firm size matters

In most LDCs the size distribution of enterprises is heavily skewed towards microenterprises and small enterprises, which typically operate in the informal sector. At the other extreme of the distribution are a small number of large firms, which are often either State-owned enterprises or large private firms, frequently owned or controlled by foreigners. These large firms tend to be found in the most profitable sectors, such as extractive industries, air transport and modern financial activities, where large size is needed to make capital-intensive investments. The "missing middle" refers to the weak or non-existent development of medium-sized domestic enterprises in the formal sector. In some cases even small-sized enterprises are rare in the formal sector of the economy. The missing middle in the LDCs — and in many other developing countries — is a result of the inability of small firms to grow and attain minimum efficient production sizes. Therefore, the dominance of large firms on the one hand, and the small size of most firms (the missing middle) on the other, partly explains the lack of formal sector job creation even during the recent boom period in the LDCs.

There are several reasons why microenterprises and small enterprises are unable to grow into middle-sized enterprises. Suboptimal size can be a constraint in itself, since it leads to lower productivity than that of larger firms, which affects profitability and makes it harder for small firms to expand the scale of production. Access to credit is another major issue, as small firms must often pay much higher interest rates even for working capital, let alone investment in fixed capital, and are constrained in the expansion of production even when there is sufficient demand for the goods or services they supply. These firms find it difficult to finance the acquisition of machinery and equipment and often cannot borrow for technology acquisition. They are also more exposed to various kinds of risk and market volatility. Weak technological capabilities and reduced access to knowledge are often combined with less developed organizational and managerial skills. All of this in turn encourages or even forces greater reliance of small enterprises on informal economic relations and family, kin or friendship networks, which only add to the legal and financial obstacles of becoming formal enterprises. As a result, they generally do not evolve into medium or large enterprises.

A typical feature of the LDCs in recent decades has been the expansion of low-productivity (informal) activities to absorb excess labour. Notwithstanding the difficulties of defining informal activities (which are also referred to as the "informal", "shadow" "parallel" or "underground" economy), they represent a substantial part of GDP. According to recent estimates, informal activities represent around 40.8 per cent of GDP in sub-Saharan Africa (Schneider et al., 2010). While the informal economy comprises a very heterogeneous group of activities in the LDCs, for the most part they can be characterized as subsistence activities. They enable those engaged in such activities to earn survival-level income at the cost of great hardship and sacrifice. The urban informal sector includes activities that rely on modern technology and generate as much income

In most LDCs the size distribution of enterprises is heavily skewed towards microenterprises and small enterprises, which typically operate in the informal sector.

The "missing middle" refers to the weak or non-existent development of medium-sized domestic enterprises in the formal sector.

A typical feature of the LDCs in recent decades has been the expansion of low-productivity (informal) activities to absorb excess labour.

as — if not more than — formal sector jobs — for example, the provision of IT-related services from home. However, the number of people engaged in such informal activities is relatively small.

Given that informal activities represent largely a survival strategy for the urban poor, they should be seen as traps from which workers seek to escape, rather than celebrated as evidence of the resilience of the poor. As suggested by the data presented in chapter 3, around 80 per cent of all employed in the LDCs are either self-employed or engaged in family work (unpaid work). The preponderance of microenterprises and small enterprises, and the large number of self-employed in the LDCs, points to a need for policies that will help enterprises grow in size, formalize and become capable of continuously upgrading their activities.

Policies aimed specifically at helping enterprises to grow in size can be divided into four categories: policies for formalizing firms, policies for financing firms, policies for strengthening the organizational and entrepreneurial capacities of firms, and policies for overcoming failures of information and cooperation (policies for encouraging networking and clustering). Some of these are discussed in greater detail in chapter 5. If successful, these policies will enable microenterprises and small enterprises to grow into medium-sized or even large enterprises. Their growth will in turn generate employment for large number of workers and will thus be employment-intensive. The simple reason for this is that in order to reach the optimal size of production, these enterprises need to increase the scale of production using existing production techniques. The benefits associated with economies of scale will then induce these firms to grow further. At the same time, the creation of medium-sized enterprises will lay the groundwork for technological progress. Once medium-sized enterprises have increased the scale of production beyond the optimal point using existing techniques, they will be forced to innovate so as to maintain their profitability.

2. TECHNOLOGICAL CHANGE AND THE EMPLOYMENT CHALLENGE: THE CHOICE OF TECHNOLOGY MATTERS

Technological change is the process of introducing new or improved goods and services, new or improved machinery, equipment and skills for production, and new or improved forms of organizing production. Technological change in the LDCs is associated primarily with the spread of new products, technologies and organizational strategies previously developed in more advanced economies. Its success depends on investments of various kinds (financial, organizational, educational, etc.) that lead to the development of competencies and capabilities at both the enterprise level and in society as a whole. In an open market environment, technological learning and upgrading by domestic enterprises is a prerequisite for becoming and remaining competitive in both domestic and external markets. Accordingly, successful economic development can be defined as the ability to create enterprises which are capable of learning and appropriating knowledge and in the longer term of generating new knowledge (Amsden, 2001). Hence, technological change in LDCs requires a greater capacity for learning and assimilation in domestic enterprises and the domestic knowledge system in which they are embedded.

Since technological learning and upgrading are critical for enterprise development and competitiveness, they will also have an impact on employment creation. The choice of technology is one of the most important determinants of the employment intensity of an economic activity. Modern technologies developed in advanced economies will be mainly of the labour-saving, capital-intensive type. The previous policy framework, which focused on the creation of the investment-growth nexus based on the open economy model, tended to

Given that informal activities represent largely a survival strategy for the urban poor, they should be seen as traps from which workers seek to escape, rather than celebrated as evidence of the resilience of the poor.

Policies aimed specifically at helping enterprises to grow in size can be divided into four categories: policies for formalizing firms, policies for financing firms, policies for strengthening the organizational and entrepreneurial capacities of firms, and policies for overcoming failures of information and cooperation.

Technological change is the process of introducing new or improved goods and services, new or improved machinery, equipment and skills for production, and new or improved forms of organizing production.

encourage investment in capital-intensive techniques in the extractive sectors. The result was limited learning and appropriation of know-how, and limited employment generation.

Yet another outcome of recent policies is the increased heterogeneity of technological development of sectors and firms in the LDCs. Most LDC economies have quite varied levels of technological development. At one end of the spectrum are the export sectors, which have to compete in international markets. Both the choice of technology and the rate of technological progress in these sectors are largely determined abroad and transmitted to the LDCs through the pressures of international competition and standards set in international value chains, rather than through domestic conditions. These pressures to adopt international technologies apply not only to exporters, but also to import-competing firms. Since enterprises whose products compete with imports are forced to be internationally competitive in order to maintain their domestic sales, technology choices (and capital-labour ratios) and other parameters of production are to a great extent determined exogenously.

Since technological learning and upgrading are critical for enterprise development and competitiveness, they will also have an impact on employment creation. The choice of technology is one of the most important determinants of the employment intensity of an economic activity.

This type of international integration leads to the adoption by LDCs of technologies that are not very far from the international technology frontier in their respective sectors and activities. Technological progress in these activities has been based on economies of scale and scope as a means of achieving higher productivity and profits, and is associated with growing labour productivity. The LDCs' export sectors typically operate with capital-intensive and high labour productivity technologies. This is generally the case with extractive industries and some service sectors, including not only those geared towards export markets (e.g. tourism), but also some sectors oriented towards domestic markets (e.g. telecommunications and parts of the financial sector). These activities form the so-called "modern" sector of these economies. Given the type of technology they use, they tend to have a very limited employment-generating effect.

The LDCs' export sectors typically operate with capital-intensive and high labour productivity technologies. Given the type of technology they use, they tend to have a very limited employment-generating effect.

As a general rule, the expansion of modern-sector activities reduces the labour intensity of economic growth (Patnaik, 2007). Some exceptions to this rule are labour-intensive manufacturing industries whose production is destined for exports. The LDCs' manufacturing export sector is included in regional and global value chains, and it must accordingly apply the international standards of quality and production processes in which those chains operate. Still, the segments of these chains that are located in LDCs are mainly the labour-intensive ones, which means that they have an important employment-generating impact on domestic economies. Commercial agriculture in LDCs — especially the farms that produce cash crops — is subject to pressures similar to those of other export industries in these countries. They are also likely to operate at productivity levels which are not significantly below international standards, although it can be surmised that they use more labour-intensive technologies than more advanced countries.

At the other end of the technology spectrum are subsistence activities, which operate with labour-intensive but low-productivity technologies. These technologies are well below the international technology frontier and generate very low earnings for their workers — many of whom are below the poverty line. This is typically the case of subsistence agriculture in LDCs. Many urban informal-sector activities also fit into this category. Some extractive-sector activities can also be labour-intensive and low-productivity. This is the case of some mining activities for which high international commodity prices induced production by less productive, marginal mines that could be operated only on a very small scale and with low-productivity techniques. Small-scale mining, often by informal miners using crude techniques and damaging the environment, is a growing phenomenon in many LDCs, especially in Africa.

At the other end of the technology spectrum are subsistence activities, which operate with labour-intensive but low-productivity technologies. These technologies are well below the international technology frontier and generate very low earnings for their workers — many of whom are below the poverty line.

The non-tradables sectors of LDCs usually operate with technologies that span the entire spectrum between the two extremes mentioned above. Some activities use technologies that are not far removed from the international technology frontier (e.g. modern services like financial services and telecommunications). These activities typically have a limited job-generating impact. Most jobs in the non-tradables sectors are thus to be found in such activities as informal services (e.g. retail trade, repair services, restaurants, transport, etc.), operating with technologies that generate low-productivity jobs and low wages. Other non-tradables sectors — such as those involving public service – are likely to use technologies that are situated somewhere between the two extremes.

There is a trade-off between remaining competitive in the tradable activities with modern, capital-intensive technologies, and choosing technologies that generate jobs in non-tradable and subsistence activities.

Given the current situation of technological heterogeneity, and the challenge of creating decent employment in sufficient quantity, the LDCs face a stark choice. There is a trade-off between remaining competitive in the tradable activities with modern, capital-intensive technologies, and choosing technologies that generate jobs in non-tradable and subsistence activities. How should an LDC that is trying to attain growth with employment in an open economy environment approach the choice of technology, production processes and technological development? Two different strategies should be followed: one for the modern sectors, involving the acquisition of advanced technologies from developed countries, and one for the other sectors, involving so-called "appropriate" technologies.

A substantial number of LDC firms and farms can learn and acquire technologies from other developing countries, rather than from advanced economies, or can develop and use home-grown technologies.

LDC firms and farms need to undertake technological learning in order to upgrade their productive capabilities. They do so primarily by acquiring more advanced technologies from abroad, generally from developed countries. In export-oriented activities, the technologies in use (largely by transnational corporations) are often not far below international standards. Exporting enterprises, as well as those engaged in import-competing activities, will thus have to continue to rely on technologies that are close to the technological frontier.

For firms and farms whose output is geared towards domestic markets, however, such advanced technologies may not always be appropriate. Domestic markets in most LDCs are small and, given lower income levels, patterns of demand are different from those prevailing in advanced economies. Hence, at least initially, they need technologies that are appropriate to their conditions. LDC firms are more likely to find such technologies in countries that are closer to them in the technology space. In other words, a substantial number of LDC firms and farms can learn and acquire technologies (such as capital equipment, organizational know-how and types of inputs used) from other developing countries, rather than from advanced economies, or can develop and use home-grown technologies.

There are several characteristics of technologies developed in other developing countries that make them more appropriate for the LDCs, at least in activities oriented mainly towards the domestic market.

There are several characteristics of technologies developed in other developing countries that make them more appropriate for the LDCs, at least in activities oriented mainly towards the domestic market. They are generally more labour-intensive, as they are developed in countries that also have surplus labour. They are also more geared towards meeting the basic needs of the large swathes of the population who cannot afford luxury goods and services. In addition, they are more appropriate, since they deal with problems that arise in similar conditions as in the LDCs, be they social, economic or climate-related. Moreover, capital equipment acquired from other developing countries is likely to be less costly than equipment imported from developed countries. Yet another desirable requirement of appropriate technologies is that they should make the greatest possible use of resources that are locally available in LDCs. The firms that use such technologies thereby strengthen the linkages with other domestic enterprises.

The choice of technology not only influences employment parameters, it also determines who will benefit from employment. Choosing appropriate technologies and local materials creates major employment opportunities for unskilled or semi-skilled workers and allows them to develop their own skills and knowledge over time. It is obviously desirable to develop technologies that give workers control over what they produce in a fulfilling manner that is not too arduous or monotonous and that also allows for a reasonable level of productivity.

South-South cooperation can be a vehicle for transferring appropriate technologies to the LDCs and also for speeding up their technological development. Although the transfer of technologies that have been developed in advanced countries will remain the focus of efforts in most LDCs for years to come, new, appropriate technologies developed for the South by the South can serve as a useful complement in the short term and perhaps as an alternative in the long term. Such technologies will be especially appropriate in the medical sciences, agriculture and food production, and alternative energy sources. There is already a substantial body of innovations by the South which address the specific issues of developing countries — issues that are frequently neglected by the North (Kaplinsky et al., 2009).

South-South cooperation can be a vehicle for transferring appropriate technologies to the LDCs and also for speeding up their technological development.

D. Structural change

1. STRUCTURAL CHANGE AND EMPLOYMENT CHALLENGE: THE THREE-PRONGED APPROACH

Structural change is a central feature of the development process. It refers to changes in the composition of production, employment, demand and trade; in the pattern of inter- and intra-sectoral linkages; and in the types of flows of goods, services, knowledge and information among enterprises (UNCTAD, 2006: 68). The relative importance of different sectors and economic activities in a national economy is transformed as a result of these processes. Generally, the weight of the primary sector in GDP decreases, while the shares of the secondary and tertiary sectors increase. In addition, there is a general tendency within the economy towards higher specialization of production. This means that production linkages within the economy become denser and more roundabout as a higher proportion of output is sold to other producers rather than to final users. In other words, the use of intermediary goods and services relative to total gross output tends to rise, as reflected in the increased density of the input-output matrix of the economy. This is a sign of evolution towards a more complex economic system with a higher degree of processing.

Structural change is a central feature of the development process. It refers to changes in the composition of production, employment, demand and trade; in the pattern of inter- and intra-sectoral linkages; and in the types of flows of goods, services, knowledge and information among enterprises.

The classic pattern in today's developed countries and some advanced developing countries has been that new economic activities with higher productivity emerge and activities with lower productivity decline or are abandoned. These transformations have been accompanied by changes in employment patterns. More people are employed in manufacturing and services, while the number of people active in agriculture declines. There has also been a process of migration from rural to urban areas as more and more employment opportunities appear in cities and towns.

The classic pattern in today's developed countries and some advanced developing countries has been that new economic activities with higher productivity emerge and activities with lower productivity decline or are abandoned.

The recent experience of most developing countries, however, has tended to diverge from these classic patterns, which now seem to be more the exception than the rule (Heintz, 2010). The process of economic growth does not necessarily follow the standard Lewis-style pattern, whereby surplus labour from the subsistence sector is drawn into the modern sector (Lewis, 1954). Rather, even when the activities of the modern sector expand, their employment-generating potential is often limited because technological choices (and thereby capital-labour ratios) are driven by global competition and thus largely determined exogenously. One of the characteristics of this different type of structural change is the transfer of labour from low-productivity agriculture to low-productivity service activities in urban areas. This entails a proliferation of low-productivity employment in non-tradable activities as workers move out of subsistence activities in agriculture, even at relatively low levels of per capita income.

The recent experience of most developing countries, however, has tended to diverge from these classic patterns, which now seem to be more the exception than the rule.

In many developing economies the services sector (tertiary sector) has recently been acquiring a greater share of GDP well before they reach the levels of per capita income at which this occurred in countries that are now developed. Various studies have suggested that this is true of a wide range of developing countries, and that the turning point at which the share of manufacturing output and employment starts to decline is now taking place at a much lower level of per capita income than hitherto assumed (Palma, 2006). This phenomenon is known as "premature deindustrialization".

One of the characteristics of this different type of structural change is the transfer of labour from low-productivity agriculture to low-productivity service activities in urban areas.

For the LDC group as a whole, the dominant pattern of structural change since the turn of the century has been a slowly declining importance of the primary sector, not in favour of manufacturing (as in the classic pattern), but in favour of mining and, in some cases, services. Examining the country-level data presented in annex table 5, from 1999–2001 to 2009–2011, the relative importance of the primary sector declined in 33 LDCs. The same number of countries had a growing mining and energy sector (including construction). The share of services in GDP also expanded in a majority (28) of LDCs over the same period. Manufacturing, by contrast, expanded by more than 2 percentage points only in the following countries: Angola, Bangladesh, Guinea, Guinea-Bissau, Lao People's Democratic Republic, Liberia, Madagascar, Myanmar and Yemen.

The most significant trend in structural change for the LDCs as a group, as analysed in chapter 1, is the slow decline in the share of the primary sector in GDP (chart 38). There has also been a very slight decline in the share of the tertiary sector and an increase in the secondary sector. However, the increase of the secondary sector is due to non-manufacturing industrial activities, whose share rose from 14.5 per cent of GDP in 1999–2001 to 22.0 per cent in 2009–2011. Manufacturing stayed the same, at around 10 per cent of GDP. This shows there has been very little structural change of the type that results in strong increases in productivity, incomes, technological intensity and high value added over the 10-year period.

The problem with the current process of structural change is that it cannot provide the surplus population released from agriculture with productive employment.

The problem with the current process of structural change is that it cannot provide the surplus population released from agriculture with productive employment. Unlike in the past, agriculture today is unable to employ more people since the general trend in the LDCs towards decreasing agricultural land per worker and a larger share of the population focused on fragile lands. In addition, the evidence from chapter 2 shows that the rate of urban population growth in these countries has been nearly three times faster than that of rural population growth. It follows that the main challenge is to provide the economically active population outside agriculture with productive employment. Unfortunately, however, current structural change has been based on growth in non-manufacturing activities in the industrial (secondary) sector, which is mostly capital-intensive. As a consequence, the informal sector has been absorbing the majority of those who were unable to find productive employment elsewhere.

The informal sector has been absorbing the majority of those who were unable to find productive employment elsewhere.

In short, the recent pattern of structural change in the LDCs has been disappointing in terms of employment creation and inclusive growth. It has resulted in a process whereby labour is released from low-productivity activities (mostly rural) only to be underemployed in other low-productivity activities (mostly, but not exclusively, urban, and in the informal sector). This shift of workers from one type of low-productivity activities to another explains why income poverty (the working poor phenomenon) is so prevalent in many LDCs, and why vulnerable employment accounts for around 80 per cent of total employment. For the LDCs as a group, then, there has been little structural change of the right type, namely, the type that results in productive employment and in substantial increases in productivity, incomes, technological change and higher value added activities.

The manner in which structural change is shaped in a given country depends on myriad factors, including the initial natural resource and factor endowments of the country, the state of external demand for its products, the international trade regime, regional integration processes in which the country participates, and so on. But government policies can also influence the process of structural change. The recent pattern of structural change in the LDCs is, in fact, a result not only of the above-mentioned factors, but also of the prevailing development strategy, together with its policy framework.

Because structural change is so critical for development and has such a major influence on the employment situation, Governments should ensure that the right type of structural change takes place in the LDCs. The first step in that direction is to recognize that economic activities are not all alike in their potential for further development of productive capacities. Since some of them result in more spill-over effects and create more linkages, it follows that production structure is not just a passive outcome of earlier growth but is also an active determinant of future growth potential. Steering structural change towards more dynamic activities is therefore crucial.

This Report has proposed a framework with a three-pronged approach to employment creation aimed at placing the economy on a jobs-rich development path. The approach is based on a pragmatic assessment of the challenges facing LDCs and on an explicit recognition that the key to inclusive development is not simply higher rates of economic growth but also a higher employment intensity of growth. Given the heterogeneity of the production structure of a typical LDC economy, with modern sectors at one end of the spectrum and subsistence activities at the other, an approach is needed that can accommodate this diversity and make sound proposals for employment creation. The three-pronged approach to employment creation thus addresses subsistence activities; tradables; and non-tradables.

It recognizes that the process of structural change should ideally be led by the consolidation and expansion of the modernizing core of the economy, composed of high-value added, knowledge-intensive and competitive activities in manufacturing, mining, mechanized agriculture and modern services. In terms of labour, structural change should ideally result in a transfer of workers from low-productivity, poorly paid work to more productive and better employment in other sectors (i.e., an intersectoral transfer of labour).

However, the expansion of the modern sector needs to be complemented by more jobs, and better jobs, in the remaining sectors of the economy. Given the prevalence of working poverty in LDCs, this will involve raising productivity in traditional activities. All possible options will have to be explored and promoted for improving livelihood opportunities and creating employment in labour-intensive activities in these other sectors.

Given the heterogeneity of the production structure of a typical LDC economy, with modern sectors at one end of the spectrum and subsistence activities at the other, an approach is needed that can accommodate this diversity and make sound proposals for employment creation.

This Report has proposed a framework with a three-pronged approach to employment creation aimed at placing the economy on a jobs-rich development path. The three-pronged approach to employment creation addresses subsistence activities, tradables, and non-tradables.

The process of structural change should ideally be led by the consolidation and expansion of the modernizing core of the economy, composed of high-value added, knowledge-intensive and competitive activities in manufacturing, mining, mechanized agriculture and modern services.

Chart 38. Primary sector as a share of GDP, 2009–2011

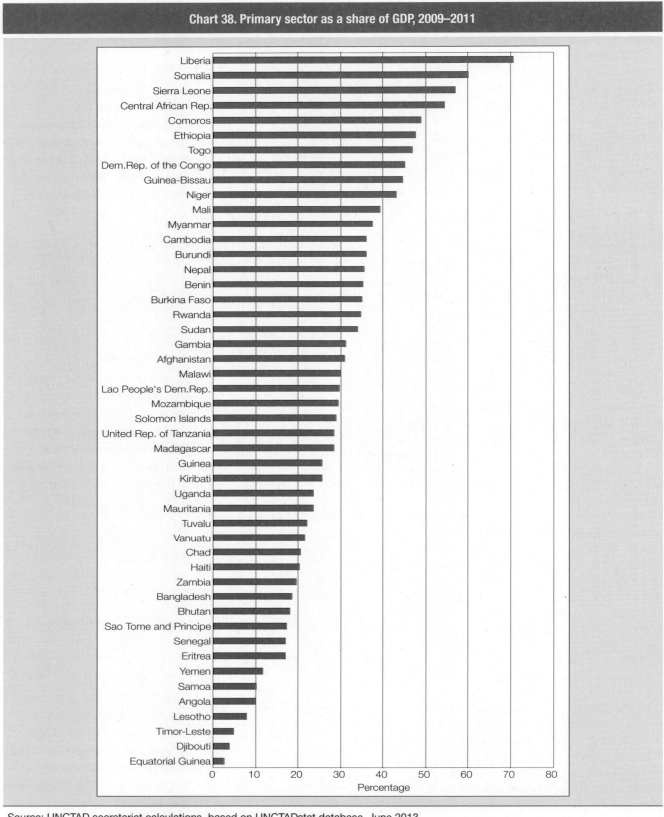

Source: UNCTAD secretariat calculations, based on UNCTADstat database, June 2013.

The logic behind the three-pronged approach to employment creation is that an increase in agricultural productivity releases labour that has to be absorbed by the rest of the economy — i.e., by tradable and non-tradable activities. Since the tradables are subject to intense competition, the extent to which they can absorb labour is limited. In other words, the choice of capital-labour ratio tends to be exogenously determined for enterprises producing tradable goods and services. Non-tradable activities would accordingly have to provide the bulk of employment opportunities both for new entrants and for workers released from agricultural subsistence activities.

Nonetheless, it is essential for policy to focus not only on employment generation, but also on productive transformation in each of these sectors and in the economy as a whole. The three-pronged approach proposed here emphasizes that employment creation is important, but that it should be pursued in parallel with the modernization of economic activities and an increase of productivity. The latter will ensure that not just the quantity of employment, but also the quality, improves.

The success or failure of the three-pronged approach will ultimately depend on whether it results in more employment creation and whether it fosters linkages in the national economy. More developed economies are invariably characterized by more dense economic structures where linkages are stronger and the production process more specialized or roundabout. This was recognized long ago by Adam Smith in his description of the process of specialization and his analysis of how it increases productivity.

Dynamic production linkage effects occur through both demand-side and supply-side relationships. For example, the multiplier effects of the export sector on the rest of the economy (demand side) will depend on the existence or absence of linkages with the rest of the national economy. If the export sector operates as an enclave within the economy, these dynamic effects will be largely absent. The effects on the supply side operate through positive externalities, economies of agglomeration, economies of specialization, and technological and knowledge spill-overs. Policies that strengthen these linkages can accelerate structural change, and with it the development of productive capacities.

2. AGRICULTURE AND THE EMPLOYMENT CHALLENGE: MODERNIZING SUBSISTENCE ACTIVITIES IN RURAL AREAS

Modernizing subsistence activities is a sine qua non for increasing productivity and improving the livelihood of the majority of LDC populations. This is particularly important in an LDC context, since a large proportion of time spent at work is devoted to subsistence activities, and since a large number of people are engaged in such activities, particularly agriculture. Broadly speaking, agriculture in LDCs comprises both subsistence activities and commercial agriculture.[11] Agricultural development policies are likely to benefit both types of activities. In the case of subsistence agriculture, they are expected to have an impact on earnings, on poverty, but also on output levels. In the case of commercial agriculture, successful policies are more likely to have broader impacts on the creation of intersectoral linkages, enhanced food security, and expansion of outputs that are traded both domestically and internationally. The importance of both types of agriculture is analysed below in the broader context of rural development, which is based not only on agricultural activities, but also on rural non-farm activities.

There are five main reasons why rural development is crucial for improving the employment situation in LDCs and why policies for employment and productivity need to target agriculture as a priority in the short term.

First, the LDC population is largely concentrated in rural areas. In 35 LDCs, more than 60 per cent of the population lives in rural areas, while less than half of the population lives in urban areas in only 5 LDCs: Djibouti, Sao Tome and Principe, Angola, Gambia and Haiti (chart 39). This means that the LDC labour supply is largely concentrated in rural areas. Policies for expanding jobs and increasing labour productivity and earnings thus need to target rural areas in the

The logic behind the three-pronged approach to employment creation is that an increase in agricultural productivity releases labour that has to be absorbed by the rest of the economy — i.e., by tradable and non-tradable activities.

Non-tradable activities would have to provide the bulk of employment opportunities both for new entrants and for workers released from agricultural subsistence activities.

Modernizing subsistence activities is a sine qua non for increasing productivity and improving the livelihood of the majority of LDC populations.

first instance. It is in rural areas that the labour force comprises workers who are already, or who could potentially become, active in both agricultural and RNF activities. If an immediate impact is to be made on poverty and unemployment, rather than leaving these problems to be resolved in the long term through the "trickle-down" effect of growth in the non-agricultural sectors, agricultural growth will have to be stepped up considerably.

Second, the primary sector (mainly agriculture) contributes the highest share of GDP in LDCs, as compared to other major groups of countries.[12] Primary activities account for over one fourth of GDP in the average LDC and in 29 of the 48 LDCs for which data are available (see chart 38).

Third, the productivity of rural activities is very low in most LDCs. The concentration of the population in rural areas — where the majority of the population in 43 LDCs lives — contrasts sharply with the contribution of primary activities to GDP (there are only four LDCs where the primary sector contributes more than half of GDP). This concentration is an indicator of very low productivity in rural activities, especially agriculture. As farm sizes are diminishing and farmers are being forced to cultivate more ecologically fragile land under increasingly uncertain climatic conditions, agricultural livelihoods have become less secure, more volatile and even less able to provide subsistence. This situation is accentuated by the heightened competition of subsistence agriculture with large-scale commercial farming, whether through more open trade or through changes in domestic property relations and land tenure patterns. The very low level of agricultural productivity is apparent not only within individual LDC economies, but also when compared internationally. Not only is there an agricultural productivity gap between LDCs and ODCs, but that gap has been widening. In 1990, the LDCs' cereal yield per hectare was only 61 per cent of that of ODCs. Two decades later, the proportion was just 37 per cent (chart 40). These very low levels of productivity, combined with the strong rural concentration of the population in rural areas, are the main explanation for the pervasive poverty in these countries (UNCTAD, 2004).

The fourth factor behind the importance of rural development to LDC employment is the current pattern of rural–urban migration in most of these countries. That pattern is driven more by expulsion forces (i.e., the dearth of gainful employment in rural areas) than by attraction forces (because of the lack of decently paid jobs in urban areas). Many LDCs are now at a critical stage in which they not only must find productive jobs and livelihoods for the millions of young people who are entering the labour force each year, but also have to confront that task in a situation where the nature of the employment challenge is changing. In the past, most of the new labour force was absorbed in low-productivity livelihoods in agriculture. Recently, however, more and more people have been seeking work outside agriculture, and urbanization is accelerating. Many LDCs have been unable either to increase agricultural productivity significantly or to generate productive jobs and livelihoods outside agriculture. In the absence of non-farm employment opportunities in rural areas, young people move to towns and cities in search of employment. This creates serious economic and social problems, such as urban poverty, growing or persistent informality, social dislocation and crime.

Fifth, most LDCs are characterized by food insecurity, which means they are highly vulnerable to developments in international food markets.[13] They are immediately affected by the negative impacts of periods of high or rising international prices, as they have been ever since the international food crisis of 2008. As high or rising international prices translate into high or rising domestic food prices, the real earnings of workers, especially the poorer among them, are lowered (UNCTAD, 2008), which also worsens their standard of living . In an economy with uncertain export prospects, ensuring adequate food availability

If an immediate impact is to be made on poverty and unemployment, rather than leaving these problems to be resolved through the "trickle-down" effect of growth in the non-agricultural sectors, agricultural growth will have to be stepped up considerably.

Many LDCs are now at a critical stage in which they not only must find productive jobs and livelihoods for the millions of young people who are entering the labour force each year, but also have to confront that task in a situation where the nature of the employment challenge is changing.

Many LDCs have been unable either to increase agricultural productivity significantly or to generate productive jobs and livelihoods outside agriculture.

Chart 39. Rural population as a share of total population, 2010–2012

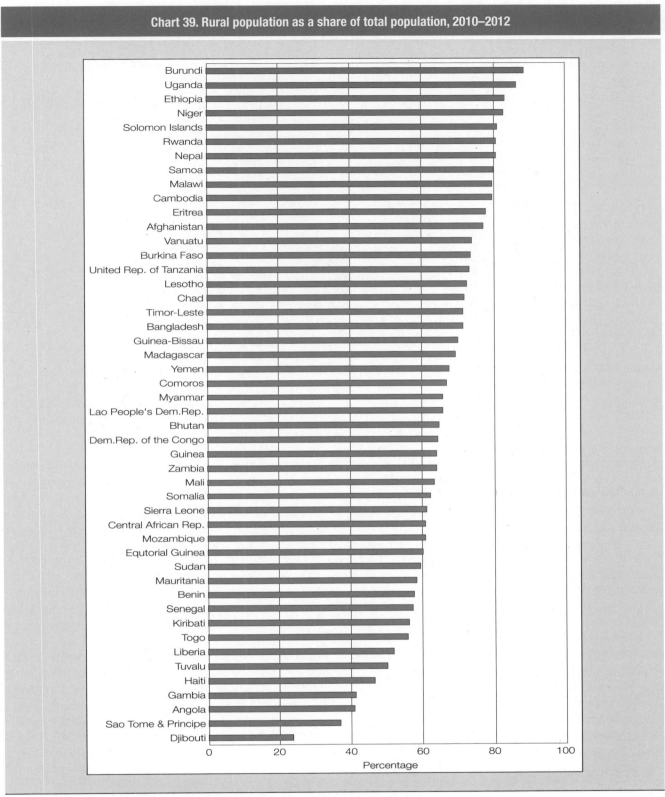

Source: UNCTAD secretariat calculations, based on UNCTADstat database, June 2013.

for the entire population — a crucial objective in its own right — calls for stepping up agricultural production, and food production in particular.

The ongoing analysis attests to the importance of rural activities — including in the subsistence sector — to employment generation, poverty reduction and more vigorous economic activity in LDCs in the short term. In future, as

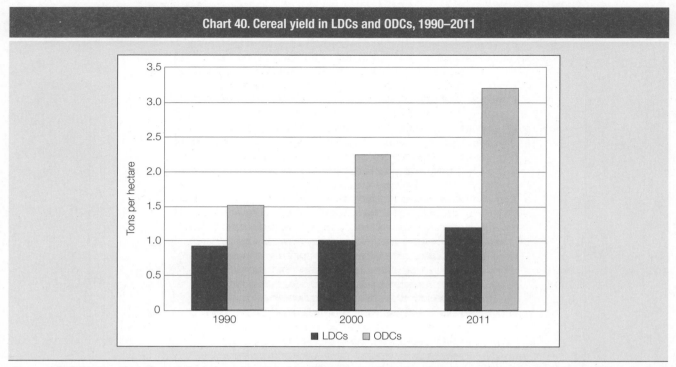

Chart 40. Cereal yield in LDCs and ODCs, 1990–2011

Source: UNCTAD Secretariat calculations, based on data from World Bank, World Development Indicators online database (downloaded in August 2013).

agriculture and RNF activities develop, rural economic activities will make a vital contribution to the development of productive capacities and to the employment generation which this process gives rise.

Indeed, agricultural development has major employment-generating effects, both in agriculture and in the rest of the economy. Strengthening linkages between agricultural and other activities also reinforces intersectoral flows of intermediate goods. The output of agricultural activities can serve as an input to incipient industrial activities, and especially to food processing industries. In fact, manufacturing activities that are not geared towards exports are highly concentrated in food processing and beverage industries. The output of industrial activities can also serve as input to agricultural production, e.g. in the form of fertilizers, agricultural equipment and machinery. Agricultural surpluses can thus be not only a prerequisite for competitive labour-intensive activities in the rest of the economy, but also an important addition to a country's exports.

Similarly, income growth in one sector strengthens demand for the output of other sectors. Higher incomes in rural areas cause the domestic market to expand, generating rising demand which can be satisfied (at least partially) by the expanding output of domestic firms in manufacturing and services. Rising income levels, combined with a growing population, will also create a greater demand for food. In other words, the economy will receive an "agricultural push" if rural incomes rise sufficiently and if strong linkages are created and maintained between agriculture on the one hand and non-farm rural activities and urban sectors on the other.

Rising agricultural production and productivity have the additional benefit of allowing LDCs to reduce food insecurity and ensure a more reliable food supply while also lessening their dependence on external sources of food supply. Although for many LDCs, the goal of self-sufficiency in food production is not immediately attainable, some progress towards food security is desirable in and of itself, regardless of the complementarities and synergies with industrial development previously described.

Agricultural development has major employment-generating effects, both in agriculture and in the rest of the economy.

The output of agricultural activities can serve as an input to incipient industrial activities, and especially to food processing industries. The output of industrial activities can serve as input to agricultural production, e.g. in the form of fertilizers, agricultural equipment and machinery.

Agricultural development should cause the relative prices of food to fall. The supply of basic wage goods is crucial for the non-inflationary expansion of employment opportunities in the rest of the economy. Since wage goods generally consist of food items, manufactured consumer goods and basic services, food prices are major determinants of the cost of living of workers and of the competitiveness and profitability of labour-intensive activities in the national economy. Lowering the cost of food amounts to increasing the real wages of workers. This in turn can have a stimulating effect on the local economy through direct demand and multiplier effects and on the investment-growth-employment nexus as well.

In short, effective rural development policies with a particular emphasis on the modernization of agriculture are likely to create opportunities for employment in both rural and urban areas. To the extent that agricultural growth leads to a diversification of the demand pattern and hence of activities that can meet domestic demand, the employment-generating potential of an "agricultural push" strategy can be quite significant.

Lowering the cost of food amounts to increasing the real wages of workers. This in turn can have a stimulating effect on the local economy through direct demand and multiplier effects and on the investment-growth-employment nexus as well.

3. Tradable activities:
THE EMPLOYMENT CHALLENGE IN AN OPEN ECONOMY

The diversification and structural change of LDC economies obviously cannot be based solely on the development of agriculture. The experience of developed countries demonstrates the critical importance of developing manufacturing activities and related producer services, so as to benefit from synergies and increasing returns to scale and to provide employment for the younger population. Modernization of agricultural production processes generates a growing surplus of labour in rural areas, and that labour surplus then seeks productive employment in urban centres. Improving the prospects for subsistence workers of finding jobs in more modern activities is essential for the structural transformation of the economy. This is the second prong of the approach outlined in this Report, focusing on employment opportunities in tradables sectors.

The experience of developed countries demonstrates the critical importance of developing manufacturing activities and related producer services, so as to benefit from synergies and increasing returns to scale and to provide employment for the younger population.

Tradable activities play a dual role in the development process. The first is that of absorbing labour that has been freed up from the subsistence sector. The second is that of generating foreign exchange revenues, which in turn is necessary for importing essential goods and servicing foreign debt. The LDCs have been focusing on the tradables sector for the past 25 years, which has meant shifting resources to encourage exports and introducing policies conducive to export-led growth. This shift has generally been successful in increasing foreign exchange earnings. Export revenues rose vigorously during the 2000s, since both the volumes exported and the prices of exported goods expanded.

In the recent past, however, the role of the tradables sector in absorbing labour freed up from subsistence agriculture has been fulfilled to a much lesser extent. Where exports are based on natural resource extraction, the employment intensity of growth has been low. In countries whose tradables sector is dominated by export-oriented labour-intensive manufactures, by contrast, more jobs have been generated.

The classic route of transferring labour from subsistence or other rural activities to more productive jobs in manufacturing has been followed in only a handful of LDCs.

The classic route of transferring labour from subsistence or other rural activities to more productive jobs in manufacturing has been followed in only a handful of LDCs, some of them in Asia, as well as Lesotho and Haiti. Bangladesh, for example, has become the world's second largest apparel exporter, surpassed only by China. Manufacturing in some other Asian LDCs has grown through participation in the manufacturing supply chains centred on China. The recent increase in China's labour costs, and the rebalancing of Chinese growth described in chapter 1, box 2, is likely to open up opportunities for labour-intensive export activities in LDCs. Hence, there is some potential for manufacturing to become one of the engines of employment creation in the LDCs in the not-too-distant future.

Clearly, the LDCs cannot afford to ignore the fact that they need foreign exchange to import capital goods, technology and other inputs required to build their productive capacities. They must also bear in mind the need to maintain or increase their export capacity. To be able to export, they may need to attract FDI, which typically chooses capital-intensive technologies that do not generate much employment. They can, however, use policies to encourage investment in export-oriented but labour-intensive activities, particularly in manufacturing, that can generate jobs while also contributing to export expansion and foreign exchange earnings.

The tradables sector comprises both export-oriented and import-substituting activities. It is true that the extent to which the LDCs can nurture the latter activities has been substantially reduced by trade liberalization. However, this does not mean that import-substituting activities are no longer feasible. They simply require different sets of policies and instruments geared towards the development of productive capacities, especially industrial policy and enterprise development policies, as analysed in the next chapter of this Report.

4. NON-TRADABLE ACTIVITIES:
THE EMPLOYMENT CHALLENGE IN LOW-PRODUCTIVITY ACTIVITIES

The final element of the three-pronged approach is to promote employment-intensive growth in non-tradables sectors. Given that the tradables sectors are less likely to provide an abundance of employment opportunities for the reasons outlined above, employment creation in non-tradable activities becomes critical. These activities include infrastructure and housing; basic services (education, health, sanitation, communication); technical services, repair and maintenance, as well as most transportation services; insurance services, property and commercial brokerage; personal, social and community services; public administration; and security and defence. Since these activities do not generally face international competition, the policy space for influencing outcomes in these sectors is larger than in tradables, and accordingly they offer much greater possibilities for increasing the employment intensity of growth.

Moreover, non-tradable activities grow as incomes grow. The share of food in the total consumption of an individual will normally decrease as income increases, leaving more space for non-food goods and services. Health and education become particularly more important as incomes grow. This means that the high growth in the LDCs over the past decade has to some extent created demand for more and better services. However, the demand for many of these services is currently met by activities taking place in the informal sector, with very low productivity and remuneration. Thus, the existence of an increasing demand for better services — a demand that is currently being matched by a supply of lower quality — points to a need for substantially upgrading the provision of many services in the LDCs.

Regardless of whether these activities are currently informal or formal, their future growth can be influenced by policies. The point is that services are mostly labour-intensive, which creates an opportunity for substantial employment creation in the LDCs. Given the importance of services for employment creation,

The recent increase in China's labour costs, and the rebalancing of Chinese growth is likely to open up opportunities for labour-intensive export activities in LDCs.

Given that the tradables sectors are less likely to provide an abundance of employment opportunities, employment creation in non-tradable activities becomes critical.

Since these activities do not generally face international competition, the policy space for influencing outcomes in these sectors is larger than in tradables, and accordingly they offer much greater possibilities for increasing the employment intensity of growth.

Governments should foster their development. For example, policies that incentivize the formalization and enlargement of enterprises in these sectors can result in rapid increases in productivity because of better use of economies of scale and scope. Increases in productivity then translate into higher incomes for workers and a broader tax base, thereby strengthening the domestic mobilization of resources. Governments can use their procurement policies, for example, to promote the development of small domestic enterprises. The use of labour-intensive techniques and domestic inputs should figure prominently among the requirements outlined in these policies.

One essential driver of the non-tradables sector is public expenditure, especially (but not exclusively) in the social sectors. This is typically much more employment-generating than several other economic activities, and also has substantial multiplier effects. Spending on the provision of proper health facilities, for example, or ensuring good-quality and universal education, has great employment-generating potential. There is thus a strong case for pursuing a growth strategy that allows and encourages labour productivity increases overall. Such a strategy should also involve a significant expansion of public expenditure and in turn of income and employment opportunities in social sectors that have a positive impact on the standard of living.

Given the greater policy space in non-tradables, that is one part of the economy on which policymakers can have the greatest influence. Specifically, they can try to put the investment-growth-employment nexus to work in the non-tradables sector, as has been described in section B. At the same time, it provides an example of how different elements of the policy framework can be combined to enhance the coherence and synergies of policies.

E. How to adjust the framework to conditions in different LDCs

The framework developed in this chapter should not be viewed as a one-size-fits-all solution for the employment challenge in LDCs. There is considerable room for diversity in its application, reflecting differences in each country's resource endowments, size, geographical location, production structure and export structure. Such diversity implies different starting positions and also different policy choices. There is some agricultural production, some manufacturing and some extraction of natural resources in all the LDCs, but the proportion of each element varies from one country to another.[14]

As argued in chapter 1, the weakness of aggregate demand in developed countries will restrict the possibilities of strong export-led growth in the LDCs for some time to come. This requires a shift towards a more domestic-demand-led growth, particularly in economies that are large enough to sustain such a shift. This rebalancing of growth can be achieved with direct redistributive policies and public expenditure on more basic goods and services. However, many LDCs are small economies and are also very specialized in their production and export structure. As a rule, small countries lacking a broad base of natural resources have to develop manufactured exports at an earlier stage than resource-rich countries, where specialization in primary commodities persists to a much later stage of development. Larger countries, on the other hand, can shift away from specialization in primary commodities through import substitution.

Given the weakness of demand in developed countries, and the small size of domestic markets, an increase in regional and South-South trade is likely to be of particular importance for the smaller LDCs. Progress towards developmental

Governments can use their procurement policies, for example, to promote the development of small domestic enterprises. The use of labour-intensive techniques and domestic inputs should figure prominently among the requirements outlined in these policies.

One essential driver of the non-tradables sector is public expenditure, especially (but not exclusively) in the social sectors.

The framework developed in this chapter should not be viewed as a one-size-fits-all solution for the employment challenge in LDCs. There is considerable room for diversity in its application, reflecting differences in each country's resource endowments, size, geographical location, production structure and export structure.

regionalism — a subject that was treated extensively in LDCR 2011 — and intensification of economic relationships between LDCs and other developing countries might help the LDCs during the current adverse economic conjuncture.

1. FUEL AND MINERAL PRODUCERS AND EXPORTERS

There are two characteristics of fuel and mineral exporters that must be considered when adapting the framework to their circumstances. The first is that the production of tradables is of an enclave type, with few linkages to the rest of the economy. These sectors have very low employment elasticity, resulting more often than not in jobless growth. The policy challenge in these countries is accordingly to ensure that higher prices of commodities and/or productivity growth in the extractive sector translate into greater domestic demand and more investment. Distribution of rents is thus crucial. Taxation systems in such economies should have two main aims: to create sufficient incentive for investors, and to secure a fair share of mining or fuel revenue for public use.

The policy challenge is to ensure that higher prices of commodities and/or productivity growth in the extractive sector translate into greater domestic demand and more investment. Distribution of rents is thus crucial.

In addition, these sectors can help generate more and better employment only indirectly, which calls for strengthening their linkages with the rest of the economy. This can be accomplished by using some of the resource revenues to improve the enabling environment for business start-ups through well-targeted investment in infrastructure. Backward and forward linkages should also be reinforced, in particular by creating natural resource-based production clusters. These are sectoral and/or geographical concentrations of enterprises engaged in interlinked activities based on the exploitation and processing of natural resources and their supporting industries (UNECA, 2013).

The second characteristic of fuel and mineral producers and exporters is that they usually have less of a financing constraint than other LDCs. The data in annex table 4, show that the resource gap of fuel-exporting LDCs is positive, which means that their savings rate is higher than their investment rate. Thus, financing public infrastructure, social services and the like should be relatively easy. However, the difficulty lies in managing the exchange rate due to the "Dutch disease" effects. The influx of foreign exchange from exports and foreign investment results in an overvalued domestic currency, effectively discouraging non-commodity exports.

The priorities for these countries should be private sector development organized around the extractive sectors with backward and forward linkages, and the investment-growth-employment nexus in non-tradables sector.

In short, the priorities for these countries should be private sector development organized around the extractive sectors with backward and forward linkages, and the investment-growth-employment nexus in non-tradables sector.

2. PRODUCERS AND EXPORTERS OF AGRICULTURAL PRODUCTS

Countries where conditions are auspicious for the expansion of agricultural and food production and exports should promote these activities by shifting the focus of public investment onto agriculture. Public investment should provide solid infrastructure to connect the producers with major centres of consumption (big cities and international markets). It should also encourage non-farm rural activities, especially those related to food processing and the provision of basic services.

Countries where conditions are auspicious for the expansion of agricultural and food production and exports should promote these activities by shifting the focus of public investment onto agriculture. Public investment should provide solid infrastructure to connect the producers with major centres of consumption.

In countries with large populations, it should be possible to combine increases in agricultural incomes with the development of domestic industries by encouraging domestic demand for intermediate and consumer goods produced by domestic industry. In such situations, industrialization can be driven by agricultural development rather than by exports.

In countries with smaller populations, the primary goal for agricultural and agro-industrial exports must be international markets. While this generates higher standards of competitiveness and quality of goods produced — and thus also entails a major role for the State in ensuring that the standards are met — recent developments are creating new opportunities for exports. One such opportunity will arise from the shift in Chinese demand for food from staples like rice to more protein-rich food obtained from livestock. A well-planned strategy to meet this growing demand could produce substantial payoffs in terms of both income and employment. Countries with small populations can also develop production for niche markets like organic food, flowers, horticulture and the like.

In short, for larger countries the development of agriculture can be coupled with the development of domestic industry, enabling them to benefit from the complementarities and synergies between the two. For smaller countries, exporting agricultural surpluses and developing production for international niche markets are viable options.

For larger countries the development of agriculture can be coupled with the development of domestic industry, enabling them to benefit from the complementarities and synergies between the two. For smaller countries, exporting agricultural surpluses and developing production for international niche markets are viable options.

3. Producers and exporters of manufactured goods

Countries that have already established internationally competitive labour-intensive manufacturing activities need to address three priority areas, each of which has contradictory impacts on employment creation. The first priority is to upgrade to more value added activities in areas where some industrial capabilities already exist. If an economy depends almost entirely on external markets for growth, its scope for employment creation is limited by the ability to benefit from demand expansion in other countries or by the ability to increase market shares. Both these options are limited in the short term, and in the longer term depend on investments in the expansion of productive capacities. Wages do not increase much in such economies, so domestic demand does not grow and employment creation is limited. Informal activities may persist and even expand in situations of relatively rapid economic growth. Industrial upgrading is thus crucial for these economies. If successful, however, it will most likely reduce employment creation since it would involve more modern technologies that generally increase the capital-labour ratio.

The first priority is to upgrade to more value added activities in areas where some industrial capabilities already exist.

The second priority for these countries is to cheapen wage goods, especially food. Since their competitiveness is based on low wages, cheapening wage goods will result in an increase in real wages, even if nominal wages do not increase. An increase in real wages can in turn stimulate domestic demand and help generate the investment-growth-employment nexus. Cheapening of food, however, requires substantial investment in agriculture. The idea would then be to promote development through an industrialization process linked in a balanced fashion to the development of the rural economy and agriculture.

The second priority for these countries is to cheapen wage goods, especially food.

Both of these processes will produce surplus labour. In order to match the number of persons released from agriculture and industry, the number of employment opportunities in services must be sufficiently dynamic. This calls for establishing the investment-growth-employment nexus in the non-tradables sector. In addition, some of the new employment opportunities will have to come from new manufacturing activities. In effect, enterprise profits from labour-intensive manufacturing exports can be invested in activities that represent backward linkages. The backward linkage dynamic is particularly important for newly industrializing countries, since their industrialization often begins with the assembly of inputs produced elsewhere. Pursuit of the backward linkage dynamic for these countries is therefore essential for achieving an industrial structure of any depth. Some of the additional employment may arise from the opportunities that will open up as Chinese unit labour costs increase (see chapter 1, box 2). As China becomes too expensive for some labour-intensive

In order to match the number of persons released from agriculture and industry, the number of employment opportunities in services must be sufficiently dynamic. This calls for establishing the investment-growth-employment nexus in the non-tradables sector.

manufacturing activities, wider opportunities will be created for other developing countries. This may give some LDCs the chance to develop much-needed industrial capabilities and become exporters of that type of goods. It may give others the chance to increase their share of international markets based on their existing industrial capabilities.

In summary, the priorities for producers and exporters of manufactured goods should be industrial upgrading of the manufacturing sector, development of agriculture and creation of the nexus in the non-tradables sector.

4. SMALL ISLAND DEVELOPING STATES

The structural characteristics of small island developing States make it extremely difficult to envisage an effective policy framework for employment creation. They are generally very small in terms of population and territory, have no natural resources that can be exploited and exported, and are generally located far away from major markets and developed countries. However, they do have a potential to develop services, such as tourism and health provision.

In many developing countries, tourism is developed in a manner that resembles the enclave economies of major natural-resource exporters, and has negligible employment effects. A more promising strategy for SIDS would be to develop tourism as a leading sector with linkages to local enterprises.

In many developing countries, tourism is developed in a manner that resembles the enclave economies of major natural-resource exporters, and has negligible employment effects. A more promising strategy for SIDS would be to develop tourism as a leading sector with linkages to local enterprises. The provision of local food, for example, could have strong employment effects on the local economy, while the provision of local cultural goods, such as music, arts and crafts, could nurture creative industries.

Another promising channel for employment creation is the provision of health and health-related services. Instead of "exporting" doctors and nurses through migration, they can try to attract clients from more developed countries.

Another promising channel for employment creation is the provision of health and health-related services. Endowed with relatively well-educated populations, especially in the health sector, SIDS have what is needed to position themselves as health tourism destinations. Instead of "exporting" doctors and nurses through migration, they can try to attract clients from more developed countries. Since doctors and nurses receive relatively high incomes, they can create demand for various types of goods and services that are available locally.

Creating linkages with a leading service sector is then a promising way to increase the employment intensity of economic activities in small island developing States.

F. Conclusions

The LDCs are likely to face an enormous employment challenge over the next two to three decades, as discussed in chapters 2 and 3. To respond to this challenge, their policymakers will have to find ways to stimulate employment creation. In addition, GDP growth rates in the current decade have so far been lower than in the previous decade, and forecasts suggest that this is likely to continue over the next three to five years. Since employment creation was inadequate even in the 2000s, the LDC employment challenge in the present decade is even more overwhelming.

The framework relates the three processes through which productive capacities develop to three main elements that must be borne in mind to formulate policies geared at job-rich growth...

The aim of this chapter was to articulate as clearly as possible a policy framework for linking employment creation with the development of productive capacities in the LDCs. The framework is based on the recognition that employment creation without the development of productive capacities is not sustainable. It relates the three processes through which productive capacities develop to three main elements that must be borne in mind in order for LDC policymakers to formulate policies geared at job-rich growth. These elements are: the investment-growth-employment nexus; enterprise development and technological change; and the three-pronged approach to employment creation.

Capital accumulation can take different forms, and in the recent past it included the investment-growth nexus, but not employment. This chapter proposes a framework that adds employment as a critical ingredient to the nexus. The focus is on setting in motion a virtuous cycle where investment boosts growth, and growth creates productive employment. Productive employment, in turn, implies increasing incomes for workers, giving rise to consumption that supports the expansion of aggregate demand. Sufficiently dynamic aggregate demand, for its part, creates incentives for new investment, repeating the cycle at a higher level of investment, growth, employment and income.

Enterprise development is the second element of the framework for maximizing employment creation. It involves the development of productive capacities through entrepreneurial capabilities and technological progress. It is argued here that successful private sector development would enable the LDCs to improve both the quantity and quality of employment creation and also to embark on a technological catch-up with more developed countries. The most important task in the LDC context is to create the "missing middle". Where technological change is concerned, policymakers need to adopt different policies and measures according to the three main sectors of the economy.

Structural change is a central feature of the development process, and its form and pace will also affect employment creation in the economy. To place the economy on a job-rich development path, the chapter proposes a framework with a three-pronged approach to employment creation. It focuses on the consolidation and expansion of the modernizing core of the economy, composed of high value added, knowledge-intensive and competitive activities in industry, mining, mechanized agriculture and modern services. However, to compensate for the often low employment intensity of growth within the modernizing core, all possible opportunities for creating employment in labour-intensive activities in tradable, non-tradable and subsistence sectors should be explored and promoted.

Finally, the chapter proposes ways to adjust the framework to different types of LDCs. As has already been noted, there is considerable room for diversity in the application of the framework across LDCs, reflecting differences in resource endowments, size, geographical location, production structure and export structure. Policymakers in each country should carefully examine the specificities of their economies and decide how to use the framework. The following chapter discusses the main policy lines required to set up the framework developed here in order to achieve employment-rich growth in the LDCs.

... these elements are: the investment-growth-employment nexus; enterprise development and technological change; and the three-pronged approach to employment creation.

One of the most important tasks in the LDC context is to create the "missing middle". Where technological change is concerned, policymakers need to adopt different policies and measures according to the three main sectors of the economy.

Policymakers in each country should carefully examine the specificities of their economies and decide how to use the framework.

Notes

1   The concept of the developmental State in the context of LDCs has been dealt with extensively in UNCTAD, 2009.

2   There is little difference in this respect between African and Asian LDCs. Both groups display a similar investment ratio, very close to the overall average. In the island LDCs, by contrast, the rate is much lower: 17.1 per cent in 2010–2011.

3   China has been excluded from the total of other developing countries because its exceptionally high investment ratio (45.9 per cent in 2010–2011) and the size of its economy bias the group average.

4   The following paragraphs draw heavily on Stiglitz et al., 2006.

5   We have used the data for Africa because more recent estimates of the LDCs' infrastructure investment needs are not available. One older estimate, provided in UNCTAD 2006, suggests that LDCs would need annual infrastructure investment equivalent to 7.5 and 9 per cent of GDP.

6   There are no available data are for several LDCs, most of them island LDCs.

7   Further details on this issue are provided in section C of this chapter.

8   In constant 2011 dollars. UNCTAD computations, based on data from the Creditor Reporting System database of OECD-DAC.

9   The Least Developed Countries Report 2006 identified the underdevelopment of the entrepreneurial sector — one particular aspect of missing institutional development, along with a deficit of infrastructure and weak (domestic) demand stimulus – as the main constraints on the development of productive capacities (UNCTAD, 2006).

10 A useful list, originally drawn up by UNCTAD, identifies five major kinds of technological capabilities: investment capabilities, incremental innovation capabilities, strategic marketing capabilities, linkage capabilities, and radical innovation capabilities.

11 This section focuses on subsistence activities within agriculture, but without neglecting the role and importance of commercial agriculture and non-farm rural activities. Chapter 5 includes a discussion of policies for creating jobs in non-farm rural activities.

12 The primary sector is made up of agriculture, forestry and fishing, with agriculture the predominant activity. The bulk of primary economic activities take place in rural areas.

13 According to FAO, as of July 2013, 23 of the 34 African LDCs , along with two Asian LDCs and Haiti, — more than half of all LDCs — required external food assistance due to critical problems of food insecurity (http://www.fao.org/giews/english/hotspots/). Moreover, three fourths (26) of the 34 countries worldwide that required external food assistance were LDCs.

14 The classification of LDCs according to their structure and employment challenges is presented on p.xii.

References

Amsden A (2001). *The Rise of the Rest: Non-Western Economies' Ascent in World Markets.* Oxford University Press. Oxford.

Barro RJ and Lee JW (2013). A new data set of educational attainment in the world, 1950–2010. *Journal of Development Economics.* 104: 184–198.

Heintz J (2010). Employment, poverty and inclusive development in Africa: policy choices in the context of widespread informality. In: Padayachee V, ed. *The Political Economy of Africa.* Routledge. London.

Kaplinsky R et al. (2009). Below the radar: What does innovation in emerging economies have to offer other low income economies? *International Journal of Technology Management and Sustainable Development.* 8(3):177–197.

Lewis WA (1954). Economic development with unlimited supplies of labour. *Manchester School.* 22(2):139–191.

McKinley T and Martins P (2010). McKinley, T. and P. Martins (2010) "Empowering MDG Strategies Through Inclusive Economic Development." Paper prepared for UNCTAD Geneva.

Palma JG (2006). Globalizing inequality: "centrifugal" and "centripetal" forces at work. Working Paper No. 35. United Nations, Department of Economics and Social Affairs.

Patnaik P (2007). Technology and employment in an open underdeveloped economy. In: Ocampo J A and Sundaram J K, eds. *Full and Decent Employment.* Orient Longman, Zed Books and Third World Nertwork. Hyderabad, London and New York, and Penang: 54–69.

Rodríguez F (2007). Have collapses in ifrastructure spending led to cross-country divergence in per capita GDP? In: Ocampo J A, Sundaram J K, and Vos R, eds. *Growth Divergences : Explaining Differences in Economic Performance.* Orient Longman, Zed Books and Third World Nertwork. Hyderabad, London and New York, and Penang: 259–284.

Schneider F et al. (2010). Shadow Economies All over the World: New Estimates for 162 Countries from 1999 to 2007. *Policy Research Working Paper No 5356.* The World Bank. Washington, DC.

Spence M (2011). *The Next Convergence: The Future of Economic Growth in a Multispeed World.* Farrar, Straus and Giroux. New York.

Stiglitz J, Ocampo JA, Spiegel S, Ffrench-Davis R and Nayyar D (2006). *Stability with Growth: Macroeconomics, Liberalization and Development.* Oxford University Press. Oxford.

UNCTAD (2004). *The Least Developed Coutnries Report 2004: Linking International Trade with Poverty Reduction.* United Nations Conference on Trade and Development (UNCTAD). New York and Geneva.

UNCTAD (2006). *The Least Developed Countries Report 2006: Developing Productive Capacities.* United Nations publication. Sales No. E.06.II.D.9. New York and Geneva.

UNCTAD (2007). The least developed countries report 2007: knowledge, technological learning and innovation for development. United Nations publication. Sales No. E.07.II.D.8, New York and Geneva.

UNCTAD (2008). *The Least Developed Countries Report 2008: Growth, Poverty and the Terms of Development Partnership.* United Nations publication. Sales No. E.08.II.D.20. New York and Geneva.

UNCTAD (2009). *The Least Developed Countries Report 2009: The State and Development Governance.* United Nations publication. Sales No. E.09.II.D.9. New York and Geneva.

UNCTAD (2010). *Trade and Development Report 2010: Employment, Globalization and Development.* United Nations Conference on Trade and Development (UNCTAD). New York and Geneva.

UNCTAD (2012). *The Least Developed Countries Report 2012: Harnessing Remittances and Diaspora Knowledge to Build Productive Capacities.* United Nations publication. Sales No. E.12.II.D.18. New York and Geneva.

UNCTAD (2013). *Trade and Development Report 2013: Adjusting to the Changing Dynamics of the World Economy.* United Nations publication. Sales No. E .13.II .D.3. New York and Geneva.

UNECA (2013). Making the most of Africa's commodities: industrializing for growth, jobs and economic transformation. Economic Report on Africa 2013.

United Nations (2011). Programme of Action for the Least Developed Countries for the Decade 2011–2020. Fourth United Nations Conference on the Least Developed Countries, Istanbul, 9-13 May 2011. No. A/CONF.219/3/Rev.1. United Nations. New York.

CHAPTER 5

POLICIES FOR EMPLOYMENT-INTENSIVE GROWTH IN THE LDCs

A. Introduction

Chapter 4 of this Report argued that in the medium to long term, the only sustainable way of ensuring that the LDC economies generate jobs in sufficient quantity and quality is through the development of productive capacities. However, while in theory the private sector should generate most jobs, it is still weakly developed in these countries. This requires a dual role for the State: enacting policies to promote output expansion and employment creation in the private sector, and directly generating jobs through the expansion of public employment in socially essential or desirable activities. Achieving these objectives will require implementing a broad range of mutually supportive policies aimed at building productive capacity and fostering structural transformation. Policy interventions should cover three broad areas: macroeconomic policies, enterprise development, and public sector investment and actions for job creation. This chapter presents the broad policy direction that LDC Governments need to follow in order to attain employment-rich growth and to establish the strong investment-growth-employment nexus described in chapter 4.

The State has a dual role: enacting policies to promote output expansion and employment creation in the private sector, and directly generating jobs.

For LDCs, there must clearly be two complementary objectives concerning employment: to expand the number of jobs, so as productively to absorb the growing labour force; and to raise the labour earnings generated by these jobs through productivity gains, which in turn implies diversifying the economy towards higher value added activities. These objectives require a range of mutually supportive policies — not just short-term macroeconomic or labour market policies, but strategies aimed at structural change. This includes longer-term policies that "should strive for an expansion of productive capacity and an increase in the employment content of growth, to the extent that increasing the employment content of growth does not jeopardize growth itself" (van der Hoeven, 2013: 22). Furthermore, given the high degree of synergy and complementarity between appropriate development policies (Rodrik and Rosenzweig, 2010), different policies (macroeconomic, sectoral, micro, social, trade and industrial policies) must be coherent and mutually supportive.

For LDCs, there must clearly be two complementary objectives concerning employment: to expand the number of jobs, and to raise the labour earnings generated by these jobs.

There are obvious constraints on policy formulation and implementation in LDCs. One important set of constraints arises from the nature of their integration with the global economy. Since LDCs tend to be open economies that rely heavily on primary commodity and low value added manufactures exports, and that are dependent on various forms of capital inflows to support the balance of payments, they are often disproportionately affected by changes in global trade and capital flows, as well as by flows in cross-border migration. National policies are thus strongly conditioned by the external environment and must also be able to respond to that environment flexibly, which often makes it more difficult to pursue them in a systematic and planned manner.

National policies are strongly conditioned by the external environment and must also be able to respond to that environment flexibly.

Another frequently mentioned constraint is the supposedly limited capacity of LDCs to design and implement policies, which is usually attributed to their dearth of technical, human, political, financial and institutional resources and/or to the prevailing type of governance. This has been used as a strong argument against their industrial policies, on the grounds that government failures are worse than market failures, especially when States do not have the capacity to design and implement industrial policy and are not competent at "picking winners". It is also argued that industrial policy is liable to corruption and rent-seeking; is associated with resource misallocation and waste; and allows the persistence of inefficient firms. However, as has been noted in previous editions of *The Least Developed Countries Report* series, several of these perceived shortcomings in LDCs are themselves due to fiscal retrenchment dating back to the structural adjustment era, weak country ownership of many policies, and lack of interest of the international community in devoting resources to capacity-building in most policymaking areas. Despite this, many LDCs do have islands of excellence in public administration or executive agencies and can build on them strategically, which would allow them incrementally to expand bureaucratic competence and gradually build developmental States using industrial policy (UNCTAD, 2009: 15–56). It should be recognized that industrial policy is a learning process (Rodrik, 2004, 2008) and that policymaking capability evolves along with productive capacities (Nelson, 1994; Freeman, 2008; Moreau, 2004; Shimada, 2013). Indeed, this has been the experience of successful latecomer industrializing countries (Chang, 2011). But donors can also play a useful role in strengthening LDC policy capacity, including industrial policy (O'Connor, 2007; UNCTAD, 2009: 46–49).

Many LDCs have islands of excellence in public administration or executive agencies and can build on them strategically, which would allow them incrementally to expand bureaucratic competence.

Yet another important background consideration involves technology choice, as discussed in chapter 4. LDC policymakers are faced with potentially contradictory priorities. On the one hand, they need to give high priority to policies that generate more jobs. On the other hand, they need to diversify their economies to increase labour productivity and labour earnings so as to alleviate the pervasive problems of poverty and underemployment. Productivity improvements are usually associated with more modern technologies which are invariably more capital-intensive and labour-saving, and which can run counter to the first objective of increasing employment. In other words, policymakers often face a trade-off between efficiency and equity. However, this need not always be the case. Ensuring adequate decent work for the labour force is possible if reasonably rapid growth of average productivity is combined with the rejuvenation of some traditionally important, employment-intensive activities (such as some forms of agriculture), expansion of service activities that meet social needs, and growth in the volume of economic activity. This has of course been the case with countries undergoing a rapid industrialization process in which manufacturing activities – which typically exhibit increasing returns to scale – render rapid growth of average productivity possible.

Ensuring adequate decent work for the labour force is possible if reasonably rapid growth of average productivity is combined with the rejuvenation of some traditionally important, employment-intensive activities.

Thus, the adoption of labour-saving technologies need not be a problem if the volume of production expands sufficiently to generate higher absolute levels of employment. Modern technologies that reduce the drudgery and arduousness of work are to be desired in their own right. It is, of course, preferable if they are associated with increases in labour productivity in society as a whole. Accordingly, the focus must not be on preventing labour-saving technological progress. It should rather be on ensuring that the surpluses from the activities carried out through labour-saving technologies are mobilized (directly through taxation or indirectly through the provision of incentives) and transferred to create demand for more labour-intensive products. These surpluses can also be used in a wide range of service activities, ranging from the provision of such essential services as health, sanitation and education to entertainment and cultural activities – anything that improves the quality of life. In this way policymakers can reach both goals: employment expansion and improving per capita incomes. Specific sectoral policies that can be deployed to ensure more employment are discussed below.

The adoption of labour-saving technologies need not be a problem if the volume of production expands sufficiently to generate higher absolute levels of employment.

With these points in mind, the rest of this chapter builds on the analytical framework developed in chapter 4. It identifies some broad policy areas that may be relevant for LDCs to consider in the light of the current global environment and their own conditions, as discussed in chapters 1, 2 and 3.

B. Macroeconomic strategies

This Report has argued that macroeconomic policies in LDCs need to be reoriented away from a single-minded focus on price stability and budget balance towards a strategy that is more focused on growth with sustainable employment creation. This is important because macroeconomic policy frequently involves trade-offs between different goals. For example, a quest for macroeconomic stability focusing on inflation control may imply sacrificing employment, certainly in the short run, and may also weaken workers' bargaining position, depress wages and therefore indirectly increase poverty. These short-run goals in turn have a bearing on development policies. The quest for macroeconomic stability may lead to less emphasis on strategies for sustainable and more inclusive development, or for improving human development and meeting broader social objectives. It is also often the case that price stability and correcting external imbalances become the dominant pursuits, such that pervasive unemployment or underemployment is allowed to persist, even though a shift in focus to make productive employment generation the most critical goal need not generate imbalances or instability.

Macroeconomic policies in LDCs need to be reoriented away from a single-minded focus on price stability and budget balance towards a strategy that is more focused on growth with sustainable employment creation.

Given the potential conflicts between goals and across instruments, the choice of policy mix is not a purely technocratic exercise, but reflects political choices and has social implications. There are strong distributional implications, especially with respect to asset and income distribution and the differential provision of public goods and services across groups in the population. These implications relate not only to differences across economic classes and social groups, but also to gender differences. Such effects may vary depending on the characteristics of the country, such as the degree of indexation of wage incomes; how investors, especially foreign ones, respond to changes in local conditions; the particular activities in which employment is generated or lost; and so on.

Over the past decade, most LDCs have followed "prudent" and fiscally restrained macroeconomic policies.

Short-run macroeconomic policies and longer-term growth strategies are inextricably linked, not separate and independent. Over the past decade, most LDCs have followed "prudent" and fiscally restrained macroeconomic policies. While some have attributed the higher rates of income growth in this period to such a strategy, it is more likely that rising commodity exports and a favourable external environment were responsible. What is clear is that if the LDCs' development strategy is to shift towards a greater emphasis on productive employment generation and sustainable economic diversification, it will require supportive macroeconomic policies. In addition, a major concern of macroeconomic policy must be the reduction of economic volatility, which is undesirable for many reasons.

Public spending and taxation are key instruments for shaping the distribution of income in the economy, strengthening the process of capital accumulation and placing the economy on a job-rich growth path.

In this context, fiscal policies become quite prominent. Public spending and taxation are key instruments for shaping the distribution of income in the economy, strengthening the process of capital accumulation and placing the economy on a job-rich growth path. They are also the main instruments for establishing linkages between enterprises in modern sectors and the rest of the economy, thus making the process of structural change more dynamic and headed in the right direction. They can help accelerate diversification of economic activities and develop sectors that are of strategic importance for national development.

Fiscal policy can favour employment-intensive economic growth particularly through investment by the State. Public investment in physical and social infrastructure is absolutely critical for LDCs, as it improves both aggregate supply and aggregate demand conditions. Public investment in roads, railroads, irrigation systems or public goods in urban areas creates physical capital, thereby expanding the country's productive capacities. Not all such investments need be executed by the public sector; they can be implemented by private involvement driven by public expenditure. This in turn provides more opportunities for private investment in activities that have become profitable because of the new infrastructure. Both of these effects expand the aggregate supply. At the same time, the employment created by public investment means additional incomes for workers, with positive multiplier effects, which boosts aggregate demand.

In many LDCs the public sector is a major purchaser of goods and services and the largest formal sector employer in the economy. So public spending in general (both investment and consumption) already has a crucial influence on many markets for goods and services, as well as on the labour market. This means that government procurement policy (relying more on locally produced inputs and output, for example) can be used to induce employment creation in the economy and create possibilities for expansion of SMEs, once again with positive multiplier effects.

Maximizing the benefits accruing from public investment and other public spending obviously requires fiscal space — the ability to mobilize resources from internal and external sources so as to meet the requirements of public expenditure. Broadening the available fiscal space in turn requires diversifying the sources of financing of the public sector and especially strengthening domestic resource mobilization (UNCTAD, 2009: 57–90). Possible actions in this regard include broadening the tax base, improving the collection system and making the tax system more progressive. Tax administration and enforcement can be improved by making more public resources available for such activities. Reforming the tax administration by improving information management and cross-checking statements and declarations leads to greater efficiency in tax collection.[1] Setting up a special unit for high-income taxpayers has also been found to be helpful. Reducing or eliminating exemptions and loopholes, as well as enticing more businesses to join the formal sector, can go a long way towards broadening the tax base. It may be useful to combine the carrots of some incentives for tax payment with sticks of better enforcement. In all cases, however, revenues will rise only if the Government has the political will, makes its intentions clear and is consistent and determined about tax administration.

It is important to diversify the sources of tax revenue rather than relying on a single indirect tax, such as value added tax (VAT). The principle should generally be to rely as far as possible on rules-based and non-discretionary tax instruments that are corruption-resistant and have lower transaction costs. Some specific tax measures that have proven effective include:

- Increasing personal income tax collection from the rich, and raising taxes on luxury consumption;

- Taxing capital more effectively without affecting investment, often simply by tightening administration and through greater use of information technology;

- Reducing VAT exemptions on non-essential goods and raising the VAT rate on luxury consumption;

- Raising excise taxes on alcohol, tobacco and vehicles;

- Reducing tax holiday and exemptions for corporations and high-income expatriates;

- Increasing taxation on urban property (where the wealthiest live);

- Revising and implementing the taxation of the financial sector (where it is reasonably developed), possibly through measures like transaction taxes on financial transactions; and

The employment created by public investment means additional incomes for workers, with positive multiplier effects, which boosts aggregate demand.

Public spending has a crucial influence on many markets for goods and services, as well as on the labour market.

Broadening the available fiscal space requires diversifying the sources of financing of the public sector and especially strengthening domestic resource mobilization.

The principle should generally be to rely as far as possible on rules-based and non-discretionary tax instruments that are corruption-resistant and have lower transaction costs.

- Refraining from further trade tariff cuts until alternative sources of revenue are put in place.

For LDCs rich in energy and mineral resources, domestic resource mobilization may be achieved particularly through improvements in the capture and redistribution of resource rents (UNCTAD, 2010a: 199–203; UNCTAD, 2010b: 155–158). It is now more widely accepted that "In cases where the allocation of exploitation rights was flawed, governments should renegotiate the concession to restore a proper balance between private return and public revenue" (Commission on Growth and Development, 2008: 80). Resource-rich LDCs can increase fiscal revenue by reversing the current practice of offering extremely favourable terms to foreign investors in agriculture and mining. In the case of agriculture, this can involve imposing a tax on land leased for large-scale investment projects or raising the existing lease on land, as well as revising the taxation on the activity undertaken by such projects. Where mining is concerned, Governments can raise their revenues by adopting higher levies, royalties, income taxes or, in specific cases, export taxes. These can be usefully directed towards strengthening human capital formation and expanding infrastructure, which provide the long-term basis for economic diversification. This is especially critical because the resources generating these rents are exhaustible.

Resource-rich LDCs can increase fiscal revenue by reversing the current practice of offering extremely favourable terms to foreign investors in agriculture and mining.

At the same time, LDC Governments can strive to strengthen the mobilization of external resources from both traditional and non-traditional sources. This includes negotiating for a non-reduction in ODA from traditional donors in the present context and, at a later stage, for an increase. A matching funds approach may also be considered, which provides an incentive for domestic revenue rising in order to obtain additional ODA. As proposed by the United Nations Department of Economic and Social Affairs, it is also worth working towards international consensus on non-traditional forms of development finance, such as a currency transaction tax; regular allocations of IMF special drawing rights (SDRs); and the use of "idle" SDRs (UN/DESA, 2012). Another non-traditional source of development finance is the channelling of a fraction of the resources of Sovereign Wealth Funds to LDCs, either directly or through regional development banks, as proposed by UNCTAD. A simple calculation estimated that through the latter alternative, if 1 per cent of the assets from those funds were directed to the capital base of regional development banks, this could mobilize an additional $84 billion in their annual lending capacity (UNCTAD, 2011: 109–123).

LDC Governments can strive to strengthen the mobilization of external resources from both traditional and non-traditional sources.

Diversification of donors is a real possibility, given recent changes in the international economy, so LDCs can look beyond traditional donors to raise more financial assistance from partner Governments in the South.[2] Multilateral financial institutions can also provide additional resources for public investment. Regional funding of infrastructure can boost labour-intensive public works projects, e.g. in the context of regional integration schemes or of internationally funded border-crossing infrastructure projects, as was the case in the Greater Mekong Subregion of South-East Asia (UNCTAD, 2011: 102–104).

Regional funding of infrastructure can boost labour-intensive public works projects, e.g. in the context of regional integration schemes or of internationally funded border-crossing infrastructure projects.

Since many LDCs continue to rely on ODA for a substantial part of their public spending, it is important to use such aid effectively. Until quite recently, aid inflows to many of these countries were not put to good use because of a fear of the adverse effects of currency appreciation and the perceived need to keep higher levels of foreign exchange reserves in order to guard against potential financial crises. While the recent decline in global economic activity has reduced this tendency to some extent, it is still essential to ensure that ODA translates into higher public investment, preferably in areas where there are shortages or which form bottlenecks for production, or in areas where existing levels of provision are socially suboptimal.

While fiscal sustainability is a crucial medium-term issue, there should be some flexibility with respect to fiscal targets, especially when deficits are the result of productive public expenditure, and during economic downswings. Rigid rules on fiscal deficits in the short run reduce the possibility of effective countercyclical policies, which are likely to become important once again in the uncertain global environment. The general rule for developing countries to maintain fiscal sustainability should be for the public sector deficit not to exceed the long-term trend growth rate of the economy, while allowing for short-term cyclical variations (UNCTAD, 2013a).

The extent to which the LDCs can use the fiscal stance to address short-run situations of excess capacity or cyclical downswing is typically more limited than in developed countries. However, even this reduced policy space can and should be used as effectively as possible. For example, many LDCs adopted countercyclical measures, mostly of a fiscal nature, during the strong downturn in 2008–2009 (Brixiová et al., 2011; IMF, 2010). A case could also be made for a fiscal deficit composed entirely of public capital investment, *as long as the social rate of return from such investment exceeds the rate of interest*, which can effectively be financed through borrowing in exactly the same way as private investors do. This is particularly important, as noted above, in physical and social infrastructure, where public investment is essential since the presence of externalities means that the private sector is not likely to invest at socially optimal levels. A simple rule would be to limit debt financing in the medium term to the level of expenditure for public investment (UNCTAD, 2013a).

Monetary policy is not only about price stabilization and inflation control, but should be an integral part of macroeconomic and overall development strategies. Particularly in LDCs, it should aim at expanding credit for investments that are considered necessary or strategic, improving livelihood conditions in sectors that employ a large proportion of the labour force, such as agriculture, and generating more productive employment by providing institutional credit to small-scale producers in all sectors. The primary function of financial markets in providing financial intermediation for development should never be forgotten.

That is why basing monetary policy solely on inflation targeting is problematic. It is true that macroeconomic instability expressed in high inflation can kill growth. However, macroeconomic stability (when broadly defined so as not to be focused on a narrow target, such as inflation) is only a necessary condition for growth, not a sufficient one. Periods of accelerated growth can be associated with moderate or even intense inflation when supply constraints are encountered. Indeed, there is no conclusive evidence that moderate inflation has adverse effects on growth (Stiglitz et al., 2006), but the distributive implications can certainly be adverse, especially in LDCs where most incomes are not indexed to inflation. In such cases, the focus of policymakers must be on preventing inflation from becoming excessive. This can be addressed by the following:

- Eliminating current and potential supply bottlenecks;

- Correcting sectoral imbalances that may add to inflationary pressure, for example in agricultural production;

- Ensuring that the growth process is not adversely affected by policies to control inflation;

- Countering possible regressive effects of inflation through specific measures directed at the poor, such as public provision of certain basic needs; and

- Ensuring that inflationary expectations and speculative tendencies do not build up in the system, thereby causing higher rates of inflation over time.

While fiscal sustainability is a crucial medium-term issue, there should be some flexibility with respect to fiscal targets.

A case could also be made for a fiscal deficit composed entirely of public capital investment, as long as the social rate of return from such investment exceeds the rate of interest.

Monetary policy should aim at expanding credit for investments and generating more productive employment.

Macroeconomic stability is only a necessary condition for growth, not a sufficient one.

One alternative to a monetary policy fixated on attaining an inflation rate in the low single digits is a macroeconomic strategy that targets those real variables that are important for a particular country. These can include aggregate growth, productive investment, employment generation and poverty reduction. Monetary policy must be part of the overall macroeconomic policy directed towards these targets, rather than operating on a separate track of addressing monetary variables only. It should be coordinated and aligned with fiscal and exchange rate policies. Since the chosen target must be met within other constraints, interest rate management will not suffice; other instruments will have to be used by the central bank, including directed credit. Policymakers should avoid being fixated on one particular target and should be prepared to adjust targets and instruments depending on the requirements of changing situations.

The volume of credit is often a more critical variable than monetary supply.

The volume of credit is often a more critical variable than monetary supply, especially in LDCs where money markets and capital markets are less developed and relatively few households and enterprises have access to borrowing from formal institutions for consumption and investment. This is especially critical for MSEs and farms that cannot provide collateral for credit and are thus deemed not creditworthy by the banking sector. Microfinance institutions are valuable channels in this respect for small enterprises to access formal credit lines. Indeed, in many LDCs, and Bangladesh in particular, such institutions have served as effective instruments for including a large group of poor people in formal financial channels. Despite their benefits, however, these channels cannot be relied on as sources of credit mobilization for productive asset creation and the development of a dynamic enterprise sector. High interest rates, short gestation periods and the small size of loans tend to militate against their usefulness in poverty reduction and asset creation. Proper financial inclusion is likely to require larger financial institutions, some form of subsidy, as well as creative and flexible approaches by central banks and regulatory regimes to ensure that different banks (e.g. commercial, cooperative, development) reach excluded groups like women, as well as micro, small and medium-sized enterprises (MSMEs), self-employed workers, peasants and those without land titles or other collateral.

Microfinance cannot be relied on as sources of credit mobilization for productive asset creation and the development of a dynamic enterprise sector.

Productive diversification involves ensuring that MSMEs receive bank loans on similar terms as large capital. To this end, policymakers need to adopt a more ambitious and creative approach to the expansion of financial service provision, which is designed to facilitate access to credit for sectors and activities that are relatively deprived but that are of great importance for the economy. Relevant policy instruments in this regard include:

Productive diversification involves ensuring that small and medium-sized enterprises receive bank loans on similar terms as large capital.

- Directed credit rules that require banks to devote some proportion of their lending to such priority sectors;

- Subsidies to cover the higher transaction costs associated with such lending;

- Public guarantees for certain types of credit;

- Direct provision of credit by public financial institutions (e.g. development banks);

- Encouragement of cooperative banks and community banks; and

- Refinancing of commercial loans where necessary.

C. Managing the external sector

Most LDCs need some flexibility in exchange rates for trade purposes, but find it difficult to deal with the consequences of high volatility. "Intermediate" exchange rate regimes, such as managed floats, thus work best, since they allow Governments to adjust the level of the exchange rate to external conditions and to the current policy priorities of the domestic economy. These managed floats are best maintained through a combination of capital account and banking policy measures, along with the more usual open market operations of the central bank in purchasing or selling currency in the foreign exchange market. To make such a regime successful, capital flows need to be "managed" through a range of market-based and other measures, in terms of both inflows and outflows, so as to prevent excessive volatility and possible crises.

Capital flows need to be "managed" through a range of market-based and other measures, in terms of both inflows and outflows, so as to prevent excessive volatility and possible crises.

A competitive exchange rate can be a crucial instrument for attaining growth with employment in a global economy (Frenkel, 2004). It changes the relative prices to a point where importing goods are expensive, thereby stimulating import-substituting activities in the national economy. It also stimulates exports, especially manufactured goods, since it makes these activities more competitive on international markets. A competitive exchange rate further facilitates a creation of linkages between the export sectors and the rest of the economy by making domestically produced inputs cheaper than imported ones. However, since a cheap currency is also a way of keeping domestic incomes lower, such a strategy needs to be carefully calibrated.

A competitive exchange rate can be a crucial instrument for attaining growth with employment in a global economy.

Indeed, since LDCs still have some leeway with respect to trade policy instruments – unlike other developing-country members of the WTO – it is useful to remember that combinations of tariffs and subsidies amount to systems of multiple exchange rates. While it is not always desirable to have too many of these operating within an economy, they can allow competitive exchange rates to be delivered to particular priority sectors without making essential imports more expensive domestically. This raises the issue of managing the trade account, an area that has been inadequately explored in recent times by LDC Governments. Most trade policies have been evaluated in terms of the extent and timing of trade liberalization through removal of quantitative restrictions, reduction of tariffs and elimination of export subsidies. This process has been accelerated by changes in the multilateral trading system, and even more by the proliferation of regional trading agreements that have pushed for greater trade liberalization. It can be argued that for LDCs the process has gone far enough, and that from the standpoint of productive diversification and in the context of the need for more domestic employment generation, there is untapped potential in terms of the flexibilities still available to LDCs in global trade. LDC Governments should accordingly consider the matter of trade policy more creatively and in an integrated manner, and look to regional arrangements as a way to stimulate the development of synergies across productive sectors.

LDC Governments should consider trade policy more creatively, and look to regional arrangements as a way to stimulate the development of synergies across productive sectors.

Since capital flows are generally procyclical (Gallagher et al., 2012), their impact on developing countries is destabilizing, fuelling excessive optimism in good times and exacerbating the bust during crises. Capital account regulations can thus be a useful and at times crucial component of maximizing the benefits while minimizing the costs of free capital flows in the LDCs. Even the IMF, which for decades insisted on full capital account liberalization, has endorsed some use of capital account regulations (IMF, 2011). The successful experience with capital account management in a number of countries (Brazil, Chile, Colombia, Malaysia, Republic of Korea and Thailand, to name a few) shows that developing countries can and should shield themselves from these external shocks. Since

Capital account regulations can be a useful component of maximizing the benefits while minimizing the costs of free capital flows.

a restrictive monetary policy will serve only to exacerbate the problem during booms (by exacerbating inflows of capital and appreciation pressures), the alternative is to adopt some form of capital account regulation to manage an open capital account. Where inflows are concerned, instruments can include minimum stay requirements, unremunerated reserve requirements, differential tax rates on returns to portfolio capital and taxes on new debt inflows. For dealing with capital outflows, instruments can include taxes on capital outflows and regulating the amounts of non-profit capital which foreigners can send abroad.

LDCs are increasingly buffeted by dramatic changes in global markets over which they have no control. Developing countries in general, and the LDCs in particular, suffer more from external shocks than developed countries. LDC economies are smaller and less diversified. They tend to be very dependent on external financing, so they are exposed to greater capital account shocks. They are also more open to trade than many developed countries, and their export structure is more concentrated in a few products. Finally, many of these countries are exposed to strong fluctuations in international commodity prices, either as exporters or importers. For all these reasons, economic volatility is greater and thus more damaging in the LDCs than in developed countries.

Within LDC economies, the distributive effects of external shocks also tend to be adverse. There are direct costs of income variability in the presence of imperfect capital and insurance markets, so that income smoothing over the economic cycle is imperfect and downswings are associated with consumption declines, especially among the poor. Generally speaking, in all countries the poor bear the brunt of economic fluctuations: They suffer most in slumps, through higher unemployment and lower real wages, and they gain the least from booms, which are typically associated with increases in wealth, in returns to capital and in salaries of professional and skilled workers.

The question is, as noted in chapter 4, how LDC Governments are to cope with such externally generated volatility. While fiscal and monetary policies remain the basic levers to ensure changes in aggregate economic activity over the course of a cycle, other measures can be quite effective. In particular there are some "automatic stabilizers" that LDCs can and should use. For example, progressive taxation that is more proactive during slumps reduces the negative fiscal impact on the poor. Welfare programmes and social protection policies — including unemployment insurance schemes, worker protection, special access to non-collateral-based credit, public distribution systems for food and other necessities, income support for female-headed worker households, and so on — all operate to ensure that consumption does not fall as much as it otherwise would during a downswing. Automatic adjustments of tariffs to external prices, for example through a variable tariff system within the tariff bindings required by WTO, can reduce the impact of global price volatility on domestic producers and consumers.

In addition to these automatic stabilizers, there are other ways of responding to booms that can potentially dampen cyclical processes. For example, a counter-cyclical tax, such as an export tax, allows Government to generate more revenue during periods of export boom, which can then be set aside for a price stabilization fund in case export prices slump in future. Taxes on capital inflows can be limited to equity and portfolio capital, as opposed to "greenfield" investment, in periods when such inflows are high. In situations of clear overheating and build-up of speculative bubbles, it is important to restrict activities that are likely to be associated with boom/bust cycles, such as speculative real estate, through such measures as the imposition of higher capital gains taxes and bank regulations that restrict the extent of lending to the real estate sector.

In some LDCs, stabilization funds may be a particularly effective instrument for managing volatility, and particularly volatility caused by strong fluctuation in international prices, which is a typical feature of commodities. They can also help insulate economies from large, destabilizing inflows of foreign exchange, in several ways. In periods of relatively large capital inflows, they can help prevent an excessive appreciation of the exchange rate, thus avoiding the detrimental effects of the Dutch disease. They can preclude the overheating of the economy during boom periods, thus helping to control inflationary pressures. They can thwart the forming of bubbles, especially in real estate, which would ideally make the economy less prone to booms and busts. Finally, by maintaining a steady level of fiscal revenue, they can smooth fiscal expenditure, so that public investment can be maintained or even increased during a major downturn, expenditure on social services does not have to be cut, and so on. Stabilization funds are especially appropriate for the large commodity exporters among the LDCs. Many large commodity exporters — such as Chile, Islamic Republic of Iran, Kuwait, Norway, Oman, Papua New Guinea, Russian Federation and the Bolivarian Republic of Venezuela — have established stabilization funds with explicit macroeconomic stabilization objectives. When the price of the commodities they export is high, revenue is accumulated in the fund. When the price is low, the accumulated revenue can be used to smooth out government expenditure.

In some LDCs, stabilization funds may be a particularly effective instrument for managing volatility, caused by strong fluctuation in international prices of commodities.

D. State-led employment creation

Given the pervasive structural weakness of the private sector in LDCs, the State needs to play a stronger role than in other developing countries in supporting employment generation both directly and indirectly (e.g. through publicly supported investment and public employment). As argued in chapter 4, the role of the State will have to be more prominent in the short to medium term in order to kick-start a growth process that can create a strong investment-growth-employment nexus. A more dynamic approach to public investment recognizes that it is not just complementary to private sector investment but may also be a necessary addition. Griffin (1996) has noted that there are many ways in which government investment in physical capital can be made much more labour-intensive, thereby increasing employment, saving on foreign exchange and raising the overall rate of return in the economy.

Public investment is not just complementary to private sector investment but may also be a necessary addition.

The role of infrastructure development in aggregate growth is widely recognized, as the provision of such infrastructure as energy (electricity provision) and transport (roads) increases market opportunities, reduces costs and raises productivity in manufacturing and services firms (Bigsten and Söderbom, 2005; Shiferaw et al., 2012a, 2012b). Usually, however, such investments are not seen in terms of their employment effects. In fact, because they appear to be mostly heavily capital-intensive in nature, it is generally presumed that their direct employment effects are negligible and that it is only indirectly, through their impact on overall development, that they can influence job creation. Nonetheless, there are several ways in which public infrastructure spending can be more directly employment-generating and can have higher multiplier effects within local economies. Infrastructure works are doubly blessed, in that they create and sustain employment while at the same time improving living conditions and laying the foundation for long-term growth. Indeed, there is much greater scope than is generally recognized for developing infrastructure by using available surplus labour in LDCs. In urban areas, for example, labour-intensive techniques can be used for such works as improving streets and access ways, water supply, sewerage, sanitation and waste management, flood protection measures, and repair and maintenance of a range of public infrastructure. In

Public infrastructure spending can be more directly employment-generating and can have higher multiplier effects within local economies.

Infrastructure works are doubly blessed, in that they create and sustain employment while at the same time improving living conditions and laying the foundation for long-term growth.

fact, labour-intensive methods can also be effective (and cheap) in operations of large-scale infrastructure works that are typically seen as the preserve of equipment-intensive companies, such as bush-clearing and digging for the construction of dams and highways. The employment creation potential of investment in irrigation, drainage, provision of feeder channels, building, local land reclamation, afforestation and so forth is considerable.

Construction is a particularly fruitful area for encouraging more labour-intensive activities through direct public procurement practices and fiscal incentives. Building activities that use local materials, local technologies and local small-scale enterprises have much greater potential to generate employment. If local and small-scale manufacturers of building materials are encouraged, they are likely to have larger multiplier effects than large-scale, capital-intensive technologies, because they are generally more likely to use locally manufactured tools and machinery and are typically marketed and transported by small-scale enterprises. All of this can reduce the overall costs of construction, lead to ecologically sounder and more appropriate types of buildings and also generate more employment. Studies in several countries and infrastructure sectors show that employment-intensive investment in infrastructure is significantly less costly in financial terms than equipment-intensive techniques, without compromising on quality. It can also reduce foreign exchange requirements substantially, create several times as much employment for the same level of investment; permit the employment of more people at all skills levels; and create strongly positive indirect income multiplier effects.

Government provision of public goods and services has been an essential part of the development process in developing countries that grew in a sustained manner over long periods in the post-Second World War period. Spending in areas such as education and health has the double economic benefit of helping to strengthen the human resources base of the economy and being labour-intensive. Governments can thus contribute directly to the generation of all kinds of jobs, unskilled, semi-skilled and skilled. Emphasizing expansion and better delivery in the provision of public services, especially in nutrition, sanitation, health and education, not only allows for improved material and social conditions, but also has positive employment effects directly and through the multiplier process. Indeed, this was an important and unrecognized feature of successful Asian industrialization, from Japan and the east Asian NICs to (most recently) China. The public provision of affordable and reasonably good-quality housing, transport facilities, basic food, education and basic health care all operated to improve the living conditions of workers. Indirectly, it helped reduce the money wages that individual employers need to pay workers. This not only cut overall labour costs for private employers but also provided greater flexibility for producers competing in external markets, since a significant part of their fixed costs was effectively reduced.

Labour-intensive public works programmes (PWPs) were initially intended more as safety nets, especially in response to natural or economic emergencies (e.g. droughts, floods or harvest failure). More recently, however, they have been increasingly adopted as labour-based infrastructure programmes in response to the situation of chronic underemployment and unemployment in LDCs. In the past decade several developing countries, including LDCs, have adopted a new generation of employment creation programmes, which pay fair wages and strive to produce useful and durable assets that benefit participants directly. In many cases they also provide training to beneficiary workers and endeavour to involve local communities in decision-making and managing projects and programmes (Devereux and Salomon, 2006). Some of these programmes are envisaged as part of national (or regional) development strategies. They have also been seen as counter-cyclical mechanisms to respond to the global financial crisis, since they stimulate domestic demand even as they generate benefits from increases

Construction is a particularly fruitful area for encouraging more labour-intensive activities.

Building activities that use local materials, local technologies and local small-scale enterprises have much greater potential to generate employment.

Employment-intensive investment in infrastructure is significantly less costly in financial terms than equipment-intensive techniques, without compromising on quality.

In the past decade LDCs have adopted a new generation of employment creation programmes, which pay fair wages and strive to produce useful and durable assets that benefit participants directly.

in infrastructure spending and provide temporary income to those affected by the crisis.

Most PWPs in LDCs are introduced and designed by donors and funded either through donor grants or loans. There are still some domestically funded PWPs in operation that were developed independently, such as the Karnali Employment Programme in Nepal. The Vision 2020 Umurenge Programme in Rwanda, which is partly donor-funded, was jointly developed with donor inputs.

PWPs tend to have as their primary objective the provision of social assistance for poor households with working-age members who are unable to find work or pursue their normal livelihood activities due to some form of acute or chronic disruption in the labour market, or a deficit in labour demand. They are typically designed to provide basic income to support household consumption and prevent the distress-selling of assets to meet subsistence needs. They frequently involve the creation or maintenance of potentially productive infrastructure, such as roads or irrigation systems, which are also meant to contribute to the livelihoods of participants and the broader community.

Public work programmes frequently involve the creation or maintenance of potentially productive infrastructure, which are also meant to contribute to the livelihoods of participants and the broader community.

PWPs that provide a single short episode of employment are usually designed for consumption-smoothing, in response to temporary labour market or livelihood disruption which may result from natural disasters (such as droughts, floods or hurricanes), humanitarian situations (such as conflict) or short-term economic crises. These programmes are primarily concerned with the provision of what are referred to as safety nets, basic "risk-coping" social protection and the prevention of distress-selling of assets. Such programmes typically offer short-term employment – in Sub-Saharan Africa, for an average of four months (McCord and Slater, 2009) – but may be extended in humanitarian situations where normal livelihood activity has been suspended. In such programmes, the objective of ensuring a timely wage transfer (in kind or cash) is more important than that of asset provision, which may in some instances be essentially a "make-work" activity carried out primarily to satisfy the work conditionality. For this reason, the quality of assets created under such programmes is often of secondary importance to the rapid provision of wage employment for those affected by a crisis. This type of programme is typical of those implemented widely in southern Asia in response to natural disasters that temporarily affect formal and informal household income-earning opportunities and subsistence production. It is also the dominant form of PWP in SSA. In that region, however, such programmes are implemented not only in response to acute crises but also in situations of chronic poverty, underemployment and unemployment, where their short duration renders them less likely to have a significant impact on poverty.

In SSA, such programmes are implemented not only in response to acute crises but also in situations of chronic poverty, underemployment and unemployment.

Other PWPs target increasing local employment opportunities, or employment created per unit invested in infrastructure provision, usually in the construction sector through the adoption of labour-intensive construction techniques. Such programmes do not necessarily require significant additional funding but rather a shift in the factor intensity of existing expenditure from capital to labour. Some infrastructure-based PWPs concern activities which are already predominantly labour-intensive, such as housing construction, and where there are only marginal gains to be made from further labour intensification (McCutcheon and Taylor Parkins, 2003). However, other infrastructure development can be made using either capital- or labour-intensive approaches. Studies carried out in Cambodia, Ghana, Madagascar and Thailand have found that labour-intensive techniques led to two to five times more employment creation than alternative techniques (Devereux and Salomon, 2006). In the case of Senegal, an estimated 13 times more jobs were created thanks to the adoption of labour-intensive techniques, than with conventional techniques (Majeres, 2003). In Cambodia, it was found

Other PWPs target increasing local employment opportunities, or employment created per unit invested in infrastructure provision.

Labour-intensive techniques led to two to five times more employment creation than alternative techniques.

that labour-based rural road works required nearly 5,000 unskilled workdays per km, compared to 200 workdays on an equipment-based operation (Munters, 2003: 45).

This approach may be particularly appropriate when used in conjunction with the large-scale investment in infrastructure that has been taking place in many countries as a stimulus in response to the global financial crisis. Obviously, the efficiency of adopting this approach rather than conventional capital-intensive approaches will depend on the nature of the assets being created. Furthermore, contractors may not always comply with contractual obligations, due to the higher cost implications of shifting factor intensity. In such cases PWPs can be implemented as a complement to private sector employment creation, so as to reach those least successful in gaining market-based employment.

If PWPs are to be part of a long-term employment strategy, there are strategic choices to be made regarding the priority group for employment. Youth might be the priority in contexts where youth not in employment, education or training are a major concern, where youth are excluded from private sector employment, and where social or political stability are key concerns. Demobilized soldiers or urban populations might be the priority in other contexts, with the poorest being selected only where poverty reduction and social protection are key policy objectives. Examples of this type of intervention include the work of the Ethiopian Rural Roads Authority, the Agence d'Exécution des Travaux d'Intérêt Public contre le sous-emploi in Senegal, the Association Africaine des Agences d'Exécution des Travaux d'Intérêt Public throughout western Africa, and ILO's Employment-Intensive Investment Programmes.

Beyond poverty alleviation and employment creation, PWPs may also have as their objectives environmental sustainability and contributing to the structural transformation of the economy. Still other objectives include skills development through work experience and on-the-job training, accumulation of financial and material assets, promotion of livelihoods, stimulation of economic growth through the promotion of demand and creation of productive assets, and maintenance of the social and political order in the context of unacceptably high levels of unemployment and poverty. While multiple programme goals relating to poverty reduction, employment creation, structural transformation and environmental sustainability are not necessarily conflicting, optimal outcomes for each may demand alternative designs.

It is often argued that the use of labour-intensive techniques entails a loss of quality of the assets created, but this need not be the case. The quality of assets depends on the correct identification, design, specification and implementation of the construction process, all of which differ if labour-intensive approaches are used. For example, executing capital-intensive designs using labour-intensive processes will not result in successful outcomes, so the whole process needs to be approached differently if good-quality outcomes are to be ensured (McCutcheon and Taylor Parkins, 2003). If the processes are appropriately designed from the outset and adequately resourced, there is no necessary trade-off between factor intensity and asset quality. Quality is also affected by the availability of agricultural and engineering capacities at local level and by the adequacy of resources allocated to the capital component of asset creation.

Coordination among different agents in the implementation of PWPs is also a critical issue. Such agents include various levels of government (national, regional, district and village); ministries and departments (such as those responsible for welfare, public works, transport, environment and agriculture); donors; civil society organizations, and so forth. This is a particularly acute challenge in LDCs, where government and donor harmonization and coordination are not always present. Coordination is an especially important

PWPs can be implemented as a complement to private sector employment creation, so as to reach those least successful in gaining market-based employment.

Youth might be the priority in contexts where youth not in employment, education or training are a major concern

PWPs may also have as their objectives environmental sustainability and contributing to the structural transformation of the economy.

If the processes are appropriately designed from the outset and adequately resourced, there is no necessary trade-off between factor intensity and asset quality.

concern when PWPs also incorporate environmental goals in their design and implementation. One example is the Vision 2020 Umurenge Programme in Rwanda, where multi-year PWP employment of the poorest is combined with the promotion of more environmentally sustainable agriculture based on the terracing of hillsides, which potentially results in sustained productivity increases and greater environmental sustainability of agriculture (depending on which crops are adopted). Environmental goals are also part of the Productive Safety Net Programme in Ethiopia. The creation of riverine protection or bunds against inundation (as in the World Food Programme's Food for Work projects in Nepal) may also generate sustained environmental benefits that can promote livelihoods over time and hence have poverty reduction benefits that accrue beyond the period of project employment.

Policymakers often hope that participation in PWPs will allow workers to "graduate" from poverty and from dependence on publicly funded jobs. However, given the structural, rather than frictional, nature of unemployment in many LDCs, it is not clear that PWP training and/or workplace experience will be sufficient to enable labour market incorporation after such employment. This is likely only where such programmes are combined with other interventions, in a broadly conducive national labour and economic context. Indeed, to the extent that such employment is well targeted at the poorest, it is less likely to result in significant graduation, while the macroeconomic and labour market outcomes are more likely to be indirect, operating through the multiplier effects of additional incomes leading to higher effective demand in the areas where the programme is implemented. There are well-documented cases of the immediate impacts of PWPs on local production; such cases involve, for example, the emergence of small-scale markets on paydays. These tend to be short-term impacts, however, since most PWPs continue for short periods. The poorer the participants and the more marginalized the area where the programme is implemented, the less likely the programme is to contribute to deliver economic spillover effects unless it is implemented on a sustained basis and a significant scale.

Even so, PWPs in rural areas have been found to contribute to rural development through public investment in agricultural infrastructure (e.g. rural roads and irrigation). This has generated greater agricultural production and productivity in the vicinity of the created assets. Moreover, improved communication and transport resulting from new or improved transport infrastructure have contributed to the creation of local markets and to better access to existing markets (Devereux and Salomon, 2006). Large-scale ongoing implementation through an employment-intensive programme (or through an employment guarantee scheme) is more likely to deliver secondary economic benefits, including an increase in the reservation wage of casual day labourers or accumulation and microenterprise development. It has been suggested that "tiny transfers equal tiny impacts, but moderate transfers can have major impacts" (Devereux, 2002: 672). Employing fewer people at higher wages for extended periods of time allows programme participants to invest in production and assets, although it may also create resentment and tension on the part of excluded community members. This means that fixing wages is a crucial aspect of PWP design and implementation.

Despite their numerous advantages, there are still several constraints in adopting and implementing PWPs effectively in LDCs. One issue is finance: Labour-intensive public works tend to be relatively costly if they are sufficiently large-scale. The cost for the Ethiopian programme, for instance, was an estimated 2 per cent of the country's GDP in 2006. Of course, if this results in significant positive multiplier effects, then some of this cost may be recouped through increased tax revenues in the subsequent period. Funding sources must nevertheless be identified, especially as the lingering effects of the 2008–2009 crisis have led to generalized fiscal restrictions (or retrenchment), making

There are cases of immediate impacts of PWPs on local production, such as the emergence of small-scale markets on paydays.

PWPs in rural areas have been found to contribute to rural development through public investment in agricultural infrastructure, which has generated greater agricultural production and productivity.

Employing fewer people at higher wages for extended periods of time allows programme participants to invest in production and assets.

it more difficult to obtain funding for PWPs in LDCs. Institutional capacity is yet another concern, since effective implementation of such programmes requires the technical and operational capacity to choose, prepare, manage and supervise the works, organize the production process, become familiar with the techniques, access the required equipment and tools, manage small-scale contracts, coordinate the actions of different government levels and channel resources to the poor.

This partly explains why it is challenging to achieve all the intended goals. In some instances the challenge of providing mass employment through PWPs has not been met. Some of these programmes have thus become de facto cash transfer programmes, providing the wage transfer without fulfilling the work requirement. In addition to issues of financing and institutional capacity, LDCs are further constrained by the orientation of the macroeconomic and other ("development") policies they have been following for over two decades. For the most part these policies are geared domestically towards macroeconomic stability and, externally, towards international integration. Employment creation is still not at centre-stage in the national policymaking of most developing countries, including LDCs. This reinforces the argument that PWPs must be part of a broader economic policy package that combines macroeconomic, trade and industrial policies to meet the basic goal of productive employment creation and diversification to higher value added activities.

PWPs must be part of a broader economic policy package that combines macroeconomic, trade and industrial policies.

Private activities account for the bulk of employment in LDCs today, and will clearly continue to do so in future.

E. Enterprise development

Private activities account for the bulk of employment in LDCs today, and will clearly continue to do so in future. The challenge for their Governments is to enable and encourage the private sector to generate more diversified and higher value added activities which will provide sufficient productive employment to the growing labour force. Three broad policy areas are relevant in this context: industrial policies, enterprise policies and rural development policies. Each of these is considered in turn.

The challenge for LDC Governments is to enable and encourage the private sector to generate higher value added activities which will provide sufficient productive employment to the growing labour force.

1. INDUSTRIAL POLICIES

Industrial policy in general refers to government attempts to change the structures and patterns of production in an economy, and in particular to diversify production towards higher value added activities. In the late twentieth century this type of intervention was frowned on in mainstream policy circles, although industrial policy remained in use in many of the more successful developing countries, such as China. Recently, however, there has been a revival of interest in industrial policies, with more analysts arguing for their usefulness and desirability (e.g. Lin and Monga, 2010; Lin, 2011; OECD, 2013). There is greater recognition that several developing countries have improved their capacity to design and implement industrial policies (te Velde et al., 2011). At the same time, the growing marketability of a new wave of innovations in green technology, energy, water, nanotechnology and genetics (Wade, 2010) has created new possibilities. But in order to exploit these opportunities, firms must be forward-looking and prepared (Pérez and Soete, 1988; Pérez, 2001). This requires the coordination of industrial policy, especially in an LDC context. New challenges — such as those resulting from climate change — require structural changes in the economy of both developed and developing countries on a scale and speed that market forces are incapable of implementing alone, which therefore requires State action. Indeed, even some developed countries have recently become much more active in their own industrial policy (Rodrik,

Industrial policy refers to government attempts to change the structures and patterns of production in an economy.

2010), under the pressures of the international economic and financial crisis, environmental challenges and concerns about their deindustrialization.

At the same time, the implementation of effective industrial policy has also become more complex and difficult in recent years, particularly in view of the fragmentation of production due to the rise of global value chains. For LDCs wishing to benefit from positive integration into such production chains, a more nuanced but still systematic approach will be required, one that encourages domestic entrepreneurship and innovation. Industrial policy must accordingly be flexible, adapted to specific contexts and constantly responding to changing global and domestic conditions. Ideally, support should be provided in a time-bound and possibly phased manner, while ensuring consistency across different sets of policies.

The implementation of effective industrial policy has also become more complex and difficult in recent years, in view of the fragmentation of production.

The broad priorities of industrial policy in LDCs can be summarized as follows (UNCTAD, 2009: 141–179; Ocampo, 2007):

- To invest in dynamically growing sectors of the economy and encourage diversification, so that at least part of the growing domestic demand is met by domestic supply, rather than by imports;

- To develop and strengthen MSMEs, where most employment is generated;

- To build linkages that can bridge the various divides that permeate the enterprise sector: micro vs. medium and large; formal vs. informal; national vs. foreign; and modern vs. traditional;

Industrial policy instruments are usually classified as being functional or selective. Functional instruments typically aim at correcting market failures and are applied throughout an economy, for example by providing credit, education and training, and by spurring competition, research and development. Once Governments have endeavoured to correct market failures, it is the firms that will decide how far they wish to innovate and upgrade technologically. Selective or vertical measures, by contrast, aim at shifting to new and dynamic activities and/or localized technological upgrading. They are targeted at specific (sub) sectors or firms. Government provides financial support for such measures during learning periods and helps start-ups with training, export marketing and the general coordination of export activities. Obviously, an important criterion for the selection of activities to be supported by industrial policy is the labour intensity of the activities and/or their potential to generate jobs either directly or indirectly.

An important criterion for the selection of activities to be supported by industrial policy is the labour intensity of the activities and/or their potential to generate jobs.

Two different but possibly complementary approaches to using such instruments can be considered. The incremental approach builds on existing activities in the economy to seek areas where backward and forward linkages and supporting activities can be developed. Agriculture, for example, can be used as the basis for developing downstream industries, such as food processing for local, regional and global markets and processing agricultural raw materials before export. Policies to encourage more local processing include bans or tariffs on raw unprocessed exports, support to industrial clusters for such activities and industrial extension services that provide both technological and marketing support. For example, export tariffs have spurred the downstream processing of cashew nuts in Mozambique and raw hides and skins in Ethiopia (Krause and Kaufmann, 2011; Altenburg, 2010). Similar policies can be devised for such other primary activities as mining, as was done for diamond processing in Botswana. Such efforts are likely to be more successful if they are combined with the development of local production clusters based on natural resources and the development of engineering capabilities for domestic production (Ramos, 1998).

The incremental approach to industrial policy builds on existing activities in the economy to seek areas where backward and forward linkages.

In such strategies, however, care must be taken to recognize situations in which upstream and downstream industries require very different endowments. The garment industry, for example, is typically labour-intensive, whereas the industry that produces textiles, yarns and accessories is increasingly capital-intensive, with large economies of scale and scope. This makes the development of backward linkages in textiles for the garments sector much more difficult in most LDCs (Adhikari and Yamamoto, 2007). Instead, LDCs are more likely to succeed by upgrading within the garment industry itself and/ or by exploiting niche markets (Altenburg, 2011). Mozambique, for instance, tried to establish backward linkages from large-scale foreign firms in mining (e.g. the aluminium smelter), but with only limited success, due to a dearth of the requisite entrepreneurial capabilities among domestic firms (Krause and Kaufmann, 2011).

LDCs are likely to succeed by upgrading within the garment industry itself and/or by exploiting niche markets.

A less traditional approach to industrial policy is more forward-looking, involving the identification of new areas of specialization, in order to enter into such activities relatively swiftly and to benefit from the rising potential in global markets for such production. In this case, because the distance in the product space between new and existing activities is large, the risk is high but the strategy potentially rewarding. Public intervention is necessary in such cases because early entrants into new products, technologies or markets have to bear all the costs of discovery but are unable to internalize all the benefits, requiring some form of State support (Hausmann and Rodrik, 2003). Government agencies typically decide what are the promising sectors or activities and concentrate their policy attention accordingly. This can, however, also be accomplished through collaboration between public and private agents, such as entrepreneurs and their representative bodies, market analysts and civil society representatives, in such forums as deliberation councils, sector roundtables and private-public venture funds, making use of internal and external expertise. This has been successfully applied in the case of the cut flower industry in Ethiopia. The initiative for exporting these products came from the private sector, but it was backed by Government, which provided low-cost access to suitable land, negotiated freight costs with the national airline and established a national horticulture development agency.

A less traditional approach to industrial policy is more forward-looking, involving the identification of new areas of specialization, in order to enter into such activities relatively swiftly.

Governments can also encourage businesses innovation (such as seeking new markets and alternative business models) through business plan competitions, coaching innovative start-up companies and offering incentives to the local business sector or the diaspora. This is the core of UNCTAD's proposal for a new international support measure for LDCs, the Investing in Diaspora Knowledge Transfer initiative (UNCTAD, 2012: 147–150), which consists of a collaborative effort between the national Government and international organizations to back the investment of the LDC diasporas in innovative and knowledge-intensive activities.

Governments can also encourage businesses innovation through business plan competitions, coaching innovative start-up companies and offering incentives to the local business sector or the diaspora.

Industrial policy formulation and execution in LDCs tends to follow a top-down approach, with Governments taking the lead on priority areas and programmes. Successful industrial policies, however, require a continuous dialogue among Governments, businesses (including MSEs) and workers. Beyond general business complaints about financing, high taxes, corruption, infrastructure services and so forth, this dialogue should highlight coordination failures that constrain enterprise development, such as the local unavailability of a low- cost input critical to a specific industry, which can in turn prompt government action to encourage production of the specific input (O'Connor, 2007). The dialogue can be especially fruitful when it is focused on specific industries and when the Government is willing to change its policies in response to specific needs. Just such continuous dialogue and interaction among the government agencies responsible for industrial policy and businesses (both sectoral chambers and

Successful industrial policies require a continuous dialogue among Governments, businesses (including MSEs) and workers.

individual firms) was crucial for structural change and upgrading in the successful industrializers of east Asia. Studies of the performance of enterprises from seven SSA countries (five of them LDCs) have found that State-business relationships enhance firm productivity by about 25–35 per cent (Qureshi and te Velde, 2012). Furthermore, some form of balance between the State and business actors is needed to avoid the State being captured by particular interests or rent-seeking (Wade, 2010). This entails ensuring that the private sector meets its commitments in exchange for receiving favourable policy measures.

It is increasingly recognized that knowledge generation and dissemination must be critical features of industrial policy, and this is very much so in the LDCs. The best way to enhance the knowledge intensity of economies is through education, technical and vocational training and skills upgrading through on-the-job training. Since LDCs are still lagging behind in these areas despite recent progress, this remains a crucial focus. In secondary and tertiary education and technical and vocational training, LDCs need to expand the supply and improve the quality of services. This includes revising curricula and teaching methods in order to make the labour force more adaptable and innovative and so as to adapt educational policies to foreseeable domestic labour market requirements. Policies must also adapt the form of education and the content of curricula so as to provide students and apprentices with such skills as "learning to learn", "learning to change" and the ability to do creative teamwork and think innovatively (Pérez, 2001; Adesida and Karuri-Sebina, 2013). Ideally, given the gestation lags in producing graduates, educational planners should have some idea of where the economy as a whole is headed over the coming 5 to 10 years in order to guide the educational system with respect to the future needs of the labour market.

The disconnect between academic research and the private sector has frequently been highlighted as a weakness in domestic knowledge systems (UNCTAD, 2006: 246–255; Adesida and Karuri-Sebina, 2013). It is therefore important for universities and research centres to strengthen their links with businesses of all sizes. Instruments to reach this goal include:

- Adopting curricula that focus on entrepreneurship development in vocational training and universities;

- Enacting tax breaks or training levies in order to fund industry-specific training of the labour force (with such training possibly provided by dedicated training centres);

- Creating (either nationally or regionally) standard-setting bodies (e.g. for quality and sanitary certification), whether by government initiative or through partnerships between Government and industry or sectoral associations.

The role of external donors deserves consideration as well, since multilateral and bilateral donors have traditionally exerted a very strong influence on industrial policymaking in LDCs. Since the structural adjustment era, these countries have been advised to avoid any industrial policy that called for greater, and more direct, State involvement in economic development. More recently, however, there has been more external support for industrial policy in LDCs, including the financing of programmes for upgrading technical and vocational training systems, cluster and value chain initiatives and building trade capacity. In some cases, industrial policy programmes are not only funded but also executed by donors. While this marks the beginning of a positive shift in donors' attitudes, it is still fraught with some of the challenges that characterize official aid more generally: for example, limited alignment with country priorities; donors establishing parallel agencies and implementation bodies that weaken State capabilities by attracting the most qualified professionals; limited coordination among donors; intensive use

Some form of balance between the State and business actors is needed to avoid the State being captured by particular interests or rent-seeking.

The best way to enhance the knowledge intensity of economies is through education, technical and vocational training and skills upgrading through on-the-job training.

Policies must also adapt the form of education and the content of curricula so as to provide students and apprentices with such skills as "learning to learn", and the ability to do creative teamwork.

It is important for universities and research centres to strengthen their links with businesses of all sizes.

of donor-related experts with limited domestic capacity-building, etc. (UNCTAD, 2008: 93–134; Altenburg, 2011). In order to contribute more effectively in this regard, donors should step up their funding of capacity-building in industrial policymaking and avoid setting up parallel structures, making greater use instead of national and local administrative structures. Most importantly, donors should align their interventions with country priorities, policies and national development plans.

Donors should step up their funding of capacity-building in industrial policymaking and make greater use of national and local administrative structures.

In a sluggish world economy, LDCs have the option of relying on regional markets as potential sources of trade expansion and growth. There is considerable potential for joint action to mobilize common resources, develop common development goals, invest in regional public goods and leverage those of development partners (including multilateral institutions, bilateral donors, and partners in the South) that are in a position to assist development-focused regional integration. While there have been some moves towards such "developmental regionalism" (UNCTAD, 2011) — notably the Greater Mekong initiative that includes Cambodia and Laos in South-East Asia – such experiences are still rare among LDCs. Regional integration in the regions where LDCs are found in larger numbers has generally been weak. Although many institutions and action plans have been established, implementation has typically been very low.

LDCs have the option of relying on regional markets as potential sources of trade expansion and growth.

At the time of writing, the Southern Africa Development Community has been holding initial discussions on the desirability of a regional industrial policy, but there has been little if any concrete action (Zarenda, 2012). In June 2010 the Economic Community of West African States adopted the West African Common Industrial Policy with very ambitious targets (e.g. raising the contribution of manufacturing to regional GDP from the current 6 per cent to 20 per cent by 2030), but its implementation is still in very early stages. However, in the specific case of agro-processing industries, African countries have launched an initiative of agricultural commodity chains of production, processing and marketing (e.g. rice, maize, wheat, sugar, meat and dairy products) that could potentially meet increasing regional demand in the context of regional integration schemes (UNECA and African Union, 2009).

Another type of industrial policy strategy is intended to change the capital-labour ratio of the economy by attracting investment in labour-intensive industries.

Another type of industrial policy strategy is intended to change the capital-labour ratio of the economy by attracting investment in labour-intensive industries like garments. This has been especially effective in creating jobs and contributing to poverty reduction in some LDCs (Bangladesh, Cambodia, Haiti and Lesotho) and several ODCs (including Viet Nam). Typically, these activities have the additional benefits of raising female participation in the labour force. By providing women with better-paid jobs, these new activities free them from subsistence activities, informal low-productivity activities or inactivity. The challenge for all these countries is to ensure the survival and possibly the expansion of these industries in the face of fierce international competition. In order to do so, they have endeavoured to keep their labour costs low (e.g. Bangladesh) or to brand their country as a "socially responsible" production location (Cambodia). Another alternative has been to exploit product niche marketing, as has been done by Sri Lanka.

Apart from goods exports, tourism is another area with potential for business expansion and employment generation in rural areas.

Apart from goods exports, tourism is another area with potential for business expansion and employment generation in rural areas. In most LDCs, where international tourism is already concentrated in rural areas, the sector can be focused to develop non-farm rural activities and generate jobs, as long as attention is given to creating backward and forward linkages and to environmental sustainability (UNCTAD, 2013c). Ecotourism is a particularly promising niche sector. Uganda, for instance, has recently implemented a set of policies for sustainable tourism that includes the promotion of local linkages through domestic entrepreneurship, the participation of local communities in both the planning and execution stages. As a result, these communities receive 20 per cent of gate fees around protected areas and are trained to act as guides and provide accommodations. Furthermore, regional cooperation is conducted by promoting the East African Community as a single tourism destination and by facilitating tourists' displacements within the region. Such cooperation also involves investment incentives for the sector (including import tariff waivers for tourism vehicles), public investment in infrastructure and close collaboration between public sectoral authorities and local stakeholders. This set of initiatives has resulted in an increase in tourist arrivals and tourism receipts since 2010, and tourism now absorbs 14 per cent of the labour force in formal employment and 21 per cent of informal sector employment (Aulo, 2013).

One recent development that may open further opportunities for some LDCs is the transition of China — by far the world's largest exporter of labour-intensive manufactures — to a different phase of development. Its labour costs are rising, and the composition of its export basket is moving towards higher value added and more knowledge-intensive products. At the same time there is an incipient movement to offshore production at the lower end of labour-intensive manufacturing to labour-abundant and low-labour-cost countries (OECD, 2013). These developments in China may make it possible for some LDCs to capture a part of this manufacturing activity. Some LDCs may take advantage of the window of opportunity presented by China's likely delocalization of the lower end of its manufacturing industry through a combination of attracting FDI and integrating domestic firms into global manufacturing value chains.

Some LDCs may take advantage of the window of opportunity presented by China's likely delocalization of the lower end of its manufacturing industry.

The LDCs that are best placed to take advantage of these changes in the geography of international manufacturing are those that present most of the following characteristics: low wages, large workforces, and the skills needed to produce goods (especially garments) rapidly and in large quantities for global retailers (*Financial Times*, 2013), as well as good transport and communication connections to other countries. These features — and especially the last one — are an advantage for those LDCs that already possess some experience of manufacturing production and exports and that are geographically close to dynamic poles of economic growth (such as Bangladesh, Cambodia, Lao People's Democratic Republic and Myanmar). However, several African LDCs — especially the most labour-abundant among them, like Ethiopia — can also take policy action to seize these opportunities. They may exploit this potential despite the fact that most of them have limited experience in large-scale manufacturing for global markets and that significant development is thus likely to take longer. Relevant initiatives include improving communication and transport infrastructure and ensuring agricultural development, both of which help to keep labour costs low. Domestically, this strategy should be complemented by policies on clustering, export promotion and labour cost containment. Labour costs can remain competitive by ensuring an adequate supply of wage goods and services, especially food (by means of agricultural policy, as explained below), transport and housing. Enacting policy measures to foster FDI, joint ventures or technology licensing is another plausible option for LDCs whose producers lack international competitiveness in basic manufacturing but have a reasonable transport and communication infrastructure (Schmitz, 2007). Preferential access to major consumer markets may constitute another favourable factor.

Several African LDCs — especially the most labour-abundant among them — can also take policy action to seize these opportunities.

Domestically, this strategy should be complemented by policies on clustering, export promotion and labour cost containment.

In the rush to seize these opportunities, however, LDCs should beware of running a race to the bottom. This may happen if they continue their present policies for attracting FDI — policies that have formed the backbone of the LDC growth model for more than two decades. Generous incentives, tax breaks and other incitements often turn out to be more advantageous to international investors than to host countries. The LDC experience shows that they have attracted substantial amounts of FDI, but that most of it went to export-oriented

In the rush to seize these opportunities LDCs should beware of running a race to the bottom.

enclaves producing primary commodities or labour-intensive manufactures. The latter type of FDI, but not the former, generates a substantial number of jobs. In both cases, however, the enclaves develop very limited linkages to the rest of the domestic economy and therefore have limited technological and productivity effects. LDCs should reorient their FDI policy to stimulate the creation of backward and forward linkages between transnational corporations (TNCs) and domestic enterprises. Such linkages would bring benefits not only in stronger employment creation, but also in technological, organizational, knowledge and other spillovers. Policymakers can enhance the benefits deriving from FDI through proper policies. They need to integrate the export manufacturing sector into national development policies and avoid the creation of export enclaves. Lall (1995) suggests the use of soft "target and guide" instruments, such as bringing in firms to make investments that fit the country's upgrading strategy and persuading them to engage in technology transfer.

The challenges for LDCs in expanding the benefits they derive from FDI are closely related to those of obtaining developmental effects from participation in GVCs.

The challenges for LDCs in expanding the benefits they derive from FDI are closely related to those of obtaining developmental effects from participation in global value chains (GVCs). GVCs are now ubiquitous in the global economy, and LDCs are increasingly a part of them. From a development and policy standpoint, the question is not *whether* these countries should participate in GVCs but *how* they should do so (UNCTAD, 2013b: 148–210). The option of joining GVCs is typically feasible for firms that have basic production skills but lack access to major markets and marketing know-how (Schmitz, 2007). Such firms tend to agglomerate in those regions within a country that are best served by infrastructure and international connections. This presupposes prior government action to ensure that these general conditions are available.

The potential benefits of participation in GVCs – employment, income, exports, technology – depend on where the country is positioned within the chain and on what type of activities it engages in.

LDCs today face three major types of risks from their form of integration into GVCs. First, some of the major benefits derived from traditional forms of industrialization (linkages, externalities, multiplier effects, etc.) are largely absent from this type of industrial growth. The potential benefits of participation in GVCs — employment, income, exports, technology and the like — depend on where the country is positioned within the chain and on what type of activities it engages in. Second, given the fragmentation of the production process and the dearth of backward and forward linkages, LDCs risk remaining locked into the lowest rungs on the GVC ladders. These are the stages that are less knowledge-intensive and that generate the least value added. Even more worrying is the fact that these stages have the least potential for upgrading. This is because the ability of local enterprises to capture value depends largely on power relationships in the chain. Since TNCs can choose suppliers from any number of countries, they are in a strong position to dictate the terms of their relationships with local suppliers in LDCs. These concerns are confirmed by an analysis of LDC export patterns, which shows that these countries do indeed remain locked into the lower levels of GVC processing and that there are very few examples of product upgrading (UNCTAD, 2007: 11–50). The third major risk of LDC involvement in GVCs is that the stages of their integration are typically labour-intensive. Although this contributes significantly to job generation, the quality of the jobs and of the associated working conditions can be appalling. The environmental and physical safety impacts have also been adverse at times. These shortcomings have been highlighted by recent accidents in firms that operate in Bangladesh and are part of GVCs.

LDCs remain locked into the lower levels of GVC processing and there are very few examples of product upgrading.

LDC policymakers can manage their country's integration into GVCs in such a way as to raise its developmental impact, by embedding GVCs in the country's overall development strategy.

LDC policymakers can, however, overcome these problems by following two parallel strategies. First, they can manage their country's integration into GVCs in such a way as to raise its developmental impact, by embedding GVCs in the country's overall development strategy, building domestic productive capacities, implementing a strong environmental, social and governance framework and synergizing trade and investment policies and institutions (UNCTAD, 2013b: 175–210). Achieving these goals is obviously difficult in view of the prevailing asymmetric power relationships, so the role of the LDC State should be to prioritize national development objectives. Authorities need to negotiate with foreign investors in order to obtain the creation of domestic linkages and technology transfer to local firms, since international integration through GVCs and FDI have a lasting developmental effect only when they are complemented by continuous technological capability-building by participating domestic firms (so as to avoid being locked into labour-intensive, lower-productivity activities). Policies should also target the creation of linkages with other domestic firms that can learn and upgrade through these linkages.

Authorities need to negotiate with foreign investors in order to obtain the creation of domestic linkages and technology transfer to local firms.

2. Policies to foster entrepreneurship

The LDCs, even more than other developing countries, have to cope with structural weaknesses and a lack of development in the private sector, which calls for policies to enhance private capital accumulation, employment generation and technological progress. Such policies must encompass different types and sizes of enterprise, since policies for MSME development obviously differ substantially from those for attracting FDI.

a. Financial services

One major element of the required policies is to enable access to finance. The failure of commercial banks to provide adequate financing to private firms in LDCs — especially MSMEs — is a major obstacle to enterprise development in these countries, as discussed in chapter 4. The State must thus play a leading role in financial allocations, not only to regulate finance and guard against financial fragility and failure, but also to use the financial system to direct investment towards sectors and technologies at appropriate scales of production. Financial policy should be designed so that financial services reach not only MSMEs, but such excluded groups as women, self-employed workers, peasants and those without land titles or other collateral. In order to lift the financing constraint on enterprise development, several alternatives can be considered by LDC policymakers. They include:

Financial policy should be designed so that financial services reach MSMEs and excluded groups.

- *State development banks.* Such banks can provide long-term financing to domestic companies (including SMEs, start-ups and innovative firms), possibly on more favourable terms than market institutions. They can supply other financial services like short-term loans and co-financing. They can help build industrial clusters to provide synergies and economies of scale to MSMEs. Effective development banks can also work closely with domestic firms by mentoring productive activities, offering other forms of SME promotion and support and helping to reduce financial volatility.

State development banks can provide long-term financing to domestic companies on more favourable terms than market institutions.

- *Venture capital.* Government can act as a venture capitalist when it finances projects by taking a participation in the firm's equity, rather than by providing loans. The stakes can be sold on the market once the company is on a solid footing. This alternative is more appropriate for larger firms and projects than for MSMEs.

- *Commercial banks.* Government can encourage lending to MSMEs by (i) providing banks with subsidies; (ii) enacting lower asset-based reserve requirements for this market segment than for other types of lending; (iii) fostering cooperation between formal and informal financial institutions, such as rotating savings and credit societies, which typically have better information on borrowers' risks and operate with lower transaction costs; and (iv) providing official credit guarantees to encourage loans to desired sectors and categories of borrowers, with a focus on neglected sectors with high employment intensity. These options are obviously more feasible where commercial banking is relatively well developed and spread throughout the country.

Microfinance per se is not an appropriate financing model for enterprise development.

- *Microfinance.* While microfinance can have a positive short-term impact on employment in petty trade and services, and often provides a safety net and consumption smoothing, microfinance per se is not an appropriate financing model for enterprise development, as it relies on interest rates that are too high and repayment periods that are too short for long-term productive investment (Chowdhury, 2009; Schoar, 2010). As noted earlier, it does not allow for productive asset creation or enable viable economic activities to flourish.

- *Ensuring financial access* on reasonable terms to households and consumers, especially through access to banking services, credit, and risk cover and insurance products. This is important because it feeds back by spurring demand and further output growth and by raising welfare.

b. Enterprise support services

Technical assistance to impart and enhance the managerial, technical and financial skills needed to establish and manage MSMEs can be crucial.

A second major element of policies to encourage entrepreneurial development in the LDCs is enterprise support services. The availability of public infrastructure is obviously a critical issue in this regard, and transport and communications infrastructure, as well as the provision of such basic amenities as electricity and water, are clearly important. Technical assistance to impart and enhance the managerial, technical and financial skills needed to establish and manage MSMEs can be crucial as well. Partnerships should be envisaged between State development finance institutions, the private sector and aid agencies to provide such services-building in managerial skills. Public authorities can also help businesses to strengthen MSME activities by establishing industrial extension services and firm support institutions, which provide advice on business development, management skills, technology options and choice. This can be further reflected in policies that encourage the expansion of those MSMEs with the most potential to grow either individually or in clusters, by giving them preferential access to credit and insurance and better access to technology, organizational systems and other useful knowledge.

c. Reaching critical firm size

Smaller firms are usually more effective in terms of the number of jobs they create per unit of investment, but they tend to lack the economies of scale that would allow them to compete effectively.

Smaller firms are usually more effective in terms of the number of jobs they create per unit of investment, but they tend to lack the economies of scale that would allow them to compete effectively in domestic and global markets. The creation of industrial clusters is one way of lessening this difficulty. Successful clusters have many positive effects for individual participating firms (UNIDO, 2009). First, there are the agglomeration effects through networks of suppliers, labour market effects, knowledge spillovers, external and scale economies, which also help to establish backward and forward linkages. Second, clusters make it easier to provide the required infrastructure and amenities that are essential for efficient production. Third, clusters help boost the productivity of MSMEs, as was evident in a study of manufacturing firms in Ethiopia (Siba et al., 2012). Fourth, clusters have positive effects on formalization. Finally, they facilitate collective action by participating firms.

LDC Governments have different alternatives for supporting firm clustering.

In this context, LDC Governments have different alternatives for supporting firm clustering. They can provide a superior supply of infrastructure, logistic, Customs, financial and legal services, offer preferential access to land and facilitate administrative procedures. They can ensure an enabling regulatory framework that facilitates the creation and operation of small firms (Schmitz and Nadvi, 1999). Several countries have established export processing zones

(EPZs), which provide a clear focus for government investment and institutional reform designed to encourage the location of firms in a particular area. Several such zones have succeeded in creating manufacturing employment and increasing exports, although they are often associated with fiscal losses because of the tax incentives provided. Another major shortcoming is that they have not been able to foster learning by domestic firms or to generate spillovers to other domestic firms (UNCTAD, 2007: 36–42). This calls for paying more attention to ensuring that clusters and EPZs are embedded in the national economy through linkages, labour movement and spillovers. Other mechanisms for encouraging clustering are firm incubators and science parks. Government measures can also provide support by boosting demand for these firms' output and by targeting public procurement to that segment in order to encourage their upgrading. This was successfully done for the government acquisition of school uniforms and furniture in Brazil (Tendler and Amorim, 1996). The extreme form of clustering is cooperatives, which are essentially another organizational form. If they are to function well and remain strong, they must be treated as the businesses they are (as associations of small producers/consumers/suppliers) and kept free of political or bureaucratic control.

One way to enhance enterprise development in LDCs is to foster the creation and strengthening of linkages between firms of different types, so as to bridge the gaps and disconnects that typically exist in the business sector of these countries and which largely explain the existence of the missing middle. Mozambique, for example, has implemented policies to foster the development of local small-scale suppliers to its large-scale aluminium smelter, although these have not yet reaped the expected benefits in terms of linkage creation and enterprise development (Krause and Kaufmann, 2011). Clearly, targets must be realistic in view of the currently limited entrepreneurial capabilities of small businesses and other constraints on their operations.

LDC policymaker need to pay more attention to ensuring that clusters and EPZs are embedded in the national economy through linkages, labour movement and spillovers.

Box 4. Focusing on smaller-scale projects to foster job creation: the case of Mozambique

Mozambique has been one of the fastest-growing LDCs of the past 20 years. Its average GDP growth has exceeded 7 per cent since 1993. Structural reforms, sound macroeconomic policies, an opening to the global economy and political stability have contributed to this growth by attracting large foreign investment projects. A major breakthrough occurred in the mid-1990s, when a consortium of investors decided to establish the large-scale aluminium smelter Mozal. More recently, other mega-projects, mostly in mining, have generated large FDI inflows.

Despite the positive contribution of these large projects, which directly and indirectly generated less than 5,000 jobs for a labour force of about 9 million people, Mozambique's development challenges remain formidable. To overcome them, UNCTAD's Investment Policy Review (IPR) of Mozambique advised looking beyond mega-projects as a source of growth, economic diversification and job creation. Promoting investment on a more modest scale, attracting smaller TNCs and building linkages with national investors were suggested as strategic priorities.

While acknowledging the importance of large projects, the IPR recognized that smaller investments can contribute more meaningfully to such social objectives as creating employment and distributing economic activity more widely. To this end, it recommended addressing the inherent regulatory bias against smaller investors. They should, for instance, have access to the same incentives as those currently reserved for mega-projects. Moreover, time-consuming and burdensome regulatory procedures should be streamlined to create a more competitive environment for smaller operators. This can be accomplished, among other things, through a review of licensing procedures and the introduction of e-governance tools.

Mozambique has a large untapped development potential for investment projects in a wide range of activities, such as agriculture, agro-processing, tourism, selected manufacturing and services, infrastructure and logistics. Placing the development of smaller projects at the heart of the investment policy debate can go a long way towards achieving the country's development goals.

Source: Based on UNCTAD (2012). *Investment Policy Review of Mozambique*. (UNCTAD/DIAE/PCB2012/1). United Nations publication, Geneva and New York. Available at http://unctad.org/en/PublicationsLibrary/diaepcb2012d1_en.pdf (14 October 2013).

d. Regulation and formalization

Economic growth on its own need not and has not reduced high informality rates, and so most employment in LDCs tends to be in informal activities. But there are high costs of informality, including the high cost of finance, less access to utilities, lack of social and legal protection and limited bargaining power or competitive edge. Formalization is often proposed as a way to assist enterprise development in LDCs, as in other developing countries. Its benefits include enforceable contracts; access to formal financial and other services; legally recognized rights; better access to public utilities, infrastructure, services, social protection; and membership in formal associations, providing "voice" (Sundaram, 2007). Ideally, formalization should help increase the productivity and competitiveness of informal firms, while offering the protection and rights that most workers in the informal sector do not have.

The best way to achieve formalization of informal enterprises is to offer them support by simplifying the path to formality.

Rather than taking a punitive approach to suppressing informality, the best way to achieve formalization of informal enterprises is to offer them support by simplifying the path to formality. Strategies can include the requirement of gradual and progressive compliance with rules and regulations, encouraged by inspections, instead of sanctions; improving business accounting; simplifying bureaucratic procedures; extending legal protection; recognizing labour relations and promoting better practices; and ensuring better access to institutional credit. In this context, a general policy orientation worth emphasizing is the need to simplify regulatory frameworks in the LDCs. Onerous procedures for setting up firms, importing machinery and intermediate goods, paying taxes and the like, discourage business activity of small and medium-sized enterprises alike. While there have been many recent efforts to improve the business and investment climate for large foreign firms, such efforts should be extended to all types and sizes of firms and not just the large ones.

While there have been many recent efforts to improve the business and investment climate for large foreign firms, such efforts should be extended to all types and sizes of firms.

e. Rural development policies

Rural development is one of the main pillars of policies to create more and better jobs in LDCs, given the high proportion of the population still living in rural areas and whose livelihood depends on the opportunities they provide. Developing the rural economy is not limited to agricultural production and productivity: Expanding RNF activities plays a substantial complementary role. Despite the importance for present and future economic and development outcomes, both agriculture and other rural economic activities have been relatively neglected in LDCs over the past 30 years. This has contributed to declining agricultural productivity, feeble agricultural production growth and depressed rural incomes (UNCTAD, 2009: 91–140). This situation must be reversed if LDCs are to promote structural change. Overturning the widespread urban bias that led to the neglect of investment in rural areas has to be a starting point for policy intervention. In recent decades, such countries as China, Viet Nam and Indonesia have reversed the previous urban bias, and all of them have benefited in terms of lifting the overall GDP growth rates. Similarly, among the LDCs, recent successful initiatives to improve agricultural productivity in Ethiopia, Malawi and Rwanda have demonstrated how agriculture can be effectively revitalized in relatively short periods of time (ILO, 2011: 27–51).

Rural development is one of the main pillars of policies to create more and better jobs in LDCs, given the high proportion of the population still living in rural areas.

Recent successful LDC initiatives to improve agricultural productivity have demonstrated how agriculture can be effectively revitalized in relatively short periods of time.

Agriculture is not a "bargain sector" in which high returns can be secured with little expenditure. Rather, as is true of industry, investment is crucial, and in the LDCs public investment is especially important in this regard. The Comprehensive Africa Agriculture Development Programme, led by NEPAD, has agreed that a targeted 10 per cent of government budgets should be allocated to agriculture. However, setting the right priorities for productive spending is equally critical, as investment in agricultural research and development, rural infrastructure and education have the greatest impact on productivity and growth.

Since the late 1990s several African LDCs have introduced programmes that heavily subsidize input price (fertilizer, and in some cases seeds) to producers, targeting smaller-scale farmers (in Malawi, Rwanda, United Republic of Tanzania and Zambia) or all farmers (in Burkina Faso, Senegal and Mali). Based on the available evidence, such programmes have been effective in raising fertilizer use, average yields and agricultural production, but their success is highly dependent on implementation. In the case of seeds, the programmes have attracted additional seed growers and expanded the number of varieties supplied. This varied experience suggests that these subsidies should not be prolonged over the long term (because of their high fiscal cost), but can and should play a role in boosting rural earnings and helping markets take off over the medium term. Procurement and distribution of subsidized fertilizers should be market-friendly, so as to enhance and not inhibit input market development. Moreover, the new generation of input subsidies ("smart" subsidies) brings innovations in design (e.g. targeting and vouchers) to support the most constrained farmers and encourage the development of input markets (Druilhe and Barreiro-Hurlé, 2012; Chirwa and Dorward, 2013). Governments may also organize bulk purchases of (imported) fertilizers in order to achieve economies of scale and reduce the price of this input.[3]

Programmes to subsidize fertilizers and seeds have been effective in raising fertilizer use, average yields and agricultural production.

In terms of improving rural infrastructure, it is increasingly evident that public investment must provide the lead in the development of transport, irrigation, warehousing, energy, marketing, communications and so forth, especially in remote areas. This is warranted on two grounds. First, it has multiplier effects, since it increases overall productivity in agriculture and thus facilitates overall structural change. Second, it develops the externalities described in chapter 4 of this Report, thereby contributing to employment generation, enterprise development and capacity-building.

Public investment must provide the lead in the development of rural transport, irrigation, warehousing, energy, marketing and communications.

As for micro- and small agricultural enterprises, access to institutional finance on reasonable terms is perhaps even more crucial to making cultivation viable. Policies are needed to make institutional credit available to all farmers, including tenants, women farmers and those without clear land titles (if necessary with some subsidies to cover the higher risks and transaction costs associated with such lending). Some strategies for expanding credit access in farming include:

- Providing seasonal and long-term finance to farmers and RNF economic agents by agricultural development banks, State banks, postal banks, community credit cooperatives (which are more familiar with borrowers' creditworthiness) and, in some cases, commercial banks. These institutions are also an instrument for mobilizing rural savings, and may sometimes establish specialized rural / microfinance units;

- Rehabilitating existing rural development banks and the creation of such institutions where none exists, in order to offer financial services not provided by commercial banks and other financial institutions;

- Encouraging the provision of financial services (credit) and extension services by means of contract farming and outgrower schemes to both smallholders and large-scale producers;

- Providing subsidies for and underwriting seasonal finance; and

- Initiating insurance and warehouse receipt schemes, which make it possible to turn agricultural produce into collateral.

Policies are needed to make institutional credit available to all farmers, including tenants, women farmers and those without clear land titles.

A major factor in the viability of cultivation is the effective use of available agricultural technologies, which means that extension services are extremely important. In order to achieve higher agricultural yields and stronger productivity growth, farmers need to learn and adopt innovations in their cultivation techniques, water management, choice of seeds and/or crops, warehousing, etc. This calls for Governments to provide support services, such as rural extension services, which diffuse new knowledge to farmers and help them learn and adopt innovations. Ideally, such services should actively involve local communities and use traditional or indigenous knowledge systems that are appropriate to smallholder farm sizes, including scale-neutral technologies. Extension activities should also encompass environmental management, which includes paying attention to conditions of land quality and water access, particularly with regard to the equitable spread of irrigation and avoiding soil degradation. However, not all technologies are developed with the specific concerns of local farmers in mind, and extension services should thus be combined with an emphasis on stronger research activities that are sensitive to local problems and requirements. To the extent possible, LDC Governments should seek to create and/or increase funding for national or regional research centres created on the basis of agro-ecological zones or strategic food commodities, and indeed many of these need not be so expensive to develop.

Agricultural extension services should actively involve local communities and use traditional or indigenous knowledge systems that are appropriate to smallholder farm sizes, including scale-neutral technologies.

In addition, agricultural policies should foster stronger backward and forward linkages of the sector. Such linkages should encompass backward linkages between agriculture and input markets, including access to appropriate inputs, so as to encourage cheaper and more sustainable input use, with better regulation and monitoring of private input supply. Forward linkages include development and proliferation of better post-harvest technologies, such as warehousing and storage, transport and preliminary processing of agricultural items. More efficient marketing channels improve access to markets and protect farmers from high volatility in output prices. This points to the need for partnerships between the State, farmers' organizations and NGOs to carry out some of the functions previously performed by agricultural marketing boards (e.g. finance and technological extension services as well as marketing). It is a mistake to believe that large corporate retail can provide an effective substitute, as the experience of several developing countries suggests otherwise. Where institutions for marketing agricultural products are missing or inefficient, and/or where local traders exert detrimental market power over small producers, Government can establish public trading facilities and market data systems, promote public cooperatives and set up warehouses in order to limit the traders' power. Some possible strategies in this regard include:

LDC Governments should seek to create and/or increase funding for national or regional research centres created on the basis of agro-ecological zones or strategic food commodities.

There is a need for partnerships between the State, farmers' organizations and NGOs to carry out some of the functions previously performed by agricultural marketing boards.

- Encouraging farmers' groups and other local cooperatives to organize the supply of inputs, machinery and credit;

- Developing local markets for the marketing of agricultural produce by investing in the physical installations and liaising with local economic agents;

- Prioritizing activities that target local and international regional markets;

- Improving the access of the rural population to product and factors markets;

- Fostering the development of common-interest producers' associations and cooperatives;

- Devising and implementing flexible and innovative cross-sectoral institutional arrangements;

- Where natural gas is present, providing industrial policy incentives for the production of fertilizers, and where it is not, organizing bulk purchase of (imported) fertilizers; and

- Using input supply and subsidies to provide credit or subsidies for seed and fertilizer acquisition.

Some of the challenges faced by agricultural development in LDCs are the security of tenure, conflict management, excessive centralization of land administration and lack of access to land. Several LDCs have tackled these challenges through such programmes and measures as decentralization of land administration to subnational levels, improved land registries and titling, establishment of institutional mechanisms to solve land tenure conflicts, and land reform. For example: The Ugandan Constitution of 1995 transferred titles from the State directly to landholders. Malawi and Mozambique both adopted land redistribution policies favouring the landless and de facto occupants, while Niger's 1986 rural code provides for mechanisms to resolve land tenure conflicts. Decentralization was achieved through land boards in Uganda, rural councils in Senegal, land commissions in Niger and land committees in Lesotho (UNECA, 2005: 129–166). Wider access to land through land reform and/or more secure rights (whether individual or collective, proprietary or not) creates better incentives for agricultural investment and is therefore likely to result in increased employment in agriculture. The mix of measures to be enacted naturally needs to be adapted to local conditions, the local institutional setting and local traditions. Nevertheless, since the mid-2000s several LDCs have been entering into lease or sale agreements involving large patches of land for commercial agriculture development by foreign investors (so-called "land grab" operations), without fully privatizing land markets. In order to reduce the conflicts and insecurities these might engender, it is important to establish new, decentralized bodies that bring local communities and customary leaders together with Government in the management of land, land rights and land disputes.

LDCs with the potential for developing cash crops for export can exploit niche markets for agricultural goods — including biofuels, "fair trade", "organic", certified timber and sustainable products — that enjoy a growing market, especially in developed countries. Coffee growers from Latin America, Africa and Asia are benefiting from this trend. One such example is the Oromo Coffee Company, from Ethiopia, which exploits ethically conscious niche markets in developed countries (Newland and Taylor, 2010). Similarly, enhancing regional cooperation in some agricultural commodity chains of production, processing and marketing (such as rice, maize, wheat, sugar, meat and dairy products) can potentially meet increasing regional demand (UNECA and African Union, 2009).

As noted earlier, the development of non-farm activities is crucial for the LDCs not just to provide other means of productive employment but also to improve the quality of life of the rural population. Employment creation in RNF activities was a crucial labour absorber during the structural transformation process in such Asian countries as Bangladesh, Viet Nam and India (Khan, 2007). Typically, government and donor interventions to support RNF employment have emphasized self-employment (Davis, 2004). The empirical evidence shows, however, that in rural Latin America and south Asia, non-farm wage employment is equally, if not more, significant (Barrett et al., 2001; Haggblade et al., 2007; Carlo Azzarri, 2009). The excessive focus on self-employment may result from perceptions of its less exploitative nature and its strategic importance for poverty reduction, but these perceptions can be debated. Greater balance between the promotion of self-employment and support to SME development has implications for the spatial focus of government interventions – for example, making greater use of rural town centres as an entry point, since SMEs tend to be located in centres where they can benefit from improved access to services, economic infrastructure, markets and labour.

Some of the challenges faced by agricultural development in LDCs are the security of tenure, conflict management, excessive centralization of land administration and lack of access to land.

LDCs with the potential for developing cash crops for export can exploit niche markets for agricultural goods that enjoy a growing international market.

Non-farm wage employment is equally, if not more, significant than RNF self-employment.

F. Summary and conclusions

Policies for employment-rich growth in LDCs should have two complementary objectives: expanding the number of jobs so as to absorb the growing labour force and the youth bulge, and raising the incomes generated by these jobs (by means of productivity gains) so as to combat the generalized prevalence of poverty and underemployment. Reaching these objectives involves implementing a range of mutually supportive policies aimed at building productive capacity and fostering structural transformation. Policy interventions should cover three broad areas: macroeconomic policies, enterprise development, and public-sector investment and actions for job creation.

Inclusive development calls for a macroeconomic policy approach that goes beyond the narrower goal of macroeconomic stability. This broader approach requires expanding the number of instruments and coordinating macroeconomic policies with other policies to stimulate the development of productive capacities. In this context, fiscal policy becomes more important than monetary policy. It should target financing public investment in physical and human capital by accelerating public investment in infrastructure and raising spending on education and training. To do so requires strengthening government capacity to mobilize and manage fiscal revenues, whether domestic or external. At the national level, this can be done initially through domestic resource mobilization, which entails changes in fiscal policy and tax administration.

Tax administration and collection can be made more efficient, by streamlining information management, cross-checking statements and declarations and setting up a special unit for high-income taxpayers. For resource-rich LDCs, fiscal revenue can be increased by modifying the extremely favourable terms currently offered to foreign investors in agriculture and mining. This may involve imposing a tax on land leased for large-scale investment projects, raising existing land taxes or revising the taxation of activities undertaken by those projects. Governments with mining resources can raise their revenues by adopting higher levies, royalties, income taxes or export taxes. LDC authorities should also boost the mobilization of external resources from both traditional and non-traditional aid donors and from multilateral and regional financial institutions.

Although fiscal policy may be more important than monetary policy in developing productive capacities, monetary policy is still critical. It should, however, be less fixated on attaining an inflation rate in the low single digits than on targeting full employment of productive resources and providing reasonable macroeconomic stability. Credit policy is also of crucial importance in the LDCs, particularly for MSMEs, which are typically credit-constrained in these countries.

Private sector development is a sine qua non for large-scale employment generation in LDCs, since it generates the bulk of jobs, both now and in the future. The main policies for developing the LDCs' private sectors are industrial policy, enterprise policy, rural development policies, and education and training policies. *Industrial policy* is designed to steer the economy towards structural transformation, by moving to higher-productivity activities both among and within sectors. There are two types of strategies that LDCs can pursue to bolster the employment intensity of growth. The first is to build on activities of existing comparative advantage, by fostering backward and forward linkages and technological upgrading in these sectors. This typically means focusing on natural resource-based activities. Agriculture can be the basis for developing downstream industries, such as food processing, geared mainly to domestic and regional markets, but also global markets.

Policies for employment-rich growth in LDCs should have two complementary objectives: expanding the number of jobs and raising the incomes generated by these jobs.

For resource-rich LDCs, fiscal revenue can be increased by modifying the extremely favourable terms currently offered to foreign investors in agriculture and mining.

LDC authorities should also boost the mobilization of external resources from both traditional and non-traditional aid donors.

Private sector development is a sine qua non for large-scale employment generation in LDCs.

A second type of industrial policy strategy aims at changing the capital-labour ratio of the economy, by attracting investment in labour-intensive industries. In this respect, some LDCs will be able to take advantage of the window of opportunity opened by China's likely delocalization of the lower end of its manufacturing industry, through a combination of integrating domestic firms into manufacturing GVCs and attracting FDI. Domestically, this strategy should be complemented by policies on clustering, export promotion and labour costs.

Effective *enterprise policy* measures for stimulating the development of urban-based MSEs include facilitating their access to capital and helping them upgrade into formal status. Policymakers need to expand the financing made available to these firms through national development banks or commercial banks. These financial institutions should select those MSEs with high growth potential, based on current profitability and entrepreneurs' profiles.

Rural development policy is a special challenge, given the dismally low level of productivity of rural areas, and requires action on infrastructure, technology and financing. The State needs to invest heavily in rural infrastructure, especially irrigation, electricity, transport, storage (warehousing) and communication (ICTs) in order to boost rural productivity and foster backward and forward linkages of farms. Rural extension services must be established or rehabilitated to provide advice and training on cultivation techniques, water management, choice of seeds and/or crops, warehousing, conditions of land quality and water access, avoiding soil degradation, and techniques for meeting market requirements.

Providing rural producers with access to capital and finance involves offering both seasonal and long-term finance to farmers and rural non-farm economic agents. This should be undertaken by agricultural development banks, State banks, post office financial services, community credit cooperatives (which have better knowledge of borrowers' creditworthiness) and commercial banks.

Most of the above-mentioned instruments of industrial, enterprise and rural development policy are targeted policies. They need to be complemented by horizontal policy measures aimed at increasing the knowledge intensity of the LDC economies, so as to make them more adaptable and better prepared to meet the requirements of a modern economy. This brings us to *education and training policy*. In primary education, the priority is to improve quality. In secondary and tertiary education and in technical and vocational training, the priority is to expand the supply and improve the quality of services. This includes revising curricula and teaching methods in order to make the labour force more adaptable and innovative, and adjusting education policies to meet future domestic labour market requirements.

Finally, in addition to involving the private sector, the State itself must play a role in generating jobs, either directly and indirectly, especially in the earlier phases of development. Since infrastructure work is a non-tradable type of activity, and since it finances the bulk of projects, the State can influence the choice of technique so as to ensure the adoption of labour-intensive production processes. These have several advantages over capital-intensive technologies: They generate more jobs, have lower costs, can contribute to local enterprise development and capacity-building, provide more readily available maintenance and repair services, and can generate foreign exchange savings.

Some LDCs will be able to take advantage of the window of opportunity opened by China's likely delocalization of the lower end of its manufacturing industry.

Rural development policy requires action on infrastructure, technology and financing.

Education and training policy should make the labour force more adaptable and innovative.

Labour-intensive production processes generate more jobs, have lower costs, contribute to local enterprise development and capacity-building, and generate foreign exchange savings.

G. International support measure: Bolstering youth employment in LDCs through private sector development

According to the current and future demographic trends in the LDCs — analysed in chapter 2 of this Report — the working-age population in these countries will increase by 15.7 million people every year, and 225 million new jobs will have to be created by 2030 to productively employ newcomers to the labour market. Even more worrying is that the LDCs youth population (aged 15–24 years), which is becoming better educated and growing fast, is increasingly seeking job in rapidly growing urban centres. The main responsibility for creating these jobs rests largely with the LDCs themselves. Nevertheless, the international community can also play a role in helping to ease the constraints faced by these countries in creating sufficient jobs.

Indeed, the international community has pledged to help implement the IPoA, which is a consensus programme aimed at transforming the LDC economies during the decade 2011–2020. One of its pledges focuses on the employment of youth and their participation in the economy. More specifically, the LDCs' development partners have committed to "provide financial and technical assistance to support least developed countries' policies and programmes that provide economic opportunities and productive employment to youth" (IPoA, para. 81 (2a)).

In line with this undertaking, the Report is proposing a new international support measure to create employment opportunities for youth in the LDCs. The support measure would involve a catalytic use of ODA for employment creation through private sector development.

The objective is to create a financing facility for private sector development in LDCs, aimed specifically at providing seed capital and training for young entrepreneurs. The ultimate goal is to create favourable conditions for the growth of local enterprises so that more employment opportunities are generated for the millions of young people who join the labour market each year. This proposal is based on the recognition that the lack of financing and entrepreneurial capabilities is one of the most critical constraints on private sector development in these countries. Investment will provide seed capital for start-ups. Training will equip young people with the requisite skills for successfully managing these new enterprises.

The financing facility would be based on a cost-sharing partnership between the international community and LDC Governments. Creating productive employment for young people in the LDCs is in the interests of the international community and of traditional donors in particular, as it would reduce the incentives for emigration from these countries. International assistance of this nature would enhance the development of productive capacities and generate desperately needed employment for LDC youth. It would have the additional benefits of improving the technical and skills base of the LDCs and of creating new forms of innovation. As such, it could be a win-win proposal for both the international community and the LDCs.

The facility would have two valuable impacts on LDC economies. First, it would enable the creation of enterprise incubators to strengthen their private sector. Unlike public works programmes, it would provide a long-term and sustainable solution to the employment challenge by fostering the development of productive capacities.

225 million new jobs will have to be created by 2030 to productively employ newcomers to the labour market.

The international community has made a pledge on the employment of youth and their participation in the economy.

The objective is to create a financing facility for private sector development in LDCs, aimed specifically at providing seed capital and training for young entrepreneurs.

The financing facility would be based on a cost-sharing partnership between the international community and LDC Governments.

Second, it would support the creation of enterprises in the formal sector of the economy. Creating formal firms would not only provide better employment opportunities for young people, but would also contribute to domestic resource mobilization by broadening the tax base.

Ownership of the scheme by the LDCs themselves is critical. It should be embedded in the national development strategy and have verifiable indicators of success. These could be specified in terms of the number of jobs created, the share of young people in the total number of employed in enterprises supported by the facility, and the like.

Financing the facility may require innovative solutions, such as a "matching fund" approach. Donors would agree to match (or exceed by a margin) the funds mobilized by LDC Governments to finance the facility. Such matching funds would provide an incentive to recipient Governments to raise more revenues for employment creation for young people. Non-traditional donors might also find the matching fund approach appealing, since the facility would be based on risk-sharing and a balance of resources.

The facility would work as follows. In the first phase, organizational and managerial training would be provided to those candidates that complied with certain requirements (such as age and educational background). After finishing the training, candidates would prepare project proposals for enterprise development in the second phase. These proposals would be screened, and the most promising would receive seed capital for concretizing their business proposals. Alternatively, funding "windows" could be provided, in which competitive bids would be offered with proposals submitted for funding under more discretionary terms, involving joint ventures and riskier capital (venture) fund approaches.

The screening would be based on the commercial benchmarks typically used by private banks, to which an additional condition could be added – namely, that a given percentage of the new firm's employees should come from the targeted age group (for example, those aged 15 to 24 years). The facility, which could be managed by a national development bank or an authorized government entity, would also fund technical and vocational education and training for new employees, enabling an ongoing increase in their skills and knowledge and increased productivity for the new enterprise.

Given the high failure rate of start-ups in most economies — a simple rule of thumb is that half of all start-ups fail during their first operating year — some form of support for new firms would have to be provided for the first three to five years. The facility could be the main source of financial and managerial support for the first two to three years (the second phase of the programme). Later on, in the third phase, Governments could provide some additional form of support, for example through financing by a State financial institution, under preferential conditions. After the last phase of the programme, enterprises would have to survive on their own.

Donors could provide not only financing for the facility, but also technical cooperation to establish enterprise incubators, as well as different types of training using their own expertise in these areas (e.g. SME support and entrepreneurship policy). In principle, the facility could finance start-ups in activities that could potentially result in the largest effect on employment creation, although Governments could gear the projects towards activities and sectors based on their national priorities and specificities (e.g. regional or sectoral development targeted by industrial policy).

When possible, LDCs might want to tape the considerable knowledge, skills, networks and other resources of their diasporas (UNCTA, 2012: 147 — 150). Participating countries could network to share best practices, particularly in monitoring the impact on the economy.

In the first phase, organizational and managerial training would be provided to those candidates that complied with certain requirements.

The screening would be based on the commercial benchmarks typically used by private banks, plus an additional condition that new firm's employees should come from the targeted age group.

Some form of support for new firms would have to be provided for the first three to five years.

Donors could provide not only financing for the facility, but also technical cooperation to establish enterprise incubators, as well as different types of training.

LDCs might want to tape the considerable knowledge, skills, networks and other resources of their diasporas.

Notes

1. The effectiveness of improving tax collection is shown by the example of Ecuador, where better access to information and monitoring of company accounts and more determined implementation of existing laws, led to a doubling of corporate income tax receipts in just five years.

2. LDC Governments can consider negotiating with these development partners on the use of local labour force in the execution of South-financed infrastructure and public works projects.

3. LDCs endowed with natural gas have a comparative advantage in the production and trading of fertilizers, and may consider adopting industrial policy measures to establish the industry.

References

Adesida O and Karuri-Sebina MG (2013). Building innovation driven economies in Africa. *African Journal of Science, Technology, Innovation and Development*. 5(1):1–3.

Adhikari R and Yamamoto Y (2007). The textiles and clothing industry: Adjusting to a post quota world. In: UN/DESA, ED. *Industrial Development for the 21st Century: Sustainable Development Perspectives*. United Nations Department of Economic and Social Affairs (UN/DESA). New York: 183–234.

Altenburg Tilman (2011). Industrial policy in developing countries: overview and lessons from seven country cases. DIE Discussion Paper No. 4/2011. Deutsches Institut für Entwicklungspolitik (DIE — German Development Institute). Bonn.

Altenburg Tilmann (2010). Industrial policy in ehtiopia. DIE Discussion Paper No. 2/2010. Deutsches Institut für Entwicklungspolitik (DIE — German Development Institute). Bonn.

Barrett CB, Reardon T and Webb P (2001). Nonfarm income diversification and household livelihood strategies in rural Africa: concepts, dynamics, and policy implications. *Food Policy*. 26(4):315–331.

Bigsten A and Söderbom M (2005). What have we learned from a decade of manufacturing enterprise surveys in africa? Policy Research Working Paper No. 3798. World Bank. Washington (DC).

Brixiová Z, Ndikumana L and Abderrahim K (2011). Supporting Africa's post-crisis growth: the role of macroeconomic policies. William Davidson Institute Working Papers No. wp1008. William Davidson Institute at the University of Michigan. Ann Arbor (MI).

Carlo Azzarri EJQ (2009). Assets, Activities and Rural Income Generation: Evidence from a Multicountry Analysis. *World Development*. 37(9):1435–1452.

Chang H-J (2011). Industrial policy: Can we go beyond unproductive confrontation? In: Lin J Y and Pleskovic B, eds. *Annual World Bank Conference on Development Economics 2011, Global: Lessons from East Asia and the Global Financial Crisis*. World Bank. Washington (DC): 83–109.

Chirwa EW and Dorward AR (2013). The role of the private sector in the farm input subsidy programme in malawi. Future Agricultures Working Paper No. 64. Futures Agriculture Consortium. Brighton.

Chowdhury A (2009). Microfinance as a poverty reduction tool: a critical assessment. DESA Working Paper No. 89. United Nations Department of Economic and Social Affairs (UN/DESA). New York.

Commission on Growth and Development (2008). *The Growth Report : Strategies for Sustained Growth and Inclusive Development*. World Bank. Washington (DC).

Davis J (2004). The rural non-farm economy, livelihoods and their diversification: issues and options. Development and Comp Systems No. 2753. EconWPA.

Devereux S (2002). Can social safety nets reduce chronic poverty? *Development Policy Review*. 20(5):657–675.

Devereux S and Salomon C (2006). Employment creation programmes: the international experience. Issues in Employment and Poverty Discussion Paper No. 24. International Labour Office (ILO). Geneva.

Druilhe Z and Barreiro-Hurlé J (2012). Fertilizer subsidies in sub-Saharan Africa. ESA Working Paper No. 12-04. Agricultural Development Economics Division (ESA) – Food and Agriculture Organization of the United Nations (FAO). Rome.

Financial Times (2013). Bangladesh garment-makers chase growth despite disasters.

Freeman C (2008). *Systems of innovation: Selected essays in evolutionary economics.* Elgar. Cheltenham.

Frenkel R (2004). Real exchange rate and employment in Argentina, Brazil, Chile and Mexico. Group of 24. Washington (DC).

Gallagher KP, Griffith-Jones S and Ocampo JA, eds. (2012). *Regulating Global Capital Flows for Long-run Development*. Pardee Center Task Force Report. The Frederick S. Pardee Center for the Study of the Longer-Range Future - Boston University. Boston (MA).

Griffin K (1996). Macroeconomic reform and employment: an investment-led strategy of structural adjustment in sub-Saharan Africa. Issues in Development Discussion Paper No. 16. International Labour Office (ILO). Geneva.

Haggblade S, Hazell PBR and Reardon TA (2007). *Transforming the rural nonfarm economy: opportunities and threats in the developing world*. Johns Hopkins University Press. Baltimore (MD).

Hausmann R and Rodrik D (2003). Economic development as self-discovery. *Journal of Development Economics.* 72(2):603–633.

Van der Hoeven R (2013). The inclusion of full employment in MDG1: what lessons for a post-2015 development agenda? The Power of Numbers: A Critical Review of MDG Targets for Human Development and Human Rights - FXB Working Paper. FXB Center for Health and Human Rights - Harvard School of Public Health - Harvard University and The New School. Harvard (MA).

ILO (2011). *Growth, Employment and Decent Work in the Least Developed Countries: Report of the International Labour Office for the Frouth UN Conference on the Least Developed Countries 9-13 May 2011 – Turkey.* International Labour Office (ILO). Geneva.

IMF (2010). Emerging from the global crisis: macroeconomic challenges facing low-income countries. International Monetary Fund (IMF). Washington (DC).

IMF (2011). Recent experiences in managing capital inflows: cross-cutting themes and possible policy framework. International Monetary Fund (IMF). Washington (DC).

Khan AR (2007). Growth, employment and poverty. In: Ocampo JA and Sundaram J K, eds. *Full and Decent Employment.* Orient Longman, Zed Books and Third World Nertwork. Hyderabad, London and New York, and Penang: 123–157.

Krause M and Kaufmann F (2011). Industrial policy in Mozambique. DIE Discussion Paper No. 10/2011. Deutsches Institut für Entwicklungspolitik (DIE - German Development Institute). Bonn.

Lall S (1995). Industrial strategy and policies on foreign direct investment in East Asia. *Transnational Corporations.* 4(3):1–26.

Lin JY (2011). New structural economics: A framework for rethinking development. *World Bank Research Observer.* 26(2):193–221.

Lin JY and Monga C (2010). Growth identification and facilitation: the role of the states in the dynamics of structural change. Policy Research Working Paper No. 5313. World Bank. Washington (DC).

Majeres J (2003). Employment-intensive investment and poverty reduction: The wide policy framework. *ASIS Bulletin.* 151–155.

McCord A and Slater R (2009). Overview of public works programmes in sub-Saharan Africa. Overseas Development Institute (ODI). London.

McCutcheon RT and Taylor Parkins FLM, eds. (2003). *Employment and High Standard Infrastructure.* Research Centre for Employment Creation in Construction - University of Witwatersrand. Johannesburg.

Moreau F (2004). The role of the state in evolutionary economics. *Cambridge Journal of Economics.* 28(6):847–874.

Munters P (2003). *Jobs or Machines: Comparative Analysis of Rural Road Work in Cambodia.* International Labour Office (ILO). Bangkok.

Nelson RR (1994). The co-evolution of technology, industrial structure, and supporting institutions. *Industrial and Corporate Change*. 3(1):47–63.

Newland K and Taylor C (2010). Heritage tourism and nostalgia trade: a diaspora niche in the development landscape. Diasporas & Development Policy Project. Migration Policy Institute and USAID. Washington (DC).

O'Connor D (2007). Policy lessons for the 21st century industrializers. In: UN/DESA, ed. *Industrial Development for the 21st Century: Sustainable Development Perspectives.* United Nations Department of Economic and Social Affairs (UN/DESA). New York: 415–422.

Ocampo JA (2007). Preface. In: Ocampo JA and Sundaram J K, eds. *Full and decent employment.* Orient Longman, Zed Books and Third World Nertwork. Hyderabad, London and New York, and Penang: xiv–xx.

OECD (2013). *Perspectives on Global Development 2013: Industrial Policies in a Changing World - Shiting up a Gear.* Organisation for Economic Co-operation and Development (OECD). Paris.

Pérez C (2001). Technological change and opportunities for development as a moving target. *CEPAL Review.* 75109–130.

Pérez C and Soete LL (1988). Catching up in technology: Entry barriers and windows of opportunity. In: Dosi G, Freeman C, Nelson R R, Silverberg G, and Soete L L, eds. *Technical Change and Economic Theory.* Pinter. London and New York: 458–479.

Qureshi MS and Te Velde DW (2012). State-business relations, investment climate reform and firm productivity in Sub-Saharan Africa. *Journal of International Development.*

Ramos J (1998). A development strategy founded on natural resource-based production clusters. *CEPAL Review.* 66105–127.

Rodrik D (2004). Industrial policy for the twenty-first century. CEPR Discussion Paper No. 4767. Centre for Economic Policy Research (CEPR). London.

Rodrik D (2008). Normalizing industrial policy. Commission on Growth and Development Working Paper No. 3. World Bank. Washington (DC).

Rodrik D (2010). The return of industrial policy April. Available at http://www.project-syndicate.org/commentary/the-return-of-industrial-policy.

Rodrik D and Rosenzweig MR (2010). Development policy and development economics: An introduction. In: Rodrik D and Rosenzweig M R, eds. *Handbook of Development Economics.* Elsevier. Amsterdam: xv–xxvii.

Schmitz H (2007). Reducing complexity in the industrial policy debate. *Development Policy Review.* 25(4):417–428.

Schmitz H and Nadvi K (1999). Clustering and industrialization: Introduction. *World Development.* 27(9):1503–1514.

Schoar A (2010). The divide between subsistence and transformational entrepreneurship. In: Lerner J and Stern S, eds. *Innovation Policy and the Economy, Vol.10.* University of Chiocago Press. Chicago (IL): 57–81.

Shiferaw A, Söderbom M, Siba E and Alemu G (2012a). Road infrastructure and enterprise development in Ethiopia. IGC Working Paper No. 12/0695. International Growth Centre (IGC). Oxford.

Shiferaw A, Söderbom M, Siba E and Alemu G (2012b). Road networks and enterprise performance in Ethiopia: evidence from the road sector development program. IGC Working Paper No. 12/0696. International Growth Centre (IGC). Oxford.

Shimada G (2013). The economic implications of comprehensive approach to learning on industrial development (Policy and managerial capability learning): A case fo Ehtiopia. *Working Papers.* Japan International Cooperation Agency (JICA) and Initiative fof Policy Dialogue (IPD). Yokohama: 341–369.

Siba E, Söderbom M, Bigsten A and Gebreeyesus M (2012). The effects of agglomeration and competition on prices and productivity: evidence for Ehtiopia's manufacturing sector. UNU-WIDER Working Paper No. 2012/85. United Nations University - World Institute for Development Economics Research (UNU-WIDER). Helsinki.

Stiglitz J, Ocampo Jose Antonio, Spiegel S, Ffrench-Davis R and Nayyar D (2006). *Stability with Growth: Macroeconomics, Liberalization and Development.* Oxford University Press. Oxford.

Sundaram JK (2007). Towards full and decent employment: An introduction. In: Ocampo JA and Sundaram J K, eds. *Full and decent employment.* Orient Longman, Zed Books and Third World Nertwork. Hyderabad, London and New York, and Penang: 1–21.

Tendler J and Amorim MA (1996). Small firms and their helpers: Lessons on demand. *World Development.* 24(3):407–426.

UN/DESA (2012). *World Economic and Social Survey 2012: In Search For New Development Finance.* United Nations publication. Sales No. E.12.II.C.1. New York.

UNCTAD (2006). *The Least Developed Countries Report 2006: Developing Productive Capacities.* United Nations publication. Sales No. E.06.II.D.9. New York and Geneva.

UNCTAD (2007). *The Least Developed Countries Report 2007: Knowledge, Technological Learning and Innovation for Development.* United Nations publication. Sales No. E.07.II.D.8, New York and Geneva.

UNCTAD (2008). *The Least Developed Countries Report 2008: Growth, Poverty and the Terms of Development Partnership.* United Nations publication. Sales No. E.08. II.D.20. New York and Geneva.

UNCTAD (2009). *The Least Developed Countries Report 2009: The State and Development Governance.* United Nations publication. Sales No. E.09.II.D.9. New York and Geneva.

UNCTAD (2010a). *The Least Developed Countries Report 2010: Towards a New International Development Architecture for LDCs.* United Nations publication. Sales No. E.10.II.D.5. New York and Geneva.

UNCTAD (2010b). *Trade and Development Report 2010: Employment, Globalization and Development.* United Nations publication. Sales No. E.10.II.D.3. New York and Geneva.

UNCTAD (2011). *The Least Developed Countries Report 2011: The Potential Role of South-South Cooperation for Inclusive and Sustainable Development.* United Nations publication. Sales No. E.11.II.D.5. New York and Geneva.

UNCTAD (2012). *The Least Developed Countries Report 2012: Harnessing Remittances and Diaspora Knowledge to Build Productive Capacities.* United Nations publication. Sales No. E.12.II.D.18. New York and Geneva.

UNCTAD (2013a). *Trade and Development Report 2013: Adjusting to the Changing Dynamics of the World Economy.* United Nations publication. Sales No. E.13.II.D.3. New York and Geneva.

UNCTAD (2013b). *World Investment Report 2013: Global Value Chains: Investment and Trade for Development.* United Nations publication. Sales No. E.13.II.D.5. New York and Geneva.

UNECA (2005). *Economic Report on Africa 2005: Meeting the Challenges of Unemployment and Poverty in Africa.* United Nations Economic Commission for Africa (UN/ECA). Addis Ababa.

UNECA and African Union (2009). *Economic Report on Africa 2009: Developing African Agriculture Through Regional Value Chains.* United Nations Economic Commission for Africa (UNECA) and African Union. Addis Ababa.

UNIDO (2009). *Industrial Development Report 2009: Breaking in and Moving up: New Industrial Challenges for the Bottom Billion and the Middle-income Countries.* United Nations publication. Sales No. E.09.II.B.37. Vienna.

Te Velde DW et al. (2011). DPR Debate: Growth Identification and Facilitation: The Role of the State in the Dynamics of Structural Change. *Development Policy Review.* 29(3):259–310.

Wade RH (2010). After the crisis: Industrial policy and the developmental state in low-income countries. *Global Policy.* 1(2):150–161.

Zarenda H (2012). A comprehensive regional industrial policy for SADC. tralac Working Paper No. S12WP10/2012. Trade Law Centre (tralac). Stellenbosch.

STATISTICAL TABLES ON THE LEAST DEVELOPED COUNTRIES

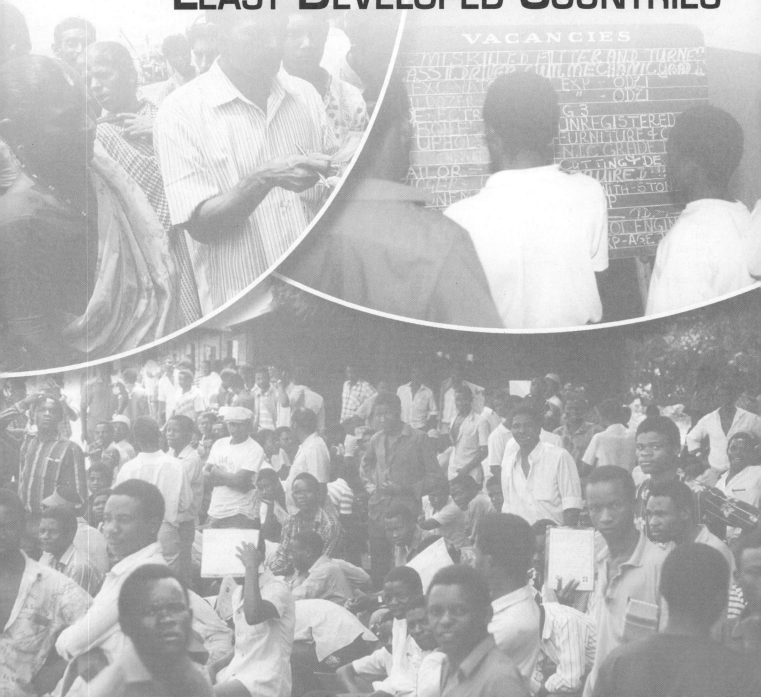

country	GNI per capita (current $)[a]	Economic Vulnerability Index[b] (EVI)	Human Assets Index[c] (HAI)	Income level	Human Development Index (HDI)		Multi-dimensional Poverty Index (MPI)[e]
		CDP 2012 review			*value*	*rank*	*value*
Afghanistan	570[a]	38.8	22.5	Low income	0.37	175	..
Angola	4'580	51.3	31.6	Upper middle income	0.51	148	..
Bangladesh	840	32.4	54.7	Low income	0.52	146	0.292
Benin	750	36.2	41.1	Low income	0.44	166	0.412
Bhutan	2'420	44.2	59.0	Lower middle income	0.54	140	0.119
Burkina Faso	670	37.5	29.2	Low income	0.34	183	0.535
Burundi	240	57.2	20.8	Low income	0.36	178	0.53
Cambodia	880	50.5	57.9	Low income	0.54	138	0.212
Central African Republic	490	35.7	21.6	Low income	0.35	180	..
Chad	740	52.8	18.1	Low income	0.34	184	0.344
Comoros	840	49.9	45.3	Low income	0.43	169	..
Dem. Rep. of the Congo	220	35.4	21.7	Low income	0.30	186	0.392
Djibouti	1'513[d]	46.3	42.4	Lower middle income	0.45	164	0.139
Equatorial Guinea	13'560	43.7	43.0	High income: nonOECD	0.55	136	..
Eritrea	450	59.0	35.6	Low income	0.35	181	..
Ethiopia	410	33.5	28.2	Low income	0.40	173	0.564
Gambia	510.0	67.8	49.2	Low income	0.44	165	0.324
Guinea	460	28.6	36.8	Low income	0.36	178	0.506
Guinea-Bissau	550	60.5	34.2	Low income	0.36	176	..
Haiti	760	47.3	35.6	Low income	0.46	161	0.299
Kiribati	2260	82.0	86.9	Lower middle income	0.63	121	..
Lao People's Dem. Rep.	1'260	37.1	61.4	Lower middle income	0.54	138	0.267
Lesotho	1'380	45.9	62.1	Lower middle income	0.46	158	0.156
Liberia	370	61.0	38.5	Low income	0.39	174	0.485
Madagascar	430	38.0	52.5	Low income	0.48	151	0.357
Malawi	320	51.9	44.1	Low income	0.42	170	0.334
Mali	660	36.8	30.2	Low income	0.34	182	0.558
Mauritania	1'110	44.2	47.1	Lower middle income	0.47	155	0.352
Mozambique	510	44.4	30.7	Low income	0.33	185	0.512
Myanmar	1'144[d]	45.0	68.8	Lower middle income	0.50	149	..
Nepal	700	27.8	59.8	Low income	0.46	157	0.217
Niger	370	38.6	24.3	Low income	0.30	186	0.642
Rwanda	560[a]	47.3	42.2	Low income	0.43	167	0.35
Samoa	3'220	51.1	92.8	Lower middle income	0.70	96	..
Sao Tome and Principe	1'320	46.1	74.9	Lower middle income	0.53	144	0.154
Senegal	1'040	36.1	47.0	Lower middle income	0.47	154	0.439
Sierra Leone	580	48.5	24.8	Low income	0.36	177	0.439
Solomon Islands	1'130	55.2	65.1	Lower middle income	0.53	143	..
Somalia	107[d]	50.1	1.4	Lower middle income	..	..	0.514
South Sudan	650	..	..		..	..	..
Sudan	1'450	44.4	52.6	Lower middle income	0.41	171	..
Timor-Leste	3'670	53.3	48.1	Lower middle income	0.58	134	0.36
Togo	500	35.4	45.5	Low income	0.46	159	0.284
Tuvalu	6'070	63.9	88.1	Upper middle income	..	..	..
Uganda	440	36.2	45.8	Low income	0.46	161	0.367
United Rep. of Tanzania	570	28.7	40.1	Low income	0.48	152	0.332
Vanuatu	3'080	46.8	77.7	Lower middle income	0.63	124	0.129
Yemen	1'110[a]	38.5	52.3	Lower middle income	0.46	160	0.283
Zambia	1'350	53.0	36.9	Lower middle income	0.45	163	0.328

Source: United Nations Committee for Development Policy (CDP) database, 2012 review ; World Bank, *World Development Indicators* database September 2013; United Nations, UNdata database, Septtmber 2013; UNDP. *Human development Report 2013*, September 2013; World Bank Economies Income classification, July 2013.

Notes: a) GNI current $ Atlas method, World Bank, WDI database, September 2013; 2011 data for Afghanistan, Rwanda and Yemen.

b) EVI: higher values indicate higher vulnerablity.See explanotory notes at http://www.un.org/en/development/desa/policy/cdp/cdp_publications/2008cdphandbook.pdf

c) HAI: lower values indicate weaker human asset development. See explanotory notes at http://www.un.org/en/development/desa/policy/cdp/cdp_publications/2008cdphandbook.pdf

d) 2011 data for Djibouti, Myanmar and Somalia. Source: Undata, National accounts main aggregates database, September 2013.

e) MPI: higher values indicate population multidimentionally poor. See explanatory notes for HDR composite indices at http://hdrstats.undp.org/images/explanations/PSE.pdf

Annex table 2. Real GDP growth rates for individual LDCs, selected years (Annual weighted averages, percentage)						
	2002–2008	2009	2010	2011	2012	2013
Food and Agriculture exporters	*5.2*	*6.1*	*6.3*	*5.4*	*2.0*	*5.1*
Guinea-Bissau	2.8	3.0	3.5	5.3	-1.5	4.2
Malawi	5.1	9.0	6.5	4.3	1.9	5.5
Solomon Islands	7.6	-4.7	7.8	10.7	5.5	4.0
Somalia						
Fuel exporters	*9.2*	*3.0*	*4.0*	*-1.1*	*2.2*	*3.9*
Angola	16.6	2.4	3.4	3.9	8.4	6.2
Chad	8.9	-1.2	13.0	0.5	5.0	8.1
Equatorial Guinea	14.9	-3.6	-2.6	4.5	2.0	-2.1
Sudan	5.9	5.2	2.5	-1.9	-4.4	1.2
Yemen	4.0	3.9	7.7	-10.5	0.1	4.4
Manufactures exporters	*6.2*	*5.3*	*5.9*	*6.5*	*6.0*	*6.1*
Bangladesh	6.2	5.9	6.4	6.5	6.1	6.0
Bhutan	8.5	6.7	11.7	8.5	9.7	6.3
Cambodia	10.4	0.1	6.1	7.1	6.5	6.7
Haiti	0.9	2.9	-5.4	5.6	2.8	6.5
Lesotho	3.8	4.8	6.3	5.7	4.0	3.5
Mineral exporters	*5.6*	*4.0*	*6.1*	*5.9*	*5.7*	*7.1*
Democratic Republic of the Congo	6.4	2.8	7.2	6.9	7.1	8.3
Eritrea	-0.5	3.9	2.2	8.7	7.0	3.4
Guinea	2.6	-0.3	1.9	3.9	3.9	4.5
Mali	4.9	4.5	5.8	2.7	-1.2	4.8
Mauritania	5.6	-1.2	5.1	3.9	6.4	5.9
Mozambique	7.8	6.3	7.1	7.3	7.5	8.4
Zambia	5.7	6.4	7.6	6.8	7.3	7.8
Service exporters	*8.7*	*7.8*	*6.1*	*6.0*	*5.7*	*5.0*
Afghanistan	7.7[a]	21.0	8.4	7.0	10.2	3.1
Burundi	4.4	3.5	3.8	4.2	4.0	4.5
Comoros	1.6	1.8	2.1	2.2	2.5	3.5
Djibouti	4.0	5.0	3.5	4.5	4.8	5.0
Ethiopia	10.3	10.0	8.0	7.5	7.0	6.5
Gambia	3.3	6.5	6.5	-4.3	3.9	8.9
Liberia	3.1	5.3	6.1	7.9	8.3	7.5
Madagascar	5.9	-4.1	0.4	1.8	1.9	2.6
Nepal	4.0	4.5	4.8	3.9	4.6	3.0
Rwanda	7.9	6.2	7.2	8.3	7.7	7.6
Samoa	3.9	-5.1	0.4	2.0	1.2	0.9
Sao Tome and Principe	5.8	4.0	4.5	4.9	4.0	4.5
Timor-Leste	5.0	12.8	9.5	10.6	10.0	10.0
Tuvalu	0.9	-1.7	-2.9	1.1	1.2	1.3
Vanuatu	5.7	3.3	1.6	1.4	2.7	4.3
Uganda	8.1	7.1	5.6	6.7	2.6	4.8
Mixed exporters	*7.8*	*4.5*	*6.0*	*5.2*	*6.7*	*6.6*
Benin	3.8	2.7	2.6	3.5	3.8	4.1
Burkina Faso	6.2	3.0	7.9	4.2	8.0	7.0
Central African Republic	2.3	1.7	3.0	3.3	4.1	4.3
Kiribati	0.6	-2.4	1.4	2.0	2.5	2.5
Lao People's Democratic Republic	7.5	7.5	8.1	8.0	8.3	8.0
Myanmar	12.1	5.1	5.3	5.5	6.3	6.5
Niger	4.7	-1.0	10.7	2.2	11.2	6.2
Senegal	4.8	2.2	4.3	2.6	3.5	4.0
Sierra Leone	6.0	3.2	5.3	6.0	19.8	17.1
Togo	2.7	3.5	4.0	4.9	5.0	5.1
United Republic of Tanzania	7.2	6.0	7.0	6.4	6.9	7.0
LDCs	*7.5*	*5.0*	*5.6*	*4.5*	*5.3*	*5.7*
African LDCs and Haiti	*7.5*	*4.2*	*4.9*	*4.4*	*4.8*	*5.6*
Asian LDCs	*7.5*	*5.9*	*6.4*	*4.6*	*5.8*	*5.7*
Island LDCs	*4.9*	*2.7*	*5.5*	*6.8*	*5.7*	*5.8*

Source: UNCTAD secretariat calculations, based on IMF, *World Economic Outlook* database, April 2013.
Notes: a 2003-2008; data for 2012 are preliminary and are forecasted for 2013.

Annex table 3. Real GDP per capita growth rates for individual LDCs, selected years
(Annual weighted averages, percentage)

	2002–2008	2009	2010	2011	2012	2013
Food and Agriculture exporters	*2.7*	*3.2*	*3.4*	*2.5*	*-0.8*	*2.2*
Guinea-Bissau	0.8	0.9	1.4	3.2	-3.4	2.0
Malawi	2.6	6.0	3.6	1.4	-1.0	2.5
Solomon Islands	5.2	-7.0	3.4	7.9	3.1	1.7
Somalia						
Fuel exporters	*6.2*	*0.2*	*1.2*	*5.5*	*-0.5*	*1.1*
Angola	13.3	-0.2	0.4	0.9	5.3	3.1
Chad	5.5	-3.6	10.2	-1.9	2.5	5.4
Equatorial Guinea	11.5	-6.3	-5.2	1.6	-0.8	-4.6
Sudan	3.2	2.5	-0.1	20.6	-6.8	-1.4
Yemen	0.8	0.8	4.6	-13.1	-2.8	1.3
Manufactures exporters	*4.8*	*4.1*	*4.8*	*5.4*	*4.7*	*5.1*
Bangladesh	4.8	4.8	5.2	5.4	4.9	4.9
Bhutan	5.9	4.8	9.8	6.7	9.0	6.0
Cambodia	8.5	-1.6	5.0	6.0	5.4	5.6
Haiti	-0.7	1.2	-4.8	3.9	-1.1	7.5
Lesotho	3.7	4.5	6.0	5.5	3.7	3.3
Mineral exporters	*2.8*	*1.2*	*3.3*	*3.1*	*2.9*	*4.2*
Democratic Republic of the Congo	3.3	-0.2	4.1	3.8	4.0	5.1
Eritrea	-4.1	0.7	-0.9	5.4	3.8	0.3
Guinea	0.5	-2.7	-0.6	1.4	1.4	2.0
Mali	1.7	1.3	2.7	-0.4	-4.2	1.7
Mauritania	2.8	-3.6	2.6	1.4	3.9	3.4
Mozambique	5.7	4.2	5.0	5.2	5.4	6.3
Zambia	3.3	3.8	5.0	4.3	4.7	5.2
Service exporters	*5.9*	*5.2*	*3.5*	*3.5*	*3.1*	*2.4*
Afghanistan	4.0 [a]	17.3	5.2	3.8	7.0	0.1
Burundi	2.2	1.0	1.4	1.7	1.6	2.0
Comoros	-0.5	-0.2	-0.1	0.1	0.4	1.4
Djibouti	1.2	2.2	0.7	1.6	2.0	2.1
Ethiopia	7.7	7.7	5.7	5.2	4.5	4.0
Gambia	0.3	3.5	3.7	-6.9	1.2	5.9
Liberia	-0.2	1.0	1.8	5.2	5.6	4.7
Madagascar	3.0	-6.6	-2.2	-0.8	-0.6	0.1
Nepal	1.8	2.7	3.0	2.1	2.9	1.4
Rwanda	6.0	4.1	5.0	6.0	5.5	5.4
Samoa	3.5	-5.1	-0.2	1.5	1.2	0.3
Sao Tome and Principe	4.2	2.1	3.2	2.5	2.2	2.7
Timor-Leste	2.4	10.2	6.8	8.0	7.4	7.5
Tuvalu	-1.2	-1.7	-2.9	1.1	1.2	1.3
Vanuatu	3.3	1.1	-0.5	-1.1	0.6	1.8
Uganda	4.7	3.7	2.2	3.3	-0.7	1.5
Mixed exporters	*5.2*	*1.9*	*3.4*	*2.6*	*4.4*	*4.3*
Benin	0.6	-0.3	-0.3	0.7	1.1	1.4
Burkina Faso	3.1	-0.1	4.7	1.1	5.6	4.6
Central African Republic	0.3	-1.9	0.5	0.8	1.6	1.8
Kiribati	-1.2	-4.3	0.4	0.0	0.5	0.6
Lao People's Democratic Republic	5.8	5.9	6.6	6.5	6.8	6.5
Myanmar	9.9	3.1	3.3	3.4	4.2	4.4
Niger	1.3	-4.3	7.3	-0.9	7.9	3.0
Senegal	2.0	-0.5	1.5	-0.1	0.8	1.3
Sierra Leone	2.5	0.7	2.6	3.3	16.7	14.2
Togo	0.1	1.3	1.7	2.6	2.7	2.8
United Republic of Tanzania	4.6	3.0	3.9	3.3	4.8	4.9
LDCs	*5.0*	*2.6*	*3.3*	*3.2*	*2.9*	*3.4*
African LDCs and Haiti	*4.8*	*1.5*	*2.2*	*3.4*	*2.1*	*3.0*
Asian LDCs	*5.5*	*4.1*	*4.7*	*2.9*	*4.1*	*4.0*
Island LDCs	*2.7*	*0.6*	*2.9*	*4.5*	*3.5*	*3.6*

Source: UNCTAD secretariat calculations, based on IMF, *World Economic Outlook* database, April 2013.
Notes: a 2003-2008; data for 2012 are preliminary and are forecasted for 2013.

Annex table 4. Gross capital formation, gross domestic savings and resource gap in LDCs , by country, and by LDC groups, selected years
(Percentage of GDP)

	Gross capital formation				Gross domestic savings				External resource gap			
	2000-2008	2009	2010	2011	2000-2008	2009	2010	2011	2000-2008	2009	2010	2011
Countries with real GDP growth >6% in 2011												
Ethiopia	23.1	22.7	24.7	25.5	6.9	5.7	5.2	8.8	-16.2	-17.0	-19.5	-16.7
Solomon Islands	17.3	19.3	37.4	21.0	4.3	-0.7	0.2	13.7	-12.9	-20.0	-37.2	-7.3
Timor-Leste	5.4	14.9	14.1	11.2	63.9	56.0	61.9	62.6	58.5	41.1	47.8	51.4
Eritrea	19.9	9.3	9.3	10.0	-21.1	-9.7	-9.3	1.2	-41.0	-18.9	-18.6	-8.8
Rwanda	16.9	21.6	21.0	21.4	2.0	2.2	0.4	2.3	-14.9	-19.4	-20.5	-19.1
Liberia	13.9	19.6	19.5	19.3	-12.3	-28.7	-26.7	-25.4	-26.2	-48.3	-46.2	-44.7
Lao People's Dem. Republic	31.0	31.5	27.3	31.1	19.1	26.2	27.7	25.3	-11.9	-5.2	0.4	-5.8
Mozambique	20.5	14.9	13.4	14.7	5.7	6.6	4.2	0.4	-14.8	-8.4	-9.1	-14.3
Equatorial Guinea	31.2	70.5	70.6	50.8	88.9	87.3	88.1	88.2	57.7	16.8	17.5	37.3
Cambodia	19.1	21.4	17.4	17.1	11.8	17.7	12.4	11.1	-7.3	-3.7	-5.0	-6.0
Democratic Rep. of the Congo	13.6	19.1	26.4	27.5	8.1	2.8	18.8	22.8	-5.5	-16.3	-7.6	-4.6
Bangladesh	23.9	24.4	24.4	24.7	19.4	20.1	20.1	19.6	-4.5	-4.3	-4.3	-5.1
Zambia	23.8	21.0	22.6	24.9	18.7	23.9	34.5	34.0	-5.1	2.8	11.9	9.1
United Republic of Tanzania	23.8	28.7	31.7	32.9	14.5	17.0	21.3	22.6	-9.3	-11.6	-10.4	-10.3
Sierra Leone	10.2	9.9	24.5	40.8	-3.5	-4.7	6.5	2.9	-13.7	-14.6	-18.0	-37.9
Countries with real GDP growth between 3% and 6% in 2011												
Bhutan	48.7	41.2	52.3	54.1	38.1	40.7	38.3	36.2	-10.5	-0.5	-13.9	-17.8
Afghanistan	17.6	17.4	17.5	15.1	-24.4	-9.9	-8.9	-8.5	-42.0	-27.3	-26.3	-23.6
Haiti	14.8	14.3	13.3	14.6	-15.7	-17.6	-44.9	-31.9	-30.4	-31.9	-58.1	-46.5
Gambia	31.8	31.1	30.2	30.7	16.0	19.1	19.1	9.1	-15.8	-12.0	-11.1	-21.6
Myanmar	13.4	18.9	22.7	19.3	13.9	15.8	21.7	19.5	0.6	-3.0	-1.0	0.2
Mauritania	34.4	20.6	18.3	25.9	12.2	0.1	4.4	15.8	-22.3	-20.5	-13.9	-10.1
Burkina Faso	22.0	24.7	28.2	26.0	7.2	9.5	22.0	12.5	-14.7	-15.2	-6.3	-13.4
Sao Tome and Principe	22.7	18.4	21.1	20.9	-19.4	-31.1	-29.6	-26.0	-42.1	-49.5	-50.7	-46.9
Togo	16.3	18.7	18.9	19.4	-2.7	3.1	2.1	3.4	-19.0	-15.6	-16.8	-16.0
Djibouti	17.9	18.8	19.1	18.9	-4.6	-4.3	-4.7	-4.6	-22.5	-23.1	-23.8	-23.5
Malawi	21.1	25.0	24.8	13.5	3.4	2.3	3.6	7.0	-17.7	-22.7	-21.2	-6.5
Guinea-Bissau	10.5	8.5	7.3	8.9	-4.5	-4.8	2.0	5.3	-15.1	-13.3	-5.2	-3.7
Vanuatu	23.3	34.1	34.1	34.1	17.4	22.3	22.3	22.3	-5.9	-11.9	-11.9	-11.9
Guinea	28.4	30.1	32.6	45.1	23.4	25.1	27.5	32.9	-5.0	-5.0	-5.1	-12.2
Burundi	16.0	24.0	22.4	22.4	-3.1	-20.1	-20.8	-19.2	-19.1	-44.2	-43.2	-41.6
Lesotho	27.5	28.0	28.0	34.3	-45.5	-43.8	-40.3	-27.8	-72.9	-71.9	-68.3	-62.1
Uganda	20.9	22.0	22.3	22.4	9.0	12.1	7.5	7.5	-11.9	-9.9	-14.8	-14.9
Nepal	25.7	31.7	38.3	32.5	10.4	9.4	11.5	8.6	-15.3	-22.2	-26.8	-23.9
Angola	13.2	16.1	16.1	16.1	39.5	15.6	35.3	40.4	26.3	-0.5	19.1	24.3
Chad	23.6	21.7	27.7	19.1	42.2	43.1	48.4	52.4	18.6	21.4	20.7	33.3
Central African Republic	9.6	11.3	14.1	14.9	3.3	-0.6	1.9	3.7	-6.4	-11.9	-12.2	-11.3
Benin	20.0	21.2	21.0	21.6	11.7	11.9	11.5	12.2	-8.2	-9.3	-9.5	-9.4
Kiribati	40.9	43.9	42.9	42.4	-30.4	-40.1	-37.1	-35.4	-71.2	-83.9	-80.0	-77.8
Countries with real GDP growth < 3% in 2011												
Senegal	24.7	22.1	22.6	22.2	7.8	5.2	7.0	4.8	-17.0	-16.9	-15.7	-17.4
Mali	21.4	21.2	24.5	22.9	16.4	20.5	22.3	21.1	-5.0	-0.8	-2.2	-1.8
Somalia	19.9	20.0	19.9	20.0	18.5	18.7	18.6	18.7	-1.4	-1.4	-1.4	-1.4
Niger	22.0	33.2	35.9	32.1	10.0	9.9	14.6	10.1	-12.0	-23.3	-21.3	-22.0
Comoros	10.5	11.5	14.3	16.9	-11.9	-22.6	-21.4	-18.8	-22.3	-34.1	-35.6	-35.7
Madagascar	24.9	31.7	18.8	14.5	7.3	2.5	1.1	0.3	-17.6	-29.3	-17.7	-14.2
Samoa	10.8	9.2	9.0	9.0	-13.8	-13.7	-13.2	-13.1	-24.6	-22.9	-22.2	-22.0
Tuvalu	57.2	55.6	53.6	51.8	-4.0	4.1	4.8	6.1	-61.3	-51.5	-48.8	-45.7
Sudan	21.5	20.5	21.7	20.6	16.6	15.7	22.4	21.6	-4.9	-4.8	0.7	1.0
Yemen	24.6	20.7	15.8	7.4	23.6	10.5	9.9	8.3	-0.9	-10.2	-5.8	0.9
Memo items:												
LDCs	21.2	22.5	23.3	22.0	17.4	14.7	19.6	20.8	-3.8	-7.8	-3.7	-1.2
African LDCs and Haiti	20.5	22.2	23.3	22.6	18.1	14.0	21.3	23.8	-2.4	-8.2	-2.0	1.2
Asian LDCs	22.7	23.1	23.4	21.3	16.0	15.5	16.3	15.1	-6.7	-7.6	-7.1	-6.1
Island LDCs	12.2	17.4	18.8	15.4	27.3	28.3	34.2	38.6	15.2	10.9	15.4	23.1
ODCs	27.8	31.2	32.0	32.8	31.9	33.4	35.0	35.9	4.1	2.2	2.9	3.1

Source: UNCTAD secretariat calculations, based on UNCTADstat database., July 2013.

Annex table 5. Share of value added in main economic sectors in LDCs, by country and country groups, 1999–2001 and 2009–2011
(Percentage of GDP)

| | Agriculture, hunting, forestry, fishing | | Industry | | | | Services | |
| | | | Manufacturing | | Non-manufacturing | | | |
	1999–2001	2009–2011	1999–2001	2009–2011	1999–2001	2009–2011	1999–2001	2009–2011
Afghanistan	56.3	30.9	16.9	13.8	6.5	9.0	20.3	46.3
Angola	6.9	10.0	3.4	6.2	67.2	55.9	22.5	28.0
Bangladesh	25.3	18.6	15.4	18.0	10.0	10.6	49.3	52.9
Benin	37.9	35.4	9.0	8.4	5.1	6.1	48.0	50.2
Bhutan	27.5	18.2	8.6	8.8	28.2	35.2	35.6	37.8
Burkina Faso	35.0	35.1	13.9	9.0	7.8	15.1	43.3	40.8
Burundi	41.4	36.1	12.9	13.5	5.6	8.7	40.1	41.8
Cambodia	38.9	36.2	16.2	15.7	5.7	7.6	39.1	40.6
Central African Republic	52.3	54.4	6.1	6.7	8.3	7.1	33.3	31.8
Chad	41.3	20.7	10.4	6.5	2.2	42.8	46.0	30.0
Comoros	45.4	49.0	4.3	4.1	7.2	6.5	43.1	40.5
Dem. Rep. of the Congo	53.9	45.1	4.9	5.4	14.8	17.7	26.4	31.9
Djibouti	3.5	3.8	2.6	2.4	12.6	17.9	81.3	75.9
Equatorial Guinea	8.6	2.8	0.2	0.2	87.3	93.6	4.0	3.4
Eritrea	19.0	17.0	10.5	6.0	11.9	17.4	58.7	59.7
Ethiopia	48.6	47.6	5.5	3.7	7.1	6.6	38.8	42.1
Gambia	23.9	31.2	6.7	5.2	8.0	7.1	61.5	56.4
Guinea	23.1	25.8	3.6	6.0	28.4	28.2	45.0	40.0
Guinea-Bissau	59.0	44.6	9.2	12.3	3.1	1.0	28.8	42.1
Haiti	23.5	20.4	10.1	9.3	22.7	24.8	43.7	45.6
Kiribati	23.2	25.7	4.9	5.2	6.6	3.3	65.3	65.8
Lao People's Dem. Republic	43.5	29.7	8.0	10.0	10.9	17.7	37.6	42.6
Lesotho	12.5	8.0	14.4	15.2	15.7	17.4	57.3	59.5
Liberia	71.8	70.6	1.8	5.8	0.9	5.6	25.5	18.0
Madagascar	28.7	28.4	12.3	14.6	3.5	5.4	55.5	51.9
Malawi	34.7	30.0	11.3	10.5	6.9	6.0	47.1	53.5
Mali	37.2	39.4	7.6	5.9	14.1	15.3	41.0	39.4
Mauritania	35.5	23.6	11.6	6.5	16.6	31.1	36.3	38.8
Mozambique	24.7	29.4	12.4	13.6	11.5	9.1	51.4	48.0
Myanmar	58.0	37.6	7.2	18.6	2.6	6.4	32.2	37.4
Nepal	37.5	35.4	9.1	6.5	8.1	8.8	45.4	49.3
Niger	43.4	43.1	6.5	5.3	6.0	10.6	44.1	41.0
Rwanda	39.4	34.8	7.6	7.0	7.6	9.3	45.4	48.9
Samoa	16.1	10.3	15.5	8.7	11.2	18.0	57.2	63.0
Sao Tome and Principe	20.4	17.4	7.7	7.0	10.3	11.5	61.5	64.0
Senegal	18.9	17.1	15.8	14.0	7.9	9.5	57.4	59.4
Sierra Leone	48.6	57.0	3.6	2.3	5.4	5.5	42.4	35.2
Solomon Islands	31.6	28.9	8.2	5.9	5.0	4.3	55.2	60.9
Somalia	60.1	60.2	2.5	2.5	4.9	4.9	32.5	32.5
Sudan	37.3	34.0	6.7	8.3	11.0	16.2	44.9	41.5
Timor-Leste	..	4.8	..	0.6	..	80.3	..	14.3
Togo	40.0	46.9	8.6	8.6	10.2	9.5	41.2	35.0
Tuvalu	18.3	22.1	1.4	0.9	12.0	8.4	68.2	68.6
Uganda	28.2	23.6	7.7	8.1	14.8	17.2	49.4	51.0
United Republic of Tanzania	33.0	28.5	9.2	9.3	9.8	14.4	48.0	47.8
Vanuatu	26.1	21.5	4.9	3.3	5.5	7.5	63.4	67.7
Yemen	12.9	11.7	5.3	7.4	33.5	28.0	48.3	52.9
Zambia	21.5	19.7	10.9	8.8	12.9	27.0	54.7	44.4
LDCs	*31.4*	*25.6*	*10.1*	*10.2*	*14.5*	*22.0*	*44.0*	*42.2*
African LDCs and Haiti	32.6	26.3	8.0	7.5	16.5	27.3	42.9	38.9
Asian LDCs	30.0	24.7	12.7	15.2	12.1	12.1	45.2	48.1
Island LDCs	28.7	13.5	8.0	2.6	7.2	51.6	56.1	32.4

Source: UNCTAD secretariat calculations, based on UNCTADstat database, July 2013.

Annex table 6. Foreign direct investment inflows to LDCs, selected years (Millions of current dollars)				
	2000–2008	2009	2010	2011	2012
Afghanistan	120.8	75.7	211.3	83.4	93.8
Angola	1'010.5	2'205.3	-3'227.2	-3'023.8	-6'897.8
Bangladesh	606.9	700.2	913.3	1'136.4	990.0
Benin	84.1	134.3	176.8	161.1	158.6
Bhutan	14.7	18.3	25.8	10.4	15.9
Burkina Faso	67.2	100.9	34.6	42.3	40.1
Burundi	2.1	0.3	0.8	3.4	0.6
Cambodia	356.1	539.1	782.6	901.7	1'557.1
Central African Republic	28.5	42.3	61.5	36.9	71.2
Chad	271.7	375.8	312.7	281.9	323.5
Comoros	1.9	13.8	8.3	23.1	17.0
Democratic Republic of the Congo	572.4	663.8	2'939.3	1'686.9	3'312.1
Djibouti	68.6	99.6	26.8	78.0	100.0
Equatorial Guinea	459.6	1'636.2	2'734.0	1'975.0	2'115.1
Eritrea	19.4	91.0	91.0	39.0	73.7
Ethiopia	321.1	221.5	288.3	626.5	970.4
Gambia	49.8	39.6	37.2	36.0	78.8
Guinea	135.6	140.9	101.4	956.1	743.8
Guinea-Bissau	6.7	17.5	33.2	25.0	16.2
Haiti	37.1	38.0	150.0	181.0	178.8
Kiribati	1.1	3.2	-6.6	-1.8	-1.7
Lao People's Democratic Republic	96.1	189.5	278.8	300.8	294.4
Lesotho	59.8	99.9	113.7	132.1	172.3
Liberia	120.6	217.8	450.0	508.0	1'354.1
Madagascar	305.7	1'066.1	808.2	809.8	894.7
Malawi	85.2	49.1	97.0	128.8	129.5
Mali	137.9	748.3	405.9	556.1	310.5
Mauritania	236.5	-3.1	130.5	588.6	1'204.4
Mozambique	289.4	892.5	1'017.9	2'662.8	5'218.1
Myanmar	357.5	972.5	1'284.6	2'200.0	2'243.0
Nepal	3.5	38.6	86.7	95.5	92.0
Niger	68.6	790.8	940.3	1'065.8	793.4
Rwanda	30.2	118.7	42.3	106.0	159.8
Samoa	9.4	9.6	1.1	12.3	21.5
Sao Tome and Principe	20.7	15.5	50.6	35.0	49.5
Senegal	140.3	320.0	266.1	338.2	337.7
Sierra Leone	47.5	110.4	238.4	715.0	740.1
Solomon Islands	24.0	119.8	237.9	146.4	69.3
Somalia	38.1	108.0	112.0	102.0	107.3
Sudan	1'711.6	1'816.2	2'063.7	2'691.7	2'466.4
Timor-Leste	12.5	49.9	28.5	47.1	42.0
Togo	53.3	48.5	85.8	171.0	166.3
Tuvalu	..	..	..	..	..
Uganda	395.5	841.6	543.9	894.3	1'721.2
United Republic of Tanzania	564.3	952.6	1'813.3	1'229.4	1'706.0
Vanuatu	33.2	31.7	41.1	58.2	37.7
Yemen	402.4	129.2	188.6	-518.4	348.8
Zambia	501.3	694.8	1'729.3	1'108.0	1'066.0
LDCs	*9'972.0*	*17'585.8*	*18'751.3*	*21'442.9*	*25'703.0*
African LDCs and Haiti	7'920.0	14'679.2	14'618.6	16'913.0	19'832.6
Asian LDCs	1'954.8	2'663.1	3'771.8	4'209.7	5'635.0
Island LDCs	97.1	243.5	361.0	320.3	235.4
ODCs	*340'732.5*	*512'703.0*	*618'311.7*	*713'769.3*	*677'122.6*

Source: UNCTAD secretariat calculations, based on UNCTADstat database, July 2013.

Annex table 7. Total workers remittances to LDCs, by country and groups
(Millions of current dollars and share in GNI)

	$ millions				Percentage of GNI			
	2000–2008	2009	2010	2011	2000–2008	2009	2010	2011
Countries with remittances > 10% of GNI in 2011								
Samoa	82.3	131.4	143.4	151.2	22.6	26.1	24.8	23.9
Lesotho	540.5	623.0	745.9	753.5	33.8	28.7	27.5	23.7
Haiti	917.8	1'375.5	1'473.8	1'597.8	23.8	23.2	24.2	23.7
Nepal	1073.0	2'985.6	3'468.9	3'951.4	13.5	23.2	21.1	21.2
Gambia	43.2	79.8	115.7	124.8	6.7	9.3	13.0	11.1
Bangladesh	4'327.8	10'520.6	10'850.2	11'989.4	7.2	10.8	10.0	10.4
Senegal	712.0	1'350.4	1'346.0	1'437.1	8.9	10.7	10.7	10.1
Countries with remittances between 5% and 10% of GNI in 2011								
Togo	175.5	334.5	333.1	345.3	9.0	10.6	10.6	9.4
Guinea-Bissau	24.9	48.9	48.1	51.1	4.7	5.7	5.9	5.7
Kiribati	7.2	8.7	8.8	-	6.1	6.1	5.1	5.1
Countries with remittances < 5% of GNI in 2011								
Uganda	391.8	778.3	914.5	937.4	4.2	4.8	5.2	4.9
Yemen	1'302.9	1'160.0	1'501.9	1'322.8	7.8	4.3	4.8	4.3
Mali	196.9	453.7	436.2	439.8	4.0	5.3	4.8	4.3
Benin	143.9	149.9	248.1	250.5	3.6	2.3	3.8	3.5
Cambodia	209.3	337.8	321.1	407.3	3.9	3.4	3.0	3.4
Liberia	57.8	25.1	31.4	27.9	12.0	2.9	3.6	3.1
Sudan	1'338.8	2'135.3	1'419.6	2'055.4	4.2	3.7	2.1	3.1
Djibouti	22.4	32.5	32.6	35.4	3.0	2.9	2.7	2.6
Sierra Leone	19.3	46.8	57.5	60.2	1.2	1.8	2.2	2.0
Comoros	12.0	12.0	12.0	12.0	3.4	2.2	2.2	2.0
Rwanda	22.5	92.6	103.1	96.5	0.9	1.8	1.8	1.5
Niger	50.9	101.7	88.0	88.0	1.6	1.9	1.6	1.4
Guinea	53.7	63.7	60.4	60.9	1.5	1.2	1.2	1.1
Mozambique	68.0	111.1	131.9	131.9	1.2	1.2	1.4	1.1
Burkina Faso	64.7	99.3	95.0	95.0	1.3	1.2	1.1	0.9
Vanuatu	13.5	5.5	6.4	6.6	3.8	1.0	1.0	0.9
Sao Tome and Principe	1.4	2.0	2.0	2.1	1.3	1.0	1.0	0.8
Ethiopia	152.8	261.6	345.2	241.6	1.2	0.9	1.3	0.8
Lao People's Dem. Rep.	3.6	37.6	40.9	44.2	0.1	0.7	0.6	0.6
Solomon Islands	4.2	2.5	1.7	2.4	1.1	0.5	0.3	0.3
Bhutan	2.9	4.9	5.7	4.9	0.4	0.4	0.4	0.3
Zambia	53.8	41.3	43.7	45.3	0.8	0.4	0.3	0.3
Myanmar	112.3	116.3	133.0	137.0	0.9	0.4	0.3	0.2
Burundi	0.8	3.6	3.6	3.6	0.1	0.2	0.2	0.2
Madagascar	14.0	6.0	10.0	13.0	0.3	0.1	0.1	0.1
United Rep. of Tanzania	14.0	23.3	24.8	24.8	0.1	0.1	0.1	0.1
Mauritania	2.0	1.9	1.9	1.9	0.1	0.1	0.1	0.0
Angola	6.9	6.0	9.0	10.0	0.0	0.0	0.0	0.0
Malawi	0.8	0.8	0.8	-	0.0	0.0	0.0	0.0
LDCs	**12'196.5**	**23'571.7**	**24'616.1**	**26'969.5**	**4.6**	**4.8**	**4.5**	**4.4**
African LDCs and Haiti	5'045.9	8'246.7	8'120.1	8'929.4	3.2	2.7	2.5	2.5
Asian LDCs	7'029.8	15'162.8	16'321.6	17'857.0	6.6	8.1	7.5	7.4
Island LDCs	120.7	162.1	174.4	183.1	7.1	6.7	6.5	5.7
ODCs	**154'741.5**	**262'716.8**	**280'581.2**	**301'557.8**	**1.6**	**1.6**	**1.4**	**1.3**

Source: UNCTADstat database, United Nations /DESA for GNI, July 2013.

Annex table 8. Selected indicators on debt burden in LDCs

	Total debt stock as % GNI				Total debt stock as % exports				Total debt service as % exports			
	2000–2008	2009	2010	2011	2000-2008	2009	2010	2011	2000–2008	2009	2010	2011
Countries with debt >100% of GNI in 2011												
Somalia	156.5	157.8	296.2	297.8	..	..	..	..	..	..	..	..
Countries with debt between 50% and 100% of GNI in 2011												
Sao Tome and Principe	295.5	81.5	90.2	93.2	1'712.4	745.0	698.1	747.5	28.4	9.8	6.4	5.4
Lao People's Dem. Rep.	127.5	101.2	84.2	79.6	447.2	384.6	245.0	..	16.0	14.8	13.2	..
Guinea	103.6	84.3	72.9	67.5	337.1	273.4	202.4	205.4	14.6	10.1	4.8	11.2
Mauritania	117.0	69.6	70.9	66.2	102.3	130.7	110.8	87.3	5.5	4.7	4.7	3.6
Samoa	48.9	53.4	58.7	60.6	117.7	139.5	161.6	180.8	4.4	4.7	5.3	5.8
Bhutan	70.5	62.4	60.6	59.9	137.6	128.7	145.2	136.1	6.5	12.8	13.5	11.1
Djibouti	64.2	79.8	63.1	56.0	164.9	211.5	173.3	..	6.7	8.5	8.1	..
Gambia	96.1	58.0	55.5	53.8	318.7	174.5	179.7	142.3	13.9	6.5	8.1	7.5
Countries with debt <50% of GNI in 2011												
Comoros	83.9	53.9	51.9	45.7	419.8	361.8	..	..	16.4	14.9	..	..
United Rep. of Tanzania	53.5	36.1	39.8	42.5	276.7	143.5	137.6	131.4	4.8	3.1	3.0	2.0
Eritrea	67.1	57.1	49.7	40.8	308.5	..	..	..	4.3	..	..	..
Solomon Islands	41.3	36.5	41.6	37.9	144.4	69.7	65.8	33.7	7.9	4.0	5.9	2.0
Dem. Rep. of the Congo	189.8	233.7	50.9	37.9	274.7	259.5	69.6	52.5	8.1	12.4	3.1	2.4
Sudan	87.2	43.6	37.3	36.2	523.6	243.2	188.5		8.2	5.6	4.2	
Sierra Leone	100.7	35.4	36.9	36.1	850.2	225.8	218.3	191.5	26.9	2.1	2.7	3.8
Cambodia	59.3	35.5	35.8	35.8	95.9	60.0	55.2	57.9	0.9	0.8	0.9	1.0
Mozambique	90.3	43.9	40.6	33.1	324.3	141.0	118.8	113.3	5.2	1.4	2.8	1.6
Liberia	879.9	183.1	37.6	31.3	842.4	391.9	97.3	..	47.1	13.6	1.4	..
Senegal	51.2	29.7	30.7	30.2	175.3	114.3	..	..	11.1	6.1	..	..
Guinea-Bissau	285.1	139.8	135.4	29.3	1'188.6	717.4	..	..	8.5	6.4	..	..
Mali	68.6	26.0	27.4	28.7	225.7	100.1	98.2	..	6.9	3.1	2.5	..
Madagascar	73.4	32.8	30.8	28.5	266.0	140.7	163.3	140.9	5.2	2.8	3.7	2.1
Lesotho	46.5	35.7	29.6	27.7	57.0	48.8	43.7	..	5.5	2.5	1.9	..
Ethiopia	51.8	16.3	24.8	27.2	365.5	152.3	157.9	147.6	8.0	3.0	3.9	6.1
Burundi	125.2	36.0	31.9	26.9	1'946.5	517.9	353.5	258.2	49.0	16.5	2.1	3.4
Central African Republic	84.0	28.8	29.2	26.5	..	..	..	..	..	..	..	..
Vanuatu	33.9	26.5	25.5	26.3	60.7	46.9	47.8	51.4	1.7	1.7	1.6	1.6
Uganda	46.9	20.5	20.6	24.6	332.8	81.6	91.6	95.1	7.5	2.1	1.8	1.7
Zambia	114.0	30.5	29.8	24.2	343.6	82.7	57.0	48.1	16.1	3.7	1.9	2.1
Niger	59.9	22.5	23.6	23.7	342.1	98.9	..	..	8.9	3.8	..	..
Burkina Faso	37.5	23.0	23.7	23.3	359.8	168.4	109.0		10.1	3.8	2.5	
Angola	66.3	24.8	25.6	22.9	72.2	40.9	36.8	31.2	15.2	8.5	4.5	4.2
Bangladesh	30.9	25.3	23.5	22.2	190.7	144.0	118.3	98.9	7.9	5.6	4.7	5.5
Malawi	98.0	23.1	19.7	21.9	405.9	84.9	85.0	74.5	8.5	2.9	1.7	1.3
Yemen	43.3	28.7	22.3	21.8	102.3	93.4	71.7	64.4	4.2	3.7	2.8	2.8
Nepal	42.7	29.0	23.6	20.7	240.1	215.6	212.9	184.0	8.9	10.1	10.5	9.5
Togo	92.9	62.0	45.0	20.1	237.2	137.3	..	..	5.1	4.4	..	..
Benin	37.4	17.5	19.8	19.6	173.0	77.1	75.4	..	6.4	2.5	2.5	..
Chad	50.5	27.4	23.1	19.0	..	..	..	..	..	..	..	..
Rwanda	57.0	16.7	16.4	17.5	621.4	165.5	147.1		11.9	2.2	2.4	
Afghanistan	17.4	22.2	17.1	14.5	..	..	..	..	..	..	..	..
Myanmar	57.5	23.4	18.5	14.0	182.7	113.7	98.5		0.9	0.2	7.1	
Haiti	38.3	24.4	16.2	11.6	250.4	151.2	118.4	72.9	9.9	4.7	15.8	0.5
LDCs	*60.4*	*32.7*	*29.0*	*26.6*	*202.1*	*114.3*	*90.4*	*67.5*	*9.2*	*6.2*	*4.1*	*3.9*
African LDCs and Haiti	76.2	36.0	32.4	29.9	230.3	106.1	83.6	..	11.0	6.5	3.8	3.7
Asian LDCs	39.8	28.4	24.6	22.3	163.7	136.7	109.3	95.6	6.1	5.3	4.6	4.9
Island LDCs	67.1	45.4	47.1	46.0	201.2	121.9	103.3	104.1	6.0	4.5	3.9	2.9
ODCs	*22.5*	*16.6*	*16.3*	*16.0*	*92.6*	*72.8*	*66.7*	*62.8*	*15.4*	*9.5*	*8.3*	*7.7*

Source: UNCTAD secretariat based on World Bank, *World Development Indicators* database, July 2013.

Annex table 9. Indicators on area and population, 2011						
	Area			Population		
Country	Land area	% of arable land and land under permanent crops	% of land area covered by forest	Density	Urban	Labor force	
	(000km2)			(pop/km2 land area)	%	agricultural	non-agricultural
Afghanistan	652.2	12.1	2.1	45	26.2	19'209	13'149
Angola	1,246.7	3.5	46.8	16	57.5	13'535	6'084
Bangladesh	130.2	65.5	11.1	1174	27.9	66'836	83'658
Benin	112.8	25.5	40.0	87	41.8	3'944	5'156
Bhutan	38.4	2.9	84.9	19	36.0	685	53
Burkina Faso	273.6	21.1	20.4	58	28.1	15'617	1'351
Burundi	25.7	51.4	6.6	372	9.8	7'638	937
Cambodia	176.5	23.5	56.5	83	19.6	9'363	4'943
Central African Republic	623.0	3.0	36.2	7	39.5	2'792	1'694
Chad	1,259.2	3.9	9.1	10	20.8	7'438	4'087
Comoros	1.9	75.2	1.4	376	30.2	519	234
Dem. Rep. of the Congo	2,267.1	3.3	67.9	28	36.3	38'434	29'324
Djibouti	23.2	0.1	0.2	37	82.4	666	239
Equatorial Guinea	28.1	7.1	57.5	26	39.7	459	261
Eritrea	101.0	6.9	15.1	59	19.5	3'976	1'440
Ethiopia	1,000.0	15.7	12.2	89	16.1	65'076	19'658
Gambia	10.1	45.0	47.6	171	58.6	1'344	432
Guinea	245.7	14.4	26.5	45	32.4	8'110	2'112
Guinea-Bissau	28.1	19.6	71.6	58	41.8	1'222	325
Haiti	27.6	46.4	3.6	364	53.9	5'895	4'229
Kiribati	0.8	42.0	15.0	123	44.7	23	78
Lao People's Dem. Rep.	230.8	6.5	67.9	28	33.0	4'700	1'588
Lesotho	30.4	10.3	1.5	67	29.8	846	1'348
Liberia	96.3	6.5	44.6	42	48.7	2'536	1'592
Madagascar	581.5	7.1	21.5	37	32.0	14'841	6'474
Malawi	94.3	39.6	34.0	164	15.6	11'123	4'258
Mali	1,220.2	5.7	10.2	12	38.4	11'764	4'076
Mauritania	1,030.7	0.4	0.2	4	39.7	1'774	1'767
Mozambique	786.4	6.9	49.4	31	30.4	18'121	5'809
Myanmar	653.3	18.8	48.2	80	30.1	32'258	16'078
Nepal	143.4	17.3	25.4	189	19.1	28'323	2'163
Niger	1,266.7	11.8	0.9	13	17.4	13'271	2'798
Rwanda	24.7	59.6	18.0	452	18.8	9'761	1'182
Samoa	2.8	10.6	60.4	66	19.5	49	135
Sao Tome and Principe	1.0	49.7	28.1	191	57.7	96	73
Senegal	192.5	20.3	43.8	69	40.7	8'925	3'843
Sierra Leone	71.6	17.2	37.8	82	40.1	3'567	2'430
Solomon Islands	28.0	3.0	78.9	19	..	372	181
Somalia	627.3	1.8	10.6	16	36.4	6'223	3'334
Sudan (former)	2,376.0	8.0	29.4	20	28.3	22'563	22'069
Timor-Leste	14.9	14.1	49.1	74	29.8	916	238
Togo	54.4	50.0	4.9	119	36.1	3'249	2'906
Tuvalu	0.0	60.0	33.3	328	50.6	3	7
Uganda	199.8	44.8	14.5	176	15.3	25'139	9'370
United Republic of Tanzania	885.8	15.0	37.3	52	26.6	33'615	12'604
Vanuatu	12.2	11.9	36.1	20	25.3	73	172
Yemen	528.0	2.8	1.0	44	34.4	9'381	15'419
Zambia	743.4	4.6	66.3	18	38.7	8'439	5'036
LDCs	*20,168.0*	*8.1*	*29.7*	*42.6*	*28.3*	*544'709*	*306'394*
African LDCs and Haiti	*17,553.7*	*7.1*	*30.0*	*31*	*28.7*	*371'903*	*168'225*
Asian LDCs	*2,552.7*	*15.0*	*26.4*	*120*	*27.6*	*170'755*	*137'051*
Island LDCs	*61.5*	*11.2*	*58.4*	*50*	*25.9*	*2'051*	*1'118*
ODCs	*56,301.8*	*13.8*	*28.4*	*85*	*49.5*	*2'007'495*	*2'777'343*
All developing economies	*76,469.8*	*12.3*	*28.8*	*74*	*46.3*	*2'552'204*	*3'083'737*

Sources: FAO, FAOSTAT , september 2013; United Nations/DESA/Population Division; World Bank, *World Development Indicators* database, September 2013.

Notes: Land area: country area excluding Inland water.

Annex table 10. Selected indicators on education and labour, 2011*

Country	Primary completion rate (% of primary school-age population)			Youth literacy rate (% of people aged 15-24)			Labor participation rate (% of total population aged 15+)		
	female	male	total	female	male	total	female	male	total
Afghanistan	18.7	48.4	34.1	..	..	..	15.7	80.3	49.2
Angola	40.0	53.2	46.6	66.1	80.1	73.0	62.9	77.1	69.8
Bangladesh	..	..	..	80.4	77.1	78.7	57.2	84.3	70.8
Benin	66.3	84.3	75.3	30.8	54.9	42.4	67.4	78.2	72.6
Bhutan	98.1	92.2	95.1	68.0	80.0	74.4	65.8	76.5	71.5
Burkina Faso	42.3	47.8	45.1	33.1	46.7	39.3	77.5	90.4	83.8
Burundi	62.2	62.1	62.1	88.1	89.6	88.9	83.7	82.1	82.9
Cambodia	89.7	90.1	89.9	85.9	88.4	87.1	79.2	86.7	82.8
Central African Republic	32.8	53.3	43.0	59.1	72.3	65.6	72.5	85.1	78.7
Chad	29.2	47.2	38.2	42.2	53.6	47.9	64.4	80.2	72.2
Comoros	65.5	83.9	74.8	85.9	86.1	86.0	35.1	80.4	57.7
Dem. Rep. of the Congo	51.0	70.8	60.9	53.3	78.9	65.8	70.2	72.5	71.3
Djibouti	44.9	46.6	45.8	..	..	..	36.0	67.2	51.5
Equatorial Guinea	52.2	51.3	51.7	98.4	97.7	98.1	80.6	92.3	86.7
Eritrea	36.4	43.2	39.8	87.7	92.6	90.1	79.8	90.0	84.7
Ethiopia	54.8	60.7	57.8	47.0	63.0	55.0	78.4	89.8	84.0
Gambia	67.2	65.5	66.3	63.6	72.6	68.1	72.4	83.1	77.6
Guinea	53.0	74.9	64.1	21.8	37.6	31.4	65.4	78.3	71.9
Guinea-Bissau	60.0	75.3	67.6	67.1	79.3	73.2	68.0	78.2	73.0
Haiti	..	..	..	70.5	74.4	72.3	60.1	70.6	65.3
Kiribati	113.1	111.0	112.0	..	..	..	..	..	..
Lao People's Dem. Rep.	89.9	95.3	92.6	78.7	89.2	83.9	76.5	79.5	77.9
Lesotho	76.8	60.4	68.5	92.1	74.2	83.2	58.9	73.4	65.9
Liberia	60.3	71.6	66.0	37.2	63.5	49.1	57.9	64.4	61.2
Madagascar	74.0	71.9	72.9	64.0	65.9	64.9	83.4	88.7	86.0
Malawi	72.4	69.9	71.2	70.0	74.3	72.1	84.8	81.3	83.1
Mali	49.5	61.0	55.4	38.8	56.0	46.9	36.8	70.0	53.1
Mauritania	71.9	68.3	70.1	66.2	71.6	69.0	28.7	79.2	53.8
Mozambique	51.6	60.9	56.2	56.5	79.8	67.1	86.0	82.9	84.6
Myanmar	106.2	101.1	103.6	95.8	96.3	96.1	75.0	82.1	78.5
Nepal	63.1	76.5	70.0	77.5	89.2	82.4	80.4	87.6	83.9
Niger	39.6	52.4	46.2	23.2	52.4	36.5	39.9	89.9	64.6
Rwanda	73.8	65.4	69.6	78.0	76.7	77.3	86.4	85.4	85.9
Samoa	102.7	94.6	98.4	99.6	99.4	99.5	42.8	77.8	60.7
Sao Tome and Principe	117.0	112.4	114.7	77.3	83.1	80.2	43.7	76.6	59.7
Senegal	64.6	61.1	62.8	56.2	74.2	65.0	66.1	88.4	77.0
Sierra Leone	71.3	77.6	74.4	52.1	70.5	61.0	66.3	69.1	67.7
Solomon Islands	..	..	..	..	..	..	53.2	79.9	67.0
Somalia	..	..	..	..	..	..	37.7	76.8	56.9
Sudan	54.9	60.8	57.9	84.5	89.9	87.3	30.9	76.5	53.7
Timor-Leste	73.6	71.4	72.5	78.6	80.5	79.5	38.4	74.1	56.5
Togo	66.8	86.5	76.6	72.7	86.9	79.9	80.4	81.4	80.8
Tuvalu	109.2	89.3	99.2	..	..	..	..	..	..
Uganda	54.2	55.7	54.9	85.5	89.6	87.4	76.0	79.5	77.7
United Republic of Tanzania	92.1	87.7	89.9	72.8	76.5	74.6	88.2	90.3	89.2
Vanuatu	83.1	83.7	83.4	94.8	94.4	94.6	61.3	79.7	70.7
Yemen	53.3	72.2	62.9	76.0	96.4	86.4	25.2	72.0	48.5
Zambia	108.3	98.3	103.3	58.5	70.3	64.0	73.2	85.6	79.4
LDCs	*59.9*	*67.4*	*63.7*	*68.1*	*77.0*	*72.4*	*65.4*	*82.5*	*73.9*
African LDCs and Haiti	*59.3*	*65.9*	*62.6*	*60.2*	*72.9*	*66.4*	*69.9*	*82.2*	*75.9*
Asian LDCs	*63.0*	*75.5*	*69.4*	*82.4*	*84.3*	*83.2*	*59.1*	*83.0*	*71.0*
Island LDCs	*78.6*	*81.5*	*80.1*	*83.7*	*85.1*	*84.4*	*43.0*	*77.5*	*60.5*
ODCs	*86.3*	*88.4*	*93.6*	*87.9*	*93.5*	*90.7*	*48.5*	*79.1*	*64.0*
All developing economies	*80.9*	*84.4*	*87.5*	*84.7*	*91.0*	*87.8*	*50.7*	*79.5*	*65.3*

Sources: UNESCO, UIS database, september 2013; United Nations/DESA/Population Division; World Bank, *World Development Indicators* database, September 2013.
*2011 or lastest year available.

Annex table 11. Selected indicators on demography in LDCs									
country	**Population total** *(thousands)*		**Life expectancy** *Male* (years)		**Life expectancy** *Female*		**Life expectancy** *Total*		**Fertility rate** *(births per women)*	
	2000	*2011*	*2000*	*2011*	*2000*	*2011*	*2000*	*2011*	*2000*	*2011*
Afghanistan	20'595	29'105	53.8	58.8	56.0	61.4	54.8	60.1	7.7	5.4
Angola	13'925	20'180	43.9	49.6	46.6	52.6	45.2	51.1	6.8	6.1
Bangladesh	132'383	152'862	65.1	69.2	65.6	70.7	65.3	69.9	3.1	2.2
Benin	6'949	9'780	53.3	57.6	57.2	60.4	55.2	58.9	6.0	5.0
Bhutan	564	729	60.2	67.2	60.4	67.8	60.3	67.5	3.6	2.3
Burkina Faso	11'608	15'995	49.2	54.9	51.8	56.0	50.5	55.4	6.6	5.8
Burundi	6'674	9'540	47.0	51.4	49.4	55.0	48.2	53.1	7.1	6.2
Cambodia	12'223	14'606	59.3	68.4	64.6	73.8	61.9	71.1	3.8	2.9
Central African Republic	3'638	4'436	42.1	47.0	45.4	50.7	43.7	48.8	5.4	4.5
Chad	8'301	12'080	45.8	49.4	47.6	51.1	46.7	50.2	7.4	6.5
Comoros	528	700	56.3	59.1	59.5	61.8	57.9	60.4	5.3	4.9
Dem. Rep. of the Congo	46'949	63'932	45.0	47.6	47.8	51.1	46.4	49.3	7.1	6.1
Djibouti	723	847	55.5	59.3	58.6	62.4	57.0	60.8	4.5	3.5
Equatorial Guinea	518	716	46.5	50.7	49.1	53.6	47.8	52.1	5.8	5.0
Eritrea	3'939	5'933	53.8	59.4	58.3	64.1	56.0	61.7	5.9	4.9
Ethiopia	66'024	89'393	51.3	60.8	53.2	63.8	52.2	62.3	6.5	4.8
Gambia	1'229	1'735	53.9	57.1	56.5	59.7	55.2	58.4	5.9	5.8
Guinea	8'746	11'162	51.2	54.8	51.3	56.4	51.2	55.6	5.9	5.1
Guinea-Bissau	1'273	1'624	50.4	52.3	52.5	55.4	51.4	53.8	5.8	5.1
Haiti	8'578	10'033	55.7	60.5	59.2	64.2	57.4	62.3	4.3	3.3
Kiribati	83	99	61.8	65.5	67.5	71.1	64.6	68.2	3.9	3.0
Lao People's Dem. Rep.	5'388	6'521	60.4	66.1	62.9	68.7	61.6	67.4	4.2	3.2
Lesotho	1'856	2'030	46.7	48.0	47.6	48.5	47.2	48.2	4.1	3.1
Liberia	2'892	4'080	51.8	59.0	53.1	60.8	52.4	59.9	5.9	4.9
Madagascar	15'745	21'679	57.3	62.4	59.7	65.3	58.5	63.8	5.5	4.6
Malawi	11'321	15'458	45.7	54.1	46.4	54.2	46.0	54.1	6.3	5.6
Mali	10'261	14'417	49.4	54.3	48.7	54.0	49.1	54.2	6.8	6.9
Mauritania	2'708	3'703	58.2	59.7	61.2	62.7	59.7	61.2	5.4	4.8
Mozambique	18'276	24'581	46.0	48.5	49.0	50.5	47.4	49.5	5.8	5.3
Myanmar	48'453	52'351	60.0	62.8	64.2	66.9	62.0	64.8	2.4	2.0
Nepal	23'184	27'156	61.2	66.5	63.0	68.7	62.0	67.5	4.1	2.5
Niger	10'990	16'511	50.7	57.3	50.7	57.6	50.7	57.5	7.7	7.6
Rwanda	8'396	11'144	46.8	61.4	48.5	64.5	47.6	62.9	5.9	4.7
Samoa	175	187	66.3	69.6	72.8	75.9	69.5	72.7	4.5	4.3
Sao Tome and Principe	139	183	61.5	64.1	65.1	68.0	63.3	66.0	4.7	4.2
Senegal	9'862	13'331	56.2	61.6	59.4	64.5	57.8	63.0	5.6	5.0
Sierra Leone	4'140	5'865	37.4	44.9	38.8	45.3	38.1	45.1	5.9	4.9
Solomon Islands	412	538	61.6	66.0	64.1	68.7	62.8	67.3	4.7	4.2
Somalia	7'385	9'908	49.3	52.8	52.5	56.0	50.9	54.4	7.6	6.8
South Sudan	6'653	10'381	48.0	53.0	50.5	55.1	49.2	54.0	6.1	5.1
Sudan	27'730	36'431	56.2	60.0	59.9	63.5	58.0	61.7	5.4	4.6
Timor-Leste	854	1'176	58.3	65.0	60.7	68.1	59.5	66.5	7.1	5.5
Togo	4'865	6'472	52.8	55.0	54.4	56.6	53.5	55.8	5.3	4.7
Tuvalu	9	10	..	..	..	..	..	..	..	..
Uganda	24'276	35'148	47.8	57.0	48.5	59.0	48.1	58.0	6.9	6.1
Tanzania	34'021	46'355	49.3	58.9	50.6	61.3	50.0	60.1	5.7	5.4
Vanuatu	185	242	65.9	69.2	69.3	73.2	67.6	71.1	4.4	3.5
Yemen, Rep.	17'523	23'304	59.1	61.4	61.9	64.1	60.5	62.7	6.4	4.3
Zambia	10'101	13'634	41.5	54.4	42.1	57.3	41.8	55.8	6.1	5.8
LDCs	*663'251*	*858'285*	*52.0*	*57.0*	*55.5*	*60.9*	*53.2*	*58.4*	*5.3*	*4.5*
African LDCs and Haiti	*400'552*	*548'513*	*49.6*	*55.0*	*51.7*	*57.4*	*50.7*	*56.2*	*6.3*	*5.4*
Asian LDCs	*260'314*	*306'636*	*60.0*	*65.6*	*62.4*	*68.3*	*61.2*	*66.9*	*3.7*	*2.7*
Island LDCs	*2'386*	*3'136*	*54.0*	*57.3*	*57.4*	*60.8*	*55.6*	*59.0*	*5.6*	*4.7*
ODCs	*4'144'079*	*4'749'170*	*62.2*	*64.1*	*66.6*	*68.5*	*64.3*	*66.2*	*2.6*	*2.4*
All developing economies	*4'807'330*	*5'607'455*	*58.8*	*61.8*	*63.0*	*66.0*	*60.6*	*63.6*	*3.0*	*2.7*

Source: World Bank, *World Development Indicators* database, September 2013

Annex table 12. LDC selected population indicators, 2012					
	Total Population ('000)	Population growth (annual %)	Population age 0-14 (% of total)	Rural population (% of total)	Urban population growth rate (%)
Afghanistan	29'825	2.5	47.4	73.3	4.5
Angola	20'821	3.2	47.6	41.9	4.1
Bangladesh	154'695	1.2	30.6	71.6	3.0
Benin	10'051	2.8	43.0	57.6	4.3
Bhutan	742	1.7	28.5	63.2	3.9
Burkina Faso	16'460	2.9	45.7	71.0	6.3
Burundi	9'850	3.2	44.2	90.1	4.6
Cambodia	14'865	1.8	31.2	80.4	2.1
Central African Republic	4'525	2.0	40.1	60.3	2.6
Chad	12'448	3.0	48.5	79.2	3.0
Comoros	718	2.5	42.2	69.7	2.9
Democratic Republic of the Congo	65'705	2.8	45.1	63.1	4.3
Djibouti	860	1.5	33.7	17.2	2.0
Equatorial Guinea	736	2.8	39.0	60.1	3.2
Eritrea	6'131	3.3	43.1	80.2	5.2
Ethiopia	91'729	2.6	43.3	83.7	3.6
Gambia	1'791	3.2	45.9	41.1	3.8
Guinea	11'451	2.6	42.5	67.1	3.9
Guinea-Bissau	1'664	2.4	41.6	57.6	3.7
Haiti	10'174	1.4	35.4	44.8	3.9
Kiribati	101	1.5	32.4	55.2	1.8
Lao People's Democratic Republic	6'646	1.9	35.6	66.1	4.7
Lesotho	2'052	1.1	36.8	69.4	3.7
Liberia	4'190	2.7	43.1	50.8	3.6
Madagascar	22'294	2.8	42.7	67.3	4.9
Malawi	15'906	2.9	45.4	84.2	4.2
Mali	14'854	3.0	47.1	60.9	4.9
Mauritania	3'796	2.5	40.2	60.2	2.9
Mozambique	25'203	2.5	45.4	69.5	3.1
Myanmar	52'797	0.9	25.3	69.4	2.5
Nepal	27'474	1.2	35.6	80.5	3.7
Niger	17'157	3.9	50.0	82.5	5.0
Rwanda	11'458	2.8	43.6	80.9	4.6
Samoa	189	0.8	37.9	80.8	-0.6
Sao Tome and Principe	188	2.7	41.6	42.1	3.1
Senegal	13'726	3.0	43.5	59.1	3.4
Sierra Leone	5'979	1.9	41.7	59.4	3.1
Solomon Islands	548	2.4	40.4	79.1	4.6
Somalia	10'195	2.9	47.3	63.3	3.8
South Sudan	10'838	..	42.3	82.1	..
Sudan	37'195	..	41.5	68.6	..
Timor-Leste	1'210	1.6	46.3	69.4	4.3
Togo	6'643	2.6	41.9	63.6	3.4
Tuvalu	10	0.2	-	49.0	1.0
Uganda	36'346	3.4	48.5	84.3	6.0
United Republic of Tanzania	47'783	3.1	44.9	72.9	4.9
Vanuatu	247	2.3	37.4	74.3	3.7
Yemen	23'852	2.4	40.7	64.7	4.9
Zambia	14'075	3.2	46.7	61.0	4.2
LDCs	*878'194*	*2.3*	*40.3*	*71.3*	*3.8*
African LDCs and Haiti	*564'085*	*2.8*	*44.5*	*71.0*	*4.1*
Asian LDCs	*310'896*	*1.4*	*32.6*	*71.9*	*3.3*
Island LDCs	*3'212*	*2.0*	*42.5*	*73.8*	*3.3*
ODCs	*4'857'463*	*1.2*	*26.4*	*49.9*	*2.4*
All developing economies	*5'735'559*	*1.4*	*28.6*	*53.2*	*2.5*

Source: UNCTAD secretariat calculations, based on UNCTADstat database, September 2013 and World Bank, *World Development Indicators* database, September 2013.

Annex table 13. New entrants to the labour market in LDCs

	New entrants (15-24) (thousands)						Share in working age population 15-64) (per cent)					
	2000	2005	2010	2020	2030	2050	2000	2005	2010	2020	2030	2050
Afghanistan	388.0	475.5	549.7	841.6	944.7	975.9	3.9	3.9	3.9	4.1	3.4	2.4
Angola	267.9	319.8	377.8	536.7	722.1	1,074.5	3.9	3.9	3.9	3.9	3.8	3.2
Bangladesh	2'764.6	2'981.5	3'070.3	3'162.7	2'943.4	2'531.5	3.5	3.4	3.2	2.7	2.3	1.9
Benin	133.5	159.8	188.0	249.6	309.9	407.9	3.7	3.7	3.7	3.6	3.4	2.9
Bhutan	11.9	15.0	15.5	14.2	13.8	11.9	3.8	3.7	3.3	2.5	2.2	1.8
Burkina Faso	236.3	271.8	311.2	419.7	544.1	785.7	4.0	4.0	3.9	3.8	3.6	3.1
Burundi	134.6	173.7	199.3	228.0	338.6	498.1	4.2	4.3	4.0	3.5	3.7	3.2
Cambodia	242.1	323.0	300.7	268.9	317.7	299.1	3.6	4.1	3.3	2.5	2.6	2.1
Central African Republic	73.3	81.5	89.5	107.4	122.2	148.8	3.8	3.8	3.7	3.5	3.2	2.7
Chad	158.2	193.9	231.8	323.9	434.3	665.9	4.0	4.0	4.1	4.0	3.8	3.3
Comoros	11.2	12.3	12.7	16.9	21.3	27.9	3.8	3.7	3.4	3.4	3.4	3.0
Dem. Rep. of the Congo	883.0	1'037.0	1'226.7	1'632.2	2'086.4	2'986.3	3.7	3.8	3.8	3.7	3.6	3.1
Djibouti	14.6	16.7	18.7	17.0	19.7	18.8	3.6	3.6	3.6	2.8	2.8	2.3
Equatorial Guinea	7.4	10.9	13.6	16.7	21.5	28.4	2.7	3.2	3.4	3.1	3.2	2.7
Eritrea	84.3	110.5	120.7	147.5	205.1	253.4	4.2	4.2	3.8	3.4	3.5	2.7
Ethiopia	1'276.8	1'490.1	1'756.9	2'433.6	2'737.5	3'204.6	3.8	3.9	3.9	3.8	3.2	2.5
Gambia	25.5	28.9	33.0	45.8	62.2	96.7	4.0	3.9	3.8	3.8	3.7	3.3
Guinea	165.3	186.4	215.5	278.9	346.3	450.7	3.6	3.7	3.7	3.6	3.4	2.9
Guinea-Bissau	24.9	28.3	31.5	39.3	48.4	64.8	3.7	3.7	3.6	3.5	3.3	2.9
Haiti	178.1	200.5	206.6	220.3	228.6	224.1	3.7	3.7	3.5	3.1	2.8	2.3
Kiribati	1.5	1.8	2.1	2.2	2.1	2.4	3.2	3.4	3.4	2.9	2.5	2.3
Lao People's Dem. Rep.	107.1	124.1	147.3	147.4	164.8	155.8	3.8	3.8	3.9	3.1	2.8	2.2
Lesotho	40.0	43.8	47.0	48.1	48.7	48.7	4.0	4.1	4.0	3.5	3.1	2.5
Liberia	58.1	64.5	75.3	102.7	128.0	173.3	3.7	3.7	3.5	3.6	3.4	2.9
Madagascar	298.9	345.7	420.6	566.3	694.6	1,022.5	3.7	3.6	3.7	3.6	3.3	3.0
Malawi	223.1	253.1	305.7	406.8	540.1	805.7	3.9	3.9	4.0	3.9	3.7	3.2
Mali	209.3	238.1	269.6	370.7	528.6	918.0	4.0	3.9	3.8	3.9	3.9	3.6
Mauritania	54.2	62.5	70.8	89.0	109.6	142.4	3.7	3.6	3.5	3.3	3.2	2.9
Mozambique	362.0	407.0	463.6	637.2	816.9	1,196.1	3.7	3.7	3.8	3.9	3.8	3.3
Myanmar	1'033.6	1'022.3	962.7	898.8	852.3	721.2	3.3	3.0	2.7	2.3	2.1	1.8
Nepal	452.2	465.7	524.9	633.0	554.4	488.4	3.5	3.3	3.4	3.2	2.5	2.0
Niger	189.6	224.5	274.8	436.5	664.3	1'411.5	3.5	3.5	3.6	3.9	4.0	3.8
Rwanda	181.2	212.6	212.9	297.8	356.8	449.9	4.3	4.2	3.7	3.7	3.3	2.8
Samoa	3.2	3.2	3.4	3.9	4.3	4.1	3.4	3.2	3.2	3.4	3.4	2.8
Sao Tome and Principe	3.2	3.6	3.7	4.3	5.8	6.9	4.4	4.3	3.7	3.3	3.4	2.8
Senegal	205.2	236.1	265.9	337.4	447.2	611.8	4.0	4.0	3.9	3.6	3.5	3.0
Sierra Leone	86.6	104.4	112.8	141.2	160.9	189.0	3.8	3.7	3.5	3.5	3.3	2.8
Solomon Islands	8.7	9.3	10.0	13.0	15.4	17.7	3.8	3.5	3.4	3.5	3.3	2.7
Somalia	134.4	156.0	182.4	260.2	343.0	540.9	3.6	3.7	3.8	4.0	3.8	3.4
South Sudan	124.8	155.0	200.3	281.9	342.2	454.5	3.6	3.7	3.7	3.6	3.4	2.9
Sudan	557.5	619.8	699.3	898.7	1'072.8	1'389.4	3.8	3.7	3.6	3.5	3.2	2.8
Timor-Leste	14.4	19.9	23.0	30.5	33.5	43.6	3.5	4.1	4.3	4.6	4.0	3.3
Togo	101.9	116.8	129.2	157.8	201.8	263.1	4.0	3.9	3.7	3.4	3.4	2.9
Tuvalu												
Uganda	476.5	570.9	683.4	968.5	1'325.0	2'062.3	4.1	4.1	4.1	4.0	3.9	3.3
United Republic of Tanzania	690.9	787.7	888.2	1'176.1	1'626.9	2'485.7	3.9	3.9	3.8	3.7	3.7	3.2
Vanuatu	3.7	4.3	4.5	5.6	6.6	7.6	3.6	3.6	3.3	3.1	3.0	2.5
Yemen	355.6	444.6	526.3	608.0	662.1	707.8	4.2	4.3	4.2	3.6	3.0	2.4
Zambia	211.9	231.5	260.2	365.2	495.9	857.8	4.1	4.0	3.9	3.9	3.7	3.4
LDCs	*13'270.7*	*15'046.1*	*16'739.6*	*20'889.7*	*24'672.6*	*31'933.1*	*3.7*	*3.7*	*3.6*	*3.4*	*3.2*	*2.8*
African LDCs and Haiti	*7'744.9*	*8'985.0*	*10'382.4*	*13'956.7*	*17'788.1*	*25'476.9*	*3.8*	*3.8*	*3.7*	*3.7*	*3.5*	*3.0*
Asian LDCs	*5'355.1*	*5'851.8*	*6'097.5*	*6'574.7*	*6'453.3*	*5'891.6*	*3.6*	*3.4*	*3.3*	*2.9*	*2.5*	*2.0*
Island LDCs	*45.9*	*54.4*	*59.4*	*76.4*	*89.1*	*110.1*	*3.7*	*3.8*	*3.7*	*3.7*	*3.5*	*3.0*
ODCs	*77'011.0*	*84'951.2*	*87'320.9*	*81'604.8*	*86'142.3*	*83'032.1*	*2.9*	*2.9*	*2.8*	*2.3*	*2.3*	*2.1*
All developing economies	*90'281.7*	*99'997.3*	*104'060.5*	*102'494.5*	*110'814.9*	*114'965.2*	*3.0*	*3.0*	*2.9*	*2.5*	*2.4*	*2.2*

Source: United Nations, DESA, Population Division (2013). *World Population Prospects:* The 2012 Revision, DVD Edition.
Note: Data reflects the cohort of new workers (aged 15-24 years) entering to the labour market or reaching the age of findings an income generating activity, which following NEPAD (2013) was 1/10 of the 15/24 year age group.

Annex table 14. Total employment trends in LDCs
(Thousands)

	2000	2005	2010	2015	2018	annual average growth rate 2000-2018 (%)
Afghanistan	5'532	6'416	7'565	9'453	10'633	3.6
Angola	4'810	5'606	6'577	7'905	8'881	3.5
Bangladesh	55'398	62'408	69'000	77'269	82'046	2.2
Benin	2'539	3'012	3'578	4'188	4'593	3.4
Bhutan	225	301	352	407	433	3.5
Burkina Faso	5'334	6'257	7'298	8'547	9'375	3.2
Burundi	2'689	3'244	3'988	4'496	4'777	3.4
Cambodia	5'629	6'772	7'839	8'648	9'099	2.7
Central African Republic	1'553	1'702	1'910	2'160	2'321	2.3
Chad	2'974	3'538	4'091	4'746	5'172	3.1
Comoros	166	195	226	260	284	3.0
Dem. Rep. of the Congo	17'192	19'961	23'447	27'752	30'603	3.3
Djibouti	..	..	..	..	..	..
Equatorial Guinea	242	290	341	387	412	3.1
Eritrea	1'521	2'005	2'395	2'801	3'057	3.8
Ethiopia	26'685	33'013	38'583	45'024	49'131	3.4
Gambia	501	590	694	816	898	3.3
Guinea	3'192	3'505	3'964	4'610	5'052	2.6
Guinea-Bissau	462	526	601	684	737	2.6
Haiti	3'001	3'418	3'813	4'336	4'625	2.5
Kiribati	..	..	..	..	..	..
Lao People's Dem. Rep.	2'413	2'728	3'125	3'518	3'738	2.5
Lesotho	531	541	680	703	729	2.0
Liberia	918	1'046	1'324	1'549	1'702	3.7
Madagascar	7'111	8'362	9'780	11'566	12'747	3.4
Malawi	4'453	5'268	6'202	7'267	7'992	3.3
Mali	2'805	3'302	3'950	4'680	5'183	3.5
Mauritania	517	634	768	899	981	3.6
Mozambique	8'059	9'140	10'250	11'582	12'523	2.4
Myanmar	23'057	24'862	26'750	28'599	29'512	1.4
Nepal	12'014	13'655	15'609	17'909	19'320	2.7
Niger	3'348	4'057	4'841	5'840	6'538	3.8
Rwanda	3'777	4'469	5'197	6'001	6'499	3.0
Samoa	..	..	..	..	..	..
Sao Tome and Principe	..	..	..	..	..	..
Senegal	3'551	4'153	4'847	5'657	6'202	3.1
Sierra Leone	1'509	1'909	2'186	2'493	2'689	3.2
Solomon Islands	149	177	206	241	263	3.2
Somalia	2'173	2'445	2'711	3'089	3'363	2.4
Sudan	9'631	11'121	13'045	15'157	16'599	3.1
Timor-Leste	221	286	310	379	422	3.4
Togo	1'985	2'344	2'717	3'127	3'385	3.0
Tuvalu	..	..	..	..	..	..
Uganda	9'813	11'218	12'857	15'260	16'881	3.0
United Republic of Tanzania	15'858	18'573	21'197	24'498	26'805	2.9
Vanuatu	..	..	..	..	..	..
Yemen	3'615	4'389	5'526	6'722	7'606	4.2
Zambia	3'898	4'163	4'844	5'515	5'988	2.6
LDCs	*261'050*	*301'605*	*345'183*	*396'741*	*429'796*	*2.8*
African LDCs and Haiti	*152'632*	*179'416*	*208'674*	*243'335*	*266'441*	*3.1*
Asian LDCs	*107'882*	*121'531*	*135'766*	*152'526*	*162'386*	*2.3*
Island LDCs	*537*	*658*	*743*	*880*	*970*	*3.2*
ODCs	*1'777'409*	*1'959'142*	*2'090'454*	*2'236'656*	*2'310'419*	*1.4*
All developing economies	*2'038'460*	*2'260'747*	*2'435'637*	*2'633'397*	*2'740'215*	*1.6*

Source: UNCTAD secretariat calculation based on data from ILO, Employment trends (EMP/TRENS) econometric models, April 2013.

Annex table 15. Countries and data sources for LDC sub-sample RNF income analysis					
Country	**Name of survey**	**Year of collection**	**Number of observations**		
			Total	*Rural*	*Urban*
Bangladesh household	Income-Expenditure Survey	2000	7,440	5,040	2,400
Madagascar	Enquête Permanente Auprès des Ménages	1993–1994	4,505	2,653	1,852
Malawi	Integrated Household Survey-2	2004–2005	11,280	9,840	1,440
Nepal	Living Standards Survey I	1995–1996	3,370	2,655	715
Source: Davis et al. (2010).